THE
EXODUS
CASE

by

LENNART MÖLLER

SCANDINAVIA

THE EXODUS CASE

A Scientific Examination of the Exodus Story
– and a Deep Look Into the Red Sea
by Lennart Möller
Copyright © 2000 Scandinavia Publishing House
Drejervej 11-21, DK 2400 Copenhagen NV, Denmark
Tel.: (45) 35310330   Fax: (45) 35310334   E-Mail: jvo@scanpublishing.dk
Text copyright © 2000 Lennart Möller
Photo copyright, see copyright list
Illustration copyright © 2000 Anni Mikkelsen and José Pérez Montero
Design by Ben Alex
Translation to English by Margaret Bäckman

Printed in Slovakia
ISBN 87 7247 230 8

CONTENTS

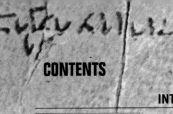

CONTENTS

PART III   AT THE MOUNTAIN OF GOD/231

CONTENTS

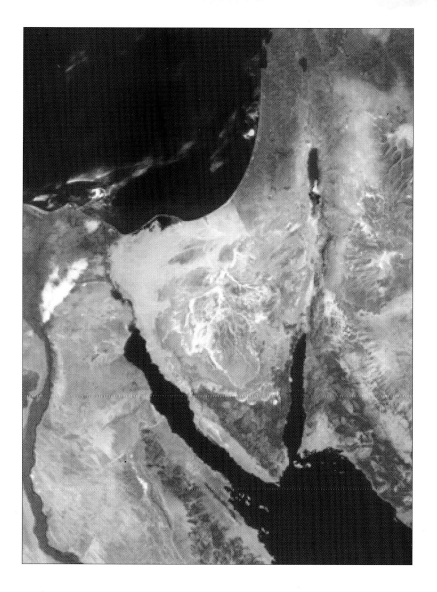

INTRODUCTION

Exodus!

*"And Moses stretched out his hand over the sea...
and the waters were divided."* (Ex.14:21)

These words and the events surrounding Moses' command have existed in our history for about 3450 years. In our subconscious, somewhere in the recesses of the brain, most of us have some sort of relation to these words.

Figure 10: Moses at Mount Sinai.

For the Jews, Moses is a symbol of the existence of this entire people. It was then that the Hebrew people ceased to be a tribe and became a people, a nation. It is here in the Pentateuch that the foundation and the identity of the Jews as a people, and Israel as a nation are to be found.

For Christians the origins of the their faith are to be found in the Pentateuch. It is here that Christians find ancient images of festivals, sacraments, and teachings, even today parts of modern worship services trace their origin to the books of Moses. In this way Jews and Christians have a common history. The legal system of the western world is based on Jewish-Christian ethics formulated, amongst other things, on the tablets of stone.

The Muslims also find their religious origins in the Pentateuch, and the Arabs' forefathers are found in the same families as those of the Jews. As an individual person, Abraham can thus take Jewish, Christian and Muslim faith and civilisation back to a common starting point.

In addition, the books of Moses have affected civilisation in most areas of the world. Naturally the degree of influence varies and is at times mainly cultural, at other times however, it is legal, historical or religious in character. At the turn of the millennium the population of the world was about six billion people. The majority of these people live in a society in some way connected with the Pentateuch.

What is our view of the Pentateuch?

Most of us have heard the story of Moses in some form or other. It is part of our cultural heritage, a legend from bygone days. Otherwise we regard these books as a powerful folk tale, containing all the ingredients one can think of: good and evil, struggles, suffering, love, absence and presence, strange events, spiritual qualities and lack of spiritual qualities, the fury of the forces of nature etc.

We can also regard these books as documents concerning a time when God manifested his presence in a special way. In Christian worship, in prayer meetings and in sermons the same benediction is used today as the one which God instructed Aaron (the brother of Moses) to pronounce over the people, according to the text:

*"The LORD bless thee, and keep thee:
The LORD make his face shine upon thee, and be gracious unto thee:
The LORD lift up his countenance upon thee, and give thee peace."*
(Numb. 6:24-26)

There are other ways of looking at the Pentateuch. These books are also the basis for various types of research. This research might be historical, linguistic, cultural or theological, to name but a few examples. Research often aims at increasing knowledge about the context, the origins of cultural expressions and the reasons for the rise and fall of civilisations. In scientific analysis one often breaks down the context into smaller parts and then tries in different ways to analyse and discuss the subject.

It is usual to differentiate between the strictly scientific method of tackling the subject and the "spiritual experience", or to express it in another way, the belief that the Pentateuch is an expression of God's action.

Figure 11: The Crossing site?

As you read this book, you already have an understanding that is more or less based on faith and science. But if we are honest, we really do not know very much - unless you happen to be an orthodox Jew who very explicitly lives with the Pentateuch in his daily life. We often base our understanding of things on random sources of information. It might be something someone has said, a newspaper article or a generally accepted cultural concept.

Your opinion might also be very emphatic: the Pentateuch is either a falsification (a historical lie that a little tribe once needed, and which has since been enlarged) or the contrary, your entire identity, and your whole soul are convinced without a doubt that this is a work of God. That God chose to manifest his presence in a special way during this period of time, and what the Pentateuch is all about affects us today.

WHO MADE THE DISCOVERIES?

There are a number of discoveries in this book. Discoveries of what once happened in ancient times. The person who made these discoveries was Ronald E. Wyatt. Wyatt was an amateur archeologist from the US, who spent over 40 years researching and made more than 100 trips to the Middle East to document the discoveries discussed in this book. He had a strong belief that the Bible text was a recording of historical events, and based on this he searched for traces and remains of these events.

Figures 12, 13: The Star of David is a symbol for Jews. The most holy place is the Western Wall of the Temple at Mount Moriah in Jerusalem.

Wyatt and the author of this book were brought together, and a decision was made that Lennart Möller should evaluate the discoveries. Wyatt and Möller have travelled together in the Middle East several times, and Wyatt has made his material available with no limitations. Based on Wyatt's discoveries, Lennart Möller has evaluated, supplemented, analysed and structured the data of the events in this book. Ronald E. Wyatt died when this book was in its final stage, in the late summer of 1999. His widow, Mary Nell Wyatt, has been of great help in criticising the manuscript, looking for references, and adding considerable knowledge on matters from the Middle East.

HOW HAS THIS BOOK BEEN WRITTEN?

Every book you read has some basis or purpose, but it is rarely clearly expressed. A textbook differs from a novel. A political manifesto is very different from a scientific article. A book for children is not the same as a book of poetry. A technical manual differs from a history book. A book of prayers is very unlike a book on archaeology. This book you are holding is presumably different from much that you have read before, and I shall explain briefly why.

The writer of this book is a scientist, but not in the field with which the book deals. My research is in the field of medicine. I work at the Karolinska Institutet in Stockholm. The Karolinska Institutet is the Medical University of Stockholm. The research in which I am involved is concentrated on DNA lesions and related illnesses e.g. cancer. Within the research group we study how substances in the environment, and oxidative stress (free radicals), can cause lesions to the genes, which can then cause or contribute to various illnesses. We develop analytical methods, keep track of illnesses and study protective factors and mechanisms within this field of research.

In this book I have tried to make use of the scientific way of working that I follow in my research. This was not always easy when matters as old as approximately 4000 years were studied.

Added to my scientific background is the know-how I have from several hobbies such as archaeology, photography, minerals and precious stones, travel in foreign cultures and scubadiving. My earlier university studies in chemistry, biology, limnology, and toxicology, as well as ecology and marine biology at the universities of Uppsala and Stockholm, have been of great help; as has the analytical laboratory research which is my profession. Where my own knowledge has been insufficient I have made use of a network of individuals with a variety of specialist qualifications.

Figure 14: Was Tutankhamun related to the events of the Exodus?

In all research a hypothesis (an assumption) is put forward and then research is carried out (which in my case is in the medical sector) with trials, experiments and analyses. Later, when results are evaluated, the hypothesis is either rejected, or it is supported and acts as a basis for further hypotheses, which are then tested. In this way the scientific process moves forward.

This book is based on the fundamental hypothesis: *The Bible texts with which this book deals (Genesis 11:27 to Exodus 40:38) are a true historical document.*

This does not mean that the book is a doctrinal document, but it means that it presupposes that the biblical passages are true, correctly recounted, and are linked to actual events.

Sometimes one reads books and articles where the author considers that it is only if one believes that something is not true, and breaks it down into small parts, that one is scientific. This is wrong. The scientific way is to clearly state the hypothesis (the premise), and then test the hypothesis. As far as possible basic data should be presented to the person reading the document, so that they can draw his/her own conclusions.

Figures 15, 16: The crucifixtion and resurrection of Jesus Christ at Mount Moriah in Jerusalem unifies all Christians. The Holy Communion is celebrated because of the events on Mount Moriah.

These conclusions can differ somewhat from the scientist's own, or in certain cases be entirely opposite. This is as it should be. In the process which follows, new hypotheses develop with the aim of strengthening, explaining or rejecting earlier hypotheses. When this process functions properly, new knowledge is continuously generated. Within experimental (laboratory) research there are in fact no incorrect results, the question is how one interprets the results. Many scholars have experienced that it was when they made a "mistake" or did something different leading to an unexpected result, that they discovered something new; something not known earlier.

I have tried to keep to these scientific criteria in my work with the book. Furthermore, I am no theologian, historian or archaeologist, and therefore am unaware of the opinion one ought to have about various things, expressions and passages in the Pentateuch. In a way this gives a sense of freedom, and explains why I sometimes see things from another perspective. Whether or not this is a true perspective can be tested as you read this book.

The critical-historical research of various books of the Bible has its origins in the Age of Enlightenment, when people began to consider these texts rationally. The problem arises when reason becomes of paramount importance. This means that something is only correct and true if it can be logically understood. That which one does not understand is untrue. If a scientist starts to think along these lines, the research comes to a halt. This happens because one sets a limit to what one understands. By definition research means to search for new knowledge, and extend the boundaries of what we understand today. Therefore, certain ways of thinking limit progress. This is also the reason why research groups often function best when they are made up of people with different qualifications and experience. New thoughts and hypotheses are born from the interaction of their different ways of thinking.

A sound attitude is to regard something as true until the opposite has been proved. This is the way it works in archaeology for instance. Law has the same basis: a person is innocent until the opposite has been proved. The strange thing is that there are a number of scholars who claim that the Bible texts are false until the opposite has been proved. Such a way of thinking could lead, for example, to the claim that since the conditions and the surroundings at the traditional Mount Sinai are of a certain nature, then the Bible texts are wrong. As a result, one begins to adjust the Bible texts.

The scientific way of tackling the matter in such a case, is to question whether one is in the right place, and how sure one can be of this. One could compare this with an orienteer who has gone astray in the forest and, instead of investigating where he/she is, begins to cut up the map and draw it differently. This attitude often leads one into error.

Throughout history things which are obvious today have been rejected because an individual's understanding has set the limits. An example of this was when, during a long period of time, church representatives could not accept that the earth was round. At the end of the nineteenth century, a person in a leading position in the country's Patent Office asserted that the office could be shut down since everything had now been invented. When computers appeared, one of the largest firms in the sector today believed that global needs could be met with just one or two computers. For a long time it was claimed in scientific circles that nothing heavier than air could fly (aeroplanes are always heavier than air). One often ends up in error if one's own reason sets the limits.

Faith in one's own reason often leads to disaster. The Titanic was unsinkable until she sank (on her maiden voyage). Many shipwrecks have occurred because of over confidence in the ability of a person, and/or the capabilities of the technique, combined with lack of experience. In news reports this is

Figure 17: The Bible, a true story?

Figure 18: Acacia, more or less the only tree in the wilderness and therefore used at the Exodus.

Figure 19: The mountains at the Red Sea.

15

Figure 20: Brick-making in Egypt according to ancient methods using clay and straw.

called "the human factor". Alcohol reinforces over confidence in one's own ability and sense of reason, and because of this most countries have established limits for the amount of alcohol drivers are allowed to have in the body; otherwise accidents occur.

One's own sense of reason is not a source of truth, but properly used it can help produce increased knowledge. However, we must not forget that there are many phenomena, which we only understand superficially today. The scientist is aware of this and expresses him/herself with caution, often by putting forward hypotheses. Hypotheses which then quickly become black and white facts in the mass media.

THE BASIC HYPOTHESIS

In order to make it really clear the hypothesis is repeated once again:

This book is based on the fundamental hypothesis: *The Bible texts dealt with in this book (Genesis 11:27 to Exodus 40:38) are a true historical document.*

A main hypothesis often leads to a number of new questions and hypotheses, and that applies to this book. You will not find all the answers you would like in this book. Remember that it covers important questions, spans a time interval of several thousand years, and that there have only been small private resources available for carrying out the work. There are no large founders, companies, authorities or sponsors behind this project. It is a good idea to state this clearly and simply. This means that as the author of the book I have not been obliged to take into consideration any hidden agenda, any list of requirements or any other form of limitation.

Figure 21: Deir-El Bahri, a temple in the south of Egypt. Is this temple related to Moses?

I would also like to state clearly that I am a Christian. This means that I believe there is a God who is greater than my own powers of reason. This is a liberating thought. For me it is a fundamental quality of God, and one of the definitions of God. If there is a God, then by definition God must be greater than I am, have a higher intellect, and my own powers of reason and logic do not extend very far in that perspective. But I would like to emphasise again that this book is not a doctrinal document.

This book is about combining scientific research methods with the hypothesis that the Bible texts recount true historical events. Therefore, this is a book about being on the spot and testing various debatable points, and is not in the first place a writing desk product. This is also the reason why there are so many illustrations and photographs. Everyone can judge the pictures for themselves. Bible passages are quoted where they are relevant to different finds and events, to make it easier to understand the course of events.

Figure 22: Fishermen using ancient methods when fishing in the Nile River.

THE NAME OF THE BOOK – THE EXODUS CASE

What is the Exodus exactly? "Exodus" is on the one hand the name of the second book of the Pentateuch, but it is also a concise designation of the flight of the people of Israel from Egypt. That the second book of the Pentateuch is called Exodus, is due to the fact that this book in the Bible deals with all the events connected with the flight from Egypt. As this is the most important part of the book, it has been named after these events.

DIVISION INTO DIFFERENT PARTS

This book is in three parts: the first part deals with the time before the Exodus, the second with the Exodus and the third with the mountain of God, Horeb (also called Mount Sinai). "The pre-Exodus period" concerns the period from Abraham to Joseph, from Genesis 11:27 to 50:26. This part is essential for an understanding of what happens later.

Part two, "Exodus", is about Moses and the departure (Exodus) of the people of Israel from Egypt as far as the crossing of the Red Sea. This corresponds to Exodus 1:1 to 14:31 in the Bible.

The third part, "At the mountain of God", deals with the time after the crossing of the Red Sea and all that happened at Horeb (Mount Sinai), and the location of this mountain. The Bible texts dealing with this are Exodus 15:1 to 40:38, in the main. However, the other books of Moses will also be commented on in part.

The aim of setting out the book in this way is to make these Bible texts easily accessible, and this is also the reason behind all the illustrations in the form of maps, tables, pictures, graphic reconstruction's and photographs. Together with the Bible texts an account is given of a number of archaeological finds and chemical analyses.

Figure 23: In the wilderness palm trees are only found in the oases.

REFERENCES

In the text, references are mainly to Bible passages. A biblical reference is given, for example, as Ex. 13:7, which means the book of Exodus, chapter 13, verse 7. The five books of the Pentateuch are found as the first books in the Bible. They are Genesis, Exodus, Leviticus, Numbers and Deuteronomy, and are also called the five books of Moses. The books of the Pentateuch are divided and numbered in chapters and verses, making it easy to find the texts. Reference is also made to several other books in the Bible, and explanations of these references are given in the list at the end of this book.

In addition to the biblical references, references are also given to the historical writer Josephus, who had access to many documents which are no longer available. The complete name of Josephus was Flavius Josephus, and he lived 37 - 100 AD. Josephus was a scholarly man who wrote several historical documents, which are now more than 1900 years old. In addition to the fact that Josephus' books are old, they are also based on sources available at that time: both oral tradition and historical documents that disappeared long ago. The translation of Josephus' books to which reference is made, is based on the 925-page, recently up-dated version of the original English translation by William Thurston (1667-1752), first published in 1736. References to Josephus are given, for example, as JA3/5:7 which means Josephus (Josephus Antiquities), book 3, chapter 5, section 7. Exact references to the works of Josephus can be found in the list of references.

There are also references to other literature, numbered in brackets in the text. The sources referred to can be found in numerical order in the list of references. This book does not claim to cover all the relevant references in this field, but gives examples for further reading. These references are also examples of other sources which can confirm the hypothesis put forward in

Figure 24: What are these structures at the base of the pyramids?

Figure 25: Light finds its way through the vegetation at Mount Moriah in Jerusalem.

this book. There are also references to figures running through the text. These figures include: maps, genealogical tables, illustrations, graphical figures, tables and photographs.

ARE BIBLE TEXTS WELL PRESERVED?

The question as to whether Bible texts are well preserved is an important one. In ancient times when the books of the Bible were copied out, it was naturally done by hand as printing processes came several thousand years later. Copying biblical texts was a special profession, and the slightest mistake was unacceptable. One small error and the whole transcript was destroyed. There were long lists of requirements to be fulfilled in order for the transcript to be approved, and the scribe had many rules to follow in his work. This very thorough control and the fact that Bible texts were considered holy means that the original texts have been preserved in a unique way.

The New Testament books of the Bible, which are about 1900 years old, have a much greater degree of precision compared with the original documents than any other antique literature. If the Greek classics are considered reliable versions of the original texts, then the New Testament texts are far and away better. In comparison, something as late as the works of Shakespeare from the eighteenth century (after the introduction of book-printing skills) have missing texts in many places. When Shakespeare's plays are performed these gaps must be filled or interpreted. There are more than 24,000 hand-written copies of the New Testament from various times, which show that nothing has been lost in the different transcripts. The oldest copies are from a time when eye-witnesses were still alive. In classical literature 1000 years may have passed from the time a work was written until the first preserved copy (1).

As for the Old Testament texts, of which the books of the Pentateuch are the first, there are a number of factors indicating that they are the original texts. They were written down by Moses, in part dictate directly by the Lord himself (according to the Bible), or y described events which Moses, as eye-witness, coul w in detail. This first transcript was a holy object, which in the Holy of Holies in the Ark of the Covenant, in the cle where only the High Priest was allowed to enter. An tribe (the tribe of Levi) had as its sole task to take care of, port and prote the Tabernacle and coi ts. Those who e into contact with the Ark in an unsuitable way e.g. during sport, died on the spot. This, to say the least, afforded special otection for these texts.

Later, those who made copies were under tight control, as has been mentioned above. One small error and the entire copy was scrapped. This was confirmed by the Qumran discoveries in 1947. At that time a document was found that was the Bible book of Isaiah. This document was about a thousand years older than the oldest copy of Isaiah then known. The texts were 95% identical, and the remaining 5% were mainly spelling variations. As far as content was concerned there were no differences (1).

There are also other demands one should make where biblical texts are concerned. Historical events and place names must be correct. This can be diffi-

Figure 26: Who are these people?

Figure 27: The Western Wall of the ancient Jewish Temple in Jerusalem.

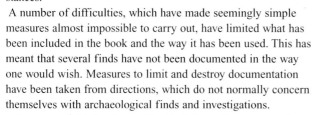

cult when languages change, develop and are influenced by others. During a mere hundred years many names of towns and places in Sweden have changed their spelling and pronunciation. Regarding the accuracy of biblical texts in relating historical events, one can say that the more archaeological finds there are, the more we understand these texts, and realise that many of the things we did not understand before, are in fact correct.

DIFFICULTIES

For those who are not familiar with the region with which this book is concerned, there is reason to briefly mention some of the conditions. It should be noted that many photographs have been taken in extremely difficult circumstances. For example, they may have been taken at great depth under the sea with powerful currents and bad light in shark infested water. Other photographs may come from inaccessible areas. A number of these pictures have been taken with very simple photographic equipment, in special circumstances.

A number of difficulties, which have made seemingly simple measures almost impossible to carry out, have limited what has been included in the book and the way it has been used. This has meant that several finds have not been documented in the way one would wish. Measures to limit and destroy documentation have been taken from directions, which do not normally concern themselves with archaeological finds and investigations.

As you read this book, consider the information you may have already encountered on this subject. Ask yourself what the hypothesis and purpose of this type of information is. Think about the character of such information, and if there are archaeological discoveries which support the hypotheses. Do not believe everything you read or hear, and be equally critical of the contents of this book, testing the hypotheses from your own experience and knowledge.

It is my hope and expectation as the author that you will gain an insight into problems and situations, about which you have not given much thought. It may also be that you have worked a great deal with these questions. In both cases I hope that you will find things which you have not read about before. Perhaps you have something to add, corrections or supplementary information. If so, write to the publisher (address on first page "Exodus/L.Möller" on the envelope) and they will forward you the.

Lennart Möller
Dr.Med.Sci./Ass

Figure 28: Hatshepsut's obelisk at the temple in Karnak.

Figure 29: There is life in the desert.

Figure 30: A deep look into the Red Sea.

PART I

THE PRE-EXODUS PERIOD

FROM ABRAHAM TO MOSES

THE PRE-EXODUS PERIOD

The story of the people of Israel begins in the first books of the Bible, the Pentateuch. It is a comprehensive genealogical chronicle which takes up generation after generation, wives, sons and daughters. Terah's genealogical record (Gen. 11:27 and onwards) concerns a family where Terah himself is the father of a well-known biblical character, Abraham, who is an ancestor of a majority of the peoples in the Middle East. This books begins with Abraham, who leaves his home and goes to the land of Canaan. This departure sets in motion a series of events which later lead to another departure, the Exodus.

Terah was according to the Bible text 130 years old when Abram (later known as Abraham), Nahor and Haran were born. The brothers were born in Ur of the Chaldees where Haran also died while still living near his father. Before his death Haran had three children, his son Lot and his daughters Milcah and Sarai. Nahor married Milcah and Abram married Sarai, who was apparently infertile for a time and could not have children. Figure 33 shows the family tree of these people who lived about 4000 years ago.

Terah took his son Abram and daughter-in-law Sarai with him and left Ur of the Chaldees to go towards the land of Canaan, but they settled in Haran, a place on the way to Canaan.

In this way the story begins about Abraham, Isaac and Jacob and what came to be the prelude to the arrival of the people of Israel in Egypt. Later on they fled from Egypt in the great migration which is called the Exodus. During their flight they come to a mountain which we know as Mount Sinai, Horeb or the mountain of God, but before we come to this there are several big events and also lesser details which are worthy of comment.

In the first part we shall follow Abraham and Sarah and their descendants' lives and travels. Much of this you will recognise since we have concepts, events and stories which live on in our culture whether or not one is Christian, Jew or Muslim. Other events will be completely new for you, and it is here that it begins to be exciting. It is strange to see how the events spanning several thousand years fit together and it is strange how archaeological finds can give rise to new insights about biblical texts and the many thousand years-old history of the Middle East.

Join in the journey which begins in Ur of the Chaldees and then continues to many other places.

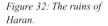

Figure 32: The ruins of Haran.

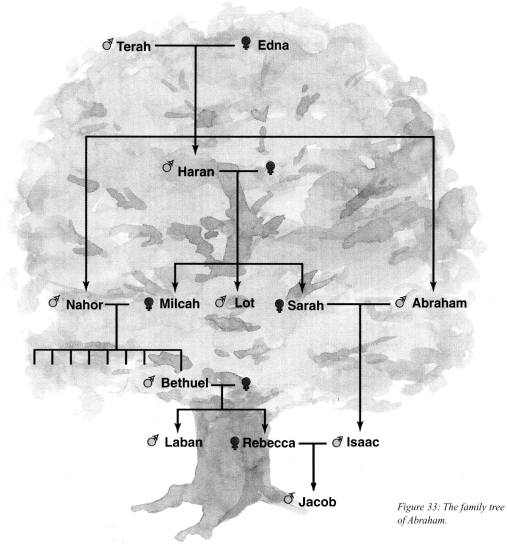

Figure 33: The family tree of Abraham.

1. WHERE WAS UR OF THE CHALDEES LOCATED?

Abram and his family left Ur of the Chaldees on their way towards the land of Canaan, but where was this "Ur of the Chaldees"? A traditional localisation of Ur of the Chaldees is eastwards of modern Israel, some-where between the Euphrates and Tigris rivers in what is Iraq at present. Archaeological discoveries have pointed out a place in southern Iraq which is called Ur. However it is unlikely that Ur in southern Iraq corresponds to Ur of the Chaldees.

1.1. WHERE WAS HARAN LOCATED?

According to the biblical chronology (see chapter 44), Abraham was born in Ur of the Chaldeans around 1996 BC, and he left the area of Ur and Haran on his departure to Canaan around 1921 BC. (Figure 1013)

The Bible text says that they were on the way to Canaan. We know the destination of their journey since Canaan corresponds to Judaea, or the area of present day Israel. They were on the way to Canaan but stayed in Haran. It is known where Haran was situated and still exists today, namely by a subsidiary of the river

Euphrates, called the river Balikh. The place of Haran is marked on modern maps as Harran in southeast Turkey (Figure 40). Haran has been an important town for several thousand years.

Figure 39: Ruins of Haran

Figures 34-38: The photographs show parts of the huge area that is the ruins of Haran.

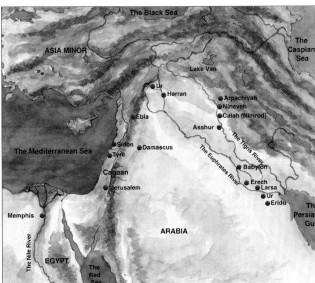

Figure 40: Places in the Middle East that are relevant to the discussion of this book. Ur and Haran referred to in the text are found in the upper middle part of the map.

At one point in time the town was protected by a fort which had 150 rooms, and a wall round the town which was 5 m high, 4 km long, with 187 watch-towers and 6 great gates. Haran was invaded and destroyed by Mongolians in 1260 AD, but a small village still exists on and beside the remains of the Harran city and fortress.

If Terah and his family were on the way to Canaan and passed by Haran, it is probable that Ur of the Chaldees lay approximately north, north-west or north-east to Haran. Otherwise it would have been a roundabout way to pass Haran on the way to Canaan. In those days it was both necessary and most practical to follow a river when one went on a journey. The land alongside rivers was flat, the risk of going astray was small and, perhaps most important of all, there was free access to water for humans, transport animals and cattle, in these often very dry regions.

Figure 41: A traffic sign on the road to Haran.

1.2. COULD URFA CORRESPOND TO UR?

If one follows the river Balikh to the north about 30 km from Haran and then about 8 km to the west, there is a town which today is called Urfa. Could this be the Ur of the Chaldees?

In "The New Encyclopedia Britannica" (2) the following is noted about the town of Urfa:

"The Town lies in the fertile plain of Haran, ringed by limestone hills on three sides... Traditions of earliest foundation associate the site with the legendary king Nimrod, and Muslim legend associates the place with Abraham; a cave beneath Urfa's citadel is said to be Abraham's birthplace. The town's modern name is derived from its early Aramaic name, Urhai"

The region of Ur of the Chaldees was probably the birthplace not only of Abram, but also of his forefathers. It is worth noting that in the area there are several villages, communities and ruins called "Serug" (Abram's great-grandfather), "Nahor" (Abram's grandfather),

Figures 42, 43: Typical huts in today's village of Haran, built on and beside the remains of the ancient Haran.

Figures 44, 45: "Tell" or "Til" means the ruins of a place. These places are often found in the form of a hill on a plain. This is because a village grew to become a city surrounded by walls. Over the ages it was conquered and destroyed. New villages and cities were built on the ruins, which were also destroyed. Finally a hill was created from the large number of ancient layers. This is commonly seen in the Middle East. The figures show an un-excavated "Til" close to Haran, and the "Til" of Haran partly excavated.

Figure 46: Todays "Nemrut" corresponds to ancient "Nimrod".

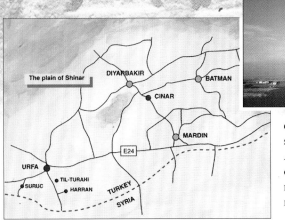

Figure 47, 48: The plain of Cinar (Shinar) with some places that are named after Abrahams family (Terah, Serug, Haran).

"Terah" (Abram's father) and "Haran" (Abram's brother). In addition, the name "Nimrod" (a fore-father to Abraham) is found in the area. These names have changed down the years. Serug is most likely the same place as the one referred to as "Sarugi" in Assyrian documents from around 700 BC and called "Suruc" today. Around 900 BC Terah is referred to as "Til-Turahi", which means the ruins of Terah (figures 44 and 45).

The place called Haran (Abram's brother's name) still exists today, situated in south-eastern Turkey, about 44 km from Urfa by the roads of today. Some of these places are marked on the map in figure 47, which shows Urfa's surroundings near the border between modern Turkey and Syria.

The cave under the town of Urfa's citadel, which according to popular tradition was Abram's birthplace, is still regarded as a holy place today (figure 49).

The city is named Sanliurfa (since 1983), but was earlier named Urfa. Urfa is related to the Hurranian state, and the city is at least from the second millenium BC. Moslems have erected a mosque over the cave, the Crusaders erected a fortress, and there are two columns from an ancient Baal temple, called Nimrod's throne, on top of the mountain. King Abgar Ukkama (9-46 AD) was the founder of Christian traditions of this city, figures 58-62.

Figure 49: The cave under the citadel of Urfa is still regarded as a holy place by Moslems. According to local traditions this was Abram's birthplace.

1.3. WHERE WAS THE PLAIN OF SHINAR LOCATED?

Earlier in the Bible text it is mentioned when the family settled in the area:

"And it came to pass, as they journeyed from the east, that they found a plain in the land of Shinar; and they dwelt there." (Gen. 11:2)

All the places referred to above should be situated on a plain in an area called Shinar. Is it possible to identify this area today, about 4000 years later?

In south-eastern Turkey just north of the Syrian border (northern Mesopotamia) there is a plain. The places referred to above are situated in this area, and in the middle of the plain lies the place called Çinar (corresponds to Shinar). It is interesting to note that Çinar is still the name of a town, as can be seen from the photograph of a modern traffic sign (figure 48). There are also other references indicating Shinar to be located in the northern part of Mesopotamia. One reference locates an area called "Sinjar" in the same area as Shinar, suggesting this "Sinjar" to be a fertile area (4). The plain of today is huge and fertile with red soil.

A further reference to Ur is made in the tablets of Ebla. In the 1970's a library containing 17,000 cuneiform tablets from around 2500 BC, was found in Tell Mardikh (Ebla) in what is now north-western Syria. In this library mention is made of a town called "Ur in the district of Haran" (5).

"It would seem to have been a Hurrian custom to call a place by what was originally the name of a person such as Nahor, Serug or Terah. What is remarkable is that all these geographical names are found in the district of Haran...."
(3)

The historical writer, Josephus, also indicated where the land of the Chaldees lay (JA1/7:2):

"...the land above Babylon, called the land of the Chaldeans... removed from that country also with his people, and went into the land then called the land of Canaan...",

Figures 50, 51: The plain of Cinar (Shinar) is fertile, especially with today's technology providing irrigation from the Euphrates.

This is a description which fits the town of Urfa, and excludes localisation in present day southern Iraq (Babylon), according to Josephus.

"The Jubilee Book" (6), containing legends some 2000 years old, makes a comment which casts light on the route followed from Ur to the land of Canaan. It says that they took the route through Lebanon to Canaan, which further supports the hypothesis that they came from the north (from present day Urfa), and not from the town called Ur in southern Iraq. Nimrod, a forefather to Abraham, is said to have created his kingdom in the "Land of Shinar" (Gen. 10:10).

Mesopotamia is defined as the area between the rivers Euphrates and Tigris. The plain of Shinar discussed in this text is located between these two rivers. It just so happens that these two rivers are close to the borders of this plain.

1.4. What does "Chaldees" refer to?

The origin of the name Chaldees is lost in obscurity. Biblical texts mention the Chaldees in various passages e.g. Stephen refers to the Chaldees in his defence speech, which begins with the story of Abram (Acts 7:1-53), and Job was attacked by Chaldeans (Job 1:17). Further reference is found in the book of Daniel in the story of Nebuchadnezzar, the king in Babylon who besieged Jerusalem. After conquering Jerusalem, Nebuchadnezzar chose several Hebrews, among them the man who became the prophet Daniel, to be taught the writing and language of the Chaldeans (Dan. 1:1-7).

However, the Chaldean language and culture referred to in the book of Daniel date back to a time approximately 600 BC, about 1300 years after Abram's migration, so these references are of no help in connecting the texts with Ur of the Chaldees.

Can the true explanation of the name Ur of the Chaldees be connected to the religion which was to be found in the area, where the town of Ur (Urfa of today) was situated? The original inhabitants of the area corresponding to south-eastern Turkey were called Hurrians and Urartuans. Inscriptions show that they had at least 79 different gods, and this collection of gods was called "Khaldis". Part of a text from the Argistis inscription reads:

"This is the spoil of the cities which I obtained for the people of the Khaldis in one year... To Khaldis, the giver, to the Khaldises, the supreme givers, the children of Khaldis the mighty..."

The remains of the temple of the god Khaldis, in Topprakkale in modern Turkey can be found near Lake Van (figure 52).

Table 1. Maps showing a city, a river and a plain with the name Sinjar (Shinar) south-east to, and on the same plain as Haran.

"Sinjac"	1784	Antonio Zatta
"Sinyar"	1808	C. S. Smith
"Sinjar" (the city)	1814	Thomson
"Sinjar R." (the river)	1814	Thomson
"Sinjar"	1816	Lapie
"Sinjar"	1820	Thomas Kelly
"Sindjar" (the city)	1822	Brué
"Sindjar" (the river)	1822	Brué
"Sinjar"	1824	A. Finley
"Sinjar"	1829	A. Macpherson
"Sinjar"	1830	M. Bull Holles
"Sinjar" (the city)	1845	G. F. Cruchley
"R. Sinjar" (the river)	1845	G. F. Cruchley
"Desert of Sinjar" (the plain)	1845	G. F. Cruchley
"Sinjar"	1855	C. B. Colton
"Sindschar"	1863	F. v. Stülpnagel
"Sindjar"	1869	Justus Perthes
"Sinjar"	1870	A. Fullerton
"Sinjar"	1947	H. Teesdale

Figure 52: The Argistis inscription is referred to in the text. On this old German map from 1805 (G.A. Oliver) a place called "Argish" was located at Lake Van ("See Wan") where the "Khaldis" religion was practiced. The colours of the map are the original colours.

Figure 53: This map was published by John Tallis around 1860 and is shown with its original colours. In the middle of this part of the map three places are located close to one another; Urfah (Ur), Harran (Haran) and Seroug (Serug). The blue coloured river to the left is the Euphrat river. On maps printed the last 200 years, Serug is most often spelled "Saruj" or "Seroug".

Figure 54: In 1845 G.F. Cruchley published this map. The map shows a region southeast of Haran but on the same plain. A city shown on many old maps is called "Sinjar". This city also gave the same name to a river ("River Sinjar") and a plain ("Desert of Sinjar"). These three names can be seen in the middle of this map section. It is possible that this plain is the plain of Shinar which the biblical texts refer to. Haran is located by the river that enters the Euphrat river from the north at "Racca" (left part of the map section).

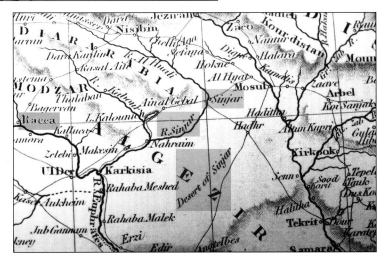

These people lived in the area where Urfa lies today. It is probable that there were several towns called Ur, and therefore it was necessary to specify which Ur was meant. It would be very convenient to indicate the religion as specification: Khaldis Ur, or as we now say several thousand years later, Ur of the Chaldees.

1.5. CAN THE ORIGIN OF "CHALDEES" BE TRACED?

Around Lake Van in today's eastern Turkey the above mentioned god "Khaldi" was worshipped. Several references have other transliteration by sound of the name of this god. Two examples are: "Haldi" in the Urartian temple of Toprakkale (8), and "Kalhu" from the northern part of Mesopotamia (9). In the area where the Urartu god "Haldi" was worshipped (south-east Turkey) the language was called "Haldian or Chaldian", today the name "Urartian" is used (7-9). In addition to this are different spellings of the place "Toprakkale", where this god had a temple. At the British Museum in London one spelling is found that sheds light on this name: "Toppra Khale" (compare to Khaldi) where the god "Haldi" had a temple. This gives a number of translations of the god/religion in the area of south-east Turkey (northern Mesopotamia); "Khaldi", "Haldi", "Kalhu", "Chaldeans" at the Urartian temple "Toppra Khale", where they spoke the languages "Haldian" or "Chaldian". It is not hard to draw the conclusion that all these very similar names refer to the same god/religion/language, especially since they refer to the same area and time in history.

> "...Nimrod, the Assyrian city of Kalhu (Biblical Calah)...." (8)

Around todays Urfa there are a large number of names and places, villages and cities that have the "Kale"-part in their names. Kale or "Khale" relates to the Khaldis cult of ancient times in south-east Turkey. Examples of these names are listed in Table 2, figures 55-57.

Figures 55-57: Examples of places in the region of Urfa that have the "kale" part in their names.

It is interesting that there are two places close to one another with similar names, Gerger and Gerger kales. This could also be written Gerger and Gerger of the Chaldees. Kale is also a name found at other places in Turkey, for instance the well known hot springs in Pamukkale.

Today Kale is under-

Table 2. Further examples of places in the region of Urfa that have the "kale"-part in their modern names.

Akcakale
Topprakkale
Direkkale
Eski kale
Kale (several places)
Rumkale
Tapkirankale
Yilani-kale
Gerger kales
Yeni kale

Figures 58-62: Urfa (Ur) is dominated by the mosque built above the cave where Abram, according to local traditions, was born. Two major minarets are raised at the mosque. In front of the mosque the "Pond of the prophet" is found with holy fish. The prophet the name refers to is Abram. Around the mountain behind the mosque a fort was erected by the Crusaders. On the peak of the mountain two columns were raised in ancient times to worship Baal. The temple of Baal was at this location named "Nimrod's throne".

stood as castle or fortress. However, in ancient times the most important place was where the gods were worshipped. That place was also protected or surrounded by a fortress. This is seen all over the world. Examples are the walled city and temple of Jerusalem, or the old churches of Sweden. These churches were grain storage places for years of famine, the only place built of rock to shield people from foreign attacks. Often the place with a tower was used to look for fires or ships from the sea. In addition to the church tower it was common to have a "kastal" (same word as castle) meaning a defence tower. Therefore, it is logical to understand the word Khale/Kale meaning the god/the church/the temple/place of worship/proteced by walls or a defence system some 4000 years ago, and that the interpretation today is more focused on the defence system (castle or fortress).

In the example in Urfa (figures 58-62), there is a place for worship (the Cave of Abraham), the mosque and a defence system (the walled part of the fortress).

1.6. THE RELIGION OF THE AREA

The Bible texts relate that Joshua indicates an approximate location of Ur of the Chaldees when he addresses the people of Israel much later in Shekem:

"Your fathers dwelt on the other side of the flood in old time, even Terah, the father of Abraham, and the father of Nachor..." (Josh. 24:2)

The river is the Euphrates and this description fits present day Urfa very well. The text also mentions the fact that both Abram and his father lived in the same area. Around Urfa there are a number of villages and other places which have the names of Abram's relatives (Nimrod, Serug, Nahor, Terah and Haran). The Prophet Joshua says something else that is worth noting:

"...and they served other gods." (Josh. 24:2)

Two things are said here. The first is that they served other gods, not another god. This fits in with the Khaldis religion, which had at least 79 gods. The second is that here there is a possible reason why Terah (who served other gods) was only allowed to reach Haran, where he died at a great age. Only Abram, called by the Lord, the one true God according to the text, was allowed to enter the promised land of Canaan, but not Terah who served other gods. This hypothesis is supported by the Bible text of Acts 7:4.

As late as 1800 years after these events legends still mentioned them. The Jubilee Book is not part of the Old Testament, but it describes the events in the books of the Pentateuch. It was written, at the latest, in the year approximately 100 BC, perhaps much earlier (10). In this book there is a comment of interest in this context. When Abram was 60 years old, he arose one night and burned down the building where all the idols were. When the people awoke because of the fire, Abram's brother Haran rushed into the burning house to save the idols, and died in the flames. The Bible text only mentions that Haran died in Ur (Gen. 11:28). Urfa of today has more than 400 000 inhabitants, while Haran is a small village built on the remains of ancient Haran (figures 42-45).

Figures 63, 64: Traffic signs showing ancient places, Suruc (Serug), Urfa (Ur) and Harran (Haran).

1.7. In summary

There are a number of indications, which together strongly support the hypothesis that it is the Urfa of today in south-eastern Turkey, which was Ur of the Chaldees; where Abram and his forefathers lived, and which they later left to journey towards the land of Canaan. These indications include the following:

♦ Urfa is situated on a plain. Two places on this plain are called Çinar and Sinjar, respectively. Ur of the Chaldees must be situated on the Shinar plain.
♦ Around Urfa there are several places, to which Abram's forefathers have given their names. Ur must be situated near such places.
♦ Local legends (popular tradition) indicate Urfa as Abram's birthplace. There is also a cave, which is still regarded as the birthplace today.
♦ The gods of the Chaldeans were worshipped in this area, which provides a probable explanation for the specification of the Ur that was meant, Ur of the Chaldees.
♦ In this area it seems that people worshipped many gods. The Khaldis cult consisted of at least 79 different gods.
♦ On the tablets of Ebla a town called Ur is indicated in the Haran district. Ur of the Chaldees (present day Urfa) is in the neighbourhood of Haran.
♦ Josephus indicates that the Chaldees were situated north of Babylon, as present day Urfa is.
♦ The direction is right if one came from Urfa and stopped in Haran on the way to Canaan.
♦ The Jubilee Book (of legends written down long after the event) indicates that they came via Lebanon, which was from the north.
♦ On the way from Urfa to Haran one could follow rivers, which was very important in these often very dry regions.
♦ Several references indicate that the god/religion "Khaldi", "Haldi", "Kalhu" or "Chaldeans", at the Urartian temple "Toppra Khale" (where they spoke the languages "Haldian" or "Chaldian"), where to be found in the plain of Shinar, where todays Urfa is located.
♦ Still today, many places in the region of Urfa have "Kale" as part of their name.

2. Who was Abram?

Terah, the father of Abram, died at the age of 205 in Haran. In those days the length of human life was becoming shorter and shorter (according to the Bible text) until the time of Moses, who lived to be 120 years old (Gen. 6:3).
When Abram is in Haran the Lord speaks directly to him and says:

"Get thee out of thy country, and from thy kindred, and from thy father's house, unto a land that I will shew thee: And I will make of thee a great nation, and I will bless thee, and make thy name great; and thou shalt be a blessing: And I will bless them that bless thee, and curse him that curseth thee: and in thee shall all families of the earth be blessed." (Gen. 12:1-3)

When the Lord says this to Abram it is around 1920 BC (chronology is discussed in detail in chapter 44). Abram, who is then 75 years old, takes with him his wife Sarai, his nephew Lot, servants (indicating that Abram is wealthy) and possessions, and he journeys on until he reaches the land of Canaan (figures 66-68). Abraham is told to leave his "father's house", but instead he allows his father to join him with the others. It is possible that this is the reason why they have to stop in Haran: to wait until his father dies (Act. 7:4).

2.1. The origin of the name of Canaan?

The land of Canaan was named after the fourth son of Ham (a person who lived earlier than Abram). The land of Canaan corresponds to what was called Judaea much later, in the time of Jesus. An area from Gaza to Egypt was inhabited by Canaanites, and called Palestine by the Greeks (JA/6:2). The Hebrews, later known as the people of Israel, received their name (according to one hypothesis) from Heber. Heber was a forefather of Abram, and lived six generations earlier, according to Josephus (JA1/6:4). According to other sources the name originates from "charibu", the ancient name of a nation in the Middle East.

Figure 65: These sheep are grazing on the ancient remains of Haran. Maybe their ancestors were the sheep of Abram?

Figures 66-68: These are probably the views Abraham saw when he entered Canaan from the north.

2.2. To Canaan and then to Egypt

Abram journeys into the land of Canaan, to a holy place called Shekem. When Abram is in Shekem the Lord appears to him and says:

"Unto thy seed will I give this land." (Gen. 12:7)

Abram builds an altar to the Lord in Shekem because it is here that the Lord appears to him and promises him a country which will belong to his descendants. Abram journeys on to Bethel where he pitches his tent. Here too, Abram builds an altar to the Lord. In figure 69 Abram's encampments and journeys can be followed.

There is famine in the land, and Abram and his retinue move on southwards to Egypt. Abram is an erudite man, who discusses with and instructs the scholars in Egypt, both in science and theology. According to Josephus, Abram introduces astronomy (the science of planets and stars) and arithmetic (basic mathematics) into Egypt; sciences which had their origins in the Chaldees from where Abram probably emigrated (JA1/8:2).

2.3. Abram and Lot go separate ways

Later on, Abram and Lot return from Egypt to the land of Canaan, very prosperous regarding cattle as well as silver and gold. There is quarrelling between Abram's and Lot's herdsmen, and they decide to go their separate ways. Abram tells Lot to choose his part of the land, and Abram will take another. Lot chooses the fertile Jordan valley, which before the Lord destroyed Sodom and Gomorrah was like the garden of Eden (Gen. 13:10). Lot chooses the whole plain of Jordan (the dramatic developments on the plain of Jordan are dealt with in chapter 3), while Abram remains in Canaan (Gen. 13:1-13). According to the Bible text the Lord speaks to Abram and says:

"Lift up now thine eyes, and look from the place where thou art northward, and southward, and eastward, and westward: For all the land which thou seest, to thee will I give it, and to thy seed for ever. And I will make thy seed as the dust of the earth: so that if a man can number the dust of the earth, then shall thy seed also be numbered. Arise, walk through the land in the length of it and in the breadth of it; for I will give it unto thee."
(Gen. 13:14-17)

Abram later settles in Hebron and there, too, he builds an altar to the Lord. Once again the Lord appears to Abram. Abram and the Lord discuss things together. The Lord promises Abram that he will be the ancestor of a great people, a people as numerous as the stars while Abram complains that he has

Figure 69: The journeys of Abraham.

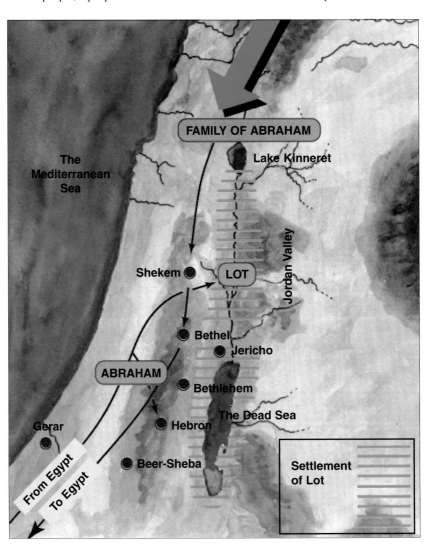

no heir. Again the promise to Abram is repeated:

"I am the LORD that brought thee out of Ur of the Chaldees, to give thee this land to inherit it." (Gen. 15:7)

2.4. A PREDICTION OF THE FUTURE

Afterwards the Lord predicts the future. Abram will not experience it, but his descendants will. It is here that the Lord predicts what this book will focus on: the life of the descendants of Abram as slaves in Egypt, and their flight, the Exodus - the great migration from Egypt.

"And he said unto Abram, Know of a surety that thy seed shall be a stranger in a land that is not their's, and shall serve them; and they shall afflict them four hundred years; And also that nation, whom they shall serve, will I judge: and afterward shall they come out with great substance. And thou shalt go to thy fathers in peace; thou shalt be buried in a good old age." (Gen. 15:13-15)

2.5. A PROMISE GIVEN TO ABRAM

The Bible text then tells us that on the same day the Lord makes a promise to Abram and says:

"Unto thy seed have I given this land, from the river of Egypt unto the great river, the river Euphrates: " (Gen. 15:18)

In their old age, Abram and Sarai are still childless. By now Abram is 85 years old and Sarai 75. It is understandable that they begin to despair, despite the Lord's promise of children. Sarai therefore gives her Egyptian maid Hagar to Abram as his concubine, so that she will give Abram a child. Hagar becomes pregnant, and an angel appears to her and says that her son is to be called Ishmael. The Lord also says that Ishmael will be at odds with his brothers. Ishmael is born when Abram is 86 years old. Ishmael in turn has 12 sons, who settle between the Euphrates and the Red Sea, which means east and south-east of present day Israel (figure 70).

Abram grows old, and when he is 99 the Lord appears to him again:

"I am the Almighty God; walk before me, and be thou perfect. And I will make my covenant between me and thee, and will multiply thee exceedingly." (Gen. 17:1-2)

Abram throws himself to the ground and the Lord continues:

"As for me, behold, my covenant is with thee, and thou shalt be a father of many nations. Neither shall thy name any more be called Abram, but thy name shall be Abraham; for a father of many nations have I made thee. And I will make thee exceeding fruitful, and I will make nations of thee, and kings shall come out of thee.
*   And I will establish my covenant between me and thee and thy seed after*

thee in their generations for an everlasting covenant, to be a God unto thee, and to thy seed after thee. And I will give unto thee, and to thy seed after thee, the land wherein thou art a stranger, all the land of Canaan, for an everlasting possession; and I will be their God. And God said unto Abraham,

Thou shalt keep my covenant therefore, thou, and thy seed after thee in their generations. This is my covenant, which ye shall keep, between me and you and thy seed after thee; Every man child among you shall be circumcised. And ye shall circumcise the flesh of your foreskin; and it shall be a token of the covenant betwixt me and you.

And he that is eight days old shall be circumcised among you, every man child in your generations, he that is born in the house, or bought with money of any stranger, which is not of thy seed." (Gen. 17:4-12)

"As for Sarai thy wife, thou shalt not call her name Sarai, but Sarah shall her name be. And I will bless her, and give thee a son also of her: yea, I will bless her, and she shall be a mother of nations; kings of people shall be of her.

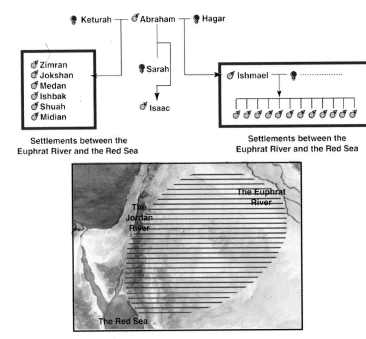

Settlements between the Euphrat River and the Red Sea

Settlements between the Euphrat River and the Red Sea

Figure 70: Abraham's family tree and areas of the settlements: east of the Jordan River, between the Red Sea and the Euphrates.

Then Abraham fell upon his face, and laughed, and said in his heart, Shall a child be born unto him that is an hundred years old? and shall Sarah, that is ninety years old, bear? And Abraham said unto God, O that Ishmael might live before thee!

And God said, Sarah thy wife shall bear thee a son indeed; and thou shalt call his name Isaac: and I will establish my covenant with him for an everlasting covenant, and with his seed after him. And as for Ishmael, I have heard thee:

Behold, I have blessed him, and will make him fruitful, and will multiply him exceedingly; twelve princes shall he beget, and I will make him a great nation. But my covenant will I establish with Isaac, which Sarah shall bear unto thee at this set time in the next year." (Gen. 17:15-21)

In this passage of the Bible, the Lord says very clearly that the sign of the covenant he has established with Abram will be circumcision. The Lord also gives Abram and Sarai new names. From now on they are called Abraham and Sarah. The covenant will be forever, and the promised land will belong

to his descendants forever, according to the Bible text. Sarah is promised a
son, which Abraham considers highly unlikely (Abraham is 100 and Sarah 90
years old at this time), but the Lord continues to talk with Abraham and
declares that the son will be called Isaac. It is with Isaac that the covenant is
established and sealed. We come back to Isaac in chapter 4.

2.6. IN SUMMARY

To summarise, the following can be said of Abraham:

◆ Abraham was a person to whom the Lord chose to speak 4000 years ago.
  In this way Abraham was chosen and became an ancestor of the peoples of
  the Middle East.
◆ Abraham's seed was promised the land of Canaan.
◆ During a time of famine Abraham emigrated to Egypt.
◆ When Abraham and Lot returned to Canaan, Abraham settled in Hebron
  and Lot in the Jordan valley.
◆ The Lord spoke with Abraham and predicted the slavery and liberation
  of the Hebrews in Egypt (Part II in this book).
◆ The Lord made a promise to Abraham, which was later established and
  sealed with Isaac.
◆ The Lord gave Abram and Sarai new names: Abraham and Sarah.
◆ The sign of the covenant between the Lord and Abraham was
  circumcision, a tradition which both Arabs and Jews still retain.

*Figure 71: Traditional farming
in Egypt very similar to ancient
traditions. Abraham stayed for
some time in Egypt.*

We shall follow Abraham's son Isaac but first we shall see what happened to
Lot, the one who accompanied Abraham and Sarah (he was Sarah's brother,
see figure 33) and settled in the Jordan valley (figure 69).

3. WHAT HAPPENED IN SODOM AND GOMORRAH?

Sodom, Gomorrah and several other towns in the valley of Jordan were so
sinful that the wrath of the Lord was aroused, according to the Bible texts.
The background is described in Gen. 18:16 - 19:28, but if we pass over this
and go directly to the biblical description of the course of events, then it
reads as follows:

*"The sun was risen upon the earth when Lot entered into Zoar. Then the
LORD rained upon Sodom and upon Gomorrah brimstone and fire from the
LORD out of heaven; And he overthrew those cities, and all the plain, and all
the inhabitants of the cities, and that which grew upon the ground." (Gen.
19:23-25)*

The passage recounts that these towns in the Jordan valley were destroyed by
fire and burning sulphur, which rained down on them. One of the towns was
Sodom, where Lot and his family lived. It is logical to assume that everything in the path of this burning-sulphur-rain was consumed by the intense
heat. In consequence, one cannot look for the usual archaeological finds in
such places.
  Masada is a large fortified mountain, with a plateau about 440 m above the
surrounding area. This mountain stands near the south-west bank of the Dead

Sea, and was the last outpost of the Jewish defence when the Romans tried to wipe them out, after the destruction of the temple in Jerusalem in 70 AD. This happened much later than the event which annihilated Sodom and Gomorrah around 1897 BC.

3.1. THE LOCALISATION OF GOMORRAH

Right up against Masada there are remains which could be one of the towns in the biblical narration. The area of approximately 3 x 2 km differs noticeably from the surroundings. With a little imagination one could picture streets, walls and sphinxes. However, these observations alone are not sufficient, and by definition are speculative.

Figure 73 shows a view of the area from the Masada plateau. Part of this area is seen in the picture marked in red. The rest of the area is partly seen in the left-hand side of the photograph, also marked in red. The coloured areas differ noticeably from the surroundings, as far as appearance and mineral type are concerned. In figure 73 this is seen as a lighter and more hilly area. The Dead Sea is seen in the background. Figure 72 shows a close-up of the red-coloured area in figure 73.

While the surrounding area is made up of large, flat surfaces with stones and gravel that are solid in character (quartz and something resembling feldspar, figures 74-75), the area in figure 72 is hilly, has vertical walls of rock and is covered in a thick layer of a heavy, fine-grained substance. This layer, which is found all over the area, is seen as drifts in figure 72. One could speculate that there has been something on this spot, which might have been a town, but it is altogether too badly destroyed to be able to judge.

The remains, which can be seen in various places in the area, are somewhat more interesting. One example is rows of stone blocks, which are probably of some quartz-based species of rock that is not destroyed by burning sulphur. These rows of stone could well have been street paving, house foundations or something similar (figures 76-77).

In other places the remains have more the characteristics of walls where right-angles can be found, something that is not so common in natural rock formations.

Figures 72, 73: The area of Gomorrah seen from the rock of Masada. In the background the Dead Sea can be seen.

3.2. SULPHUR BALLS

The mineral is noticeably eroded and what differs from the surroundings are the ash-like remains, which encase all the raised parts. However it is not ordinary ash, but a heavy ash-like substance. What is odd about the area is that there are large quantities of sulphur balls, which range from a few

centimetres in diameter to the size of a tennis ball. These sulphur balls are only spread over this special site, within the area that looks different (coloured area in figure 73).

In figure 85 there are a number of these sulphur balls with a diameter of between one and eight cm. These sulphur balls have melted into the rock species, and one can trace how the sulphur has penetrated into the mineral at a high temperature, which shows that the sulphur has burned. This can be seen in figures 79 and 80. The block of stone is divided into two parts. On the right is the channel through which the sulphur ball has melted down through the stone. When the sulphur had passed through, the channel sealed itself together again and, with the lack of oxygen, the fire of the sulphur went out.

The heat has caused changes in the mineral, and these can be seen as brown rings in the mineral encompassing the sulphur ball. These rings are clearly seen in figures 81 and 82. The sulphur ball has later been encased in a shell, formed by the high temperature followed by cooling, which is also seen in figures 88 and 89. The points of impact of the sulphur are marked like "machine-gun fire" over the whole area. This is most clearly seen in figure 78, which shows a large number of shell-covered sulphur balls where the surrounding mineral has eroded.

Figures 74, 75: The normal ground material, found in the area of the Dead Sea.

The mineral has crumbled away in many places in the area. However, the shells round the sulphur balls have been more resistant to erosion. This can look as in figure 78, with perhaps a hundred or more shell-covered sulphur balls on a very small surface. Each rounded, raised object in the picture is a shell-covered sulphur ball, and here too the size varies from about 1 to 10 cm in diameter. If a shell is broken up, the sulphur ball can be seen clearly. If the balls are picked out, they look like those in figures 85 and 89.

The sulphur is found not only in the loose, eroded material, but also in blocks of stone and rock faces, which have not yet eroded (figure 83). In the example from figure 83, the yellow ball was tested on location to see if it was sulphur. The ball was set alight when the flame of a cigarette lighter was held to it, the ball then burned with a strong smell of sulphur while giving out intense heat. Figure 83 shows the sulphur ball in place in the rock face, while figure 84 shows the same sulphur ball burning. A further indication that there have been high temperatures in the area is the shape of the rock faces, which seem to have bulged out due to great heat, as can be seen in figure 86.

3.3. Fruit-like remains

The historical writer Josephus makes an interesting, 1900 year-old note (11). He recounts how beautiful it was before everything burned up, and how rich the towns were in the area. Rich towns imply the existence of large buildings, temples, walls etc. Josephus describes what happened:

Figures 76, 77: Could these solid rocks, in different patterns within the "ashes" of Gomorrah, have been some kind of construction?

"Now this country is then so sadly burnt up, that nobody cares to come to

Figure 78: There are a high number of sulphur balls in the area. Each formation seen in the picture is a sulphur ball covered with a shell.

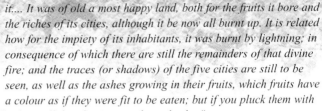

it.... *It was of old a most happy land, both for the fruits it bore and the riches of its cities, although it be now all burnt up. It is related how for the impiety of its inhabitants, it was burnt by lightning; in consequence of which there are still the remainders of that divine fire; and the traces (or shadows) of the five cities are still to be seen, as well as the ashes growing in their fruits, which fruits have a colour as if they were fit to be eaten; but if you pluck them with your hands, they will dissolve into smoke and ashes"*.

This description fits in very well with the appearance of the area in figure 72. It is also very easy to associate the sulphur balls with a pale yellow citrous fruit with a thin, rough skin which crumbles easily in one's fingers. What crumbles away (minerals and sulphur balls) is like ash, and so fine-grained that it is difficult to brush off one's clothes. In figure 87 a "peeled fruit" is held in the hand.

3.4. A DESCRIPTION OF THE AREA

Josephus makes another note in the section quoted, namely that the remains of these towns can be seen as shadows. In order to cast a shadow an object must be higher than its surroundings, and this is precisely how it looks in the place where these sulphur balls are situated (figures 73 and 90-92).

Immediately before the section of Josephus quoted above, it is stated that the district of Sodom and Gomorrah lies very near the

Figures 79, 80: The burning sulphur ball has melted its way down through the rock. Due to the heat the canal has sealed and with no oxygen there is no further combustion (fire). The mineral close to the sulphur ball is relatively resistant to erosion, and thereby forms a shell.

Figures 81, 82: The heat of the burning sulphur has coloured the surrounding material.

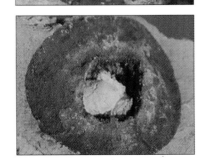

Figures 83, 84: A sulphur ball in the rock material and the same sulphur when burning.

Figure 85: Examples of sulphur balls. Approximate sizes are 1-10 cm in diameter.

Dead Sea. This description also fits the localisation of the area in figure 73, where part of the Dead Sea can be seen in the background.

Figure 86: This pattern of the rock suggests strong heat at formation.

3.5. CHEMICAL REACTIONS IN CONNECTION TO BURNING SULPHUR

Samples were collected from different places in this area in order to analyse the rock species and minerals. The analyses imply that what happened with the burning sulphur was as follows:

Samples from the outer area (not exposed to the intensive heat) are mainly limestone or, to use more chemical terms, calcite or calcium carbonate ($CaCO_3$). This corresponds to the building materials most common in the region, but differs from the surrounding area which consists of quartz and feldspar minerals.

As far as the sulphur balls are concerned, the mineralogist who was to analyse these samples did not believe that it was sulphur, since this form of sulphur is not like the sulphur otherwise found in nature. However the analyses showed that it was pure sulphur (S).

Figure 87: "...which fruits have a colour as if they were fit to be eaten..." as stated nearly 2000 years ago.

The mineral samples that came from the hot area where the sulphur balls were, were found to be gypsum, or in chemical terms calcium sulphate ($CaSO_4$).

All the analyses were carried out with X-ray crystallography, liquid chromatography and atom absorption spectrophotometers, by qualified geological and analytical chemistry laboratories, who knew nothing about the identity of the samples to be analysed.

The results from this analysis mean that one can explain in simple chemical terms what is most likely to have happened in this place, according to figure 93. According to the figure, CO_2 (carbon dioxide) is released from $CaCO_3$ (the limestone) under intensive heat (in this case burning sulphur). At the same time the sulphur (S) is oxidised to sulphur dioxide (SO_2), which reacts with water to form sulphate (SO_4^{2-}). The calcium ion (Ca^{2+}) can then react with the sulphur ion (SO_4^{2-}) and form calcium sulphate ($CaSO_4$). Calcium sulphate is what we call gypsum. Analyses of the dominating mineral in this area show that it is gypsum.

Then what is the so-called "ash" found in the area? It is seen in figure 94 as an eroded material lying in drifts below all the raised parts. The "ash" is very fine-grained and it clings to clothing, being very difficult to brush off. It can best be compared to coarsely ground flour. The colour is grey with particles

Figures 90-92: The "ash-like" remains of the probable location of Gomorrah.

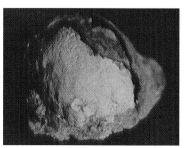

Figure 88: A sulphur ball surrounded by a thin shell.

Figure 89: An opened shell with a sulphur ball.

41

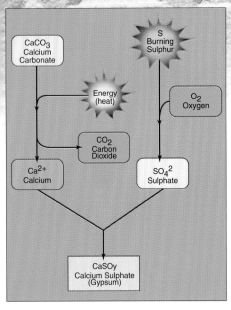

Figure 93: The probable scheme of chemical reactions of the disaster that struck this place.

Figure 94: The "ash-like" remains lying in drifts below all raised parts.

of a lighter tone. A faint smell of sulphur can be discerned.

3.6. WHAT IS THE "ASH"?

Chemical analysis shows that the "ash" contains a relatively large amount of sulphur (4.5 %), which stems from the erosion of the sulphur balls described earlier. As far as other minerals are concerned the "ash" consists of the following on a diminishing scale: $CaCO_3$ (aragonite and calcite), $CaSO_4$ (gypsum) and SiO_2 (quartz); lesser quantities of NaCl (salt) and $CaMg(CO_3)_2$ (dolomite) and possibly a small quantity of CaF_2 (fluorite).

These analyses show that the "ash" contains the same minerals as the solid matter of which the area consists, and that in the eroded material there is also a large amount of sulphur. Even the eroded matter has consisted earlier of fixed structures of limestone, which to a large extent have been transformed to gypsum on exposure to burning sulphur. The salt, which is found in lesser quantities in the "ash", exists in the whole area round the Dead Sea. The Dead Sea itself has approximately 25-28% solid material, mainly salt, which corresponds to a salt-saturated solution. The normal proportion of salt in the earth's oceans is approximately 4%. The high salt content of the Dead Sea is the reason for the absence of life in the lake ("Dead"), and why people have problems swimming since they "float" on top of the water.

All of this means that the analyses indicate that the limestone was exposed to burning sulphur, which to a great extent has transformed the limestone to gypsum. Gypsum wears away easily and is one of the main components in the "ash" lying in large drifts in the area.

If the analysis of sulphur content is representative of historical times, sulphur fell over the area in an amount corresponding to at least 5% of the amount of solid rock in the area. It was definitely much more, since a large portion of the sulphur either reacted with calcium (forming gypsum, the dominating material in the area) or disappeared as gas (sulphur dioxide). Thus, the total sulphur exposure to the area was enormous.

3.7. CHARACTERISTICS OF THE AREA

The minerals usually found in the region round the Dead Sea are stone and gravel composed of several species of rock such as quartz and feldspar. In this limited site with a surface of about 3 x 2 km there is an area which differs from the surroundings: it is composed of another mineral, is higher than the surrounding area, looks different from the surrounding area, and it feels as if one is walking in heavy ash or sand when one climbs the eroded sides. In addition, the limited area looks as though it has been subjected to "machine-gun fire" of sulphur.

Part of the sulphur melted its way into the limestone, and when the melted path closed up again the sulphur remained and the fire went out because of the lack of oxygen. Following the erosion of surrounding matter, these balls have appeared all over the area, partly in severely eroded sections and partly as sulphur balls with a shell made of the surrounding mineral that had previously melted down.

The chemical analyses (and not least by simply looking around the place) indicate that burning sulphur rained down on this limited area. Further confirmation that it is sulphur found in the area, is that it can be set alight. The effect of an open flame held to one of the sulphur balls is shown in figures 83 and 84. The sulphur catches fire immediately, and burns for a relatively long period of time, giving out intense heat.

3.8. THE ORIGIN OF THE SULPHUR?

The occurrence of sulphur cannot be compared with what is normally found in nature. If gases from springs or volcanoes condense, crusts of sulphur are often formed consisting of small crystals or amorphous structures (figure 95). Sulphur can also be found in crystalline form with beautiful crystals of bright yellow colour (figure 96). Otherwise, sulphur is most commonly found in reaction products with other substances, for example as sulphides and sulphates. Only on occasion, have very small particles of solid sulphur been found.

One form of sulphur which is often found in connection with fossils is iron sulphide (FeS_2). Iron sulphide has a characteristic brassy yellow or gilt metallic lustre. It is not uncommon that the inexperienced observer confuses iron sulphide, which is also called pyrite, with gold. In figures 97 and 98 fossils of once living organisms can be seen with remains of sulphur in the form of lustrous gold like iron sulphide crystals (pyrite), from the Swedish island of Gotland.

The sulphur (in the form of sulphur balls) which occurs near the Dead Sea is only found in these specific locations, which differ greatly from the surroundings. Sulphur is not present together with, or adjacent to, fossils which have not been found in these places where discoveries have been made. The sulphur differs from what is usually found near volcanoes (crusts of sulphuric crystal mass, individual crystals or in the form of sulphur minerals), or in connection with fossils (sulphides e.g. pyrite crystals). The sulphur occurs as pure sulphur, in a compressed powder form. The area has been volcanic, but this was a very long time ago, even in geological terms.

Figure 95: The structure of amorphous sulphur.

It is most likely that the sulphur in these places has had such a high temperature that it has melted its way through the mineral on the spot, and later died out because of the lack of oxygen. The sulphur is not in the form of crystals, crusts nor iron sulphide, but is more in the form of balls of compressed powder rather like blackboard chalk.

All things considered, it can be said that the character of the area and chemical analyses indicate that burning sulphur has "rained" down on the place. The high temperature of the burning-sulphur-rain (together with lightning according to the Bible text) makes normal archaeological finds impossible, but there are other finds that are worthy of comment.

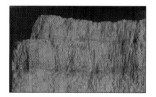

Figure 96: Crystalline structure of sulphur.

In several places there are rows of stones, of more stable rock species (quartz and feldspar), within the gypsum and calcite. The rows of stones

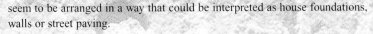

seem to be arranged in a way that could be interpreted as house foundations, walls or street paving.

3.9. ORGANIC MATERIAL

Organic material is found at the outer edges of the area (colder areas), and this seems to have melted together with other minerals (non-transformed limestone). That temperatures have been lower in the outer areas is supported by the fact that there is less occurrence of sulphur, there is a relative abundance of limestone and that carbon is found in a tar form or a form resembling coke. Tar was an important product in this area. Earlier the Dead Sea was called the "Asphalt Sea" due to the abundance of asphalt-like tar, which floated up to the surface (11). This tar was an important commodity, which generated income for the area (Hes.16:49). Figure 99 shows an example of coke-like tar, which has melted together with limestone.

Figures 97, 98: Fossils from Sweden that have formed pyrite from sulphur, seen as gold-like crystals.

3.10. IRON

Iron is a metal which occurs in nature as a reaction product with other substances (e.g. iron ore). If pure iron is found in nature it is almost always of human origin. Melted metal has been found in the area. In figures 100-101 an example of this is shown. The figures show a piece of metal, which is distinctive as it is pure iron (magnetic as well as chemical analysis) oxidised in the outer parts. The piece of metal seems to have been exposed to a high temperature, and in a molten state has run over an edge and then set. This suggests human activity, before the rain of burning sulphur.

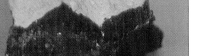

Figure 99: Limestone and carbon (organic material) that have "melted" together.

3.11. SKELETAL REMAINS

In the area something which is probably pieces of a partly cremated skeleton has been found (figures 102-109). If this is a skeleton, the being (larger mammal or human) lay stretched out (figure 102) and was hit partly by burning sulphur and probably falling "ash", which protected parts of the skeleton. These parts probably represent pieces of the backbone, parts of the pelvis bone and parts of the femur bones. Added to the fact that the skeleton parts have been exposed to high temperatures, is that they have also become petrified (changed into stone) and/or been cintered.

When a skeleton is heated to high temperatures the vertebrae and pelvis bones are those best preserved, while remaining parts of the skeleton break down into a dusty powder. This has been shown when attempts have been made to copy pre-historic cremation. Furthermore, parts of the skeleton are transformed at combustion, and become first formable (can change in form and appearance) and then take on a cintered form of something which resembles cement. Under intense heat the vertebrae burst in a characteristic way, which is seen from the circle-shaped cracks often in a terraced pattern (13).

It is feasible that the pieces which are probably skeletal that have been found in the area, represent those parts that normally best withstand burning: vertebrae and pelvis bones. Furthermore, what looks like petrification may well be a question of cintring, a process that is completely different from that of petrification, but which also gives rise to a stone-like material due to

Figures 100, 101: Solid iron that has been exposed to high temperature, and in a molten state has run over an edge and then set.

intensive heat, and does not absorb water.

The structures which resemble vertebrae have cracked in a circular pattern (figure 107), something one expects of vertebrae that are exposed to high temperatures. The skeleton parts have changed form somewhat, but it can still be seen that certain pieces of bone have had a hollow structure (figures 103 and 108). This find could very well be a skeleton, but it is difficult to prove this on account of the heat to which these finds have probably been exposed. No organic substance remains in the material for possible analysis.

Figures 105 and 106 shows what possibly is the femur joint. The analyses discussed below were performed on the inner part of the joint. Figure 104 display a section of the possible backbone. In figure 109 a human vertebrae is shown compared with a possible vertebrae from the parts seen in figure 108.

Figure 102: Quite probably a partly cremated skeleton of a mammalian. The remains represent parts of the backbone, pelvis bone and the femur bones.

3.12. CHEMICAL ANALYSIS OF THE SKELETAL REMAINS

Analysis of the composition of minerals in these finds could give an indication of whether they are skeletal parts. Since these skeletal parts have been exposed to special treatment (burning sulphur and semi cremation), analysis has been done of both these finds and of surrounding minerals, to discover if there is any difference in composition or simply a formation due to the substances surrounding. These finds show the following:

◆ There is a large amount of quartz (+770%) and aluminum oxide (+680%) in the surrounding minerals, in comparison with the presumed skeletal parts. This shows that the surrounding minerals originate from different rock species, while the skeletal parts have much lower values. Skeletons should have lower levels of these minerals. This result shows that the skeletal parts and the surroundings are most likely to be of different origins.

Figures 103, 104: Details of the probable backbone seen across and from the side. Note the hollow structure, the circular cracks and the similarity with a human vertebrae (figure below).

◆ Sulphur is found in organic material e.g. skeletons, but there should be a much higher content in the surrounding minerals because of the large amount of sulphur that has fallen over the area. The surrounding substances have a much higher sulphur content (+1100%). This further confirms that these

Figure 107: Cracking in circular patterns is a typical characteristic of partly cremated human (mammalian) vertebrae.

Figures 105, 106: Details of the probable femur joint covered by layers of minerals.

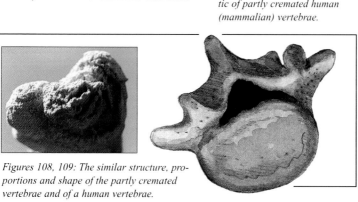

Figures 108, 109: The similar structure, proportions and shape of the partly cremated vertebrae and of a human vertebrae.

finds, which are probably skeletons, do not originate from the surrounding substances.

◆ Fluorine is an element found in nature but above all in bones and teeth. The presumed skeletal parts have a high content of fluorine (+216%) in comparison with the surrounding substances, which supports the hypothesis that they are skeletal parts.

◆ Calcium (Figure 110) is an important constituent of the skeleton, but also a main component of the limestone mineral found abundantly at this place. If data is calculated based on expected calcium contents (13), the presumed skeletal parts are closer to the expected value for skeletons than the value in the surrounding minerals. This indicates that they most probably are skeletal parts.

◆ Magnesium (Figure 111) is found in various minerals and rock species, as it is in the skeleton. Analysis shows that the magnesium content in the presumed skeletal parts is much lower than in the surrounding minerals, but very close to what is expected (13) in the skeleton. This is a further indication that the presumed skeletal parts really are skeletal.

Altogether these analyses show that a number of factors support the theory that these are skeletal parts. These factors are:

◆ Appearance and size (backbone, parts of the pelvis bone and femur bone). These parts are the most resistant when the skeleton is heated and therefore, should still be found.
◆ The hollowness which can be discerned at the edges of the vertebrae. Vertebrae consist of the body of the vertebra (vertebral frame), a

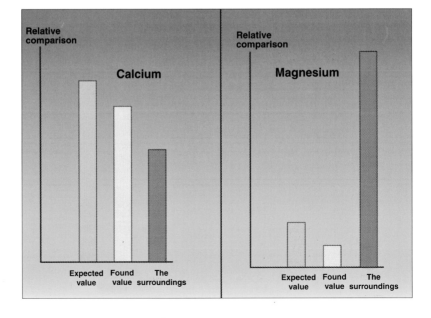

Figures 110, 111: Expected value; human skeleton, found value; analysis of the probable mammalian skeletal remains, the surroundings; analysis of surrounding material.

crosswise outgrowth and a cavity for the spinal cord (nerve-system). The finds show regular outgrowths (bulges) and are hollow.

◆ The cracks in the vertebrae are similar to those which appear when heat is applied (circular cracks in a terrace pattern).

◆ Analyses establishing the content of quartz, aluminum oxide, sulphur, fluorine, calcium and magnesium show that the presumed skeletal parts differ greatly from the surrounding material, and further support the hypothesis that they are skeletal parts.

3.13. IN SUMMARY

To sum up, it can be said that this place shows the following finds and analysis data:

◆ The area is raised and differs from the surroundings (makes shadows).

◆ The entire area seems to have been exposed to a rain of burning sulphur with a large number of sulphur balls still to be found in the area.

◆ The sulphur balls have melted down through the limestone and then stopped burning.

◆ The outer parts of the area consist of limestone, while the central part is dominated by gypsum.

◆ If limestone is exposed to burning sulphur then gypsum is formed.

◆ The sulphur balls with their encasing shells look like citrous fruit, which is what 1900 year-old notes assert about the places where the remains of the towns hit by burning sulphur were to be found.

◆ The surrounding area has a completely different appearance, and contains no sulphur balls.

◆ The site corresponds to where the biblical texts and the historical writer Josephus indicate Sodom and Gomorrah were situated.

◆ Rows of stones are to be found in the mass of gypsum.

◆ The ash-like substance in the area consists of a mixture of limestone, dolomite and gypsum. In addition, there is a high proportion of fine-grained sulphur.

◆ The sulphur differs from the sulphur forms found near volcanoes or with fossils.

◆ Coke-like tar is found in the cooler parts of the area.

◆ Melted metal samples of pure iron have been discovered.

◆ Fragments that are probably skeletal, have been found in the area. These have been exposed to high temperatures, and have disintegrated in the same way as skeletons do (particularly vertebrae) at high temperatures.

◆ Analyses support the hypothesis that these really are skeletal parts.

4. WHO WAS ISAAC?

We now return to Abraham and Sarah. The Lord manifests himself again and still Sarah does not believe that she will give birth to a son. The Lord then says:

"Is any thing too hard for the LORD? At the time appointed I will return unto thee, according to the time of life, and Sarah shall have a son." (Gen. 18:14)

4.1. The birth of Isaac

Abraham and Sarah are 100 and 90 years old, respectively, when the promised son is born, the son who receives the name Isaac at the Lord's command. Isaac is circumcised on the eighth day, and this has been the custom ever since among Jews. Arabs, who are descended from Isaac's brother Ishmael, are circumcised at the age of 13 as it was at that age that Ishmael was circumcised.

Earlier in the Bible (Gen. 16:12) there is a prophecy which corresponds very well with the situation today, namely the strife between descendants of Ishmael living east and south-east of present day Israel (the Arab world) and descendants of Isaac, the Jews (Israel).

"And he will be a wild man; his hand will be against every man, and every man's hand against him; and he shall dwell in the presence of all his brethren." (Gen. 16:12)

4.2. The "sacrifice" of Isaac

The Lord appears to Abraham on several occasions. At one time the Lord tests Abraham's fidelity by asking him to sacrifice Isaac, his only son with his wife Sarah. Abraham makes all the preparations and goes to the mountain which the Lord points out to him. There he builds an altar for the sacrifice, and is about to sacrifice Isaac when an angel of the Lord calls out to him. He receives a ram to sacrifice instead. Through this test the Lord sees that Abraham holds the Lord's commands in high esteem, even putting them before his son's life. This event becomes the confirmation of the promises given to Abraham, according to the text:

"And God said, Sarah thy wife shall bear thee a son indeed; and thou shalt call his name Isaac: and I will establish my covenant with him for an everlasting covenant, and with his seed after him." (Gen. 17:19)

Figure 112: Mount Moriah, on which the old Jerusalem is built.

The mountain on which Abraham built the sacrificial altar is called Moriah. It is the same mountain on which Jerusalem and the temple were built later on, and the same mountain on which Jesus Christ was sacrificed and crucified (figure 112). Today this area mainly consists of old Jerusalem and its vicinity. Figure 113 depicts Mount Moriah at these various points of time.

Yet again the Lord repeats his promises to Abraham that he will be the forefather of a great people. At this time Abraham lives in Beer-Sheba, just to the north of the Negev desert.

4.3. Hebron and Machpelah

Sarah dies in Hebron (figure 114) at the age of 127. Abraham wants to buy the Machpelah cave from Ephron to use as a grave for Sarah and also as the family grave, but he receives it as a gift from Ephron. As a gift in return Abraham gives the value of the cave and field in silver to Ephron (Gen. 23:1-19).

Today there is a building in Hebron that is regarded as holy by both Jews and Muslims. According to tradition the building is erected over the cave

Figure 113: Abraham was ready to sacrifice his son Isaac on the peak of Mount Moriah. Later the Temple was erected on the same mountain, and further, Jesus Christ - the Son of God according to the Bible - was sacrificed on the very same mountain peak. These events span approximately 2000 years.

Figure 114: Hebron of today.

Figure 115: Muslims praying at the mosque in Hebron.

which became the family grave of Abraham, Isaac, Jacob and their offspring. Figure 115 shows Muslims praying inside this building, which for Muslims is a mosque. Probably in older times the Machpelah cave looked like figures 116-118, a cave with some sort of roof built of the stone, found in the area. It is unlikely that any evidence can be found to show if any of these places is the actual Machpelah cave, for four reasons:

1. Most graves have been plundered during the centuries and millenia that have passed since these events took place.
2. If the exact locality of the Machpelah cave was known (which it was for a long time) then it is certain that many would want to have bones and other items from the graves as relics.
3. During all the wars that have taken place over several thousand years, an enemy may well have destroyed the grave and its contents to take revenge and/or to annihilate important places.
4. If any of the given places is Machpelah, then it is most probably empty, based on a Bible passage from much later. In Matt. 27:51-54 it is written that many saints arose at the time of Jesus' resurrection. If there are any in the history of Israel who might belong to this group, then it is those who were buried in the Machpelah cave. In this case the Machpelah cave would be empty, which according to popular tradition the cave in Hebron is said to be. But no one is allowed to go down into the cave to check if this is true or not.

4.4. Rebecca, the wife of Isaac

Abraham grows older and gives his eldest servant the task of bringing back a wife for Isaac from the home of Abraham's relatives. The servant finds Rebecca by a well in Haran, Abraham's hometown. Rebecca is a grandchild of Abraham's brother Nahor. The servant presents the bridal gifts, and they feel convinced that it is the Lord's guidance. So Rebecca, with her companions, goes back with the servant to Isaac and becomes Isaac's wife.

Figures 116-118: A possible design and interior of the Macpelah cave.

4.5. THE BROTHERS OF ISAAC

Ishmael, was the brother to Isaac, born by Hagar. Abraham took another wife, Keturah, with whom he had six sons, amongst them Midian. Isaac was the main heir, so while Abraham was still alive he singled out the sons he had with Keturah and gave them gifts. Later they moved eastwards and settled in Arabia and down by the Red Sea, including his son Midian. In chapters 13 - 15 we return to the question of where Midian and his descendants settled.

Abraham died at the age of 175, and was buried in the same cave in Hebron as his wife Sarah. Abraham's sons Isaac and Ishmael arranged the burial. Ishmael himself lived to be 137 years old.

4.6. IN SUMMARY

The chapter about Isaac can be summarised as follows:

◆ Isaac was the son of Abraham and Sarah.
◆ Isaac's brother Ishmael gave rise to many Arab peoples.
◆ Abraham was prepared to sacrifice his son Isaac on Mount Moriah. Mount Moriah later became the site of the Jewish temple, Jesus' crucifixion and present day old Jerusalem.
◆ Isaac found his wife, Rebecca, in Haran (currently south-eastern Turkey), the town from which Isaac's relatives originated.
◆ Isaac's half-brother Midian gave rise to the Midianites, who later settled in Arabia, east of Canaan in present day Jordan and Saudi Arabia.
◆ The Lord's promise to Abraham was repeated, confirmed and sealed with the "sacrifice" of Isaac.

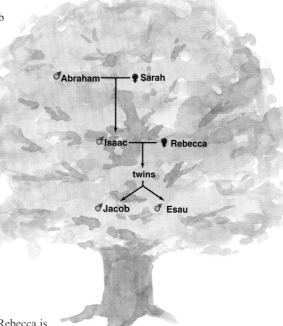

5. WHO WAS JACOB?

Isaac is 40 years old when he marries Rebecca. Rebecca is barren and Isaac prays to the Lord for her. When Isaac is 60 years old Rebecca gives birth to twins, the firstborn is called Esau and the one born after is called Jacob (figure 119). The Lord speaks to Rebecca about the twins before they are born:

Figure 119: Parents, wife and off-spring of Isaac.

"Two nations are in thy womb, and two manner of people shall be separated from thy bowels; and the one people shall be stronger than the other people; and the elder shall serve the younger." (Gen. 25:23)

Esau is not interested in his birthright and agrees to sell when Jacob offers to buy it. Esau spends most of his time in the open, hunting wild animals.

5.1. ISAAC IN GERAR

There is famine in the country, as in the time of Abraham, and Isaac wants to travel down to Egypt. When he reaches Abimelech, who is the king of the Philistines, the Lord appears to Isaac and says:

"And the LORD appeared unto him, and said, Go not down into Egypt; dwell in the land which I shall tell thee of: Sojourn in this land, and I will be with thee, and will bless thee; for unto thee, and unto thy seed, I will give all these countries, and I will perform the oath which I swear unto Abraham thy father; And I will make thy seed to multiply as the stars of heaven, and will give unto thy seed all these countries; and in thy seed shall all the nations of the earth be blessed; Because that Abraham obeyed my voice, and kept my charge, my commandments, my statutes, and my laws." (Gen. 26:2-5)

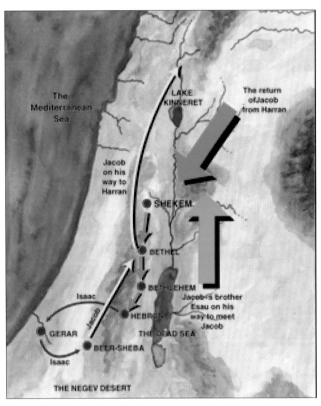

Figure 120: The journeys of Isaac according to the biblical texts.

Isaac stays in Gerar, and is under the protection of Abimelech. Isaac has good harvests, his herds of cattle increase and he becomes more powerful. Finally, he becomes so powerful that Abimelech asks him to leave the area. Isaac moves on from place to place. According to the Bible the Lord appears to him again, and confirms the covenant made with Abraham. Isaac's servants find water when they dig a well, and the name they give the place remains to this day: Beer-Sheba (figure 120) in the northern part of the Negev desert in present day Israel.

5.2. THE BLESSING OF ISAAC

Isaac grows old, his eyes grow weak and he becomes blind. Jacob deceives Isaac into thinking that he is Esau, and he receives his father's blessing. This type of blessing implies a sort of will and when it is given, it is given. Esau becomes angry and disconsolate. On the advice of his mother, Jacob takes himself off to his mother's and forefathers' hometown Haran to find a wife. Isaac tells Jacob that he may not take a wife from among the people of Canaan, but that he must look for a wife among his cousins (Laban's daughters).

5.3. JACOB'S LADDER

When Jacob is on the way to Haran, he stops at the holy place called Bethel. He lies down to sleep and the Lord speaks to him in a dream. Jacob sees a ladder stretching up into heaven with angels ascending and descending the ladder. According to the Bible the Lord says to Jacob:

"I am the LORD God of Abraham thy father, and the God of Isaac: the land whereon thou liest, to thee will I give it, and to thy seed; And thy seed shall be as the dust of the earth, and thou shalt spread abroad to the west, and to the east, and to the north, and to the south: and in thee and in thy seed shall all the families of the earth be blessed. And, behold, I am with thee, and will keep thee in all places whither thou goest, and will bring thee again into this land; for I will not leave thee, until I have done that which I have spoken to thee of." (Gen. 28:13-15)

Jacob promises the Lord that if his journey goes well (see the map in figure 120) and he is able to return to Isaac's house, the Lord will be the God of Jacob.

5.4. The family of Jacob

When Jacob comes to a well in the area of Haran he meets Rachel who keeps her father Laban's sheep and has taken the sheep to the well for water. By working for Laban for seven years Jacob receives, through a trick, not Rachel but Rachel's

Figures 121, 122: These sheep are eating the grass that grows on the ruins of Haran. They are probably very similar to Laban's sheep that were in this area when Jacob came to look for a whife among his relatives.

sister Leah as his wife. However, by promising to work seven more years for Laban, Jacob receives Rachel as his wife too.

Leah gives birth to Reuben, Simeon, Levi and Judah. Rachel is barren and gives her maid Bilhah to Jacob as his wife so that she can bear children for Rachel. Bilhah gives birth to Dan and Naphtali. Then Leah gives her maid Zilpah to Jacob as his wife so that she can bear more children for Leah. Zilpah gives birth to Gad and Asher. Afterwards Leah gives birth to Issachar, Zebulun and a daughter called Dinah. Rachel later becomes fertile, and gives birth to Joseph.

With these eleven sons: Reuben, Simeon, Levi, Judah, Dan, Naphtali, Gad, Asher, Issachar, Zebulun and Joseph and the only daughter Dinah, Jacob leaves his father-in-law Laban. For twenty years he has served Laban, who has deceived him several times. Jacob takes with him his wives, sons, servants, his cattle and sheep, and journeys back to the land of his father Isaac.

5.5. The name Israel

In one place Jacob wrestles with the Lord, and the Lord says to him:

"Thy name shall be called no more Jacob, but Israel: for as a prince hast thou power with God and with men, and hast prevailed." (Gen. 32:28)

Jacob meets his brother Esau and gives him a generous gift in the form of camels, asses, rams, sheep, goats and oxen. Later Jacob takes another route and makes camp in Shekem. Jacob raises an altar in this place to which he gives the name El-Elohe-Israel (God, Israel's God). The Lord protects Jacob in different ways, and speaks with him on several occasions. Jacob, with his people and his herds, goes up to Bethel to pray to the Lord. In Bethel the Lord confirms the promise he gave to Abraham and Isaac:

"Thy name is Jacob: thy name shall not be called any more Jacob, but Israel shall be thy name: and he called his name Israel. And God said unto him, I am God Almighty: be fruitful and multiply; a nation and a company of nations shall be of thee, and kings shall come out of thy loins; And the land which I gave Abraham and Isaac, to thee I will give it, and to thy seed after thee will I give the land." (Gen. 35:10-12)

Jacob receives the name "Israel", of whom (progenitor) Judah is one of twelve sons (tribes). The other 11 tribes are scattered across wide areas and are no longer found as a clearly defined group, but have long since been assimiliated into other ethnic groups. The Bible relates:

"I am the Lord God of Abraham thy father, and the God of Isaac. The land whereon thou liest, to thee will I give it, and to thy seed. And thy seed shall be as the dust of the earth, and thou shalt spread abroad to the west, and to the east, and to the north, and to the south, and in thee and in thy seed shall all the families of the earth be blessed." (Gen. 28:13-14)

5.6. RACHEL'S GRAVE
While Jacob and his family are moving about, it is time for Rachel to give birth. Rachel does not survive the delivery, but dies immediately after the birth of her son. She gives her son the name Ben-oni (Jacob calls him Benjamin). Rachel is buried on the way to Ephrath near Bethlehem. This grave is still there today, close to Bethlehem, and is a sacred place for Jews. In figure 123, the outer part built to protect the grave can be seen. Jews visit this place to pray both beside and in front of the grave.

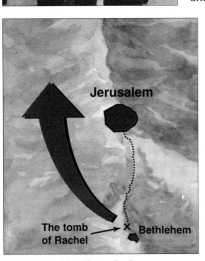

Figures 123, 124: The tomb of Rachel still exists outside Bethlehem. The photograph shows the building surrounding the tomb.

5.7. THE 12 TRIBES
So Jacob comes with his people to his father Isaac in Hebron. Jacob has his twelve sons with him, who will give rise to the twelve tribes of Israel: Reuben, Simeon, Levi, Judah, Issachar and Zebulon, the sons of Leah; Joseph and Benjamin, the sons of Rachel; Dan and Naphtali, the sons of Bilhah and Gad and Asher, the sons of Zilpah (figure 125). Isaac dies at the age of 180, and is buried in Hebron by Jacob and Esau.

Esau's family, which was large, settled in Edom because there was not enough land for both Jacob and Esau. There are many tribes and princes descended from the family of Esau. Among them were prince Amalek, who became the forefather of the Amalekites, and prince Zepho. One of the kings of Edom was Baal-Hanan. These names are mentioned here because they are connected with later events during Israel's flight from Egypt.

5.8. IN SUMMARY
The history of Jacob, so far can be summarised as follows:

◆ Isaac's wife Rebecca has two sons, Esau and Jacob.

- Jacob has the oath of the Lord to Abraham and Isaac repeated for him by the Lord himself.
- Jacob's father has a well dug and in this way lays the foundations of the town of Beer-Sheba, which is still a lively town in southern Israel today.
- Jacob goes to Haran to find a wife from among his relatives.
- The Lord reveals himself to Jacob in a special way (Jacob's ladder).
- Jacob is the one who receives a new name from the Lord, Israel.
- Jacob becomes the forefather of the twelve tribes of Israel.
- The grave of Rachel (Jacob's wife) still exists today just outside Bethlehem.
- Jacob's brother Esau is the forefather of the people of Edom, and the Amalekites.

We have now come to an important stage in the story of the people of Israel. We have followed the story of Abraham, Isaac and Jacob, and have now reached the 37th chapter of the book of Genesis. God has chosen his people, according to the Bible text, and we have seen how the twelve tribes of Israel have been founded through the birth of the twelve sons of Jacob. What happens now are the events which lead to the people of Israel ending up in Egypt. The Egypt that many years later they leave in the massive migration we know as the Exodus.

6. How did Joseph come to be in Egypt?

Joseph is the second youngest of the twelve sons of Jacob. He is born to Rachel when Jacob, the father, is old. Rachel is the woman Jacob loves above all others. Jacob has two wives, one he has been forced to marry (Leah), and Rachel, the woman for whom he had worked 14 years at his father-in-law's home in order to gain her as his wife. In addition, Jacob has two concubines, Bilhah and Zilpah, who are maids of Rachel and Leah. These four women are the mothers of Jacob's twelve sons. Joseph is his father's favourite, and it is probable that Jacob likes Joseph and Benjamin more than the other sons because Rachel is their mother.

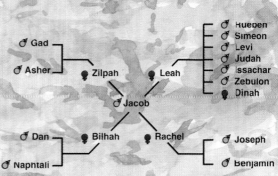

6.1. Joseph's dream

Joseph receives a special garment from his father, and this makes the other brothers very envious. Besides this Joseph has dreams. These dreams are prophetic (predictions of the future), and Jacob no doubt feels that these dreams are important since he keeps them in mind, while the brothers hate Joseph for the content of the dreams (Gen. 37:1-11).

One dream concerns sheaves bound in the field. The

Figure 125: The concubines, wives and children of Jacob. The sons gave rise to the 12 tribes of Israel.

sheaves symbolise the brothers. One sheaf, which represents Joseph, stands up and the other sheaves bow to Joseph. The second dream is about the sun (the father) and moon (the mother) and eleven stars (the eleven brothers), who bow to Joseph. Jacob rebukes Joseph when he narrates his dreams, and the brothers hate him even more. Joseph is 17 years old when this takes place. In modern times sheaves are still the symbol for Joseph, as can be seen on an Israeli postage stamp (figure 127).

Figure 126: One of Joseph's dreams: sheaves bowing to Joseph.

6.2. JOSEPH'S SEARCH FOR HIS BROTHERS

On one occasion, Jacob sends his son Joseph from Hebron to Shekem. Jacob wants to know how things are with the brothers, and the flocks of sheep that are grazing in Shekem. Joseph does not find them in Shekem, but is told that they have moved on to Dothan (figure 128). They recognise him as he approaches, and they begin to plan to kill Joseph. The eldest brother, Reuben, persuades them not to shed blood but to throw him into a dry pit in the desert. Reuben said this because he wanted to save Joseph.

When Joseph reaches them, they strip him of his fine garment and throw him into the empty pit. The brothers sit down to eat, and just then a caravan of camels arrives. The caravan is a group of Ishmaelites (Midianites) on the way from Gilead to Egypt with goods to trade (Gen. 37:25). The historical writer Josephus (JA2/3:3) states that these Ishmaelites are Arabs. In other words, they are distant relatives of Jacob's sons living east of Canaan.

The goods for trading were rubber and balsam. Balsam was a sweet-smelling resin or incense, which was used as ointment, and as a remedy for pain. They also had with them laudanum, which is a sweet-smelling resin from the citrus plant and had similar uses to those of balsam, however it was first and foremost used in treating coughs.

Figure 127: Sheaves are still a symbol for Joseph as seen on this Israeli stamp.

6.3. JOSEPH IS SOLD AS A SLAVE

Judah has the idea of selling Joseph to the merchants instead of leaving him to die in the pit. They pull Joseph out of the pit, and sell him for 20 pieces of silver.

Reuben returns and discovers that Joseph is no longer in the pit. He is furious, tears his clothes, and asks his brothers what they have done. To cope with the situation they kill a goat and dip Joseph's clothes in the blood. Then they send the bloody clothes to Jacob, and ask if he recognises them. Jacob recognises the clothes, and concludes that a wild animal has taken Joseph. Jacob is heart-broken, he mourns his son for a long time, and no one can comfort him.

The Ishmaelites who buy Joseph take him to Egypt and sell him to Potiphar, who is an officer at the court of Pharaoh. The Bible narrates how the Lord is with Joseph just as he had been with Abraham, Isaac and Jacob. Joseph succeeds in all that he does, and after a time becomes responsible for Potiphar's household and all his possessions. The account of how Joseph is sold into Egypt by his brothers is found in Gen. 37:12-36.

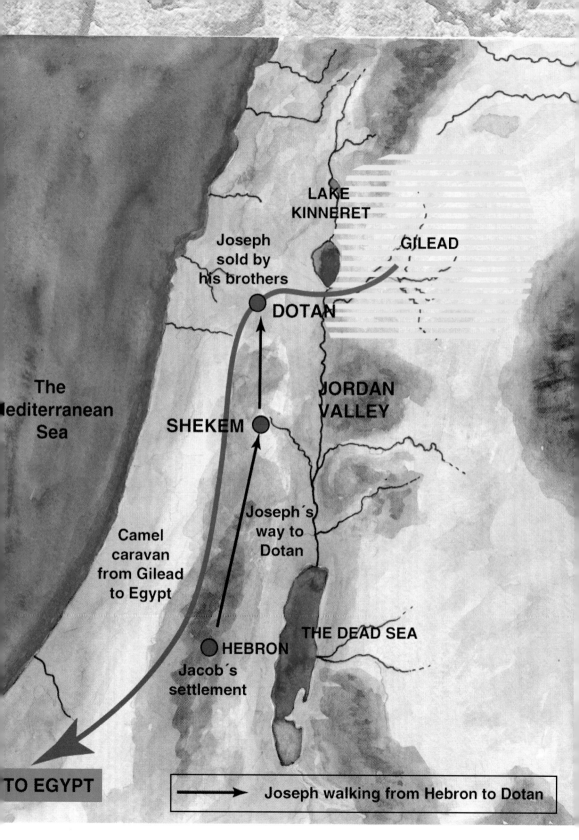

LAKE
KINNERET

GILEAD

Joseph
sold by
his brothers

DOTAN

The
Mediterranean
Sea

SHEKEM

JORDAN
VALLEY

Joseph's
way to
Dotan

Camel
caravan
from Gilead
to Egypt

THE DEAD SEA

HEBRON
Jacob's
settlement

TO EGYPT

Joseph walking from Hebron to Dotan

Figure 128: Joseph left Hebron to look for his brothers. In Dotan the brothers
sold Joseph to merchants of a caravan on its way to Egypt.

6.4. JOSEPH INTERPRETS DREAMS

Through no fault of his own Joseph is put in prison, but even in prison things go well for him, and he is given great responsibility. God gives him the gift of interpreting dreams, and he is able to help some influential people (who happen to be in prison at the time) to understand their dreams.

Some time later, it so happens that Pharaoh has a dream which he does not understand. Pharaoh calls together all the sages in Egypt, but no one can help him interpret the dream. Then one of the influential people at court, who was in prison for a brief time, remembers that Joseph can interpret dreams. Joseph is hastily brought out from the prison and taken to Pharaoh (Gen. 39:1 - 40:23).

The Bible texts recount Pharaoh's dream:

Figure 129: Joseph was bought by Ishmaelites, who were on their way to Egypt with a camel caravan.

"And it came to pass at the end of two full years, that Pharaoh dreamed: and, behold, he stood by the river. And, behold, there came up out of the river seven well favoured kine and fatfleshed; and they fed in a meadow. And, behold, seven other kine came up after them out of the river, ill favoured and leanfleshed; and stood by the other kine upon the brink of the river. And the ill favoured and leanfleshed kine did eat up the seven well favoured and fat kine. So Pharaoh awoke." (Gen. 41:1-4)

The dream continues on the same theme, but with ears of corn instead of cows. Joseph interprets Pharaoh's dreams (figure 130), which signify that there will be seven years of good harvests in Egypt followed by seven years when the crops will fail.

6.5. JOSEPH PROMOTED TO A HIGH POSITION

Joseph goes on to give advice about what should be done in order for Egypt to cope with the crisis. Pharaoh's reaction is:

"Can we find such a one as this is, a man in whom the Spirit of God is?" (Gen. 41:38)

Pharaoh realises that Joseph is protected and guided by God, and therefore Pharaoh gives Joseph the task of being the highest administrator in the country, second only to Pharaoh himself. Pharaoh gives him his own signet ring, dresses him in fine clothes and hangs "the gold chain round his neck" (Gen. 41:41-42). In figure 131 there is an example of what could be a similar gold chain.

Pharaoh gives Joseph the Egyptian name Zaphenath-Paneah and a wife called Asenath, the daughter of a priest. When this happens Joseph is 30 years old. Things turn out just as Joseph's interpretation of the dream indicated: beginning with seven years of plenty, when Joseph makes sure that the whole of Egypt stores up food in readiness for the years of famine to come. During the years of good harvests Joseph has two sons, Manasseh and Ephraim (figure 132). The famine which follows affects not only Egypt, but all the countries in the region. Therefore, people come to Egypt to buy seed and food, because in Egypt they had prepared for it due to Joseph's administration.

Figure 130: Joseph interprets the dream of the ruling pharaoh.

6.6. Joseph's brothers go to Egypt

Jacob, Joseph's father, sends his sons to Egypt to buy grain because there is also a great shortage of food in the land of Canaan. Ten of Jacob's sons, all who are left except Benjamin, go down to Egypt.

Israel's sons come to Egypt, to the chief administrator who is responsible for all the sales of grain. They bow to Joseph and beg to buy grain for their people in the land of Canaan. Joseph recognises them but they have no idea that he is Joseph. Joseph speaks roughly to them, saying that they are spies planning for an attack on Egypt (figure 85). He talks to them through an interpreter, but of course he understands what they say to each other.

Reuben says that this is their punishment because they showed no mercy to Joseph when they sold him. Joseph turns away in tears, and remembers the prophetic dreams of his youth about his brothers bowing down to him. Joseph makes one condition, which is that one brother, Simeon, is held prisoner until Benjamin too comes to Egypt. According to the historian Josephus, Joseph chooses Simeon because he was the one who urged the other brothers to betray Joseph (JA 2/6:5). Joseph arranges for them to receive all the grain they want to buy, and also puts their money back into the sacks of grain.

On the way home one of the brothers discovers the purse of money in a sack. They are terrified and wonder what God has done to them (Gen. 42:28). The brothers come home to their father Jacob and tell him all that has happened, and then they find money in all the sacks of grain. Jacob is in despair and says:

Figure 131: The gold chain of the Pharaoh was given to Joseph. The photograph shows an ancient gold chain from a royal tomb of Egypt.

"Me have ye bereaved of my children: Joseph is not, and Simeon is not, and ye will take Benjamin away: all these things are against me." (Gen. 42:36)

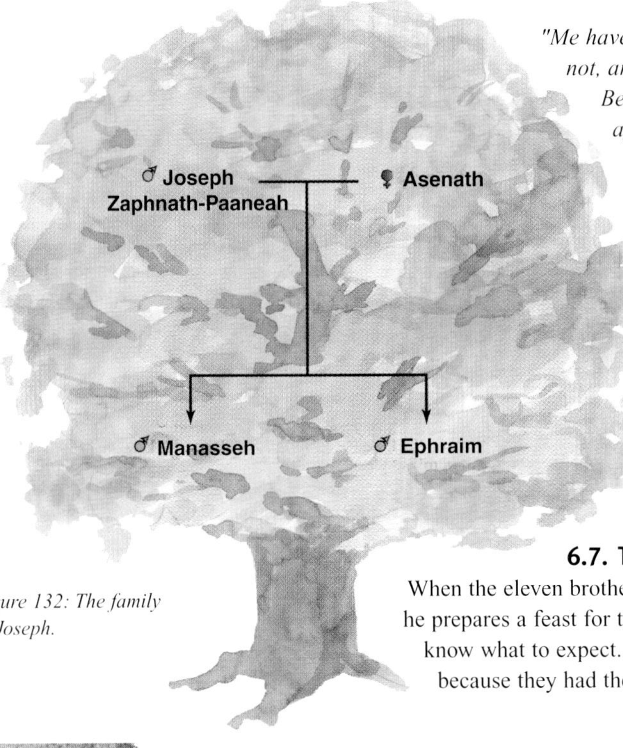

♂ **Joseph**
Zaphnath-Paaneah ———— ♀ **Asenath**

♂ **Manasseh**   ♂ **Ephraim**

Reuben promises his father that if he does not bring Benjamin home from Egypt, he can kill both of Reuben's children . Jacob does not want to send Benjamin because he says *"his brother (Joseph) is dead and he alone is left"* (Gen. 42:38). This implies that Jacob prefers two sons to all the others, Joseph and Benjamin, the only sons of the woman Jacob loved – Rachel.

6.7. The silver cup

When the eleven brothers come to Joseph in Egypt once again, he prepares a feast for them. They are terrified, and do not know what to expect. They believe they are to be punished because they had the money with them when they returned

Figure 132: The family of Joseph.

home the time before. The first thing Joseph does is to ask after Jacob. He is told that all is well with him. Then when Joseph sees Benjamin he is moved to tears, goes into his room and weeps. Then Joseph returns to the meal, and it becomes a real feast.

When they return home the same thing happens again. They receive their grain and the money is put back in each sack. In additon, Joseph puts his silver cup in one of Benjamin's sacks. Silver was worth more than gold since silver was imported into Egypt. The silver cup belonging to the second-in-command in Egypt commands a high price, as well as being a sign of authority and power (figure 133).

Joseph then sends his steward after them and accuses them of stealing the silver cup. They deny taking it and offer themselves as slaves if the cup is found in their sacks. The cup is found in Benjamin's sack and they return to Joseph, who speaks roughly to them but says he would be satisfied if Benjamin alone becomes his slave. Then Judah begs Joseph to let him be a slave instead of Benjamin because Jacob would not survive if he were to lose Benjamin too.

Joseph can no longer hide his true identity and he orders all except his brothers to leave the room. Then Joseph bursts into tears and the whole house can hear him crying. Then he says:

"I am Joseph; doth my father yet live? And his brethren could not answer him; for they were troubled at his presence. And Joseph said unto his brethren, Come near to me, I pray you. And they came near. And he said, I am Joseph your brother, whom ye sold into Egypt. Now therefore be not grieved, nor angry with yourselves, that ye sold me hither: for God did send me before you to preserve life. For these two years hath the famine been in the land: and yet there are five years, in the which there shall neither be earing nor harvest. And God sent me before you to preserve you a posterity in the earth, and to save your lives by a great deliverance. So now it was not you that sent me hither, but God: and he hath made me a father to Pharaoh, and lord of all his house, and a ruler throughout all the land of Egypt. Haste ye, and go up to my father, and say unto him, Thus saith thy son Joseph, God hath made me lord of all Egypt: come down unto me, tarry not: And thou shalt dwell in the land of Goshen, and thou shalt be near unto me, thou, and thy children, and thy children's children, and thy flocks,

Figure 133: In a tomb beside the Step pyramid in Sakkara, a high ranking official of the royal court is described in reliephs. The central relieph covers the entire wall. The person holds a (silver?) cup in his hands. Could this be Joseph?

and thy herds, and all that thou hast: And there will I nourish thee; for yet there are five years of famine; lest thou, and thy household, and all that thou hast, come to poverty. And, behold, your eyes see, and the eyes of my brother Benjamin, that it is my mouth that speaketh unto you. And ye shall tell my father of all my glory in Egypt, and of all that ye have seen; and ye shall haste and bring down my father hither." (Gen. 45:3-13)

Then he hugs his brothers, first Benjamin and then the others, and weeps.

When Pharaoh hears that Joseph's brothers are in the country he is very glad, he orders them all to come, and says that they will receive the best that Egypt can offer. They are provided with gifts, chariots and all that they need to move to Egypt with all their family.

6.8. JACOB AND HIS FAMILY MOVE TO EGYPT

When the brothers return to Jacob in Canaan with all this, and tell him about Joseph, the biblical texts say that Jacob's heart stands still and he cannot believe them. But Jacob revives from the shock and comes to a decision:

"And Israel said, it is enough; Joseph my son is yet alive: I will go and see him before I die." (Gen. 45:28)

Now the decision is made. Jacob and his family move to Egypt (figure 136). Jacob brings everything that belongs to him and all his family. In all there were 70 people from the house of Jacob who came to Egypt. When Jacob and his retinue come to Beer-Sheba, he makes a sacrifice to God. In Beer-Sheba God speaks to Jacob in a vision in the night:

Figures 134, 135: Goshen, a very fertile part of the Nile River delta region, was to become the home of Jacob and his family.

"Jacob, Jacob. And he said, Here am I. And he said, I am God, the God of thy father: fear not to go down into Egypt; for I will there make of thee a great nation. I will go down with thee into Egypt; and I will also surely bring thee up again: and Joseph shall put his hand upon thine eyes." (Gen. 46:2-4)

Here God himself promises that he will not only accompany Israel to Egypt, but he will also bring him out of Egypt again, according to the text.

We have now followed the story of how Joseph and his family came to be in Egypt (Gen. 37:1 - 46:34). The story continues with Joseph and his descendants in Egypt.

6.9 JOSEPH'S ASSIGNEMENT

Joseph has a very special assignment:

◆ He is born to the wife his father loved and he is given a special garment.
◆ Already in his teens he has prophetic dreams about the future.
◆ Joseph is sold by his brothers to be a slave in Egypt.
◆ Joseph has considerable responsibility as administrator of all the property of an officer at the court in Egypt.
◆ Joseph is put in prison on false accusations, and there too he is given special tasks e.g. interpretation of dreams.
◆ Pharaoh has a dream about the future which he wants the sages of Egypt to interpret, but they are unable to do this.
◆ Joseph is the only one who can interpret Pharaoh's dream, and he is given responsibility as the chief administrator over Egypt, second only to Pharaoh.
◆ The dream concerns the whole region, which will experience seven good years followed by seven bad years of famine.

- ◆ At the beginning of the period of famine Joseph's brothers come to Egypt to buy grain.
- ◆ After a number of events Jacob and his retinue move to Egypt, and live there under the protection of Joseph and Pharaoh.

The people of Israel are now in Egypt, and after a time there is the great migration – Exodus, but first we shall see what really happened in Egypt.

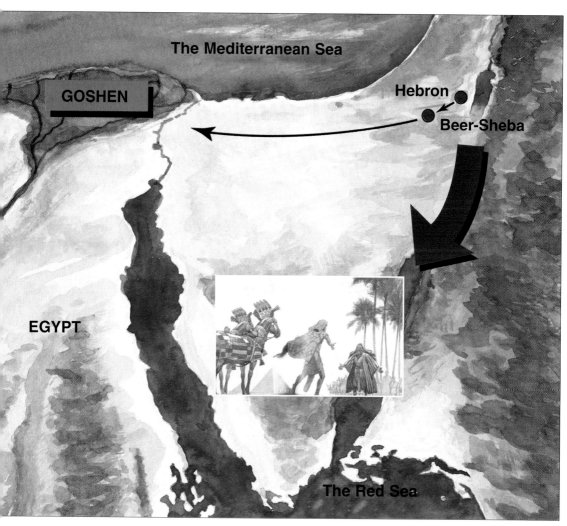

Figure 136: Jacob and his family of 70 moves from his tent-camp in Beer-Sheba to the Nile river delta region, known as Goshen.

7. WHERE DID JACOB'S FAMILY SETTLE?

Judah goes first, and tells Joseph that the family is coming. So Joseph goes to meet them, and joins the whole family in the Egyptian town of Heliopolis (JA 2/7:5). On Joseph's invitation, Jacob and his retinue settle in the land of Goshen (Gen. 45:10, 46:28, 34 and 47:1, 4, 6). Goshen is not a town, as some hypotheses claim, but it is an area of land, the land of Goshen (figure 138). The fact that it is an area of land is repeated each time Goshen is named.

Figure 137: A shepherd with his flock in Goshen.

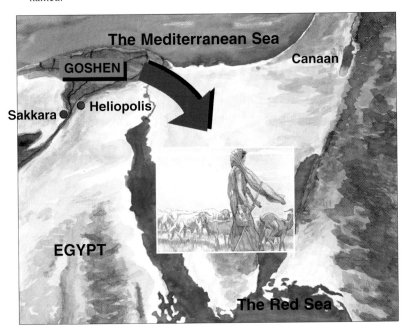

Figure 138: The very fertile land of the eastern part of the Nile river delta was called Goshen. Goshen was not a town, but an area of land.

7.1. JACOB'S FAMILY SETTLES IN GOSHEN/RAMESES

Joseph instructs his brothers to say clearly that they are herdsmen when they are called by Pharaoh. Then, says Joseph, you will be allowed to live in the land of Goshen, because all shepherds are "an abomination to the Egyptians". This is what Pharaoh then commands. When they settle in Egypt and Jacob stands before Pharaoh, Jacob is 130 years old.

It is important to note that in the same passage in which the land of Goshen is mentioned several times, this area is also given another name: the land of Rameses. That this is the same area of land is confirmed in several ways:

Figure 139: There are several harvests each year around the Nile River.

◆ In the same passage, the land of Goshen and the land of Rameses are referred to as two names for the same area (Gen. 47:1-12).
◆ They were to live in the best part of the land. Pharaoh gives the command that they are to live in "the best of the land ... in the land of Goshen" (Gen. 47:6) and a little further on the text reads "…gave them a possession in the land of Egypt, in the best of the land, in the land of Rameses…" (Gen. 47:11).
◆ Pharaoh had commanded that they should live in the land of Goshen, (Gen. 47:6) and later in the text it says "in the land of Rameses as Pharaoh

had commanded" (Gen. 47:11).

From the biblical texts it is clear that both names, Goshen and Rameses, indicate the same place, and that this is within a larger area. The area of land referred to is the Nile delta (figures 140-142). Probably it is the eastern part of the Nile delta that is meant.

7.2. Jacob is buried in Hebron

Jacob dies at the age of 147, after 17 years in Egypt. Joseph takes Jacob's body to Hebron and buries him there, according to Josephus "at a great expense" (JA 2/8:1). In chapter 4 there is a more detailed description of the family grave, which was located in Hebron.

All the brothers are buried in Canaan except Joseph. The bones of Joseph are taken to Canaan later, when they flee from Egypt, as Joseph is given an oath by the people of Israel that this will be done at the Exodus. Joseph was well aware that the stay in Egypt was only temporary for the people of Israel, and that God had promised the land of Canaan to Abraham for the Israelites.

7.3. In summary

To summarise, the following happened with the family of Jacob:

◆ Jacob's family settles in the fertile Nile delta.
◆ The area in which they live is called Goshen, but is also known as Rameses.
◆ They are given an area of land, not a town.
◆ Goshen is the best part of the country (fertile area).
◆ Pharaoh commands that they should live in Goshen.
◆ When Jacob dies Joseph buries him in the family grave in Hebron.

Figures 140-142: Still today, the land of Goshen is a very fertile area with a constant supply of water.

8. Does Joseph exist in Egyptian history?

The Bible tells how Joseph came to Egypt, and came to play a prominent part as administrator and ruler over Egypt directly under Pharaoh. The question one naturally asks is if such an important person is also named in the history of Egypt. If so, are there archaeological discoveries which confirm this hypothesis?

8.1. Imhotep

During the third dynasty a very special person called Imhotep (figure 143) appears in the history of Egypt. This is also confirmed in archaeological discoveries. For many years there have been doubts as to whether Imhotep was an actual person since it was difficult to believe that one single person could possess so many qualities and talents. At times Imhotep has been called the Leonardo da Vinci of Egypt. But Imhotep was more than this. Leonardo da Vinci was a genius in many areas while

Figure 143: This statue shows Imhotep, but the statue was made long after he lived.

Imhotep, in addition to being called a genius, was also regarded as a god. The Egyptian priest Manetho wrote:

"...during his (Pharaoh Djoser of the 3rd dynasty) reign lived Imouthes (Imhotep), who, because of his medical skill has the reputation of Asclepius (the Greek god of medicine) among the Egyptians and who was the inventor of the art of building with hewn stone." (The author's explanations in brackets).

8.2. IMHOTEP AND JOSEPH - A COMPARISON

When excavations were carried out at the Step Pyramid in Sakkara (figure 144), about 15 km south of the great pyramids in Giza, remains of a statue with only the feet remaining, were found (15). There on the foundations was carved the name of Djoser and of:

Figure 144: The Step Pyramid of Sakkara.

"...Imhotep, Chancellor of the King of Lower Egypt, Chief under the King, Administrator of the Great Palace, Hereditary Lord, High Priest of Heliopolis, Imhotep the Builder, the Sculptor, the Maker of Stone Vases..."

Could this description fit Joseph?

"And the thing was good in the eyes of Pharaoh, and in the eyes of all his servants. And Pharaoh said unto his servants, Can we find such a one as this is, a man in whom the Spirit of God is? And Pharaoh said unto Joseph, Forasmuch as God hath shewed thee all this, there is none so discreet and wise as thou art: Thou shalt be over my house, and according unto thy word shall all my people be ruled: only in the throne will I be greater than thou. And Pharaoh said unto Joseph, See, I have set thee over all the land of Egypt. And Pharaoh took off his ring from his hand, and put it upon Joseph's hand, and arrayed him in vestures of fine linen, and put a gold chain about his neck; And he made him to ride in the second chariot which he had; and they cried before him, Bow the knee: and he made him ruler over all the land of Egypt. And Pharaoh said unto Joseph, I am Pharaoh, and without thee shall no man lift up his hand or foot in all the land of Egypt. And Pharaoh called Joseph's name Zaphnathpaaneah; and he gave him to wife Asenath the daughter of Potipherah priest of On (Heliopolis). And Joseph went out over all the land of Egypt." (Gen. 41:37-45)

Figure 145: An ancient golden signet ring (seal) from Egypt.

It is probable that Joseph was the only person to gain the confidence of a Pharaoh to this degree. Joseph received every authority apart from becoming Pharaoh himself, in spite of the fact that he was not of royal blood, and that he belonged to another nationality.

The seal of a ruler constitutes the power, and is a confirmation that a person has authority. This is found in most cultures, although today it is most common that the signature of a president or prime minister in front of international media has replaced the importance of a seal.

So the fact that Pharaoh's own signet ring (seal) was handed over to Joseph meant that he had unlimited power (figure 145). Joseph's role was mainly that of minister of state, and Imhotep seems to have been the first to have such wide and comprehensive authority in ancient Egypt. There is a striking resemblance when comparing these two persons.

8.3. Imhotep and Joseph - an inscription

An inscription which links together Joseph and Imhotep exists on the island of Sihiel, just below the first cataract of the Nile (15). This inscription claims that it is a copy of a document written by Pharaoh Djoser in the 18th year of his reign. This copy was carved more than a thousand years after the events it claims to cite. The inscription tells of seven meagre years and seven rich years. Let us compare certain parts of this inscription with some biblical texts:

Figure 146: The Nile River is central to Egypt, the most important places have always been situated near it (Sakkara, Giza, Thebes, Luxor).

1. *" I was in distress on the Great Throne..."* (Inscription).

"And it came to pass in the morning that his spirit was troubled..." (Gen. 41:8).

2. In the text of the inscription Pharaoh is worried about the coming famine, and asks Imhotep who the god of the Nile is, so that he can pray to this god. "...I asked him who was the Chamberlain, ... Imhotep, the son of Ptah... What is the birthplace of the Nile? Who is the god there? Who is the God?" Imhotep answers: "I need the guidance of Him who presides over the fowling net..." (Inscription)

Joseph answers Pharaoh:

" And Joseph answered Pharaoh, saying, It is not in me: God shall give Pharaoh an answer of peace." (Gen. 41:16).

In the Egyptian text Imhotep is called the son of Ptah, who was the Egyptian god known as the greatest god, creator of all, including other gods. Joseph professed faith in the one and only God, creator of all things. In that sense Joseph was different because he only prayed to the one God, creator of all things. The God who was over all other gods in Egypt was called Ptah. It is then logical that Joseph is given the title of the son of Ptah in accordance with Egyptian custom. The god like character of Joseph was most likely given to him long after his death. It should be noted that the inscription asserts that Imhotep and the son of Ptah are one and the same person.

3. In the inscription Imhotep answers Pharaoh's question about the Nile god and describes where he lives. In the biblical text Joseph explains Pharaoh's dream. The text of the inscription relates that while the king slept the Nile god, Khnum, appeared to him in a dream and promised that the Nile would give its water, and that there would be famine for seven years followed by seven good years.

This corresponds in detail to the dream that Joseph interpreted for Pharaoh except that the order is reversed. The Bible speaks of seven good years followed by seven years of famine (Gen. 41:25-32). Bad years occur now and

Figure 147: The meaning of
the dream is not only found in
the biblical text, but also in
the history of Egypt.

then, but there is only one occasion spoken of in the history of Egypt when seven years of plenty were followed by seven very difficult years of famine, even if the order is reversed sometimes, as in this inscription for example.

It should be noted that the biblical text has greater credibility in stating that seven years of plenty are followed by seven years of famine than the reverse in the inscription, since this was made about 1000 years after the event. Egypt and all the countries around were almost destroyed in spite of the preparatory measures taken during the seven good years. Had they not taken these measures the entire eastern Mediterranean region would have been wiped out. During the seven years of famine they could neither sow nor reap. Without enormous stocks of grain and other food, no nation could have survived those seven years of famine.

4. The inscription goes on to tell of Pharaoh Djoser's promise to the Nile god, Khnum, that the population, with the exception of the priests in the god's house, would be taxed 10% on all that was harvested.

"Let Pharaoh do this, and let him appoint officers over the land, and take up the fifth part of the land of Egypt in the seven plenteous years." (Gen. 41:34)

"And it shall come to pass in the increase, that ye shall give the fifth part unto Pharaoh, and four parts shall be your own, for seed of the field, and for your food, and for them of your households, and for food for your little ones." (Gen. 47:24)

"Only the land of the priests bought he not; for the priests had a portion assigned them of Pharaoh, and did eat their portion which Pharaoh gave them: wherefore they sold not their lands." (Gen. 47:22)

Here we have an inscription that relates how Pharaoh Djoser asks Imhotep to help him with the coming seven years of famine. Imhotep answers that he must communicate with God as he does not have the answer himself. Pharaoh has a dream foreseeing the event (in reverse order). Imhotep taxes the people 10%, with the exception of the priesthood, in order to cope with the crisis.

All these components are in the biblical account. Pharaoh asks Joseph what he must do to survive the coming seven years of famine. Joseph relied solely on God in all that he did. This occasion arises because Pharaoh has a dream which Joseph interprets. During the seven good years Joseph imposes a 20% tax on the people, with the exception of the priesthood, in order to cope with the crisis.

All the biblical components of the story are there, however the account is "Egyptianised" in order to fit in with the Egyptian system of gods. For example, the god Khnum was responsible for seeing that the Nile produced its annual flooding, leaving mud which provided the right conditions for good harvests. Low water in the Nile and no floods were also the work of the god Khnum, in the view of the Egyptians.

The inscription is thought to have been made during the second century BC by the Khnum priests, to show that they had rights to certain privileges. Part of the inscription maintains that Pharaoh gave some of the land and tax rights to their god. This is not the only account. There is a similar inscription on the island of Philae in the Nile (17), but there it is the priests of Isis who claim that Pharaoh Djoser granted the same privileges to their god. In other words, the same story occurs in different connections to justify the privileges of various groups of Egyptian priests (15, 16).

8.4. IMHOTEP AND JOSEPH
- THE MEDICAL CONNECTION

Imhotep is the earliest doctor written about in historical documents. Imhotep is on a par with the Greek god of medical skills, Asclepius. No mention is made of Joseph being a doctor, but the biblical text has an interesting note:

"And Joseph commanded his servants the physicians to embalm his father: and the physicians embalmed Israel." (Gen. 50:2)

Figure 148: To the west of Sakkara is the entire Sahara desert.

In other words, Joseph had doctors in his service. When later on, Imhotep becomes the god of healing, the way in which he heals can be linked with Joseph. In ancient Greek texts (19) an important holy place in Memphis is mentioned (an Egyptian town besides Sakkara), to which people came from all around to be healed by Imhotep. They prayed to him, made sacrifice and then spent the night in the holy place. While they slept the god Imhotep came to them in their dreams and healed them.

What was behind the very prominent role Joseph played in Egypt was precisely his ability to dream prophecies about the future, and to interpret the dreams of others. In other words, Joseph had two qualities which link him to the art of healing, firstly that he had doctors in his service, and secondly that through his dreams God could perform strange miracles and signs.

Figure 149: To the east of Sakkara is the fertile Nile river valley.

8.5. IMHOTEP AND JOSEPH - THE WORDS OF WISDOM

Joseph is pointed out by Pharaoh as being a very wise person:

"And Pharaoh said unto Joseph, Forasmuch as God hath shewed thee all this, there is none so discreet and wise as thou art." (Gen. 41:39)

Attention is also drawn to Joseph as a wise man in the 105th psalm, in the Book of Psalms. The following line is found there:

"...and teach his senators wisdom." (Ps. 105:22)

Figure 150: The Giza pyramids seen from a satellite.

Imhotep is known as the one who had many words of wisdom. One example is: "Words of Imhotep" where it is written: "I have heard the words of Imhotep" (wise saying). The wise sayings of Imhotep were spoken about at that time. The writings of Imhotep no longer exist, but there are five known counsellors of Pharaoh with the title of Ptah-hotep. There are wise sayings dedicated to this (or these) Ptah-hotep, all of them priests in Heliopolis. It could be that Imhotep's successors continued the tradition of words of wisdom, but their origins were lost through the years. Therefore, these words of wisdom were attributed to the one who had the same function that Imhotep, and later the various Ptah-hotep had (15).

Further to this wisdom, it can be mentioned that there are several similarities between passages in the Book of Proverbs in the Bible, and Imhotep's wise sayings. This can be explained in two ways, either the Book of Proverbs, which is a collection of wise sayings, originates from Egyptian tradition, or vice versa. It could very well be that Joseph (Imhotep) was the one who gave rise to the Book of Proverbs, which later went in two directions. On one hand, these wise sayings were incorporated into Egyptian tradition as the spoken word of the son of the only god (Imhotep, Ptah's son), on the other hand the people of Israel took these sayings with them, and later on they became part of the Bible. The Bible does not indicate any author of the words of wisdom in the Book of Proverbs, but it consists of several sections, many of which are attributed to the wise king Solomon.

Figure 151: The well-known pyramids of Giza are located some 15 km north of the Step Pyramid of Sakkara.

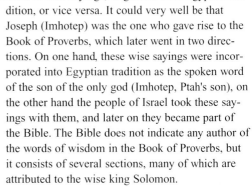
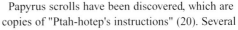

Papyrus scrolls have been discovered, which are copies of "Ptah-hotep's instructions" (20). Several passages of these texts are worth noting. At the end of the manuscript the author says that he is near death after a life of 110 years, and that he had received recognition from the king (Pharaoh) such as no-one prior to him had received.

We know from the Bible that Joseph was received by Pharaoh in a remarkable way, limited only by the fact that Pharaoh retained his position, everything else was Joseph's. Pharaoh went so far as to give him his personal signet ring and unlimited authority (Gen. 41:37-45). The Bible also recounts that Joseph knew he was dying, and that he died at the age of 110:

"And Joseph dwelt in Egypt, he, and his father's house: and Joseph lived an hundred and ten years. And Joseph saw Ephraim's children of the third generation: the children also of Machir the son of Manasseh were brought up upon Joseph's knees. And Joseph said unto his brethren, I die: and God will surely visit you, and bring you out of this land unto the land which he sware to Abraham, to Isaac, and to Jacob. And Joseph took an oath of the children

of Israel, saying, God will surely visit you, and ye shall carry up my bones from hence. So Joseph died, being an hundred and ten years old: and they embalmed him, and he was put in a coffin in Egypt." (Gen. 50:22-26)

During the third dynasty there cannot have been many people with this unique position in Egypt, who had written all these wise sayings, who conclude their authorship at 110 years of age, and then die. The resemblance's between Imhotep and Joseph are striking from this point of view too.

One hypothesis claims that 110 years was a symbolic age for a powerful person. If this is true, then Imhotep and Joseph have received the same mark of honour. However, it is most probable that it is an actual age that is given since the biblical texts continually record the age of each person. For example, Abraham lives to the age of 175 years, Isaac 180 years and Jacob 137 years. If 110 years was a fictitious age to honour a person, then these too would have been given that age.

8.6. IMHOTEP AND JOSEPH - THE POINT IN TIME

We know that the Pharaoh who was in power at the time Joseph came to Egypt, had had that position for an unknown length of time before Pharaoh and Joseph met. When Joseph came to interpret his dreams, Pharaoh was established and had great power and highly-developed authority.

It was the same for Pharaoh Djoser's counsellor Imhotep. There is nothing written about Imhotep from the early part of Djoser's time as Pharaoh. Nothing on monuments or similar things. For example, Imhotep was not the architect of Djoser's grave at Beit Khallaf, a building that was surely begun as soon as Djoser came to power. At this place there is a clay seal with Djoser's name, his mother's name

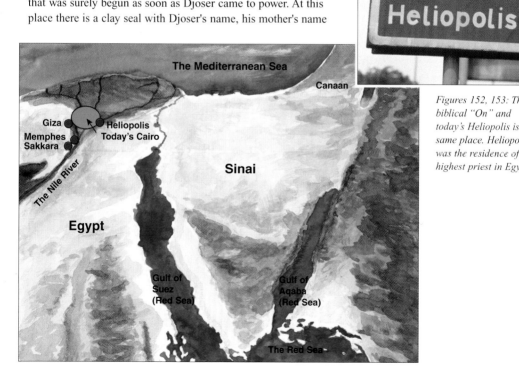

Figures 152, 153: The biblical "On" and today's Heliopolis is the same place. Heliopolis was the residence of the highest priest in Egypt.

and the names of a number of people who held office during his reign, but Imhotep is not mentioned.

This implies that Imhotep - that godlike counsellor - had not yet entered the picture. It was usual that the new Pharaoh appointed those in high offices (with his own family highest of all) immediately on coming to power. Both Imhotep and Joseph seem to have come to power in a similar way, some time after the reigning Pharaoh had begun his rule. It is also important to note that Imhotep was the first one to have such a position in the history of Egypt.

Certain inscriptions point to another important fact: Imhotep's titles in certain inscriptions indicate that he was not a member of the royal family, but was someone who had attained his position on his own merits. This was unique because the one who usually had the role of Pharaoh's foremost adviser and co-ruler was Pharaoh's son. On this point too Imhotep and Joseph are very similar.

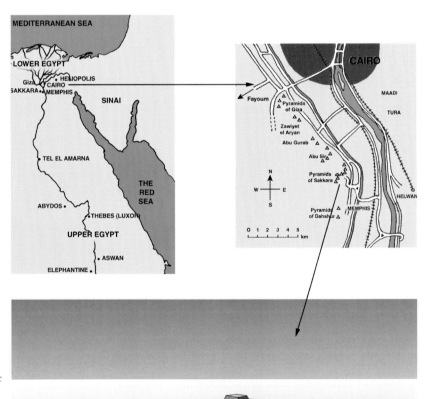

Figures 154-156: The Sakkara complex and the Step Pyramid, the square, buildings etc. that were surrounded by a magnificent wall with only one entrance.

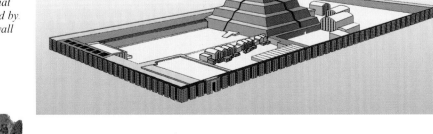

8.7. IMHOTEP AND JOSEPH
- THE PRIESTLY CONNECTION

Imhotep was a priest in the town of Heliopolis (the biblical "On") which lies on the outskirts of modern Cairo.
Joseph's father-in-law, Poti-Pherah, was the priest in On at
the time of Joseph's marriage to Asenath (Gen. 41:45).
Since Asenath was grown-up when she married, her father
must have been at least 40 years old. In ancient Egypt

Figure 157: The wall and the only entrance to the Sakkara complex.

people did not often live to be older than 50. On the other hand, Joseph lived
to be 110 years old.

It is not unlikely that Joseph became a priest in On after the death of his
father-in-law. It is perhaps even probable since Joseph held the highest position in the country (apart from Pharaoh himself), and was considered by
Pharaoh to be a man of god who had great wisdom. In Egypt the rulers were
representatives of different gods. The priest in On was not the priest of a special god, but it seems to have been a position of honour given to a chosen
person with great political influence. Both Joseph and Imhotep therefore had
direct links with the priestly office in Heliopolis.

8.8. IMHOTEP AND JOSEPH - THE PYRAMIDS

It was Imhotep who had the honour of having designed the first pyramid, and
who began to build with cut stone instead of clay bricks. If we look at
Egyptian history, it can be seen that it was during the reign of Djoser that
Egypt became a great power. For one thing great riches had accumulated during the seven years of famine when grain was sold to fellow countrymen, and
to the countries around Egypt.

Figure 158: A part of the wall around the Step Pyramid.

During the seven years of plenty with good harvests, an administrative centre had been established under Joseph's leadership, which could handle the
storage and sale of large quantities of grain, according to the Biblical
account. Archelogical investigations have revealed a big complex, which
included a burial place for Pharaoh, and even included large silos situated in
an area surrounded by a wall. The name of this place is the Step Pyramid in
Sakkara (figure 156), which we shall consider in detail.

Figure 159: The 40 columns inside the entrance to Sakkara.

The first pyramid to be built was the Step Pyramid. Around this pyramid,
and the parts pertaining to it, is a beautiful, ornamented wall (figures 157
and 158). At the main entrance in the eastern wall one comes into a long hall
with 40 columns, 20 on each side (figure 159). Each column is joined to the
main wall by a vertical partition, which means that there is a space between
each column. When one has passed these columns, one comes to a number of
very large shafts going deep down into the ground.

The hypothesis of today claims that these shafts are burial chambers, but
they are exceptionally large, far bigger than any other burial chamber, and
different in shape and function (figures 160-163). All these shafts are connected to each other by a central tunnel (figure 164). The shafts reach up
above the surface of the ground, and one shaft has a stairway (figure 165)
that goes right down to the bottom.

It is most unlikely that these are graves because of their tremendous size,
and because they have large openings upwards above the ground. No attempt
has been made to hide these shafts, as one did otherwise with all burial

Figures 160-163: Examples of the large, deep shafts at Sakkara. The upper photograph shows the part of the shaft seen above ground-level, surrounded by a wall. The other three are photographs of the shafts cut into the rocky ground of Sakkara.

chambers. Hiding the entrances to burial chambers became the system in Egypt as the dead were buried together with great riches. Furthermore, the dead were held in great respect since they were representatives of the gods and should be allowed to rest in peace, protected from all grave-robbers.

In addition, it should be noted that all the other graves in the vicinity are shaped in the traditional way, which means small graves with hidden entrances. There is only one place in Egypt which has these shafts, and so it is most unlikely that these are graves. The argument that the state of the ground and the rock in this place led to a different way of making graves, does not stand in view of the fact that all the other graves in this area are constructed in the traditional way.

These shafts with large openings upwards, above the ground, must then have been something quite different. In Pharaoh's grave, which lay under the pyramid, there are also the traditional storage places for food for the dead, which also clearly indicates that the shafts were used for some other purpose.

The Bible shows how Joseph acted and organised the grain storage throughout the country:

"Now therefore let Pharaoh look out a man discreet and wise, and set him over the land of Egypt. Let Pharaoh do this, and let him appoint officers over the land, and take up the fifth part of the land of Egypt in the seven plenteous years. And let them gather all the food of those good years that come, and lay up corn under the hand of Pharaoh, and let them keep food in the cities. And that food shall be for store to the land against the seven years of famine, which shall be in the land of Egypt; that the land perish not through the famine." (Gen. 41:33-36)

"And Joseph gathered corn as the sand of the sea, very much, until he left numbering; for it was without number." (Gen. 41:49)

This was carried out, and it must have been an exceptionally big project to build all these silos and corresponding stores. In order to cope with storing the grain for several years it was necessary to have a cool, dry environment in these store rooms. Underground silos in the dry, desert region with openings above the ground, presumably covered by a wooden roof, would effectively meet these requirements. The seven years of famine affected Egypt and the whole region of surrounding countries, the Bible tells the story:

"And the seven years of plenteousness, that was in the land of Egypt, were ended. And the seven years of dearth began to come, according as Joseph had said: and the dearth was in all lands; but in all the land of Egypt there was bread. And when all the land of Egypt was famished, the people cried to Pharaoh for bread: and Pharaoh said unto all the Egyptians, Go unto Joseph; what he saith to you, do.

And the famine was over all the face of the earth: and Joseph opened all the storehouses, and sold unto the Egyptians; and the famine waxed sore in the land of Egypt. And all countries came into Egypt to Joseph for to buy corn; because that the famine was so sore in all lands." (Gen. 41:53-57)

When foreigners came to Egypt to buy grain, the biblical texts say that they had to go to Joseph:

"And Joseph was the governor over the land, and he it was that sold to all the people of the land: and Joseph's brethren came, and bowed down themselves before him with their faces to the earth." (Gen. 42:6)

Joseph's brothers come straight to Joseph to buy grain. It is probable that they arrived in Sakkara, where even today we can see the archaeo-logical remains in the form of the complex around the Step Pyramid. In all probability Pharaoh Djoser's minister of state (Joseph) had at least 11 huge shafts built in which to store grain, or silos as we call them today. This amount of grain was more than an individual town needed, and all the towns of Egypt had their own grain stores. Since there is a large area around the Step Pyramid which has not yet been excavated, one can speculate that there were even more silos in the area. The complex around the Step Pyramid was probably an international trading place for grain, with Joseph himself in charge.

Figure 164: The display at Sakkara showing how the shafts are connected.

Figure 165: One of the shafts has a staircase all the way down to the bottom.

Since large quantities of goods and gold accumulated as payment for all the grain (Gen. 45:6), this was another reason for having high walls as protection (figures 166 and 167). The Sakkara complex had only one entrance, which implies that there were reasons for security. In comparison, the pyramids in Giza, including the mighty Cheops pyramid, are not surrounded by a wall.

The 11 shafts which are just inside the columns are extremely large, with a volume that meant they could hold about 40 000 cubic metres of grain alto-gether (corresponding to approximately 4 000 trucks each loaded with 10 cubic metres). All the shafts are linked by an underground tunnel, and one shaft has a stairway leading to the bottom of the shaft system. When the shafts were filled to the top they were probably sealed with timbers and blocks of stone.

Figures 166-167: Design and decorations at the Sakkara complex.

Remains of grain have been found at the bottom of these shafts, but no dis-coveries have been made that might imply that these shafts could have been burial chambers. One shaft has a stairway down to the tunnel complex. This stairway was probably used to get down to the place where the sacks were filled. There is a tunnel, which then leads out from the area. Part of this silo system has been drawn on a picture displayed in present day Sakkara (figure 164).

The complex of buildings at Sakkara is unique, nothing like it has been found elsewhere. Hayes describes it in the following way: "... a veritable city

in itself, planned and executed as a single unit and built of fine white limestone from the nearby Mukattam hills" (22).

The construction and application of the Sakkara complex fits in very well
with Joseph's role in Egypt. Joseph needed an administrative centre for the
enormous assignment that had been given to him: to save all Egypt and the
surrounding countries during seven years of famine after seven years of good
harvests.

The Bible tells of how Joseph himself took charge of the international contacts (the national distribution was delegated to the storehouses built in the
towns), and in this way came into contact again with his own brothers.
Joseph's brothers were also suffering from the famine and journeyed down to
an administrative centre in Egypt, where there were large amounts of grain
and a trading place. In addition, the second highest man in Egypt, the administrator and owner of Pharaoh's signet ring, had his administrative seat precisely there.

There is also a further connection here to Imhotep. Imhotep
was called the "builder" and the "inventor of the art of building with cut stone". Without doubt Joseph initiated extensive
construction work all over Egypt. These constructions were
different in various ways. They were large constructions and
the purpose was to store grain and other foodstuffs during a
long period of time. The building had to be done quickly as it
was necessary to hurry to collect up the food during the good
years. Orders to build were sent throughout the country, and
every town was to have its own stocks. Certainly Joseph stood
out as a builder of a type seldom seen.

*Figure 168: The ibis bird is
a bird species very closely
connected to Sakkara.
Mummified ibis birds were
sacrificed to the god-like
character Imhotep (long
after his death), in the hope
that the giver of the sacrifice would be healed in or
by their dreams.*

From Sakkara we can also note that the building material in this administrative centre was of good quality, was pleasant to look at, and was built in cut
stone. This too agrees with the description of Imhotep. If these events are
correct - and there is much that supports this - then this also means that
Joseph built the first pyramid, the Step Pyramid.

The Step Pyramid in Sakkara is situated within the complex containing the
grain shafts, and according to Egyptian history, Imhotep, Pharaoh's minister
of state, was the builder.

*Figure 169: The cartouch
(seal) of Pharaoh Djoser.
Djoser was the Pharaoh
who had Imhotep as his
minister of state.*

8.9. IMHOTEP AND JOSEPH - THE BURIAL PLACE

Imhotep was an extremely important person in ancient Egypt with great
influence and a very high position. Thus, according to tradition his grave
should have been impressive, and should have been found amongst the other
graves that have been discovered. However Imhotep's grave has never been
found. Or has it?

When Joseph died at the age of 110, he was embalmed and placed in a coffin and buried in Egypt (Gen. 50:26). Where should he have been buried if
not in Sakkara? Joseph must definitely have had a royal funeral. We know
too that Joseph made the sons of Israel take an oath that they would carry his
bones with them in the coming departure from Egypt (Gen. 50:22-26).

Later on, when Moses led the Exodus (departure from Egypt), he kept the
oath and took Joseph's bones with them (Ex. 13:19). This was in line with
what later became Jewish custom. A person was buried and after a time the

bones were dug up and placed in a smaller wooden box (casket), which was usually placed in a cave. The people of Israel had to swear with an oath that they would take Joseph's bones, according to the biblical text.

Earlier on we took up the question of Imhotep as a great doctor. Ancient Greek texts describe a place to which pilgrimages were made not far from Memphis. Sakkara is situated near Memphis. When excavations were being carried out in Sakkara, just by the Step Pyramid, to find the grave of Imhotep, archelogists had a surprise. An extensive labyrinth of underground tunnels was found full of mummified ibis birds and bulls in separate galleries.

Inscriptions and coins found there show that people from different countries came there to be healed. After being put on a par with the Greek god of healing, Imhotep was given the title "highest ruler of Ibis". In other words, this was the place of Imhotep, where the Greeks record people went on pilgrimage to be healed. An anonymous inscription of a Greek who came to this place tells how he was healed through a dream.

Up to a million ibis birds (figure 171), mummified and laid in brick piping, had been brought to Imhotep to honour him, and to this day the tunnels are full of them. Later it was discovered that these tunnels were linked to a shaft leading to a burial chamber, which was not empty but contained a sealed and empty coffin (17). The burial chamber had not been plundered, but contained an empty coffin. Close to this burial chamber there was another chamber full of broken earthenware pots. In this room there were pots bearing Pharaoh Djoser's seal (figure 169).

This grave had belonged to a very important person, who had the seal of Pharaoh Djoser on his pots. The person was no longer in the grave but the empty coffin remained. Most probably this was Imhotep's burial chamber. But what happened to Imhotep?

Figures 170, 171: The holy ibis bird. The upper photograph is from Deir-El Bahri.

Here there is a very clear connection with Joseph. Joseph was buried in a coffin in Egypt. It must have been an impressive grave in view of the important role Joseph played in Egypt. When the people of Israel fled from Egypt, they took Joseph's bones with them, but probably not the coffin. At the time of the Exodus Joseph, who is very likely to have had Sakkara as his administrative centre, would have left behind an empty coffin in exactly this place.

If the hypothesis holds that Joseph and Imhotep are the same person, then Joseph would have been buried in Sakkara, where years later the ancient Egyptians offered the sacred ibis birds in honour of Imhotep. It is exactly there that the burial chamber with the empty coffin is found, in Sakkara, quite close to Pharaoh Djoser's pyramid, in the galleries of sacred, embalmed, ibis birds (figure 170).

Behind these galleries the possible burial chamber of Joseph is found. The biblical text (Gen. 41:41-42) says clearly that Joseph received the ruling Pharaoh's signet ring (the seal of Pharaoh), when he attained his position of authority at the age of 30. Since Joseph lived another 80 years, it is most likely that he retained his seal during the reigns of several pharaohs.

In this burial chamber a number of artifacts have been found. Examples are pottery and other items that would contain food, and important things for the

A comment on the shafts: "This is the so-called south tomb, whose significance has not yet been clearly determined...." (21)

journey of the dead. These containers have the seal of Paraoh Djoser (Figure 169).

If this grave belonged to Joseph, and there is a great deal that points to this, then there is a very clear connection here between Joseph and the pharaoh Djoser. Djoser's minister of state was Imhotep, who in turn was Joseph.

This burial chamber differs from the pharaohs' burial chambers in another way. The pharaohs' burial chambers always faced eastwards, towards the rising sun, while this burial chamber faced northwards. This implies that the person buried in this place did not worship the gods of Egypt, which also indicates Joseph.

We see here further clear links between Imhotep and Joseph. Imhotep should have been buried in this area, most probably in the place to which many people, a long time later, came to be healed by him, adjoining the galleries of ibis birds. The ibis bird was included in one of Imhotep's titles. In this place healing came through dreams. We know about Joseph's supernatural power of working through dreams from the biblical texts. We have also gone through the hypothesis based on Sakkara being Joseph's administrative centre, with all the grain silos and other indications.

Both Joseph and Imhotep could, with good reason, have been buried here. The burial chamber suggests that it was of a high dignitary, confirmed by the seal of Pharaoh Djoser. Why was Imhotep's grave empty (just an empty coffin), but not plundered? We know that Joseph's bones were moved by the people of Israel, but probably not his coffin. In other words, there would have been an empty coffin left in this place if Joseph had been buried there.

Could it be that Imhotep and Joseph are the same person? If this is the case, and many indications point to this, then suddenly it is much easier to see both Joseph's and Imhotep's role in Egypt.

8.10. Imhotep, known under several names?

Well-known characters, and especially leaders of nations, have always been known by a variety of names. This is particularly evident in the royal families in Europe. There are several similarities between these families and the families which ruled Egypt. The most important similarities are that power is inherited, and that they are given many titles.

If we take the Swedish royal family as an example, the name of a sovereign could be:

> Carl-Gustaf Bernadotte
> Crown prince Carl-Gustaf
> Duke of Jämtland
> King of Sweden
> Carl XVIth Gustaf
> King Carl-Gustaf
> Holder of the Serafim Order
> Chief of State

All these names are correct. They distinguish themselves from each other by representing different periods in a person's life, e.g. crown prince and king. They also differ in that they indicate the name, the authority or the succession. Other titles and functions could be added to the list.

Many different names are the rule rather than the exception amongst national leaders, and it is especially clear when it is a matter of families in which power is inherited. In addition, a number of sovereigns often have somewhat similar names, and so a number is given as a supplement to the name. In the example above from the Swedish royal family, the number "16" (XVI) has been added to specify exactly the person referred to. It can in no way be taken for granted that this follows a logical numerical order. The present king in Sweden is called Carl the 16th Gustaf, while his predecessor (who was his grandfather) was called Gustaf the 6th Adolf.

Carl the 16th Gustaf has the same name (Gustaf) as his great grandfather Gustavius the 5th, although a different spelling. The two last kings during this century have double-names, while the two first have single names. The number given to these four kings, ruling one after the other, were II, V, VI and XVI, respectively. King Oscar II was king of Sweden and Norway, while the others were kings only of Sweden. The next regent in Sweden will be a queen. With all these variables it becomes complicated and this, it should be remembered, is an example of a royal family currently ruling (figure 172).

Figure 172: The four kings of Sweden that ruled during the 20th century; Oscar II, Gustavius V, Gustav VI Adolf and Carl XVI Gustaf. The next ruler will be Queen Victoria. The kings are represented by coins from each period of rulership.

There is no reason to assume that it should be otherwise in the various Egyptian dynasties. The difference is that when it comes to the history of Egypt there is very limited information, which must also be interpreted and translated from a dead language based on symbols. Everything must be founded on ancient documents or inscriptions that are several thousand years old, and which in most cases cannot be dated by objective methods. In other words one cannot determine the exact date with any measuring technique, but various contexts lead to a hypothesis, which often must be corrected and modified as new knowledge is generated. In addition, it is known that all Egyptian regents had several names, and that Egypt had one to three regents at the same time.

Often the scientist is aware of this uncertainty, and defines his result as a hypothesis or, expressed in another way, an assumption or premise. However, it is not completely unusual that the more popular type of book defines these hypotheses as being the truth. This is pointed out as background to the possibility that Imhotep had several names.

In this section we have studied all the similarities between Joseph and Imhotep. Let us for a moment assume that this is quite correct. In this case Joseph had many names:

1. Joseph, the name he received from his family (Gen. 35:24).
2. Zaphenath-Paneah, the name Pharaoh gave Joseph when he assumed his position (Gen. 41:45).
3. Imhotep, the name Joseph possibly received when he was appointed minister of state.

Added to this another name would fit Joseph, namely:

4. Ptah-hotep. The first part in this name indicates which god the person represented, or to which they belonged. Ptah means the greatest god, creator of all things. According to the biblical texts, Joseph never relinquished his faith in one god, God the creator of all things. In this respect Joseph differed most markedly from other ministers of state and pharaohs, who prayed to many gods and considered that they were gods themselves.

It is worth noting that amongst other things Imhotep was given the title "Ptah's son". Discoveries have been made in Sakkara in which a scribe is holding a sacred object representing Ptah.

Let us see what Imhotep's titles were: "…and I asked him who was the Chamberlain, the Ibis, the Chief Lector Priest Imhotep, the son of Ptah…" (15) These titles signify that the person spoken of was a minister who was god-like, who was connected with the sacred ibis bird, a priest (who tells what God says), Imhotep (with all the qualities that Imhotep had), son of the only God (creator of all things).

Apart from indicating the extremely high rank the person enjoyed, this is an excellent description of Joseph. Probably Imhotep (Joseph) received the name Ptah-hotep after his death. Joseph, who during his lifetime prayed to the only God (Ptah), saved the entire nation of Egypt in the name of the only God, and in addition brought them tremendous riches: when they sold their grain during the seven difficult years.

Joseph lived 110 years, 80 years after becoming minister of state. Joseph thus had many years to serve under several pharaohs; all the time solely worshipping the one God. It is not difficult to think of adding to all the other titles Joseph had that of Ptah-hotep.

Figure 173: King Solomon began the construction of the Temple in Jerusalem, in the fourth year of his reign, 480 years after the Exodus, according to the biblical texts.

8.11. IMHOTEP AND JOSEPH - THE PERIOD OF TIME

In the summary of chapter 8 important characteristics of Imhotep and Joseph are summarised and compared. The list includes 27 characteristics, of which 25 are common to both Imhotep and Joseph. This list contains very special and unique qualities. It is hard to believe that two such remarkable and unique individuals, with such an important role in the history of Egypt can be so alike in so many ways and yet be two different people. We must not forget that it was only within an exceedingly small group of people in Egyptian history that Joseph and Imhotep could be found.

Then the final question is, did Joseph and Imhotep live during the same period of time in Egypt? Two people with this type of power and authority, and these qualifications could not have lived in Egypt at the same time, unless they were one and the same person.

We begin with the biblical texts to see if a date can be established for Joseph's arrival on the Egyptian scene as minister of state over Egypt. It is relatively easy to indicate this with the help of a few pieces of the puzzle. With the date of when the Babylonian ruler Nebuchadnezzar conquered Jerusalem and destroyed the temple, the books of the Old Testament give the answer.

Several historical sources consider that the destruction of Jerusalem and the temple, followed by the captivity of Israel in Babylon, took place in 586 BC.

In the books of Kings in the Bible every ruler and the length of his reign are mentioned. Israel was divided into two kingdoms for many years, the kingdoms of Israel and Judah. This means that there were two parallel royal lines with a large number of cross-references, so that the time-axis becomes like a ladder with a number of steps. This means that certain ambiguities in one royal line can be corrected with the help of the other royal line.

Thus the chronology can be traced backwards with great precision through the entire history of the people of Israel. When one comes to the powerful and wise King Solomon, an exact date is given. King Solomon began the construction of the temple in the fourth year of his reign, which was 480 years (1 Kings 6:1) after the Exodus, the great migration. (figure 173)

By using these three factors: the time when the temple was destroyed by Nebuchadnezzar, the royal lines in the kingdoms of Israel and Judah, and the time indication of the beginning of the temple construction in relation to the Exodus, then the year of the Exodus is calculated to be around 1446 BC.

By calculating the time in Egypt with the help of indications found in the books of Genesis and Exodus, and the fact that Joseph was 30 years old when he was appointed ruler in Egypt, the life of Joseph can be dated to around 1745-1635 BC. The measure of uncertainty regarding this date can be in the order of 10-30 years. In the last 2000 years the measure of uncertainty is around 4 years (our modern era after the birth of Jesus), and there are uncertainties in the above calculation, e.g. when a sovereign dies in the second year of his reign, does this mean after 13 months or after 24 months? This type of uncertainty can generally be corrected, but when it is a matter of a number of steps in the calculation then one should add a decade or two to allow for the factor of uncertainty.

The books of the Bible together with other historical sources (concerning Nebuchadnezzar's entry into Jerusalem) give us the basis for a relatively well-founded time-axis. Considering that this spans almost 1800 years plus 2000 years of our modern era, in all almost 4000 years, one must realise that these are very precise estimates. More details regarding these calculations of time are to be found in chapter 39.

So what can we say about the points in time which are given regarding the history of Egypt? To put it simply, the basic material is very difficult to use for exact estimations. There are several reasons for this:

1. It is not at all clear how many people have actually been rulers in Egypt. When several names occur, it could mean that there are a number of different people, or several people who are given different titles in different contexts, or they could refer to one and the same person. As it can be seen from the example of the Swedish royal family and all the names which can be used, uncertainties easily arise. We also know that the Egyptian rulers had many titles, one example was given above (15):

Figure 174: The chariots of ancient Egypt enable dating due to the number of spokes. This is discussed in chapter 49.

Figure 175: The ancient Egyptian language is hard to understand since it is based on symbols and not letters.

"...and I asked him who was the Chamberlain, the Ibis, the Chief Lector Priest Imhotep, the son of Ptah..."

In this example four different names for one person have been used at the same time. Another example is Tutankhamun, who had at least five different names: Tutankhamun, Nebkheprure, Renpkhau sehetepnetjeru, Neferhepu segerehtawy and Kanakht tutmes.

The knowledge we have of the names and titles of each ruler, his family and ministers, during several thousand years, leave room for a great deal of uncertainty.

2. In one inscription seals have been preserved as a sort of Egyptian royal line (43). It should be noted that the inscription is not complete (it is damaged), and it may be that several seals belong to the same person. It is natural to assume that a person changes his seal as he moves on from being the heir to the throne to joint ruler with the pharaoh, and later becomes Pharaoh. It is not unlikely that several people, other than the sovereign, are named in this type of tabulation e.g. the monarch and the heir to the throne. Altogether this gives rise to a great deal of uncertainty in establishing dates.

It should be noted that the joint ruler, before taking over as Pharaoh in Thebes, was Pharaoh in Memphis. In other words, there could be two pharaohs in office at the same time, one being superior (Thebes) to the other (Memphis). Several texts speak of the Egyptian leaders in the plural, "Egyptian kings". One example is the Bible text of Jeremiah (Jer. 46:25).

Figure 176: Tutankhamun is known for his exceptional tomb with a 10.3 kg golden death mask.

3. The language is a further difficulty, partly because it is based on symbols (figure 175) and not on letters in the ordinary sense, and partly because it is a dead language. This leads to problems of interpretation and understanding. There is an inscription with the same text in two different languages (with two varieties of hieroglyphs) which is fundamental for an understanding of the Egyptian hieroglyphs, the so-called Rosetta stone (26). It should be noted that only one or two of all the pharaonic seals are included in this inscription.

4. The main source of information regarding the history of Egypt is found in the graves of the pharaohs. With only a few exceptions all these graves have been plundered. This means that certain information is brought to the fore because more is known about that particular example, while there are long periods of time about which there is little knowledge.

Tutankhamun has been brought to the fore very markedly, and his beautiful and valuable death mask (in gold and the semi-precious stone turquoise) has become a modern symbol for Egypt (figure 176). The reason for this is that Tutankhamun's grave was one of the few that had not been plundered, and therefore contained all the valuable objects of gold. In addition, everything else that a royal personage would take with him on his journey of death was intact. On the other hand, the degree of magnificence with which

Tutankhamun was surrounded is surprising in view of the fact that he was only around 18 years old when he died.

The importance accorded him today is due not to his political significance, his long reign, the knowledge of him as a great leader in history or anything of this nature, but to the fact that his death mask and other other items in the untouched grave were so magnificent and had not been stolen (approximately 700 objects were found in the grave). The next question one can ask oneself is if this was the rule for all royal burials or only for Tutankhamun, since there is so little with which to compare it as most other graves have been plundered.

5. In one inscription (43) there is a special reference to a constellation of stars. From this a date can be calculated, but there are one or two factors of which one must be aware if the information is to be rightly interpreted. Firstly, the exact position from where the constellation of stars was observed is needed. This is not given in the inscription, and so there can be great uncertainty in calculating the date. An even more important factor is that constellations of stars go in cycles and are repeated at certain intervals. This means that the constellation could fit with several periods of time. The period selected would then entail a subjective choice.

6. In ancient times Egypt was divided into upper (southern) and lower (northern) Egypt, upper and lower respectively were in relation to the river Nile. These two regions had their own pharaohs, but during certain periods of time the land was united. During other periods the Nile delta had its own pharaoh or king. Combined with the lack of knowledge concerning certain periods, this makes dating very uncertain.

If one calculates dates for Norway and Sweden during the last two centuries based solely on the lines of kings, one meets problems for two reasons. For one thing, the king of Norway was in exile during the second world war (which the Swedish king was not), but above all Sweden and Norway formed a union during the period 1814 to 1905, when the king of Sweden was also king of Norway.

After a long period of time, and with very limited information factors such as these can lead to great uncertainty in calculating dates.

7. Pharaohs who fell from grace, or in other ways did not fit in, have been removed from various inscriptions listing cartouches (royal seals) from different pharaohs. It is common to find notes in the literature on how certain statues, inscriptions etc. were systematically destroyed by rulers in Egypt. This "falsification of ancient history" naturally makes things very difficult, when it is a matter of obtaining a clear picture of different eras up to 5000 years ago.

8. There are several different opinions about epochs in time and chronologies with regard to Egypt's pharaohs. This in itself indicates that the chronologies contain uncertainties.

9. One example of uncertainty is mentioned when discussing how long

Figure 177: The Nile River, and the mountains where the Valley of Kings and Deir-El Bahri is located, just opposite Luxor. This is the place where many pharaohs were buried.

"Even with the chronological information available...it may come as a surprise to realize that it is extremely difficult to fix true or absolute dates in Egyptian chronology." (43)

Pharaoh Djoser reigned. Djoser is regarded to have reigned for 19 years. At the same time the Step Pyramid in Sakkara (Djoser's mausoleum) was constructed and built by Imhotep. Probably Imhotep attained his position a number of years after Djoser had attained to his position, so the actual time for construction, organisation, and building of this extremely large edifice was perhaps only 10 years.

In one comment surprise is expressed that the first pyramid could be built in only 19 years, but the question as to whether the dating is completely correct is not raised. Nor is the method indicated by which the date was determined. Djoser is said to have had several names: Djoser, Zoser, Netjeri-khet and Tosorthos, which can also create uncertainty. Nonetheless, the exact period of Djoser's reign is given to the year (2668-2649 BC) in spite of the fact that there are only a few references to Djoser, and that it concerns events of approximately 4600 years ago, according to Egyptian chronology.

10. A further aspect of the uncertainty involved in calculating the dates of the early Egyptian dynasties is presented in E.A.Wallis Budge's book (most recent revision 1989) (28). The following passage is found in this book:

Figure 178: The Hatshepsut obelisk at the Karnak temple in Luxor. Luxor was the residence of the pharaoh of upper Egypt.

"The dates that he and others have assigned to the first dynasty depend upon the numbers of the years that they have assigned to these two intervals. But these dates – Lepsius BC 3892, Bunsen BC 3623, Lieblein BC 3893, Brugsch BC 4455 or 4400, Meyer BC 3315, Breasted BC 3400, Hall BC 3500 – are only indexes to the opinions of those who propose them, and it is quite possible that every one of them is wrong in point of actual fact. The material for fixing with certainty the date of the first dynasty does not exist at present."

The span of time indicated for this point in Egyptian history varies considerably between the authors mentioned, 1140 years to be precise. Wallis' book gives several examples of extensive differences in estimated dates, and mentions that the Egyptians did not keep their own chronologies in the way that we do today, and therefore generally speaking it is difficult to draw specific conclusions about dates and periods of time.

The reign of Pharaoh Djoser was during the third dynasty. There is a great deal of uncertainty about the dating because of the reasons given above, and therefore it is difficult to compare them with the comparatively exact time-axis which the biblical texts set up.

It should then be more important to relate events to each other, and this also gives a greater degree of certainty when the older Egyptian dynasties are discussed. For example, it may be that dating done with the help of constellations of stars (discussed earlier) could change the Egyptian time-axis with around 1000 years, depending on which constellation cycle one chooses.

There is a much greater degree of precision in the statement that the events regarding seven years of famine occurred during the reign of Djoser, when Imhotep was the second man in the realm of Egypt, and that this period of famine was connected with a sort of contract agreement with God (15).

The answer to the question whether Imhotep and Joseph were alive during the same period of time (in other words were the same person), cannot be given on the basis of a calculation of the exact years because of the lack of an Egyptian time-axis which, in a way that inspires confidence, can indicate the dates of the older Egyptian dynasties. On the other hand, events during the reign of pharaoh Djoser show a remarkable number of similarities with descriptions in the Bible (in the books of Genesis and Exodus), similarities which do not exist with other pharaohs.

8.12. Joseph - according to popular tradition

Towards the end of the 19th century when investigations and archaeological excavations were being carried out in Egypt, a note concerning Sakkara was made. At that time there was no knowledge of the hypothesis that Joseph would have had Sakkara as his administrative centre, and everything else mentioned in chapter 8 of this book. At the end of the 19th century very few amongst the local Egyptian population in the area were literate, and even fewer were familiar with historical documents. It is this background that makes the comment on the tradition of the local population interesting (28).

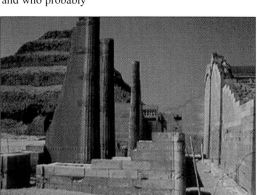

"The Pyramid of Teta...is one of the southern group of pyramids in Sakkara. The Arabs call it the "Prison Pyramid", because local tradition says that it is built near the ruins of the prison where Joseph the patriarch was confined"

Figure 179: Local tradition at the end of the 19th century says that Joseph was in prison in the Sakkara area.

We know that Joseph was imprisoned in Egypt (Gen. 39-41). We also know that he became the supervisor and manager of all the property of a wealthy Egyptian. A wealthy Egyptian who was a state official, and who probably lived near the administrative centre of Egypt, which at that time was the Memphis/Sakkara area. (figures 179, 180)

When Joseph landed in prison, it is probable that it was the nearby prison. It is possible that this prison was not for the lowest ranks in society, but for political prisoners. Presumably it corresponded to what we call house-arrest today, i.e. when political opponents are allowed to live freely in a house but not allowed to go outside the house. The Bible implies this since high dignitaries seem to have been able to go in and out of this prison depending on the political situation (Gen. 39-41). In one place it is stated that the prison was the house of the captain of the guard (Gen. 41:10).

Figure 180: A part of the Sakkara complex.

The biblical texts and popular tradition support the hypothesis that Sakkara was the place where Joseph spent most of his life. To this will be added all the other indications in chapter 8.

8.13. Famine - an inscription in Sakkara

Famine and crop failure often occurred in the region. There are many documents that tell of certain years when there was drought or failure of the crops. The Bible also speaks of this, one example being when Abraham goes down to Egypt on an earlier occasion:

"And there was a famine in the land: and Abram went down into Egypt to sojourn there; for the famine was grievous in the land" (Gen. 12:10)

It was certainly hard on the people of that region when there was a year of drought and difficulty. But they were also used to this, which meant that they had stocks of various products. They were also mobile, especially those who had cattle and sheep. At ordinary times they had to move around to accompany the animals (or lead their flocks) where there was grazing and water.

They had another alternative, which was to move towards the coast where fishing and trade could facilitate matters. There was a great deal of trade in the region and when the famine had been going on in Canaan for two of the seven years, Jacob not only had money but also honey, almonds, pistachio nuts, balsam, tragacanth gum and ladanum to take with them (Gen. 43:11-12). It was also possible to survive periods when the crops failed by eating from the herds of cattle and sheep.

However, the period of famine which hit Egypt and the region around was completely different. If there is crop failure for seven years in succession, all human life in the area is extinguished. No ordinary reserves can cope with this. If such a drought and failure of crops were to occur today in Europe or the USA, entire countries would be laid waste. Quite simply, there are not sufficient reserve stocks of these dimensions. Current grain reserves at global level are in the order of a few weeks' consumption.

It was the same situation in Egypt. When Pharaoh and Joseph discuss the extent of the approaching famine, they are faced with the country's ruin. When Joseph suggests how to cope with this he says:

"And that food shall be for store to the land against the seven years of famine, which shall be in the land of Egypt; that the land perish not through the famine." (Gen. 41:36)

Figure 181: A very special inscription was found in Sakkara showing a lot of starving people. This type of inscription is very rare (if any others exist at all) and indicates that Sakkara played an important role in a major period of famine.

In Genesis chapter 47 one can read how all the countries in the region are hard hit by the famine. Many come to Egypt, which is the only place where there is food. All the money, cattle and farming land in Egypt fall to Pharaoh when Joseph exchanges these for the grain he administers. They survive the seven long years of famine solely because the preceding seven years had given very good harvests, which were put aside in huge stores. This famine

was extraordinary and differed greatly from "normal" years of crop failure. More than a thousand years later inscriptions were made referring to this special period (section 8.3.).

Making inscriptions about ordinary crop failure, which was part of the living conditions in the region, would not have been particularly interesting and there is very little of this found. It is probably true to say that there are no carvings which show this. Except one.

There is one very long carving, which shows only a large number of starving people. People who are suffering extreme starvation. This carving exists in one place - Sakkara. In figure 181 there is a picture of a small part of this carving. The carving shows a number of people in an advanced state of deprivation. The fact that this carving was found in Sakkara is a further indication that Sakkara had a very special position regarding food supplies and starvation. This carving also includes depictions of grain, sacks that are carried up steps (compare with the steps down into the silo-shaft mentioned earlier)... and food distribution... (compare with how Joseph's brothers obtain grain in sacks).

In the history of Egypt, the one who had special ability and a god-like position, and who had his administrative centre in Sakkara was Imhotep. There is only one person who can have organised the survival of such a terrible period of famine in the history of Egypt and its neighbouring countries. The Bible says that it was Joseph, and Egyptian history refers to the reign of Djoser when Imhotep was minister of state with the status of a god.

Both Joseph and Imhotep ruled as prime ministers during a period of seven good years and seven years of famine. This is yet another indication that Joseph and Imhotep were the same person.

It should be noted that there is no other period of famine of 7 + 7 years described in the history of Egypt except the one for which Imhotep was responsible. Similarly there is only one period of famine of 7 + 7 years described in biblical texts, the one for which Joseph was responsible. The Bible gives a comprehensive description of how this took place in Egypt.

8.14. IN SUMMARY

A summary of comparisons between Imhotep and Joseph shows that there are many likenesses between these two people. More details are found in the text in chapter 8. In the table Im = Imhotep and Jo = Joseph.

Table 3. A comparison of Imhotep and Joseph

1-Im. Minister of the king of Lower Egypt (= the northern part of Egypt where, for example, Sakkara is situated) (29).
1-Jo. "And Pharaoh said unto Joseph, See, I have set thee over all the land of Egypt.", " ..and he made him ruler over all the land of Egypt." (Gen. 41:41,43).

2-Im. Foremost under the king (18, 19, 29).
2-Jo. "…and according unto thy word shall all my people be ruled: only in the throne will I be greater than thou." (Gen. 41:40).

3-Im. Administrator of the great palace (29).
3-Jo. "Thou shalt be over my house," (Gen. 41:40).

4-Im. Ruler by inheritance (29).
4-Jo. "And Pharaoh said unto Joseph, I am Pharaoh, and without thee shall no man lift up his hand or foot in all the land of Egypt." (Gen. 41:44). By this statement Joseph was granted the status of being the son of Pharaoh. The Pharaoh actually granted Joseph a higher status than a son, when all these matters are considered.

5-Im. Priest in Heliopolis (19, 29).
5-Jo. Married to the daughter of the priest in Heliopolis (Gen. 41:45). With the status Joseph had as representative of the only God and political leader, it is not unlikely that he also succeeded his father-in-law as priest in Heliopolis.

6-Im. Builder and architect (18, 19, 28, 29, 43).
6-Jo. Joseph had all the storehouses and silos in Egypt built to store the grain and other food for the entire country and surrounding countries, during a period of seven years. Gen. 41:35-36, 47-49, 41:57 and other passages.

7-Im. Discoverer of the art of building with cut stone (14, 19, 28).
7-Jo. See point 6-Jo. If the hypothesis that the Sakkara complex was Joseph's administrative centre is correct, then these buildings were in cut stone. They were also the first of this sort in Egypt, so the builder of Sakkara was also the discoverer of this building art.

8-Im. Sculptor and creator of stone vases (29).
8-Jo. Is not mentioned in relation to Joseph.

9-Im. Exalted to be of godly character (14, 19, 28).
9-Jo. "And Pharaoh said unto his servants, Can we find such a one as this is, a man in whom the Spirit of God is?" (Gen. 41:38).

10-Im. It is not stated that people fell down before Imhotep but it is very probable that this was the case considering Imhotep's position in society.
10-Jo. People fell down before Joseph (Gen. 41:43).

11-Im. Great medical skill, is compared to the Greek god of healing, Asclepius (14, 18, 19, 28, 43).
11-Jo. Had doctors in his service, and worked by performing miracles and signs from God (Gen. 50:2).

12-Im. Was active during a period with seven years of famine followed by seven years of good harvests (15, 16, 19, 43).
12-Jo. Was active during a period with seven good years followed by seven years of famine (Gen. 41:1-32, 47-57).

13-Im. "I need advice from God" (15, 16).

13-Jo. "And Joseph answered Pharaoh, saying, It is not in me: God shall give Pharaoh an answer of peace." (Gen. 41:16).

14-Im. Called the son of Ptah, the creator of all things (15, 16, 18, 19, 28).
14-Jo. Professed faith in the only God, creator of all things (Gen. 40:8, 41:16, 41:25).

15-Im. Gives Pharaoh advice (16).
15-Jo. Gives Pharaoh advice (Gen. 41:1-57).

16-Im. Comes to Pharaoh when Pharaoh is distressed (16).
16-Jo. Comes to Pharaoh when Pharaoh is worried (Gen. 41:8,14)

17-Im. Decides on the tax rate (10%) to cope with the seven year-long famine (16).
17-Jo. Decides on the tax rate (20%) to cope with the seven year-long famine (Gen. 41:34).

18-Im. The tax law does not apply to the priests (16).
18-Jo. The tax law does not apply to the priests (Gen. 47:26)

19-Im. Becomes the god of healing and comes to people as they sleep (18, 19).
19-Jo. Performs miracles in the lives of others, and is characterised by having dreams that come true and the ability to correctly interpret the dreams of others (Gen. 37:5-11,20, 40:5-23, 41:1-36)

20-Im. Realises when he is dying (20).
20-Jo. Realises when he is dying (Gen. 50:24)

21-Im. Has written many words of wisdom (28, 43).
21-Jo. "And Pharaoh said unto Joseph, Forasmuch as God hath shewed thee all this, there is none so discreet and wise as thou art." (Gen. 41:39). There are also great resemblances to the Book of Proverbs. In the Book of Psalms it says of Joseph: "...and teach his senators wisdom" (Ps. 105:22).

22-Im. Dies at the age of 110 (20).
22-Jo. Dies at the age of 110 (Gen. 50:22-26).

23-Im. Was probably not appointed and in service until Pharaoh Djoser had reigned for a time.
23-Jo. Was appointed some time after Pharaoh had established himself as ruler in Egypt (Gen. 41:37-45).

24-Im. Was not of royal blood but attained his position on his own merits.
24-Jo. Was from another nation, was not of royal blood and attained his position through the qualities God had given him (Gen. 37:1 - 41:57).

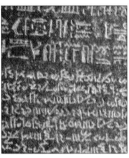

Figures 182, 183: The Rosetta stone, found in 1799, has a similar text in Greek and two types of ancient hieroglyphs. This made it possible to understand the Egyptian language based on hieroglyphs.

25-Im. Imhotep devoted time to writing and was an author (19, 28).
25-Jo. With his wisdom, long life and administrative ability it is very probable that Joseph wrote a great deal. It may even be that Joseph is the author of certain parts of the Book of Proverbs (see "21-Jo").

26-Im. Is called "Ibis", in other words the one to whom all the ibis birds were sacrificed in Sakkara (15, 43).
26-Jo. In a burial chamber inside the galleries of about a million mummified ibis birds, there is an empty coffin. This fits with what Joseph's grave would have looked like: an empty coffin since the people of Israel had taken his bones with them (Gen. 50:22-26).

27-Im. Pharaoh Djoser reigned during the seven year-long famine. The one who was minister of state with the status of a god was Imhotep (19, 28, 43).
27-Jo. The Bible states that, under the reigning Pharaoh, Joseph was minister of state with the status of a representative of God, who solved the problem of the approaching seven years of famine disaster (Gen. 41:37-45).

It is unlikely that there were two such individuals with so many qualities in common. Moreover they lived during a very special period of time. It is easier to accept the hypothesis that Joseph and Imhotep are one and the same person than to insist that there are two different people with these qualities, social position and god-like functions. That these two people by chance should happen to be so alike on so many unique points, with a very limited circle of people from which to choose, and whom were active during a period of unique events, may be seen as highly improbable. Either Imhotep and Joseph are the same person, or the history of Egypt and/or the biblical texts are a falsification.

9. THE PYRAMIDS AND THE ART OF CONSTRUCTION - HOW AND FROM WHERE?

If the hypothesis is correct that Imhotep and Joseph are the same person, then Joseph was the one who introduced the art of building with cut stone into Egypt. This is the art of construction we mainly see today in the form of the pyramids. There are many theories as to how these huge constructions could be built at all, so long ago. The biggest problem in these theories is how all these massive blocks of stone could be raised to such a height without modern techniques.

In this case, how could Joseph introduce such a technique? And from where did it come?

The key may lie in a hieroglyph.

Figure 184: The Egyptian language is constructed with symbols.

9.1. SIMPLIFIED SYMBOLS

The hieroglyphs developed as simplified symbols, which were later given a distinct meaning so that these symbols could represent both symbols/events/-hierarchies as well as letters and numbers.

Today we have simple symbols on road signs: a spoon and fork which indicate that there is a restaurant, or a telephone receiver which indicates that there is a payphone. What distinguishes these symbols is that a small part that everyone recognises has been used. A spoon and fork signify that one can eat lunch at the place. Although the sign does not show it, one eats from a plate, drinks from a glass and sits on a chair at the table etc (figures 185, 186).

If the spoon and fork symbol signifies a restaurant, the symbol could be developed further and later come to signify "R". The symbol can then be used equally well in a running text, and signify "R" as in symbolising restaurant or to eat. Most languages have developed in this way.

The Chinese language is still based on symbols. In order to be read the Chinese language requires knowledge of approximately 3000 symbols. However, to cover the entire language one needs to understand far more than 10 000 symbols. The advantage of a language built up from letters which can be combined in different ways is that for most languages one only needs to know about 25 letters.

The difficulty with a language built up from symbols is to understand what a symbol really means. If we return to the "restaurant symbol" with a spoon and fork, it is clear that it concerns food if one usually eats with a spoon and fork. If on the other hand we think about a person from Asia, who comes from a cultural region with few external contacts and where one usually eats with chopsticks, then the symbol means nothing. Or vice versa, not many people in Chicago would associate a sign showing two chopsticks with a restaurant symbol.

Figures 185, 186: Symbols are only relevant within a certain cultural group. Outside this group the symbols could mean totally different things - or nothing at all.

9.2. UNDERSTANDING LETTERS AND SYMBOLS

For this reason we have a limited understanding of Egyptian hieroglyphs. Ordinary hieroglyphs which are repeated in different situations, and build up different words can then receive the significance of a certain letter. While this can be completely correct, the same hieroglyph can also be used as a symbol to signify something entirely different. We use our letters as a matter of course, but very few know the background to why the letters have the appearance they have today.

The Egyptian language is an ancient language, in which the hieroglyphs have a significance both as letters and as symbols. This has meant that this dead language has been very difficult to understand. It was only when the Rosetta stone was found, with the same passage written in hieroglyphs (simplified and ordinary hieroglyphs) as well as in Greek that an understanding of the language became possible.

But it must be noted that the language is dead, which naturally makes it difficult to understand. Furthermore, not all the hieroglyphs are to be found on the Rosetta stone. Nor is it easy to decipher the hieroglyphs, even with the Rosetta stone. It was found in 1799 in the area of the Nile delta by a French officer, but it took until 1822 before the hieroglyphs were translated. During the whole of the 19th century parts or variations of the translation work, which was carried out in many different places, were published. The Rosetta stone is a fragment of a stela inscribed with a priestly decree around 200 BC (26).

This is the reason why it can be difficult to understand the symbol of a

Figures 187, 188: The lifting device hieroglyph is often shown in groups of three. Three means plural or many in the ancient Egyptian language.

hieroglyph, even when one can understand which letter it represents. A hieroglyph can be included in a Pharaoh's seal and can be connected with this Pharaoh, but at the same time it can be difficult to know exactly what the hieroglyph represents.

9.3. A CERTAIN HIEROGLYPH

There is a hieroglyph which is not particularly common, and which is mainly found in three different contexts: buildings, the pharaohs' pyramids and in the cartouches (seals) of Osiris, Isis and Horus. The hieroglyph is shown in different contexts in Sakkara, which can be seen in figure 189. The pyramid symbol is easily recognisable, close to this there are three hieroglyphs which are not particularly common. They have often been given the meaning of throne or throne-stool because they occur in connection with pharaohs, rulers and buildings such as pyramids. It is clear that the symbol is connected with important people, but why give it the meaning of a throne?

Figures 189, 190: The lifting device hieroglyph is common in Sakkara. It is also often shown with the symbol of a pyramid. Three repeated symbols means "many" in the Egyptian hieroglyphic language.

The following will describe a hypothesis which has resulted in the construction of an implement for lifting large blocks of stone. Therefore, it is probable that the "throne hieroglyph" is part of this implement, which was crucial in the building of pyramids solely for pharaohs and their families. We shall look more closely at the argument in order to assert that this hieroglyph may well be a construction tool and not a throne.

1. The first comment is that the hieroglyph does not look like a throne. There are also other hieroglyphs which symbolise a throne, and they are more in proportion and have a quite different appearance (33).
2. The connection with certain pharaohs and pyramids implies a connection with the pyramids as such.

3. That the hieroglyph is chiefly found in Sakkara makes it interesting since this was the site of the first pyramid, which according to the hypothesis in chapter 8 was Joseph's administrative centre.
4. The connection with the ancient gods/the pharaohs Osiris, Isis and Horus may have something to do with the connection with

Figures 191, 192: The lifting device hieroglyph as it normally looks (upper), and a variety from Abydos (lower).

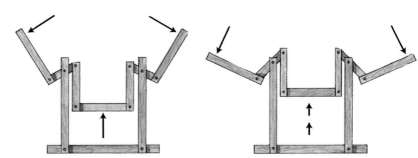

Figure 193: The basic principle for a lifting device based on the "lifting device" hieroglyph.

Mesopotamia; the part of the world from
which Joseph and his family came.

The first comment about the hieroglyph not resembling a throne will be left
at that statement.

9.4. A LIFTING DEVICE

In another hieroglyph from Abydos (30) further details are given which can
be seen in figure 192. The hypothesis that this was an implement for pyramid
construction work, and the connection with the quotation below from
Herodotus (died 425 BC) provided the inspiration to construct a lifting tool.
Since Herodotus lived long after the pyramids were built, his descriptions of
how they were built have not been taken seriously, but the important thing is
that he collected verbal information and had access to many documents
which have disappeared in modern Egypt.
Herodotus writes about the construction of the
pyramids (31):

*Figure 194: Tutankhamun had
many things with him for his
stay in the kingdom of the dead.
Among other things were the
crucial parts of a lifting device.*

*"The method employed was to build it in steps,
or, as some call them, tiers or terraces. When
the base was complete, the blocks for the first
tier above it were lifted from ground level by
contrivances made of short timbers; on this first
tier there was another, which raised the blocks a
stage higher, then yet another which raised
them higher still. Each tier, or story, had its set
of levers, or it may be that they used the same one, which, being easy to
carry, they shifted up from stage to stage as soon as its load was dropped
into place..."*

*Figure 195: The basic principle
for a lifting device constructed
to lift heavy pieces of rock. The
holes in the ground were aimed
to stabilise the whole construction.*

Based on this information the principle outline in figure 193 was drawn up.
With the help of a find in Tutankhamun's burial chamber (figure 194), which
is now in the Egyptian museum in Cairo, the outline was completed to look like figure 195. This find must have been important for
Tutankhamun's journey of death as were other items such as chariots, weapons, thrones and food. This part has not been successfully
identified regarding its function, but it has been assumed that it
was part of a sledge used to draw blocks of stone for building pyramids.

This is the reason why it is hanging upside down in the museum,
quite simply it is not really known what it is. It can be said that this
construction could not possibly have belonged to the working parts
of a sledge - the runners. In figure 195 the part found in
Tutankhamun's burial chamber is noted in the lifting construction.

According to this hypothesis, the find in the burial chamber could
be the key function in the lifting construction which made the
building of the pyramids possible. When a pharaoh was buried the
burial chamber was filled with important objects to cope with the journey to the realm of death (e.g. food), and so that he could participate

*Figure 196: The lifting devices connected
in series to enable lifting of heavy blocks
of rock.*

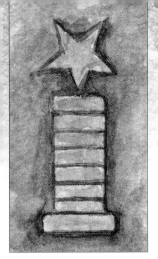

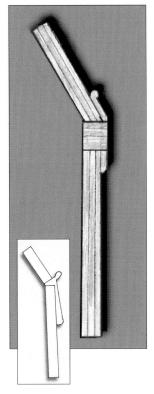

in the more important functions as Pharaoh. Thus for instance thrones, war chariots and the key function (lever) were needed in order to be able to build pyramids and temples.

In figure 196 a large block of stone is shown which, resting on logs, has been rolled into the lifting device. To give lifting force several levers have been placed side by side, and ropes have been connected to a log-type roll, in order to be able to lift all the levers at the same time and at the same speed. In that way the blocks could be rolled over to another lifting device, and step by step lifted up to the required height.

9.5. ADDITIONAL HIEROGLYPHS

There are two other hieroglyphs which might be connected with this lifting device. The first is a hieroglyph which resembles a cotton reel. Presumably this hieroglyph depicts the log round which the rope was wound as the block was lifted. A further indication of this use is that which may have been the handle, the winch arrangement, or the rotating part held as a handle when the rope was wound up, depicted as part of the hieroglyph. The hieroglyph is found in figure 197 where a lifting device is shown, here one can see what this hieroglyph might depict. (figure 202)

The second hieroglyph (figure 199) looks like a direct representation of the wooden construction found in Tutankhamun's burial chamber (figure 198), which in the hypothesis of this chapter is connected with a lifting device. The hieroglyph appears to be a direct copy of that device regarding proportions, angles in curves, and in small but essential details such as the protruding part which probably functioned as a brake in the lifting arrangement. In the lexi-

con this hieroglyph is said to represent a wooden construction consisting of pieces of wood joined together (32), which is precisely what the hypothesis of this book claims the part of the lifting device is (figure 124).

The "throne" hieroglyph (figure 189) is also found in another variant where a rope with a ball has been added. Here the hieroglyph lexicon (33) indicates that this is a building tool with a plummet. This

Figures 197-199: A wooden model of the lifting construction. The crucial parts are probably found as hieroglyphs. The unknown star-like hieroglyph could illustrate the timber to roll on the rope, with star-like handles. The bent hieroglyph is also unknown but looks very much like the lifting device. In the literature the hieroglyph is suggested to illustrate a wooden artifact with unknown function.

Figures 200-202: A wooden model of the lifting device.

94

Figure 203: A full scale model but with smaller dimensions compared to the devices to lift blocks of rock, makes it relatively easy to lift a van straight upwards.

Figure 204: How could all these blocks of stone be placed in position?

is most likely a correct description. In this context the plummet would be crucial in ensuring that the lifting device was standing level so that a block of stone on the log rolls would not roll off as it was lifted.

The remarkable thing is the interpretation, that if the plummet is removed from the work tool which this hieroglyph most likely symbolises, then it would represent a throne. It is more natural that the plummet was part of the hieroglyph, and that it was simplified at a later date. Irrespective of whether the hieroglyph symbolises the less probable - a throne - or the important implement for building pyramids, it is natural to associate the symbol with the highest leadership.

9.6. THE LIFTING DEVICE

Does this implement for lifting work in practice? In figures 200-202 a small wooden model is shown in a stationary position, and in a position of maximum elevation. A simplified full scale model was built with planks and joists to lift a van. Four people, two at each rope so that they could pull evenly, were able to lift the vehicle easily as can be seen in figure 203.

Loading estimates show that to lift a 25 ton block of stone with this construction 8 pairs of levers are needed with the dimensions these devices probably had in ancient time.

So that such a heavy construction (blocks of stone as well as the lifting device) would not be moved out of position, a locking arrangement was needed. At the foot of the Cheop pyramid (figure 204) holes have been made in the rock foundation (figure 205 and onwards). These round or square holes are of a size that would fit logs or heavy timber to stabilise the lifting device described above. In this way the lifting device could have been made fast to cope with extremely heavy loads (figure 195).

The entire pyramid is surrounded by round and square holes in symmetrical

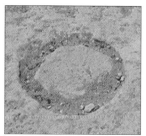

Figures 205, 206: The Cheop pyramid is surrounded by a system of holes in the ground.

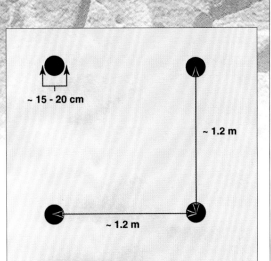

Figure 207

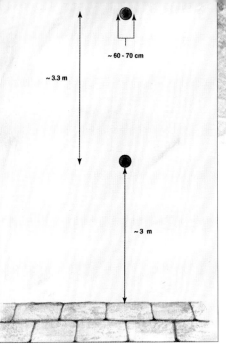

Figure 208

Figure 209

Figure 210

Figures 207-211: The Cheop pyramid is surrounded by holes. Today the holes are filled with gravel and pieces of rock. There seems to be a system in how the holes are arranged, suggesting a function to secure some kind of lifting devices.

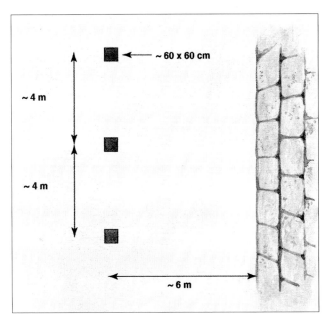

Figure 211

patterns (figures 205-211). The round holes vary from roughly 15-20 cm to 60-70 cm in diameter. In several cases holes of 15-20 cm in diameter lie in square-shaped patterns with approximately 1.2 m between the holes. The larger round holes (diameter 60-70 cm) lie with approximately 3.3 m spaces between them and approximately 3 m from the foot of the pyramid. In figures 205 and 206 these holes can be seen.

To prevent people from falling into the holes they have been filled with blocks of stone. Figures 207 and 208 show the pattern of how the holes have been cut in the rock. The square-shaped holes are roughly 60 x 60 cm (figures 209 and 210) and lie in a line with approximately 4 m space between them (figure 211). The line of holes lies parallel with the pyramid approximately 6 m from the foot of the pyramid. Some of the four-sided holes are roughly 60 x 80 cm.

Altogether, there are more factors which indicate that the "throne hieroglyph" represents the lever of a lifting device (for building pyramids), than there are factors that indicate it represents a throne. The hypothesis that a hieroglyph depicts a lever in a lifting device, which can lift extremely heavy blocks of stone, has been shown to work in practice with models of different scales, even lifting up vehicles. Calculations show that up to 50 ton stone blocks could be lifted in this way. This also fits the description Herodotus gives in one of his texts (31).

Further, it is common that three lever hieroglyphs are found in connection to a pyramid hieroglyph (figure 189). This fits very well with the hypothesis that the lever hieroglyph is related to the construction of pyramids and that several levers were needed. The numbers of three has a meaning of "several" in Egyptian hieroglyphs. If the lever hieroglyph symbolised a throne it would suggest several thrones in the cartouche of a pharaoh, which is probably not what the pharaoh would have liked (one pharaoh – one throne).

9.7. THE OSIRIS CONNECTION

Both the Bible and the Koran have a story about a powerful king called Nimrod (a fore-father to Abraham), who ruled in Mesopotamia (in the Euphrates-Tigris area). This Nimrod, who is also connected with Haran, the place from which Abraham came, founded a town which was given the name of Babel. In Babel a tower was built which was to reach up to heaven, the tower of Babel. The aim was that the tower would be a protection for humankind in a new flood. Nimrod claimed that he was the highest of the gods, which Osiris was in Egyptian history.

According to stories from Assyria and Babylon, Nimrod was murdered and his body hacked to pieces. His wife was called Semiramus, whose son Tammuz was concieved as well as born after Nimrod was murdered. Thus Tammuz was regarded as an incarnation (re-birth) of Nimrod. These divine characters are to be found, with the same course of events, as the well-known divine characters in Egyptian history. The only difference is that they have Egyptian names (Table 4).

Here we see two identical narratives. The difference is that these divine characters have received different names in the different cultures, or more correctly, when they are likely to have entered into Egyptian culture from Mesopotamia, they received Egyptian names.

9.8. Joseph and Mesopotamia

Joseph's relatives came from the cultural sphere in Mesopotamia where Nimrod was a well-known figure. It was Abraham who left this area when he moved to the land of Canaan, where later Isaac was born. Isaac was Joseph's grandfather. This could very well be the link which connects the Mesopotamian art of construction with the "discovery" in Egypt of how to build pyramids; through the sale of Joseph to Egypt, where he later became the highest in the land under Pharaoh. Joseph had every possibility to bring over as a skill the building technique he had from his family tradition. We also know that Joseph was considered to be a great builder. According to the Bible, the Lord also gave Joseph a great deal of knowledge, not least through dreams.

The connection with Mesopotamia could explain the sudden discovery of how to build pyramid-like structures in Egypt, and also explain how this knowledge was brought from Mesopotamia to Egypt. The pharaohs/divine characters with origins in Mesopotamian culture also have the "throne hiero-glyph" (or, more probably, the "lever hieroglyph") in their cartouches (seals), which further supports the hypothesis of a connection with these characters.

To this can be added an important comment about the hypothesis that Joseph had his administrative centre in Sakkara. It was there that the central power of Egypt created enormous wealth by selling grain to the entire Egyptian nation and to neighbouring countries and areas, thus providing the financial possibilities for carrying out these huge construction projects.

Table 4. The connection between the divine figures in Babylon and in Egypt.

Name in Babel Characteristics	Name in Egypt Characteristics
Nimrod	*Osiris*
Highest of the gods	Highest of the gods
Murdered	Murdered
Body hacked to pieces	Body hacked to pieces
Builder of the first ziggurat	Brought knowledge of
(pyramid-like structure)	the art of building pyramids
Semiramus	*Isis*
Wife of Nimrod	Wife of Osiris
Tammuz	*Horus*
Son	Son
Born after the father's death	Born after the father's death
Regarded as father's	Regarded as father's
reincarnation	reincarnation

9.9. In summary

The hypothesis that the art of building pyramids is connected with Imhotep/Joseph is supported by:

◆ The building technique may have its origins in Mesopotamia, the cultural sphere from which Joseph and his family came, where ziggurats, pyramid-like structures, and high towers were built.

◆ The leading figures in Egypt, who have similar backgrounds to the corresponding figures in Mesopotamia, have the "lever hieroglyph" in their seals.

◆ The "lever hieroglyph" can be directly connected with building technique through the related hieroglyph equipped with a plummet, and indirectly through the constructed lifting device.

◆ The "lever hieroglyph" is often found in connection with pyramids.

◆ The "lever hieroglyph" is relatively unusual except in Sakkara, the starting point for pyramid construction. According to the hypothesis in chapter 8, Sakkara is also Joseph's administrative centre.

◆ Herodotus' collection of knowledge (writings and oral traditions) on the technique of building pyramids in Egypt, written about 2300 years ago, agrees with the hypothesis of a lifting device.

◆ A lifting device based on the "lever hieroglyph" and a find from Tutankhamun's grave functions both as a model and in full-scale. Calculations also show that it can function with blocks up to 50 tons in weight.

◆ The inscription from Sakkara with three (meaning several) lever hieroglyphs together with a pyramid hieroglyph support the hypothesis that it is a lifting device and not a throne (or several thrones).

Altogether, there are good grounds for connecting the "lever hieroglyph" with both Sakkara and Joseph, and with a functioning lifting device for building pyramids, for example. The hypothesis is supported by the fact that the Greek historian, Herodotus, describes a similar method of building pyramids, and the fact that stabilising holes are found around the Cheop Pyramid, which are well adapted for stabilising these lifting devices.

Figure 212: Is there actually a connection between the Egyptian pyramids and Joseph?

THE PRE-EXODUS PERIOD
A SUMMARY

The first part of this book covers the biblical texts from Gen. 11:27 - 50:26. The period of time covered is from around 1996 BC (the birth of Abraham) until the death of Joseph around 1635 BC (figure 213).

In part I we have followed Abraham, Isaac and Jacob from Ur of the Chaldees to Canaan. There is good reason to suppose that Ur of the Chaldees corresponds to present day Urfa in Turkey and to no other place that has been suggested e.g. in southern Iraq. These patriarchs later moved around in the land of Canaan and amongst other things we have followed the remarkable events that occurred in the Jordan valley with rain of burning sulphur in a place which, as far as description and localisation are concerned, tallies with Sodom and Gomorrah.

Furthermore, we have pursued the places and names of places that still exist today. In the same way several of the places can be identified, for example Rachel's grave near Bethlehem. Rachel was the mother of Joseph. Joseph's role in Egypt is noteworthy and tallies very well with the knowledge that is available regarding the god-like figure, Imhotep, in the history of Egypt.

If this hypothesis is correct, that Joseph and Imhotep are one and the same person, then the whole history of Egypt suddenly opens with narratives and archaeological remains so that biblical texts can be directly linked with developments and people in the history of Egypt. If Imhotep and Joseph are the same person this also means that there is a great deal more in Egyptian history which can be linked with Joseph and his people. It is with this that part II of this book deals.

Figure 213: A summary of the family of Abraham until Joseph.

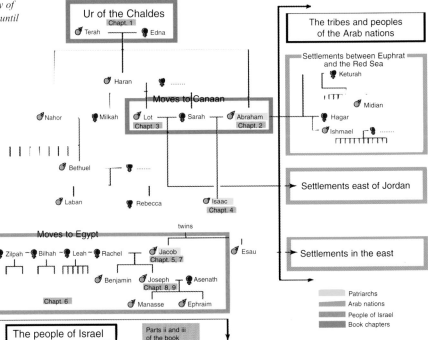

PART II

THE
EXODUS

FROM EGYPT AND
THROUGH THE RED SEA

THE EXODUS

We have now followed Abraham, Isaac and Jacob, forefathers of most of the peoples in the Middle East region, through biblical texts and comments on archaeological finds. We have also followed in detail the people of Israel through Abraham, Isaac and Jacob, father of the twelve tribes of Israel.

Jacob's son, Joseph, became the ruler of Egypt, subordinate only to Pharaoh himself. Joseph brought his father and his brothers with their families to Egypt during the years of poor crops and great famine. In Egypt Jacob's family increased during many years and became very large, consisting of its twelve tribes. It became more and more difficult for the people of Israel to live in Egypt.

According to the Bible text God gave his promise to Abraham and his successors. The text further explains how God helped his chosen people by sending them a powerful leader: an Egyptian heir to the throne, general, politician and leader. But before he is mature enough to lead the people of Israel out of Egypt, he must learn to listen to the voice of God.

Moses enters the scene and the people of Israel are made ready for the Exodus.

10. WHAT HAPPENS AFTER THE DEATH OF JOSEPH?

Many years had passed and Jacob's family increased greatly in Egypt. The children of Israel were fruitful, lived in the very fertile part of Egypt (figures 216, 217), had large families with many children and grew to become a great people.

10.1. THE HEBREWS BECOME NUMEROUS IN EGYPT

The Bible states that the country was overrun by them.

"And the children of Israel were fruitful, and increased abundantly, and multiplied, and waxed exceeding mighty; and the land was filled with them." (Ex. 1:7)

They become so numerous and so influential that the Pharaoh who reigned, long after the Pharaoh who had Joseph as his chief administrator, begins to curtail their freedom of movement. This Pharaoh is afraid that the people of Israel will be able to unite with an enemy and in this way overpower Egypt.

10.2. THE HEBREWS AS SLAVES

Pharaoh places officers over the people of Israel and they are treated like slaves. They are forced to build towns for Pharaoh (Pithom and Raamses). But the people of Israel continue to increase and the oppression increases with the growth in numbers. They are forced to become brickmakers and are made to carry out many forms of heavy labour. Amongst other things they have to dig canals and build walls round the cities (Ex. 1:8-14).

Figures 216, 217: The people of Israel lived in the very fertile delta region of the Nile river.

"Therefore they did set over them taskmasters to afflict them with their burdens. And they built for Pharaoh treasure cities, Pithom and Raamses." (Ex. 1:11)

10.3. THE CHILDREN WERE KILLED

At this time Pharaoh orders the midwives to kill the newborn boys while the girls are allowed to live. But the Bible text narrates that the midwives obeyed the Lord rather than Pharaoh and let the children live.

The people of Israel continue to multiply and become very numerous. Then Pharaoh orders all newborn boys to be thrown into the Nile (Ex. 1:15-22). If a family does not obey, then the whole family is to be executed, according to the historical writer, Josephus (JA 2/9:2). The people of Israel now undergo extremely hard times. They are not only slaves but Pharaoh actively tries to reduce the growth of the people by killing the children.

"And there went a man of the house of Levi, and took to wife a daughter of Levi. And the woman conceived, and bare a son: and when she saw him that he was a goodly child, she hid him three months. And when she could not longer hide him, she took for him an ark of bulrushes, and daubed it with slime and with pitch, and put the child therein; and she laid it in the flags by

the river's brink. And his sister stood afar off, to wit what would be done to him." (Ex. 2:1-4)

This is the well-known story of Moses in the bulrushes. The ark that is mentioned was more of a basket and the bulrushes were a type of reed. The mother of Moses simply made a little reed boat for her baby. This reed basket may have looked like that in figure 218.

It is now approximately 180 years since the people of Israel came to Egypt and around 80 years before the Exodus, the great migration (the chronology is discussed in chapter 44). The one who will lead the Exodus is the baby boy in the woven reeds on the shores of the Nile. According to the Bible text, God has a clear plan for this infant from the tribe of Levi.

The biblical text relates that the Hebrews grow to become a great people very quickly. This becomes a threat to the Egyptians who finally make the entire people slaves. This is not sufficient and Pharaoh, in various ways, has all newborn males killed in order to stop the vigorous increase. It is during this difficult period that Moses is born.

Figure 218: This is what the reed boat, that Moses was placed in, could have looked like. The basket is from the times of the Pharaoh's.

11. WHO WAS MOSES?

Moses' father was the Levite Amram and his mother's name was Jochebed (Ex. 6:20). Amram suffered with all his people and cried out to God. Josephus describes Amram as a man of prayer with great compassion for his people. At this time, 80 years before the Exodus, Israel is a great people. They are no longer referred to as a family or kindred but as a people.

11.1. THE BIRTH OF MOSES

According to the Bible, God comes to Amram in a dream and says that he sees the suffering of his people and that God has arranged it so that Israel has grown to be a great people. God goes on to say that the child to whom Jochebed will give birth will be protected from those who want to kill him, that the child will grow up in a surprising way and that the child will be given the task of liberating the Hebrew people. God also mentions his brother Aaron who will maintain the priestly function. Amram shares this dream (which is also referred to as a vision) with his wife and they are both happy and afraid

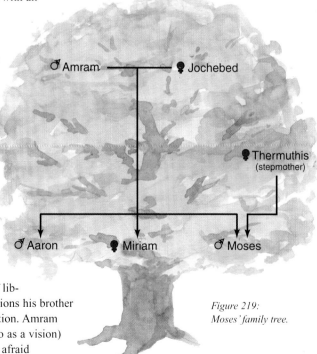

Figure 219: Moses' family tree.

because they realise the situation in which they find themselves.

The child is born and for three months they look after the baby secretly in their home. According to the decree of Pharaoh, all newborn Hebrew baby boys should be drowned in the Nile. Amram and Jochebed make a decision.

11.2. MOSES, SAVED BY THE PRINCESS

It is not possible to hide the child indefinitely. If God has manifested his will regarding the child then he will also protect him. They make what they call an ark of rushes or bulrushes which they smear with tar. The ark is big enough to carry a little baby and they put the little ark, or basket, in the Nile. The Bible relate what follows:

"And the daughter of Pharaoh came down to wash herself at the river; and her maidens walked along by the river's side; and when she saw the ark among the flags, she sent her maid to fetch it. And when she had opened it, she saw the child: and, behold, the babe wept. And she had compassion on him, and said, This is one of the Hebrews' children. Then said his sister to Pharaoh's daughter, Shall I go and call to thee a nurse of the Hebrew women, that she may nurse the child for thee? And Pharaoh's daughter said to her, Go. And the maid went and called the child's mother. And Pharaoh's daughter said unto her, Take this child away, and nurse it for me, and I will give thee thy wages. And the women took the child, and nursed it. And the child grew, and she brought him unto Pharaoh's daughter, and he became her son. And she called his name Moses: and she said, Because I drew him out of the water." (Ex. 2:5-10)

Figure 220: All newborn Hebrew baby boys were supposed to be drowned in the Nile River at the time when Moses was born.

This part of the Bible narrative is about Pharaoh's daughter taking the baby and adopting him as her own child, thus saving him from being killed or alternatively from drowning. Thanks to Moses' sister's (Miriam) suggestion, Pharaoh's daughter gives Moses' own mother the task of breast-feeding him and moreover is paid for it. It is not enough that the child's life is saved, he is also brought into Pharaoh's family and through this adoption becomes a very important person in Egypt. Moses will receive the best available education and will lack nothing in material goods. Furthermore he will receive power.

Josephus gives the name of Pharaoh's daughter and states that she is called Thermuthis (JA 2/9:4-5) and he gives the following explanation as to why the child was given the name Moses. Pharaoh's daughter Thermuthis, who is childless herself, gives the child this name. The Egyptians called water "mo" and those who had been rescued from the water were called "uses", so the name the child received was Mouses (JA 2/9:6). This explanation to the name of Moses fits the biblical text very well:

"And she called his name Moses: and she said, Because I drew him out of the water." (Ex. 2:10)

At the time of Moses' birth we have come to approximately 1526 BC. After this the Bible does not mention any details of Moses' childhood and adolescence except that he grew up at the Egyptian court. It is first when Moses is 40 years old that the biblical texts continue the decription of events. For

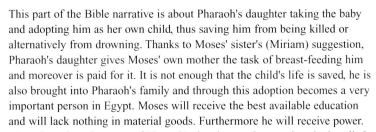

some unknown reason the Book of Exodus is very brief regarding Moses' first 40 years at court, probably because what happened then was not crucial to his real assignment, the Exodus, the assignment to lead the entire people of Israel out of Egypt.

11.3. MOSES FIRST 40 YEARS AT THE THE EGYPTIAN COURT

We do not know exactly what happened during the first 40 years of Moses' life but the historical writer Josephus tells us the following: When Moses became adult Egypt was attacked by Ethiopia. The Ethiopians were victorious and took more and more liberties in Egypt and finally could reach the Mediterranean Sea.

In this strained situation the Egyptians turned to their oracles and prophets and were told to make use of the Hebrew, Moses. Pharaoh then appointed Moses as general in command of the Egyptian army. Moses did not enter the Nile valley as the Ethiopians had done but chose a completely different strategy. It was difficult to go via the desert and carry out encircling tactics because there were poisonous snakes in these areas.

Moses therefore took with him his ibis birds (figure 221), the snakes' worst enemies. Moses had the birds with him in cages and let them out in the places where the snakes were numerous. In this way the Egyptian army was able to take an unexpected route and travel faster than would have normally been the case. Moses won a decisive victory and later wins one battle after the other. Faced with the prospect of becoming slaves in Egypt, the Ethiopians flee back to their own capital city, Sheba.

Figure 221: The ibis bird helped Moses in the victory over the Etiopians according to the historian Josephus.

Many of the Egyptian leaders became afraid of Moses. For one thing Moses was a foreigner (Hebrew) and represented the people of Israel who had grown to be very numerous, and for another Moses had become very powerful because, as general of the Egyptian army, he had defeated the Ethiopians. Moses' innovative talents also frightened many who feared that he would introduce new customs into the country. In a mixture of envy and fear many people, even Pharaoh, wanted to kill Moses. Moses knew that people were looking for a pretext to kill him. In this situation Moses makes a mistake (summarised from JA 2/9:7-10:2).

In Stephen's defence speech about 1500 years later Stephen relates the history of Israel and mentions some of Moses' background:

"In which time Moses was born, and was exceeding fair, and nourished up in his father's house three months: And when he was cast out, Pharaoh's daughter took him up, and nourished him for her own son. And Moses was learned in all the wisdom of the Egyptians, and was mighty in words and in deeds." (Acts 7:20-22)

Without knowing exactly how Moses' first 40 years at court passed, we can take it for granted on good grounds that he received the education and training that only very few in Egypt came anywhere near.

11.4. MOSES MAKES A BIG MISTAKE

Moses is now visiting among the Hebrews and sees an Egyptian ill-treating a Hebrew (figure 222). During this period the Hebrews were slaves under the Egyptians and were treated very badly. Moses becomes angry and kills the Egyptian.

Rumours of the incident spread and soon Pharaoh also learns about it. Through this event Pharaoh has a reason to kill Moses. Moses does the only thing he can in this situation, he flees. The roads were watched so Moses fled through the desert, through areas where his enemies could not conceive that he would be found. This shows that Moses was familiar with the desert and able to find his way in a terrain where even today we have great difficulty in orienting ourselves. Finally Moses reaches the land of Midian and at this point he is 40 years old (Ex. 2:11-15).

11.5. IN SUMMARY

Moses grew up in very special circumstances:

◆ Moses was born during the time when all newborn male infants among the Hebrews were to be killed.
◆ When he is three months old, Moses' parents put him in a little reed boat in the Nile.
◆ Thermuthis, the childless heiress to the throne of Egypt, finds Moses and rescues him.

Figure 222: The people of Israel were treated as slaves during the time when Moses grew up at the Egyptian court.

◆ Through the intervention of Moses' sister Miriam, Moses' biological mother breast feeds Moses.
◆ Josephus explains Moses' name by saying that his adoptive Egyptian mother combined "mo" (water) with "uses" (name given to those rescued from the water) which became Mouses.
◆ Moses' first 40 years at the court of Egypt describe a person with access to all possible learning and training. As general in command of the Egyptian army, Moses rescues Egypt from the attacks of the Ethiopians.
◆ Moses becomes a threat to the Egyptians and makes a serious mistake when he kills an Egyptian to save a Hebrew slave.
◆ Moses flees at the age of 40 years to the land of Midian.

12. Does Moses exist in Egyptian history?

Is Moses to be found in Egyptian history? Moses was "only" heir to the throne and, according to Josephus, general in command of the Egyptian army, and there are many pharaohs who are mainly unknown. However Moses was a very prominent person and it can be assumed on good grounds that the life of Moses was documented in various ways as the lives of all other important people were documented in Egyptian society.

Two questions are of importance. On the one hand what Egyptian name could Moses have had, and on the other whether any historical information about this person has been preserved. As will be seen in chapters 44 and 49, the hypothesis is that Moses appeared during the 18th dynasty.

Here it should be noted that the dynasties of Egypt are a relative concept but they have come to be considered as indicating different eras of time. The dynasty concept will be used for the sake of simplicity but it can be worthwhile to see what Breasted (34) writes about the dynasties as a concept.

"A more or less arbitrary and artificial but convenient subdivision of these epochs, beginning with the historic age, is furnished by the so-called dynasties of Manetho. This native historian of Egypt, a priest of Sebennytos, who flourished under Ptolemy I (305-285 BC), wrote a history of his country in the Greek language. The work has perished, and we only know it in an epitome by Julius Africanus and Eusebius, and extracts by Josephus. The value of the work was slight, as it was built up on folk tales and popular traditions of the early kings. Manetho divided the long succession of Pharaohs as known to him, into thirty royal houses or dynasties, and although we know that many of his divisions are arbitrary, and that there was many a dynastic change where he indicates none, yet his dynasties divide the kings into convinient groups, which have so long been employed in modern study of Egyptian history, that it is now impossible to dispense with them."

Figures 223, 224: Brickmaking in today's Egypt according to ancient traditions. Clay and straw were used as raw material and the bricks were dried in the sun.

Tyldesley (35) have the following comments related to the 18th dynasty:

"The surviving archaeological evidence is therefore strongly biased towards religion and death; we have for example, two tombs, three sarcophagi and several temples built by Hatshepsut, but little trace of the palaces where she lived her life. Overall we are left with the misleading impression that the Egyptians were depressingly gloomy and morbid race."

And further, in a general comment to the Egyptian history:

"...we should never lose sight of the fact that the written record is incomplete, randomly selected, and carries its own biases. The monumental inscriptions, for example, are basically a mixture of religious and propaganda texts which tell the story that the king him - or herself wished to convey, and which cannot be taken as the literal truth. The translators of these inscriptions are faced with problems not just of accuracy but of interpretation..."

Figure 225: Bricks made from clay and straw from the time of Moses.

And a comment to Egyptian chronology:

"However, there was no ancient equivalent of our modern calendar, and year numbers started afresh with every new reign."

And a final comment on Egyptian names:

"Manetho, working in approximately 300 BC, compiled a detailed history of the kings of Egypt. This original work is now lost, but fragments have been preserved in the writings of Josephus (AD 70), Africanus (early third century AD), Eusebius (early fourth century AD) and Syncellus (c. AD 800). These preserved extracts do not always agree, and the names given are often wildly incorrect, but students of Egyptian history still acknowledge a huge debt to Manetho, the 'Father of Egyptian History'."

13. THE CONNECTION WITH THE HYKSOS PEOPLE

The 18th dynasty is characterised by the fact that at least two and probably three pharaohs or rulers reigned in Egypt at the same time. The reigning Egyptian family lived in Thebes, the pharaoh who would take over lived in Memphis, while another ruler controlled the northern delta region. The Egyptians considered the delta people to be foreigners. There is good reason to believe that it was the Hebrews, descendants of Joseph, who were the foreigners who had settled in the delta region on the orders of the pharaoh reigning at the time. It is probable that other tribes as well had moved into this fertile region of the country, tribes who gave rise to the name Hyksos.

Figure 226: The Karnak temple in Luxor has (according to the hypothesis of this book) many references to the stepmother of Moses.

From the beginning, the Hebrews in the delta area received royal status on account of Joseph's contributions as minister of state when he saved Egypt from the seven years of famine. This is clear not least from the way in which Joseph's father, Jacob, was embalmed after his death. In Gen. 50:1-14 this is described as 40 days of embalming, a 70-day period of public mourning in Egypt and a large Egyptian retinue present at the interment in Hebron. The Hebrews received a royal position and from the texts in the Book of Exodus we see how this family very quickly grew to be an entire nation.

It is therefore probable that those whom the Egyptians called foreigners and who lived in the delta region with the name of "Hyksos" were Hebrews intermingled with other tribal peoples from Asia. Moreover it can be added that they had a different religion from the Egyptians, which also tallies with the hypothesis that it was the Hebrew people, probably with other tribes too, with a relatively independent leadership.

Inscriptions exist which in different ways mention these "shepherd kings". This too, that they are called "shepherd kings" implies a group of people with the predominating occupation of being shepherds, which is how the biblical texts describe the Hebrews and which was also the reason that Pharaoh gave them the delta land in which to settle (Gen. 46:31-34).

There is an interesting inscription (23) of queen Hatshepsut during the 18th dynasty which refers to the time when the Hyksos people had been driven out of the country: "I have restored what had decayed, I annuled the former privileges since the Asiatics were in the region of Avaris of Lower Egypt (the delta). The immigrants among them disregarded the tasks which were assigned to them, thinking Re would not consent...." The text in brackets is the author's comment.

The evidence is lacking to what really took place but the Egyptian records suggests that a warrior people (Asians, barbarians) lived among the Northland people (the Hebrews). The Asians (barbarians) were driven out by the Egyptians and a situation arose which most probably was threatening to the Hebrews. They were shepherds and had no possibility of defending themselves. Not least the biblical texts indicate that their position was weak and led them to become slaves, which shows how weak they were as a warrior people (Ex. 1-14).

The Egyptians wanted to be rid of the "barbarians" but considered the shepherd people (the Hebrews) as manpower to use for rebuilding the country. "I have restored what had decayed" says the inscription. The Bible tells us that as slaves the Hebrews were forced to work very hard at building. A new ruler comes to the fore in Egypt who says:

"Come on, let us deal wisely with them; lest they multiply, and it come to pass, that, when there falleth out any war, they join also unto our enemies, and fight against us, and so get them up out of the land. Therefore they did set over them taskmasters to afflict them with their burdens. And they built for Pharaoh treasure cities, Pithom and Raamses." (Ex. 1:10-11)

"And they made their lives bitter with hard bondage, in morter, and in brick, and in all manner of service in the field: all their service, wherein they made them serve, was with rigor." (Ex. 1:14)

When the barbarians are driven away, the Hebrews are allowed to remain, they had received the right to live there from Pharaoh himself, but their rights were taken from them and they became a slave people. Slaves to restore "what had decayed" and presumably to build many other things too, since the Hebrews were numerous at that time (figure 227).

Figure 227: The Hebrews were forced to built cities for the Egyptians. In this work they were treated as slaves.

14. Who were the Pharaohs during the time of Moses?

During the 18th dynasty the Pharaohs are said to have been called or entitled Amenhotep or Thutmosis. This hypothesis can be questioned as the name alternates between Amenhotep and Thutmosis. The pharaoh was the embodiment of the most important god and this god was then the highest god for the entire royal family reigning at the time. Since the pharaohs during this dynasty belonged to the same family it is hardly likely that one pharaoh would consider Thot (Thutmosis) was the highest god while another pharaoh considered Amen (Amenhotep) the highest.

Inscriptions found in temples and graves imply rather that "Thutmosis" is a name (title) which a pharaoh might have, and in the same way "Amenhotep" was a further title. It is probable that several pharaohs had the title of both "Thutmosis" and "Amenhotep" depending on the stage at which they were in their careers. See chapter 8.10. for a more detailed discussion about royal names that are still applied today.

The general understanding of this period has confused many scholars, one stating in a comment on other egyptologists that they are "unaware of the complexities of the Tuthmoside succession" (35).

It may be that the co-ruler was "Thutmosis" during the time he reigned together with Pharaoh who was "Amenhotep". When the co-ruler later became the pharaoh he also became "Amenhotep". One can only speculate as to whether the pharaoh first became "Thutmosis" and later "Amenhotep" or vice versa. However Amen is yet another name for the Egyptians' most important god (the sun god), which means that it is more probable that Amenhotep was the Pharaoh's title while the co-ruler had to be content with a lower "god title" (Thutmosis).

To this can be added that the sun god Ra was over the other gods and consequently pharaoh could also add this title to his row of designations. In this context Ra becomes Rameses. Rameses was a title used by many pharaohs, they were all an incarnation of the sun god, as the son of the sun god, or Rameses. This creates some confusion when Rameses II is pointed out as the great pharaoh with all the temples, statues and much more. Particularly when one looks at the statues representing Rameses II. They seem to represent different people. What one should also note is that inscriptions mention the title Rameses on many statues, temples and graves but not with the specification "II". That is a later idea.

The following is a hypothesis concerning which pharaohs reigned during the time of Moses, with their "double names" according to where in their careers they found themselves at different times (Table 5).

Is there any information in the biblical texts which can be linked with the hypothesis presented in Table 5 about the succession to the throne? It is likely that there is a link. In the First Book of Kings the biblical text is as follows:

"And it came to pass in the four hundred and eightieth year after the children of Israel were come out of the land of Egypt, in the fourth year of Solomon's reign over Israel, in the month Zif, which is the second month, that he began to build the house of the LORD." (1 Kings 6:1)

Figures 228-230: Deir-El Bahri was the temple built for Hatshepsut, located close to Luxor. Did Moses build this temple?

"The family relationships of the Tuthmosid rulers are a genealogical nightmare." (57) Could an explanation be the theory of chapter 14?

Here we have a very precise indication of the date of the beginning of the construction of the temple in Jerusalem. Most often the fourth year of king Solomon's reign is given as approximately 966 BC (ref. 36 and the chronology in chapter 44). If one counts back 480 years from the year mentioned, this places the Exodus in approximately 1446 BC. Can this date be verified?

In the Encyclopedia Britannica (2) the following stands:

> "The next date is given by a medical papyrus, to which a calendar is added, possibly to insure a correct conversion of dates used in the reciepts to the actual timetable. Here it is said that the 9th day of the 11th month of year 9 of King Amenhotep I was the day of the helical rising of Sothis, i.e. 1538 BC. This date, however, is only accurate provided the astronomical observations were taken at the old residence of Memphis; if observed at Thebes in Upper Egypt, the residence of the 18th dynasty, the date must be lowered by 20 years, i.e. 1518 BC."

Figure 231: A statue of Queen Hatshepsut of the Karnak temple in Luxor.

The chronology which is described more closely in chapter 44 (drawn up long before reference 2 was found) shows that year nine for Amenhotep I occurred around 1519 BC which coincides amazingly with the approximate date 1518 BC from reference 2. Here an astronomic observation can be linked with the chronology mentioned in Table 5 and with great precision place the 18th dynasty within the period of time used in this book.

The following hypothesis (chapter 15) is based on the chronology in Table 5 and therewith the astronomic observation in reference 2.

15. WHO WAS PHARAOH'S DAUGHTER?

By Pharaoh's daughter is meant here the person who found Moses in the reed basket in the Nile and who later adopted him according to the biblical text in Exodus 2:1-10.

The question then arises if, during the 18th dynasty, there was a Pharaoh who had no son who could inherit the throne but who had a daughter who played this role. Thutmosis I/Amenhotep I tallies with this description. He lacked a male heir but had a daughter who is very well-known in the history of Egypt. Her name was Nefure and Hatshepsut. In earlier inscriptions when she is a princess she is referred to as Nefure. Later when she becomes queen probably her name/title changes to Hatshepsut.

Figures 232, 233: Do these block statues illustrate Nefure and Senmut or Senmut and Nefure?

According to this hypothesis, when Moses was born Amose reigned and lived in Thebes. Thutmosis I lived in Memphis and acted as co-ruler. Both of them could be called Pharaoh. Pharaoh comes from the word "pero" meaning "big house", which implies that the title was a mark of power and influence. Thutmosis I was probably the one who acted as Pharaoh in

Table 5. Egyptian titles/names of the people referred to in the Bible, according to the hypothesis presented in chapters 14-16.

Person in the Bible texts	Name/title	Pharaoh
Pharaoh at time of Moses' birth	Amose	Amose
Co-ruler, with daughter	Thutmosis I	
Pharaoh, with daughter	Amenhotep I	Amenhotep I
Pharaoh's daughter, princess	Nefure	
Pharaoh's daughter, queen	Hatshepsut	
Moses, heir to throne	Senmut	
Moses, co-ruler	Thutmosis II	
Co-ruler (succeeded Moses)	Thutmosis III	
Pharao	Amenhotep II	Amenhotep II
Co-ruler	Thutmosis IV	
Pharaoh at time of Exodus	Amenhotep III	Amenhotep III
Firstborn son of Pharaoh at time of Exodus, co-ruler	Tutankhamun	

Figure 234: Hatshepsut's obelisk at the Karnak temple in Luxor.

Memphis and who was the father of Nefure, the person who most likely found Moses and adopted him.

On several statues a young woman with a little child is to be seen (figures 232, 233). The wording on these statues indicates that it is Nefure and Senmut. The child is wearing a royal ornament on its head indicating royalty, in this context a future heir to the throne. An heir to the throne was always a man, hence these statues represent a little boy.

Nefure is known as a princess and the daughter of Pharaoh Amenhotep I. It is then probable that it is princess Nefure who found the baby Moses in the Nile reeds and adopted him to have an heir to the throne. Other hypotheses claim that these statues represent a man (Senmut) who is responsible for the child Nefure, which the statues do not imply since it is difficult to understand how the older person in these statues can be seen to represent a man. Similarly it is unlikely that the child was a girl as this would be contrary to the custom in Egypt that the heir to the throne was always a man.

Senmut is an important name for Moses as it has a special meaning, namely "mother's brother". This name goes back to the Egyptian gods (and royal family according to Egyptian custom) Osiris, Isis and Horus. In this family in a complicated way, the son of Isis, Horus, becomes his mother's son and his mother's brother since he was a reincarnation of Isis' dead husband, who in turn was Isis' brother. In other words, Horus was also the brother of Isis (his mother's brother). This was to show that Isis was the rightful heir to the throne in spite of the fact that his father was dead when he was born.

In the same way Moses needed to have a rightful identity in order to be heir to the throne. His adoptive mother is thus depicted with Moses, who is then called his "mother's brother" (Senmut) and thereby receives the right to inherit the throne since his mother is the bearer of this right (although she cannot become Pharaoh). It is another way of saying that Moses, in the same way as Horus, was born into the royal family without a father. In this hypothesis Senmut is not a formal name for Moses but should perhaps be translated as "adopted son" in our everyday language. In another Bible passage (Heb.11:24) it is related that as an adult Moses refused to call himself the son of Pharaoh's daughter, which is understandable in view of his adult life (figure 235).

Figure 235: A woman with royal status holding a male child, heir of the throne. The statue is approximately 3,500 years old and from the Memphis/Sakkara area. Could this be Moses and his step-mother?

There is an interesting comment about Senmut in the literature (37); "It is probable that Senmut abused his power and that at a particular point in the reign of Hatshepsut he fell into disgrace, as demonstrated by the damage done to most of his monuments." This is exactly what happened to Moses according to the Bible text: From an Egyptian perspective he fell into disgrace when he escaped from Egypt and it is obvious that a person, the heir to the throne, doing this would have everything in terms of monuments, statues, scrolls etc., destroyed. A person doing what Moses did, must, according to Egyptian traditions - be erased from the history.

Tyldesley writes a chapter on Senmut in the interesting review of Hatshepsut (35). A number of known, strange and in many cases unclear facts related to Senmut are discussed. In the following table some of these characteristics of Senmut will be commented in relation to the hypothesis that Senmut and Moses were the same person.

Table 6. A comparison of Senmuts characteristics from ref 35 in relation to Moses as described in the Bible texts, mainly the book of Exodus (B), and in some cases in relation to descriptions by Josephus (J).

Figure 236: The temple Deir-El Bahri was built by Senmut (Moses) for Hatshepsut (Moses' stepmother).

SENMUT	MOSES
"...son of humble parents."	Son of hebrew slaves (B).
"Unfortunately, we have no means of knowing when Senmut had started his illustrious royal career."	Moses was found in the reeds of the Nile river at the age of three months by the princess at the royal court (B).
"Driven by a burning desire to shake off his lowly origins..."	Lowly origins (slaves) (B).

"He rose rapidly through the ranks..."	Become heir to the throne (B).
"...before quitting the army..."	Was a general (J).
"...to join the palace bureaucracy..."	Was trained to be pharaoh (B).
"...now took the calculated decision to link his future totally with that of Hatshepsut."	His only link to the royal court was via his stepmother, the princess who adopted him (B).
"...he was a close personal friend to the royal family."	He was adopted by the royal family (B).
"...most typically holding the infant Nefure in his arms."	According to the hypothesis of this book the statues shows Nefure holding Moses in her arms.
"...sitting with Nefure...held at right angles in his lap, a position hitherto reserved for women nursing children."	According to the hypothesis of this book it was Nefure holding Moses, according to Egyptian customs.
"Effectively, Senmut was ruler of Egypt".	He was to become the ruler and was, before his escape, co-ruler (B).
"The discovery of the shared tomb of Ramose and Hatnofer, Senmut's parents, confirms that Senmut was not of particulary high birth."	Moses parents were slaves (B).
"Ramose and Hatnofer...did not play a prominent role in public life."	Moses parents was not public people in Egypt (B).
"Nor is there any evidence to suggest that Senmut ever married..."	Moses was not married during his time in Egypt (B, J).
"...remain single, he must have been an oddity, one of the few..."	He married first when he arrived to Midian (B).
"...evidence that Senmut's immediate family had been struck by sudden catastrophe."	Not known. But could definetely be a possibility when Moses escaped from Egypt.

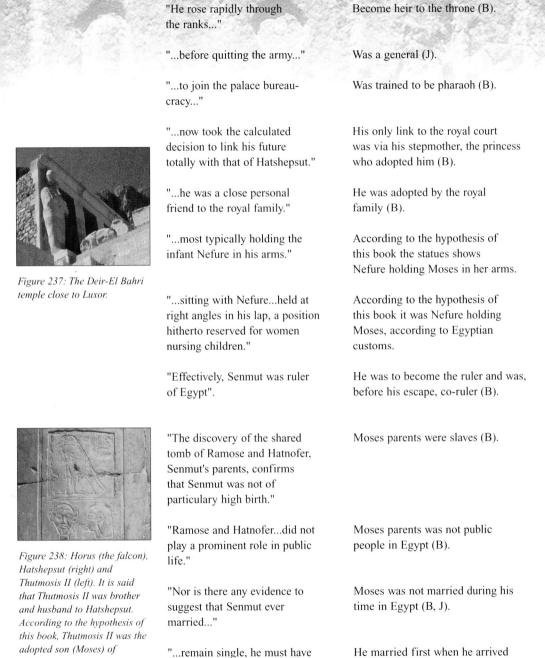

Figure 237: The Deir-El Bahri temple close to Luxor.

Figure 238: Horus (the falcon), Hatshepsut (right) and Thutmosis II (left). It is said that Thutmosis II was brother and husband to Hatshepsut. According to the hypothesis of this book, Thutmosis II was the adopted son (Moses) of Hatshepsut, expressed as "mother's brother" in Egyptian tradition.

"...badly damaged fragment... includes the words 'capture' and 'Nubia', is positioned next to images of running soldiers"

He was a general and organised war campains in Nubia (Ethiopia), and he led his army to victory (J).

Senmut is busy in the palace and related to Nefure and Hatshepsut "dating to the period before Hatshepsut's accession"

Moses grew up in the palace (B), adopted by the princess (Nefure) that later become queen Hatshepsut.

"...indicating that Senmut was in royal service during the reign of Thutmosis I..."

Not known from the Bible, but this is according to the hypothesis of this book. See figure 245.

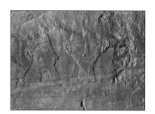

Figure 239: Hatshepsut (left) and Thutmosis II (right) at Deir-El Bahri. Thutmosis II was probably Moses.

"...Senmut's shrine omits the customary earthly and funerary feasts and includes instead a depiction of Hatshepsut being embraced by the crocodile-headed god..."

Moses origin was that he was found in the Nile river (B), where the crocodiles were found. Hatshepsut was probably the childless woman that found Moses in the river. Therefore she was in a symbolic way blessed by the god(s) related to the Nile river.

"Senmut was instantly stripped of all his privileges and disappeared in mystery circumstances."

Moses had to escape from Egypt due to his mistake to kill an Egyptian (B). He disappeared to Midian and lost everything he had in Egypt in a few days (B).

Figure 240: Horus (the falcon), Thutmosis II (upper left) and Hatshepsut (lower left) at Deir-El Bahri. According to Egyptian custom, Thutmosis II (Moses) was his "mother's brother" (see the text) and in this way heir to the throne (brother), but was also adopted. "Mother's brother" which is the meaning of "Senmut".

"His unused tombs were desecrated"

His tombs were unused since he died in todays Jordan (B).
His tombs would definetly be desecrated due to his escape, or betrayal of the Egyptian court (B).

"...his monuments were vandalized and his reliefs and statues were defaced in a determined attempt to erase both the name and memory of Senmut from the history of Egypt."

Would be expected due to his betrayal of the Egyptian court (B). The memory of Moses in Egyptian has been lost.

"At least twenty-five hard stone statues of Senmut have survived the ravages of time. This is an extraordinarily large number of statues for a private individual..."

He was heir to the throne, not a private individual (B).

"...we must assume that most, if not all, were the gift of the queen..."

The princess (who later was queen) was the stepmother of Moses (B).

"An intimate relationship with the queen would account for the rapid rise in Senmut's fortunes..."

Intimate in terms of mother - son relation (B) (several hypotheses suggests that their relation was as lovers).

"...being near to the gods was purely a royal prerogative..." (a remark of confusion)

He was a part of the royal family (B).

"...Hereditary Prince..." (a remark of confusion)

Yes (B).

"What is surprising is that Senmut was able to acquire any form of hard stone sarcophagus." (only for royalties)

He was a part of the royal family (B). It was to be expected.

"Senmut's tomb was substantially complete when all building work ceased"

Moses escaped the country (B) and betrayed the Egyptian royal court.

"...tomb 71 suffered a great deal of damage." "...other damage appears to have been entirely deliberate..."

Moses escaped the country (B) and betrayed the Egyptian royal court. To destroy tombs and other objects related to Moses could be expected.

Figures 241, 242: At Deir-El Bahri there are several examples of erased illustrations and carvings of both Hatshepsut and Moses (Thutmosis II), as can be seen above.

"The historical record is tantalizingly silent over the matter of Senmut's death."

The Egyptian historians did not want to know what happened to Moses, and they had no idea what was going on (B).

"What could have happened to him? The enigma of Senmut's sudden disappearance is which has teased egyptologists for decades..."

It is most likely that what the book of Exodus is focused on. The life of Moses (B).

"Many of Senmut's monuments were attacked following his death, when an attempt was made to delete his memory by erasing both his name and his image."

Moses has disappeared from the history of Egypt.

"Each of these descriptions has been based on four surviving ink sketches of Senmut's face."
"...high-bridge nose..."
"...aquiline nose..."

Moses was adopted, but genetically he was a hebrew (B). Hebrews are in many cases characterised having an "aquiline nose" which was not a character of Egyptians.

In summary; all these 35 comments on Senmut fits Moses very well.

The Bible relates that Moses' biological mother was allowed to breast-feed Moses, very probably she was allowed to bring him up until he was considered old enough to begin his training at the palace.

"And the child grew, and she brought him unto Pharaoh's daughter, and he became her son. And she called his name Moses..." (Ex. 2:10)

Probably at the same time his Egyptian "maternal grandfather", Thutmosis I/Amenhotep I, became the ruler of all Egypt, which meant that they moved to the palace in Thebes. When Moses was about 18 years old he probably was appointed heir to the throne with his foster mother, Nefure, as regent. Probably from this point in time Nefure was called Hatshepsut and queen. Senmut (Moses) had several titles as "superintendent of the grain stores, of the lands, of the livestock..." (37) .

A woman could not embody the gods but could be the wife of a Pharaoh and, if there were no heir, could carry out the functions until an heir had reached a mature age. In Hatshepsut's temple, Deir El Bahri, there is a wall where the birth of the heir to the throne is portrayed. Certain hypotheses claim that this is the birth of Hatshepsut, which becomes complicated since the child is a boy which one source tries to explain by saying that the one who made the inscription was confused. Another illustration on this wall shows the child in Hatshepsut's arms.

A number of hypotheses claim that Hatshepsut declared herself to be king, which is based on the inscription "king Hatshepsut Xnem Amen/MaatKaRe". The claim is that this is Hatshepsut with further additions to her name. "Hatshepsut Xnem Amen" means "Hatshepsut united with Amen". "Amen" is the principal god during the 18th dynasty and another name for the sun god (Ra). The name means that the "king" with this name is the product of Hatshepsut in union with the god Amen, or the offspring of the union between Hatshepsut and the god Amen.

According to the hypothesis in this chapter, this "king", or rather heir to the throne, was Moses with Hatshepsut as his co-ruler. When someone is appointed heir to the throne, then inscriptions refer to this person as "king". Moses was very closely connected to Hatshepsut since she was his only link to the royal family. In order to justify his accession to this elevated position it was important to observe protocol at every step so that Moses would be accepted in the existing system (figure 245).

It is said that Senmut had a high-bridge (aquiline) nose. Note the difference between Hatshepsut's nose (Moses' stepmother) and the nose of Moses (Thutmosis II) at the Deir-El Bahri temple in figures 239-240.

A long wall at Deir-El Bahri illustrates how Hatshepsut touches the hand of a god (=sexual relation). The next illustration shows her being pregnant, followed by a series of illustrations of a small boy growing to become a teenager. This is according to the tradition to explain an adoption. The hypothesis of this book is that Hatshepsut's son was Moses.

Figure 243: The pregnant Hatshepsut.

16. WHO WAS THUTMOSIS II?

When Moses is finally appointed co-ruler at the age of 33 years he becomes Thutmosis II. What happens later when Moses is 40 years old is dealt with in chapter 11 and also in chapter 17 and onwards.

Near to Thebes there is a beautiful building called "Deir El Bahri" (figure 246), which, according to this hypothesis, was the temple Moses built (as architect) for his stepmother Nefure. Above this building there is a grave (grave number 71) with a statue that was never completely finished. This statue is carved out of the rock and depicts a woman holding a little child. With the hypothesis presented in this chapter it is logical that this represents Moses in the arms of his stepmother Nefure.

This building was probably begun when Moses was about 18 years old - it was probably then that he was appointed heir to the throne with Nefure as regent. The names found in this grave are Nefure and Senmut.

Immediately under this grave a chamber has been found in which there are two mummies with the names Hatnofer and Ramose, most likely the Egyptian names for Moses' biological parents. Here one can see that Moses was given a god-like position in Egyptian society by giving his biological father the name of Ramose, since Ra was the greatest god among the Egyptians.

Hatnofer was embalmed and received a royal burial, indicated by the fact

Figure 244: Hatshepsut and her son.

Figure 245: A suggested system that places all these pharaohs, other people at the royal court, years and events into one system. See the text for comments.

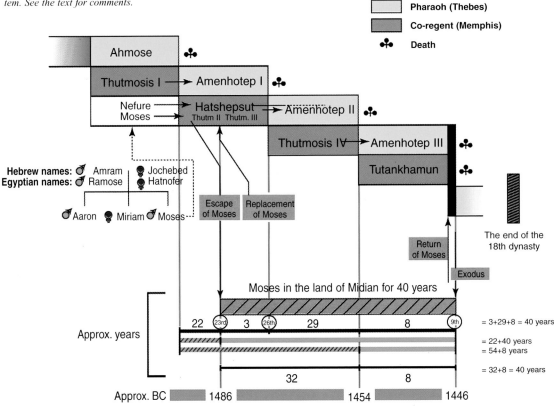

that she received this place as her burial place and that her death occurred when Moses was between 18 and 40 years old. Since the building was begun when Moses was around 18 years old it is likely that Moses' mother died when Moses was between 25 and 40 years old. She can definitely not have had this burial after Moses became 40 years old when a sentence of death was pronounced against Moses and he had to flee the country. Moses' father, Ramose, probably died before Moses was 18 years old since he received a more simple burial and was placed at Deir El Bahri after having been moved from another grave.

Figure 246: Deir El Bahri probably built by Moses according to the hypothesis of this book.

Moses' grave was never finished and no-one was buried in it. One reason may be that the building of an even grander grave was begun when Moses became Thutmosis II at the age of 33 years.

Grave number 353 is interesting because no-one was ever buried in this burial chamber. This was probably the second burial chamber built for Moses and in this case would represent the royal grave. When one goes down into this grave it can be seen that it is unfinished and those who carved the reliefs stopped at a certain point and it looks as though they had just finished their work for the day (figure 247). Nearby there are plans for future work with inscriptions drawn in black texts on the wall.

Figure 247: Moses grave was never finished and it looks like the workers just have left.

It can be noted that in Egyptian graves the dead person was depicted in different situations with his wife and others in the family. In this burial chamber the dead person (Moses) is depicted solely with his parents, Hatnofer and Ramose. According to the Bible, Moses had no family of his own when he lived in Egypt.

16.1. Who takes Moses'place when Moses flees?

Moses flees in tremendous haste from Egypt when he is 40 years old. The question then arises concerning who became Pharaoh when Moses disappeared from the Egyptian leadership and his future place on the throne.

The pharaoh at that time, Amenhotep I, was old and during 22 years had prepared for Moses to take over the throne (figure 245). What was to happen in this acute situation?

In Memphis there was a man who had been prepared to become co-ruler with Moses when Moses ascended the throne. Probably this man was promoted to become co-ruler with Amenhotep I with the same name (rank/title) as Moses, Thutmosis. Documents show that he received his position in his 22nd year. A co-ruler begins to count his years when he receives the position of co-ruler. This year then becomes the first year. Here we have a person who attains his position in his 22nd year with the same Egyptian name as Moses (Thutmosis).

It should be noted that the number of years may be counted from when the person becomes heir to the throne, crown prince or co-ruler. Then, when he becomes emperor he begins to count his years again. This leads to two lengths of rule, each as a different "god" authority. This is the reason why Thutmosis III states his reign as 54 years, while Amenhotep II's is 26-32 years (depending on the source). Thutmosis II, who is the one who takes Moses' place, is distinguished in that there is no trace of him as he rises in rank but he suddenly becomes co-ruler in his 22nd year (figure 245).

Figure 248: Pharaoh Akhenaten, one of many that were depicted on the statues with all his positive and negative characteristics.

What happened when Moses was suddenly forced to flee the country, was that the Egyptian authorities were obliged to find a replacement who could embody the god Thot (with the title/rank Thutmosis). In order not to break the "line of succession", the successor assumed the role of Moses and the years he had had in that post. Usually when a member of royalty died the god flew up to the heavens and was later reborn in the person who received the same position after a time. In this case no-one died and an immediate transfer was necessary. Everything that belonged to Moses was probably transferred to this new person (Thutmosis) and things continued without a break. This new person is called Thutmosis III. Presumably however, most of the statues said to represent him really represent Moses.

Thutmosis III was said to have reigned for 54 years, however 22 of these years were really the years Moses had in the position of Thutmosis. If these 22 years are subtracted from the 54 years, then that makes 32 years in power. In one text it is stated that Thutmosis III "passed away after a rule of 32 (some say 54) years".

The connection between these years is shown here, otherwise it is very complicated to understand since it is difficult to find a point of reference from which to start counting. This person, who reigned for 32 years as Amenhotep II before he died and was succeeded, was a great and mighty ruler in Egypt, the super power at that time.

Moses' foster mother, Hatshepsut, lived for many years after the flight of Moses and is called "queen" on the monuments in the later years of the reign of Amenhotep II, only Cleopatra being more well-known among women in leading positions in Egypt.

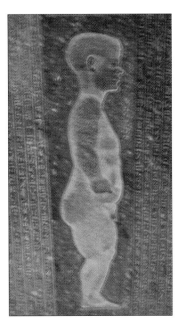

Figure 249: This person, a dwarf, is depicted in detail according to the portrait-like traditions among the Egyptian artists.

16.2. WHO DOES THUTMOSIS II REPRESENT?

The statues and images in ancient Egypt show an amazing portrait-like resemblance. All the people depicted are not idealised, but they often have not just one but several characteristics, both positive and negative. Examples of this are Pharaoh Akhenaten (figure 248), who had a very peculiar build, others are dwarves (figure 249), have physical features such as obesity, varying skin colour, height and, to say the least, are very different in appearance. Even when army units were made as statuettes, all the soldiers were different. This is mentioned as background to the well-founded assumption that artists and sculptors tried to achieve a portrait-like resemblance.

The following observations are speculative but may be interesting to note. The Egyptians, and in particular the leaders, have certain traits in common. One such trait is that they have straight noses (figures 250-253).

In this book the hypothesis that Thutmosis II was Moses is stated. So what do the statues of Thutmosis II look like? Moses was not an Egyptian, as far as his genes were concerned, but a Hebrew. Sometimes Hebrews can be described as having more of a hook nose than others. It is interesting that the statue representing Thutmosis II has a more distinct hook nose compared to other statues, as can be seen in figure 254. If this was done purposely by the sculptor with the aim of making the representation of Thutmosis II as portrait-like as possible, then this means that the statue in the figure probably represents Moses.

16.3. WHO WAS PHARAOH AT THE TIME OF THE EXODUS?

When Amenhotep II died, according to the hypothesis in this book, his co-ruler of 29 years, Thutmosis IV, succeeded as Pharaoh with the pharaonic title Amenhotep III. When Amenhotep III became Pharaoh he appointed his eldest son, although very young, as crown prince as was the custom. The young person who received this role was about 10 years old at the time and we know him as Tutankhamun. Amenhotep III later reigns for about 8 years before the time of the Exodus occurs.

Amenhotep III is interesting from a special point of view. It would seem that he was not intended for the throne of Egypt since he was not the eldest son through the royal mother, whom custom decreed should become Pharaoh. In the Sphinx inscription, which can still be seen between the paws of the Sphinx (figure 169) by the pyramids in Giza outside present day Cairo, a remarkable story about Thutmosis IV is told. One day Thutmosis IV fell asleep in the shadow of the Sphinx and dreamt that the sun god came to him, and said that if he removed all the sand from around the Sphinx he would become king.

This story would not have needed to be told if he had received the right to the throne

Figures 250-253: The Egyptians had one trait in common, their straight noses. Noses were depicted in the traditional way - as similar as possible to the person that was depicted.

Figure 254: Figures 248-249 show that statues were made according to a tradition to make the statue resemble the living person as closely as possible. This photograph shows Thutmosis II, who according to the hypothesis of this book (Figure 245) was Moses. This statue has a hook nose, typical of the Hebrews. Moses, although adopted by an Egyptian princess, was a Hebrew in terms of his genes. In addition, there are notes that Sannut had an aquiline nose (table 6), and Thutmosis II is depicted with a big nose on reliefs (figures 238-240).

Figure 255: The Sphinx, close to the pyramids of Giza, outside Cairo.

in a traditional way - by being the eldest son. It may have been that Amenhotep II was also childless, or that for some reason the eldest son could not become Pharaoh. That son could have died young, for instance. For reasons which we shall discuss in chapter 27, we know nontheless it was very probable Amenhotep III was not the eldest son, while Tutankhamun, heir to the throne after Amenhotep III, was the eldest son of Amenhotep III.

Tutankhamun was co-ruler and in an inscription on the statue of a lion, which Tutankhamun dedicated to the Soleb temple, he calls his father Amenhotep III (37), which confirms the relation between these two people.

16.4. CAN WE IDENTIFY THE MUMMIES THAT HAVE BEEN FOUND?

There are many mummies in Egypt and there are also problems in connecting a specific mummy to a specific Pharaoh. One example is the mummy that is supposed to be Thutmosis·I who reigned for 21 years, according to inscriptions. The following is said about the mummy supposed to belong to Thutmosis I: "However, several eminent physical anthropologists who have seen these X-ray plates have been absolutely convinced that this mummy is that of a young man, perhaps 18 years of age, certainly not over twenty." (39). Several such examples can be given, but there are also explanations.

1. That the name lived on was of primary importance. The worst thing that could happen, was for the name to be removed from inscriptions etc. It was not so important that it was precisely the right mummy because the body was dead and it was the spirit that needed a body - any body.
2. Many grave robberies (in general most graves have been robbed) have led to the contents of graves being scattered.
3. Many mummies have disappeared to be used as medicines. An ingredient in many European prescriptions in the Middle Ages was part of a mummy as they were held to have a magical effect.
4. Later pharaohs who restored graves that had been plundered, put in another mummy.

Thus, there are many uncertainties regarding the identity of mummies that have been found. It is probably only the mummies of Amenhotep I, Amenhotep II and Tutankhamun from the 18th dynasty, who are the individuals with whom they are connected. With regard to Tutankhamun, the grave is one of the few which has not been plundered. The mummy of Amenhotep I shows a common genetic defect (protruding teeth) which existed in the family, which means that this mummy can be connected to the 18th dynasty. The other mummies are probably mixed up or placed there at a later date (e.g. after a grave robbery) since they are found in the wrong graves and/or have not received a royal burial.

Moreover, according to the hypothesis in this book, there should not be any mummies of Thutmosis II, who was Moses, nor Amenhotep III, who drowned in the Red Sea. Furthermore, according to the same hypothesis, there should only be one mummy from the name-pair Thutmosis/Amenhotep since this was one and the same person (figure 245).

17. To where does Moses flee?

Moses flees to the land of Midian. The question of where the land of Midian lies, is a key in the whole question about the Exodus, which will be shown in the following chapters. It is clearly expressed in the Bible that it was to the land of Midian that Moses fled:

"Now when Pharaoh heard this thing, he sought to slay Moses. But Moses fled from the face of Pharaoh, and dwelt in the land of Midian: and he sat down by a well." (Ex. 2:15)

Figure 256: The mountains in the land of Midian.

17.1 To the land of Midian

This question is not controversial. Both the Bible and the historian Josephus (Ex. 2:11 - 6:30 and JA 2/12-13, respectively) base their accounts on the fact that during his flight Moses finds himself in the land of Midian on a recurring number of occasions. It should be noted that it states Moses came to the land of Midian and not to some encampment, grazing place, or area of interest as a trade route that the Midianites had. The Midianites moved about over a large surface in various connections e.g. the biblical text mentions that Joseph was bought by Midian merchants, who passed by Shekem on their way from Gilead to Egypt with goods to trade:

"Then there passed by Midianites merchantmen; and they drew and lifted up Joseph out of the pit, and sold Joseph to the Ishmeelites for twenty pieces of silver: and they brought Joseph into Egypt." (Gen. 37:28)

17.2. Where was the land of Midian located?

When Josephus relates these events there is a further comment that these merchants came from Arabia (JA 2/3:3). During his flight Moses came to the land of Midian, the question is where did this land lie? We have already noted that Josephus indicates that the home of the Midianite merchants was in Arabia. Josephus also indicates that the land of Midian was situated on the Red Sea coast, and he also names the town of Midian (JA 2/11:1).

The Gulf of Aqaba on the coast of the land of Midian is part of the Red Sea. Josephus also states that the area belonged to the descendants of Keturah. It is not known that any towns were built in the Sinai desert. In northwestern Saudi-Arabia there is a town which today is called Al Bad. Several sources refer to Al Bad as the home of Jethro (Moses' father-in-law) in which case it was also the home of Moses for 40 years.

Abraham took the children he had with his concubines, gave them gifts, and sent them eastward, and in that way separated them from Isaac. One of the sons of Abraham and Ketura was called Midian, who gave rise to the Midianites who settled in the "land of the East" (Gen. 25:5). Josephus states among other things that Ketura's sons settled in Arabia down towards the Red Sea (JA 1/15). Most biblical maps covering this area at this period also place the land of Midian on the eastern side of the Gulf of Aqaba, which today corresponds to north-western Saudi-Arabia (figure 257).

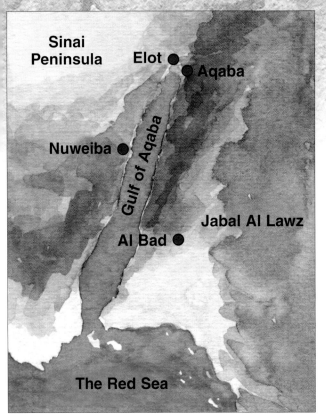

Josephus comments that it was the custom among the Troglodytes for young unmarried women to tend the flocks of sheep. Among the first people Moses meets in Midian are the women who are going to give their sheep water, and he then makes reference to the fact that they are of this nation (Troglodytes). When Abraham makes gifts to his sons with Keturah, one of whom is Midian, it is mentioned that the sons claimed amongst other things the Troglodytes' area in Arabia by the Red Sea (JA 1/15, 2/11).

17.3. OLD MAPS AND INVESTIGATIONS

When investgating where Midian was located on old maps from 1654 up until modern times, there is only one answer. Midian has always been located on the east coast of the Gulf of Aqaba. In Figure 258 a part of a map from 1719 (Chatelain) is shown. Midian (spelled

Figure 257: The land of Midian was located in the north-western part of Saudi-Arabia. Al Bad is the only settlement in that area. Land in ancient times referred to an area to dwell in, like an area for a tribe. Countries - in our context of today - did not exist during this time.

Madian) is on the east coast. In addition, Jethro is said to have had his home in Midian. Further, the "Almond mountain" is located east of Jethro's settlement. This is, according to the hypothesis of this book, where Jethro was supposed to have Al Bad as his settlement, with Jabal Al Lawz to the east of that settlement. Jabal Al Lawz means the "Almond Mountain".

Figure 259 shows a much more modern map from 1911 (H. Mielisch). The quality of the map is much better due to the increase in knowledge of how to determine localizations. Here Midian is located on the east coast (called Madiana). "Bed" is the place that is called Al Bad today, which probably was the place where Jethro lived.

18 maps from 1654 to 1911 were studied and all locate Midian to the east coast of the Gulf of Aqaba.

In 1878 an investigation took place to make a good

Figure 258, 259: The maps (from 1719 (above) and 1911 (right)) display Midian on the east coast of the Gulf of Aqaba

Figures 260, 261: R.F. Burton's map after the first detailed investigation of the land of Midian (1878).

map of the land of Midian (Figure 260). This was probably the best investigation made in modern times, and the map can still be used today to find the way through the wadis and along coast lines. It was officers of the Egyptian General Staff, under the command of officer R.F. Burton that made this investigation. There are some interesting observations worthy of note (Figure 261):

They locate Madiama but refer to a specific place, and the general area is called the land of Midian. The Wadi of Al Bad (El Bada) is located in the same place as it is found today. Al or El both mean "god". In this book Al Bad is the suggested place where the priest of Midian - Jethro - lived. Jethro was Moses' father in law, which means that Moses also lived in this place for 40 years. This is the only place in the area where permanent settlements are possible due to access to drinking water.

This was how Moses met one of Jethro's daughters. According to the biblical text they met at a well, Moses needed water and Jethro's daughters needed water for their sheep.

When Burton and his officers were in Midian, they found a well very close to Al Bad. Guided by the local bedouins, they defined this well as "the well of Moses". Burton also located the highest mountain in the area further to the east, Jebel El Lauz, today called Jabal Al Lawz. Burton also noted the mountain in parenthesis, "Almond Mtn". That is still the interpretation of the name of that mountain: "The Almond Mountain". The investigation and map were generated during a time when almost everyone considered Mount Sinai to be located on the Sinai peninsula.

Figure 262: Hagiar is a mountain range located in Arabia (according to old maps). This map is by R. de Vaugoudy (1761).

17.4. THE HOME OF MOSES AND AGAR

In the Christian tradition, the prophecy of Isaiah about the birth of Jesus is read together with the Christmas gospel. In the Old Testament passage, read at this time, Isaiah 9:2-7, the fourth verse reads:

"For thou hast broken the yoke of his burden, and the staff of his shoulder, the rod of his oppressor, as in the day of Midian." (Is. 9:4)

The Bible passage describing the flight of Moses continues:

"Now when Pharaoh heard this thing, he sought to slay Moses. But Moses fled from the face of Pharaoh, and dwelt in the land of Midian: and he sat down by a well." (Ex. 2:15)

This means that Moses fled from the region where Pharaoh had influence. It also means that Moses must have fled from Sinai (called "the wilderness of the Red Sea"), since Pharaoh had considerable interests under military guard on this peninsula because of deposits of the semi-precious stone turquoise (figure 263) and copper mines (figure 264).

Figure 263: Egypt had important turquoise mines in the southern part of the Sinai peninsula, guarded by the army.

The Sinai peninsula cannot have been a very safe place during 40 years of flight for the extremely well-known Moses: as a refugee with the armed forces of Egypt on his heels. Moreover Moses lived quite openly all the time, and did not try to conceal his identity. This would not have been possible for any length of time in Sinai, especially in the vicinity of the traditional Mount Sinai which was not far from the Egyptian mines under military guard.

The Sinai peninsula has always belonged to the Egyptian sphere of interest and it was called "Msr" which means "Misraim" or Egypt (41).

In Stephen's defence speech, before he is stoned (approx. 1500 years later), he goes through the important parts of Hebrew history in the presence of the high priest and mentions among other things the flight of Moses from Egypt:

Figure 264: The Sinai peninsula is rich in copper containing minerals, like turquoise. The photograph shows genuine copper as it can be found in nature.

"Then fled Moses at this saying, and was a stranger in the land of Madian, where he begat two sons." (Acts 7:29)

In the Swedish Bible commentary to this text it says: "This land probably lay in the northern part of the Gulf of Aqaba".

Further, in the Bible it says that an Egyptian man (Moses) helped the women to water their sheep (Ex. 2:19), which means that Moses must have been in another country, otherwise they would not have said "an Egyptian man".

Again, in his letter to the Galatians Paul says:

"For this Agar is mount Sinai in Arabia, and answereth to Jerusalem which now is, and is in bondage with her children." (Gal. 4:25)

This comment of Paul can be interpreted in two ways, either as a direct reference to the fact that Mount Sinai lay in Arabia, or more symbolically that the law in Arabia is represented by Hagar, Abraham's concubine. The text may also have both these meanings.

Interestingly, old maps show a mountain east of Midian (in Arabia) named "Hagiar" (Chaletain 1719 and R. de Vaugondy 1761). This is seen in figure 262. Could this be the "Agar" mountain mentioned in the biblical text?

17.5. IN SUMMARY

To summarise, the Bible and historical sources mention the following key words regarding where Midian was situated: outside Egypt's sphere of interest, out of reach of Pharaoh's army, by the Red Sea, towards the northern part of the Gulf of Aqaba, where the descendants of Keturah lived (east of Jordan down towards the Red Sea in the land of the East) and in Arabia. The eastern coastal area of the gulf of Aqaba as the site of Midian is not contradicted by these sources, quite the contrary, they support the hypothesis.

In the text that follows a number of questions arise which further support the hypothesis that Midian was situated in north wetern Saudi-Arabia. However it is clear that Moses fled to the land of Midian, and there are a number of references which recur from various sources indicating that this land was sitauted to the east of the Gulf of Aqaba, which means in north-western Saudi-Arabia.

18. WHAT HAPPENS IN MIDIAN DURING MOSES' TIME AS A REFUGEE?

The first thing that happens in the land of Midian is that Moses finds a well. Then seven women, daughters of the priest in Midian, come to fetch water for their sheep. Shepherds arrive and want to drive the women away but Moses intervenes and helps the women. Their father Reuel (also called Jethro) wonders how the women could have returned so quickly that day, and so they tell of the help they received from Moses. Reuel then tells them to go and find Moses and invite him home to Reuel (Ex. 2:16-20).

They are not in a temporary camp but near the well where they used to water their sheep, and Moses is invited home to Reuel's house. There are very few wells in the area and it is near these oases that permanent settlements developed. The text also mentions a scarcity of water and it seems as though it took most of the day to find a place to water the sheep.

The priest in the land of Midian was probably to be found in the land of Midian in order to exercise his office there. This is further confirmation that Moses was in the land of Midian. The Bible also tells us that Moses remained in the land of Midian (Ex. 2:15).

This visit to the home of Reuel led to Moses becoming responsible for Reuel's sheep (Ex. 3:1, JA 2/11:2), and later also marrying one of the daughters, Zipporah (Ex. 2:22). Zipporah gives birth to two sons. The first receives the name Gershom (the name means foreigner) since Moses is in a country where he is a foreigner (Ex. 2:22), in other words outside Egypt.

A long time passes (about 40 years), and Moses minds the flocks of sheep while the children of Israel groan more and more. One day Moses comes to Mount Horeb with the sheep (Ex. 3:1).

19. WHERE IS HOREB?

Before addressing the question of where this mountain is situated, we shall see how the biblical texts and the historical writer Josephus state the identity of the mountain.

19.1. SEVERAL NAMES OF THE MOUNTAIN

This mountain has several names. In Exodus 3:1 two of these names are mentioned in the same verse:

Figure 265: Moses left the fertile Nile River Valley around Luxor with all the temples and luxury, for a life in the wilderness.

"Now Moses kept the flock of Jethro his father in law, the priest of Midian: and he led the flock to the backside of the desert, and came to the mountain of God, even to Horeb." (Ex. 3:1)

Thus two of the names are mentioned, the "mountain of God" and "Horeb". Josephus tells about the same mountain but calls it Sinai (JA 2/12:1). When Paul refers to this mountain in his letter to the Galatians he writes:

"... mount Sinai in Arabia, and answereth to Jerusalem which now is, and is in bondage with her children." (Gal. 4:25)

When the story of the prophet Elijah wandering to Horeb is related in the First Book of Kings, it reads:

"And he arose, and did eat and drink, and went in the strength of that meat forty days and forty nights unto Horeb the mount of God." (1 Kings 19:8)

In Psalm 106 in the Book of Psalms, the time of the Exodus is spoken about: when the people of Israel are in camp after having passed through the Red Sea:

"They made a calf in Horeb, and worshipped the molten image." (Ps. 106:19)

The book of Deuteronomy tells about the covenant the Lord made with the people of Israel:

"The LORD our God made a covenant with us in Horeb." (Deut. 5:2)

When the story of King Solomon is told and when the ark of the covenant is taken into the temple, it says in the First Book of Kings:

"There was nothing in the ark save the two tables of stone, which Moses put there at Horeb, when the LORD made a covenant with the children of Israel, when they came out of the land of Egypt." (1 Kings 8:9)

When Moses was up in the mountain and received the tablets of stone, the book of Exodus tells:

"And the glory of the LORD abode upon mount Sinai, and the cloud covered it six days: and the seventh day he called unto Moses out of the

midst of the cloud." (Ex. 24:16)

A little later in the book of Exodus when the receiving of the tablets of stone is taken up again, it says:

"And he gave unto Moses, when he had made an end of communing with him upon mount Sinai, two tables of testimony, tables of stone, written with the finger of God." (Ex. 31:18)

Moses blesses the tribes of Israel shortly before his death and the beginning of the benediction is:

"And he said, The LORD came from Sinai, and rose up from Seir unto them; he shined forth from mount Paran, and he came with ten thousand saints: from his right hand went a fiery law for them." (Deut. 33:2)

In Stephen's defence speech, approximately 1500 years after the Exodus, Stephen gives an account of Moses in connection with the events in the desert:

"This is he, that was in the church in the wilderness with the angel which spake to him in the mount Sinai, and with our fathers: who received the lively oracles to give unto us." (Acts 7:38)

Altogether these texts give a clear answer that the mountain had at least three different names: mountain of God, Mount Sinai and Mount Horeb.

19.2. WHERE WAS THE MOUNTAIN LOCATED?

The Mount Horeb that Moses visited with his sheep on that occasion, was situated in the land of Midian. We can establish this from the biblical texts, since Moses lived with his family at the home of his father-in-law Reuel, who was the high priest in Midian. Moses was responsible for the flocks of sheep, which gives us more information about the location of Horeb. This was a permanent settlement, as far as Moses was concerned, for forty years. The settlement existed before the arrival of Moses and after he had left the area.

The only places in this desert region which had a fixed population were in the vicinity of water, since there are no lakes or permanent rivers in the region. In this context water was the groundwater in wells that had been dug out. Surface water in different watercourses is not found and rainwater is so rare that it cannot be counted on as a source of drinking water. These wells that had been dug were used to the full, which can be deduced from the crowding that occurred round the wells (Ex. 2:15-19). When Moses was near Mount Horeb with his flocks of sheep, it cannot have been too far from the permanent settlement with access to water.

Since Al Bad is a very old settlement with wells, and really the only permanent settlement in the region (along the southern part of the east coast of the Gulf of Aqaba), it is probable that the high priest Reuel had Al Bad as his home. If one assumes that Al Bad was where Reuel, Moses and the rest of

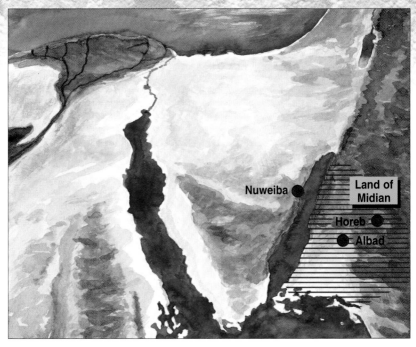

Figure 266: The land of Midian refers to an area for a tribe. One can compare this with the small land of Israel that was divided into the lands of the 12 tribes. Today we talk about countries, but in ancient times countries as we know them did not exist. The highest mountain ridge in the region separates Al Bad and the camp site on the eastern side of Mount Sinai (Horeb).

the family lived, and we know that on this occasion Moses had all the flocks of sheep with him, then the possibilities are limited regarding which mountain might be Horeb.

Josephus makes a further note that the mountain was the highest in the area (JA 2/12:1). On the east coast of the Gulf of Aqaba, and especially in the southern area near Al Bad, there is only one mountain range which tallies with this description. This mountain range is called Jabal Al Lawz today, it lies in the vicinity of Al Bad and is the highest in the area with its 2580 metres above sea-level (figure 266).

Josephus makes another note concerning this mountain: that one did not go there because the shepherds regarded it as a sacred mountain where God had his dwelling (JA 2/12:1).

On relatively good grounds we can assume that Moses was now at the mountain range which today is called Jabal Al Lawz in Arabic. A mountain that lies east of the Gulf of Aqaba, on the southern coastal area, in present day northwestern Saudi-Arabia. The mountain that is called "the mountain of God", "Mount Sinai" or "Horeb" in the Bible. Several of the following chapters will further develop the hypothesis that Mount Sinai is really situated in Saudi-Arabia, but now we shall go back to the events Moses experienced at this mountain.

Table 7. Mount Horeb, east of Midian on old maps.

Mountain	Source and year
"M. Oreb"	Gerard Mercator, 1512-1594*
"Mount Oreb"	Pierre Mariette, 1654*
"Haura"	Nicolas Sanson, 1705
"Hawra"	H. Mielisch, 1911

* Very old and not exact maps

20. WHAT HAPPENS AT MOUNT HOREB?

The biblical texts relate that an angel of the Lord appeared to Moses as a bright light or a fiery flame that leapt up from a bush. We know this incident as "Moses and the burning bush" (Ex. 3:2 and onwards).

20.1. WHAT KIND OF FIRE WAS THERE WHEN THE BUSH WAS BURNING?

The bush is not burnt up by the fire. This is because when the Holiness of the Lord is manifested, according to the Bible, it is often as a bright light (a flame of fire) but not the fire we know which burns up and destroys organic material. A clear example in the Christian tradition is when the disciples of Jesus experience the outpouring of the Holy Spirit at the first Pentecost:

"And there appeared unto them cloven tongues like as of fire, and it sat upon each of them." (Acts 2:3)

We can exclude an ordinary fire in a bush because the bush does not burn up, it is completely untouched by the "fire":

"Now Moses kept the flock of Jethro his father in law, the priest of Midian: and he led the flock to the backside of the desert, and came to the mountain of God, even to Horeb. And the angel of the LORD appeared unto him in a flame of fire out of the midst of a bush: and he looked, and, behold, the bush burned with fire, and the bush was not consumed. And Moses said, 'I will now turn aside, and see this great sight, why the bush is not burnt.'" (Ex. 3:1-3)

There are at least five reasons why it is not an ordinary bush which is burning:

1. The main character and eye-witness, Moses, does not believe it is.
2. Moses becomes curious just because the bush is burning without being burnt up.
3. It would not have been burning slowly since these bushes are very dry and moreover contain various volatile oils which together would make a bush burn up very quickly. The conversation in its entirety between Moses and the Lord takes a long time and the bush is "burning" throughout this conversation.
4. The bush speaks to Moses (see the text below).
5. The consequences of the conversation which is carried on, with which the rest of this book deals.

20.2. WHAT HAPPENS AT THE BURNING BUSH?

Moses becomes curious and goes towards the light/fire. Then the Lord calls to Moses and Moses answers. According to the text, the Lord then says to Moses:

"And he said, 'Draw not nigh hither: put off thy shoes from off thy feet, for the place whereon thou standest is holy ground. Moreover he said, I am the

God of thy father, the God of Abraham, the God of Isaac, and the God of Jacob.' And Moses hid his face; for he was afraid to look upon God." (Ex 3:5-6)

Moses understands immediately that it is the Lord speaking and he hides his face.

Figure 267: The mountain ridges surrounding the Red Sea.

"And the LORD said, 'I have surely seen the affliction of my people which are in Egypt, and have heard their cry by reason of their taskmasters; for I know their sorrows; And I am come down to deliver them out of the hand of the Egyptians, and to bring them up out of that land unto a good land and a large, unto a land flowing with milk and honey; unto the place of the Canaanites, and the Hittites, and the Amorites, and the Perizzites, and the Hivites, and the Jebusites. Now therefore, behold, the cry of the children of Israel is come unto me: and I have also seen the oppression wherewith the Egyptians oppress them. Come now therefore, and I will send thee unto Pharaoh, that thou mayest bring forth my people the children of Israel out of Egypt.'" (Ex. 3:7-10)

It is interesting to note that the Lord calls the people of Israel to a spacious land. This means that Egypt must have been over-crowded for the people of Israel. This implies that in Egypt the people of Israel consisted of a huge number of men and women since the delta region of the Nile is very large.

20.3. THE DISCUSSION BETWEEN THE LORD AND MOSES

So the Lord calls Moses to lead the people of Israel out of Egypt. Moses believed that he was ready about 40 years earlier when he was at the height of his power and glory. It is true, from a human view-point Moses had everything: he was general and commander of the Egyptian army, he had great knowledge and wisdom and he was heir of the Egyptian empire.

But before he was qualified to be the Lord's instrument to lead the people of Israel out of Egypt, 40 years were needed as a shepherd in the desert. Moses is now 80 years old. It seems that life is moving towards its end, nevertheless Moses will not act in his own strength but in the strength of the Lord, according to the text. Then God speaks, loud and clear. Moses receives his marching orders. "You shall lead my people Israel out of Egypt," says the Lord. Moses is doubtful, "Who am I" he says and then God answers:

"And he said, 'Certainly I will be with thee; and this shall be a token unto thee, that I have sent thee: When thou hast brought forth the people out of Egypt, ye shall serve God upon this mountain.'" (Ex. 3:12)

The mountain of which God speaks is Horeb. In other words Moses receives very clear instructions that he must return to this mountain. The mountain to which he had come with his father-in-law Reuel's sheep, Reuel who lives in Midian. Thus from this moment Moses knows where he will go with the people of Israel. He will return to Mount Horeb! The Lord says this very clearly in the bible text. Firstly, the people of Israel will leave Egypt (see the earlier discussion in chapter 17 regarding the extent of Egypt's sphere of interest) and secondly, that on this mountain where Moses stands they will worship God. Mount Horeb in Midian.

This is important to note. During the entire Exodus (migration) Moses knows where his final destination with the people of Israel is. In spite of this Moses will become both confused and in despair during the Exodus, when the Lord leads him along what he feels are mistaken ways. Added to this Moses knows that the land of Canaan was the promised land for the people of Israel and their final goal. The Lord also says something strange when he calls Moses:

"And he said, 'Certainly I will be with thee; and this shall be a token unto thee, that I have sent thee: When thou hast brought forth the people out of Egypt, ye shall serve God upon this mountain.'" (Ex. 3:12)

How can worshipping God on Horeb be a sign? The Lord knows, but not Moses. Not yet. Then a discussion between the Lord and Moses follows. The Bible relates:

"And Moses said unto God, 'Behold, when I come unto the children of Israel, and shall say unto them, The God of your fathers hath sent me unto you; and they shall say to me, "What is his name?" what shall I say unto them?' And God said unto Moses, 'I AM THAT I AM': and he said, 'Thus shalt thou say unto the children of Israel, "I AM hath sent me unto you."' And God said moreover unto Moses, 'Thus shalt thou say unto the children of Israel, "the LORD God of your fathers, the God of Abraham, the God of Isaac, and the God of Jacob, hath sent me unto you": this is my name for ever, and this is my memorial unto all generations.'

'Go, and gather the elders of Israel together, and say unto them, "The LORD God of your fathers, the God of Abraham, of Isaac, and of Jacob, appeared unto me, saying, I have surely visited you, and seen that which is done to you in Egypt: And I have said, I will bring you up out of the affliction of Egypt

Figure 268: The promised land. The land that was promised to Moses as the land the people of Israel should emigrate to. The land that was granted to the seed of Abraham. The land that corresponds to today's Israel.

unto the land of the Canaanites, and the Hittites, and the Amorites, and the Perizzites, and the Hivites, and the Jebusites, unto a land flowing with milk and honey."'

And they shall hearken to thy voice: and thou shalt come, thou and the elders of Israel, unto the king of Egypt, and ye shall say unto him, "The LORD God of the Hebrews hath met with us: and now let us go, we beseech thee, three days' journey into the wilderness, that we may sacrifice to the

LORD our God." And I am sure that the king of Egypt will not let you go, no, not by a mighty hand. And I will stretch out my hand, and smite Egypt with all my wonders which I will do in the midst thereof: and after that he will let you go.

And I will give this people favor in the sight of the Egyptians: and it shall come to pass, that, when ye go, ye shall not go empty. But every woman shall borrow of her neighbor, and of her that sojourneth in her house, jewels of silver, and jewels of gold, andraiment: and ye shall put them upon your sons, and upon your daughters; and ye shall spoil the Egyptians." (figure 268)

And Moses answered and said, 'But, behold, they will not believe me, nor hearken unto my voice: for they will say, "The LORD hath not appeared unto thee."' And the LORD said unto him, 'What is that in thine hand?' And he said, 'A rod.' And he said, 'Cast it on the ground.' And he cast it on the ground, and it became a serpent; and Moses fled from before it. And the LORD said unto Moses, 'Put forth thine hand, and take it by the tail.' And he put forth his hand, and caught it, and it became a rod in his hand:

'That they may believe that the LORD God of their fathers, the God of Abraham, the God of Isaac, and the God of Jacob, hath appeared unto thee.' And the LORD said furthermore unto him, 'Put now thine hand into thy bosom.' And he put his hand into his bosom: and when he took it out, behold, his hand was leprous as snow. And he said, 'Put thine hand into thy bosom again.' And he put his hand into his bosom again; and plucked it out of his bosom, and, behold, it was turned again as his other flesh. 'And it shall come to pass, if they will not believe thee, neither hearken to the voice of the first sign, that they will believe the voice of the latter sign.

And it shall come to pass, if they will not believe also these two signs, neither hearken unto thy voice, that thou shalt take of the water of the river, and pour it upon the dry land: and the water which thou takest out of the river shall become blood upon the dry land.' And Moses said unto the LORD, 'O my LORD, I am not eloquent, neither heretofore, nor since thou hast spoken unto thy servant: but I am slow of speech, and of a slow tongue.' And the LORD said unto him, 'Who hath made man's mouth? or who maketh the dumb, or deaf, or the seeing, or the blind? have not I the LORD?

Now therefore go, and I will be with thy mouth, and teach thee what thou shalt say.' And he said, 'O my LORD, send, I pray thee, by the hand of him whom thou wilt send.' And the anger of the LORD was kindled against Moses, and he said, 'Is not Aaron the Levite thy brother? I know that he can speak well. And also, behold, he cometh forth to meet thee: and when he seeth thee, he will be glad in his heart.

And thou shalt speak unto him, and put words in his mouth: and I will be with thy mouth, and with his mouth, and will teach you what ye shall do. And he shall be thy spokesman unto the people: and he shall be, even he shall be to thee instead of a mouth, and thou shalt be to him instead of God. And thou shalt take this rod in thine hand, wherewith thou shalt do signs.'"
(Ex. 3:13 - 4:17)

20.4. IN SUMMARY

The conversation between the Lord and Moses speaks for itself. A few notes:

- The people of Israel are well organised with a system of elders.
- Moses and the elders will ask to be allowed to go on a three-day journey into the desert to worship their God, which included sacrifices forbidden in Egypt.
- When they leave Egypt the people of Israel will receive many gifts from the Egyptians.
- Moses receives three signs to show the people of Israel (the staff, his hand and the blood).
- Aaron, Moses' brother, will speak on behalf of Moses.
- Aaron is already on his way to Moses, which means that he has communicated with God himself, which is also confirmed later in the text (Ex. 4:14).

After this conversation the preparations started for what has later been called the Exodus.

21. What does Moses do after meeting God on Mount Horeb?

Moses goes to his father-in-law Reuel, and according to the custom asks permission to return to his people in Egypt. Reuel gives him his blessing and wishes him well. The Lord speaks again to Moses and says:

"And the LORD said unto Moses in Midian, 'Go, return into Egypt: for all the men are dead which sought thy life.'" (Ex. 4:19)

Moses receives his marching orders from the Lord. The assignment begins with Moses' return to Egypt. Once again it is emphasised that Moses is not in the land of Egypt and its sphere of interest (the Sinai peninsula). Moses takes his wife Zipporah and their two sons on an ass, and returns to Egypt on foot (Ex. 4:20).

The Lord speaks to Aaron, Moses' brother, and tells him to go and meet Moses in the desert. Aaron must have received much more information from the Lord, or alternatively Horeb was known to the people of Israel as the mountain of God, because Aaron meets Moses on Mount Horeb, the mountain of God. Moses relates what God has said and what assignment he has received. Later they return to Egypt together and assemble the elders of Israel. Aaron talks about what Moses has seen and the assignment he has received. Moses shows the signs that will confirm the assignment (the staff, his hand and the blood). The elders of Israel believe that God has spoken to Moses, and when they hear that God had seen their suffering, they fall down and worship the Lord (Ex. 4:27-31).

The biblical texts relate that Moses now has the Lord's assignment, and has the elders and the people of Israel with him. Now the struggle between good and evil begins. Through Joseph the Lord has given Egypt unbelievable prosperity. By following Joseph's advice to stock grain and other food during the seven good years in order to distribute and sell it during the seven difficult years, Egypt has amassed enormous wealth. In order to survive, people both within and outside the country sold everything of value to the Egyptian rulers in exchange for food. But not so very long after the death of Joseph

the people of Israel begin to be treated as slaves.

The people of Israel suffer increasing hardship. Finally Pharaoh orders all new-born Israelite boys to be killed so that the people of Israel will die out. According to Josephus, Moses, rich in wisdom and knowledge, saves the Egyptians when the Ethiopians force their way into the whole of Egypt. But as soon as Moses has rescued them they look for a pretext to kill him. Moses makes a serious mistake, flees and things become worse for the people of Israel. The new Pharaoh (figure 269) sitting on the throne of Egypt will have many opportunities to allow the people of Israel to depart. The struggle between good and evil will become increasingly intense. Moses is prepared for this, not by his 40 years as heir to the throne and general at the court, but by his 40 years in the desert as a shepherd.

According to the bible text, the assignment is given to Moses, and Moses is once again in Egypt, this time on the Lord's commission.

Figure 269: This pharaoh is Thutmosis IV. According to the hypothesis of this book, it was Thutmosis IV that was the ruler of Egypt during the time of the Exodus. See the earlier figure 245.

22. DOES PHARAOH ALLOW THE PEOPLE OF ISRAEL TO DEPART?

Moses and Aaron go to Pharaoh as the Lord told them. The following converstion is carried on:

"And afterward Moses and Aaron went in, and told Pharaoh, 'Thus saith the LORD God of Israel, "Let my people go, that they may hold a feast unto me in the wilderness."' And Pharaoh said, 'Who is the LORD, that I should obey his voice to let Israel go? I know not the LORD, neither will I let Israel go.'

And they said, 'The God of the Hebrews hath met with us: let us go, we pray thee, three days' journey into the desert, and sacrifice unto the LORD our God; lest he fall upon us with pestilence, or with the sword.' And the king of Egypt said unto them, 'Wherefore do ye, Moses and Aaron, let the people from their works? Get you unto your burdens.'

And Pharaoh said, 'Behold, the people of the land now are many, and ye make them rest from their burdens.' And Pharaoh commanded the same day the taskmasters of the people, and their officers, saying, 'Ye shall no more give the people straw to make brick, as heretofore: let them go and gather straw for themselves.

And the tale of the bricks, which they did make heretofore, ye shall lay upon them; ye shall not diminish ought thereof: for they be idle; therefore they cry, saying, "Let us go and sacrifice to our God." Let there more work be laid upon the men, that they may labor therein; and let them not regard vain words.'" (Ex. 5:1-9)

The officers force the people of Israel to collect their own straw for making bricks and they spread out all over Egypt to look for straw. But the quota must be filled nontheless, in spite of all the extra work, and they are hit and beaten. Moses is in despair. His own people curse him, and he has only done what the Lord called him to do. Moses turns to the Lord, and the Lord answers:

"Then the LORD said unto Moses, 'Now shalt thou see what I will do to Pharaoh: for with a strong hand shall he let them go, and with a strong hand shall he drive them out of his land.'" (Ex. 6:1)

"And God spake unto Moses, and said unto him, 'I am the LORD: And I appeared unto Abraham, unto Isaac, and unto Jacob, by the name of God Almighty, but by my name JEHOVAH was I not known to them. And I have also established my covenant with them, to give them the land of Canaan, the land of their pilgrimage, wherein they were strangers.

Figure 270: Traditional production of clay bricks according to ancient Egyptian traditions. The raw material is straw mixed with clay, which is then dried in the sun.

And I have also heard the groaning of the children of Israel, whom the Egyptians keep in bondage; and I have remembered my covenant. Wherefore say unto the children of Israel, "I am the LORD, and I will bring you out from under the burdens of the Egyptians, and I will rid you out of their bondage, and I will redeem you with a stretched out arm, and with great judgments:

And I will take you to me for a people, and I will be to you a God: and ye shall know that I am the LORD your God, which bringeth you out from under the burdens of the Egyptians. And I will bring you in unto the land, concerning which I did swear to give it to Abraham, to Isaac, and to Jacob; and I will give it you for an heritage: I am the LORD."'" (Ex. 6:2-8)

Moses and the Lord often have long discussions, and often Moses resists while the Lord gives him knowledge, power to perform miracles and a leadership, which means that Moses himself is weak and the Lord is strong. Moses has not only Pharaoh and the whole of Egypt against him, but his own people are very critical because conditions are increasingly difficult for them under Pharaoh's terror. Pharaoh refuses stubbornly and contemptuously to release the people of Israel.

23. What happens in Egypt?

In all, Pharaoh was given ten opportunities to release the people of Israel:

23.1 The actions of Pharaoh

1. When Moses and Aaron stood before Pharaoh and showed him the sign with the staff that became a serpent: Pharaoh did not listen to them (Ex. 7:13).
2. When all the water in Egypt was turned to blood. Pharaoh turned away and went home, and did not care (Ex. 7:23). The water tasted very bitter to the Egyptians, but tasted normal to the people of Israel.
3. When the frogs covered Egypt: Pharaoh said that Moses should ask the Lord to remove the frogs and then Pharaoh would let the people go. Moses prayed to the Lord, and the next day all the frogs died. Then Pharaoh went back on his promise (Ex. 8:8-9, 15).
4. When the mosquitoes were everywhere in Egypt: "This is God's finger," say Pharaoh's magicians, but Pharaoh did not listen (Ex. 8:19).
5. When the flies swarmed over Egypt: "I will let you go," says Pharaoh, but when Moses asked the Lord to remove the flies, Pharaoh went back on his promise (Ex. 8:32). There were no swarms of flies in Goshen where the people of Israel lived.
6. When the cattle suffered from the plague: But Pharaoh did not release the people of Israel (Ex. 9:7). The plague did not affect Goshen.
7. When everything living suffered from abscesses and blisters. But Pharaoh did not listen to Moses (Ex. 9:12). Abscesses and blisters did not affect the area of Goshen.
8. When violent hailstorms fell on Egypt: Everything living that was out of doors was killed. Pharaoh said that he had sinned and that it is the Lord who is righteous. Pharaoh promised that they would be allowed to leave the country, but even this time Pharaoh broke his promise after Moses asked the Lord to stop sending the hail (Ex. 9:27-28, 34-35). The hail did not fall on Goshen.
9. When locusts covered Egypt: After this Pharaoh offered to allow only men to leave Egypt, but Moses did not accept this. Locusts covered Egypt when Moses stretched out his hand at the Lord's command. Pharaoh repented, and said that he had sinned against both Moses and the Lord. Once again Pharaoh begged Moses to remove the plague. Moses prayed to the Lord and the locusts disappeared. Pharaoh went back on his promise yet again (Ex. 10:16-17, 20).
10. When thick darkness settled over Egypt for three days: Pharaoh promised that they would be allowed to leave the country, but without their cattle. Moses did not agree to this, so Pharaoh said that Moses was not to come into his presence again, otherwise he would be killed (Ex. 10:28-29). Darkness did not descend on Goshen.

Ten times Pharaoh was thus given the opportunity to let the people of Israel go out into the desert to worship God. Pharaoh did not listen and/or gave a promise which he broke time and time again. Pharaoh was informed beforehand about these disasters, but still allowed them to happen.

23.2. WERE THERE NATURAL CAUSES BEHIND THESE EVENTS?

Possibly one can think of natural explanations for all these disasters. The following point to the fact that this could not have been the case:

a) Pharaoh's own magicians believed that it was the Lord's doing, and they were the last people to believe in the Lord, the God of the Hebrews (Ex. 8:19, 10:7).

b) Everything that happened, happened on the Lord's command, from one day to the next. No natural ecological changes occur so quickly.

c) The water which turned to blood could have been a reddish algae bloom, even if the explanation sounds a little far-fetched. However it so happened that all water was affected (algae blooms are not found in wells and pots). Furthermore, according to Josephus the water tasted bitter and gave the Egyptians stomach pains, but tasted normal to the Hebrews (JA 2/14:1). The text also says that the water became blood, and did not just taste bad and look like blood (Ex. 7:14-25). It is difficult to find a natural explanation for this.

Figure 271: The water of the River Nile turned to blood.

d) Seven days later Egypt suffered a plague of frogs, which covered the whole land. Frogs exist naturally but they live in or near water, and all the fish in the Nile died when the water changed to blood. The frogs should also have suffered from this poisoning if they and their spawn were there. Only seven days later everywhere was crawling with frogs, all over Egypt. One day later all the frogs except those in the Nile died. At the same time the water was completely restored. These are not natural processes. (Ex. 8:1-15)

e) The swarms of mosquitoes all over the country could perhaps be explained by saying that they came from the rotting frogs. The problem is that mosquitoes lay their eggs in water, larvae develop which later become mosquitoes. In order for there to be such enormous swarms of mosquitoes there must already be enormous numbers of female mosquitoes to lay the eggs (and this is not so according to the text). Moreover. we must not forget that all the water was poisoned. It is hard to explain the swarms of mosquitoes as a natural phenomenon. (Ex. 8:16-19)

f) On the other hand, the flies could well have come from all the frog corpses since flies willingly lay their eggs in dead animals. An abundant supply of nourishment for the eggs could give rise to an explosion of flies. The problem is that Goshen (the Hebrews' land in Egypt) also had dead frogs but no flies. Moses had said that this would be the case. Furthermore, every single fly disappears at one sweep. It is not easy to find natural explanations of this either (Ex 8:20-30).

g) The plague which attacked the cattle could be a natural disease. Different illnesses caused by virus or bacteria are usually species-specific i.e. one species is affected, while another is untouched. Here was a disease which caused boils on horses, asses, camels, cows and sheep. All this happened simultaneously (it happened in one day), and not one animal in Goshen dies, while the animals of the Egyptians are badly hit. This does not tally with normal diseases among animals (Ex. 9:1-7).

h) Next, both humans and animals were troubled with abscesses and blisters.

This could have been a natural disease although it is rather strange that both animals and humans were affected. The remarkable thing is that the people of Israel were not affected. Here again we have an illness which deviates from what we regard as normal. For example, it is difficult to imagine a virus which attacks cows and Egyptians but not Hebrews. Nor did the Egyptians connect this to normality, but blamed it on Moses' command that this was to be (Ex. 9:8-12).

i) Hail occurs naturally more or less all over the world. Special weather conditions are necessary with rain and upwinds. The drops of water are blown upwards and freeze to ice at high altitudes, then fall down as hail. If the upwinds are very strong the hailstones can can be blown upwards several times, becoming larger until they become too heavy for the wind to hold up and they fall down to the ground. Hail often occurs during the warm season of the year (it is spring in Egypt when this happens). In this case, the hail fell in Egypt but not in Goshen. This could be completely natural since hailshowers are often very localised in nature. That Moses on the previous day said this would happen could be coincidence, or it would have been a very qualified meteorological guess. That, as Moses said, it would be the worst hailstorm in the history of Egypt is not easy to predict. Many believed Moses and took both cattle and servants inside. The hailstorm is described as absolutely unbelievable. Everything outside on the ground, crops, people and livestock were beaten down. Even the trees were shattered. The remarkable thing was the size of the hailstones (figure 272), the fact that the whole of Egypt was affected (and not just a limited area), that Goshen was not affected, that Moses predicted it all and later, by stretching out his hands, brought it to an end at once. It was definitely no ordinary hailstorm (Ex. 9:13-35).

Figure 272: Hail can be very big. Now and then hail grows to a very large size. If hail reaches the size shown it can destroy anything in its way.

j) Swarms of locusts occur naturally in the region and they come suddenly to affect a region, if the places where they breed are not under control. Even before the swarms of locusts descended on Egypt, Pharaohs counsellors were desperate. They realised what Moses could achieve on the Lord's orders, and the country was laid increasingly in ruins. But Pharaoh was obstinate, and so Moses predicted it would happen the following day. The swarms of locusts were unimaginable. The ground could not be seen because of all the locusts, and they filled all the houses. Later, when Pharaoh in desperation begged Moses to remove them, Moses prayed to the Lord and a mighty wind came which took away every single locust in Egypt and blew them out into the Red Sea. This is not the normal behaviour of swarms of locusts (Ex. 10:1-20).

k) Later, darkness covered the whole country. We know about eclipses, but they only reduce the sunlight for a moment, and do not give compact darkness. This was a matter of thick darkness for three days throughout the land, except in Goshen! It was light where the people of Israel lived. What could be a natural explanation of such a phenomenon as this? (Ex. 10:21-29)

l) Added to this are the strange events immediately preceding the Exodus, and the entire Exodus with its remarkable events. More of this in the following chapters.

m) In addition to this, that all these incredible events occured after Moses gave the order for them, and that everything happened immediately and disappeared just as quickly when Moses asked the Lord to remove the plague, is difficult to explain, to say the least. To suppose that all these events happened by chance in the order in which they occurred is statistically unlikely.

There can be no other conclusion than: either everything is a fabrication or everything happened exactly as it is described.

24. The Ipuwer papyrus

Are there any other sources concerning these disasters which Egypt experienced? There are several reasons why there should be very little information regarding these events. They happened approximately 3450 years ago and there are not many documents preserved from that time. Furthermore, there were two different sorts of people who could write. Only a limited élite in the country were privileged in being able to write, and this important education was probably given to the eldest son (the firstborn). We know from the biblical texts that all firstborn Egyptians died at the Exodus of the people of Israel. If one was not a scribe because one was firstborn then one was a scribe because one was in service with important people in Egypt anyway. These important people belonged to the ruling class as administrators or military officers. The entire Egyptian army with its officers and lower ranks that followed the people of Israel went down in the Red Sea. Of those who remained in Egypt the scribes either had no-one for whom to work or, more probably, the country was in complete chaos.

If a country suffers from a great disaster in nature or extensive warfare or something similar, the most important thing is to survive and not to document different events. In addition it may be noted that the whole course of events was hardly something to be proud of. And thus we have a political/historical reason for those in power later on to surround this crisis with silence. To these reasons can be added a psychological reason. Very few leaders (perhaps not even one) confess to defeat. We can see this in what happens today, when it is quite clear that a country has lost a war. But for his own people the Leader points to total defeat as a victory.

24.1. An ancient papyrus

Although there are many reasons for not finding any documentation of the dramatic course of events in Egypt, nontheless the question remains whether there is any written record.

There is a document which is probably a description of these events, which Egypt had to experience before the people of Israel were allowed to leave. It is an ancient papyrus document from Egypt. The document was written during the 19th dynasty, the dynasty that took over shortly after the events of the Exodus. The papyrus document is called "Admonitions of Ipuwer" and is 347 cm long (42). The Ipuwer document is one long description of a society in total crisis. It has more the character of a poetic description, with many repetitions, than of a news report.

It is debatable whether this is a description of actual events, or merely a fictitious story. One reason that it is said to be fiction, is that the country (Egypt) is suffering total disaster while the slaves have become rich with the wealth of their former owners.

Based on the biblical texts this is exactly what happens when all the slaves (the entire people of Israel) take with them all imaginable riches as gifts from the wealthy Egyptians, while the Egyptian upper class has either perished in the Red Sea or remains at home in a situation that can only be described as one of total disaster. According to the biblical texts precisely this argument, which is put forward as an argument against the text describing an event that really happened, is an argument for this text describing the disaster that befell Egypt.

The Bible tells of the wealth of the slaves (the people of Israel) immediately after the disasters in Egypt:

"And the Egyptians were urgent upon the people, that they might send them out of the land in haste; for they said, 'We be all dead men.' And the people took their dough before it was leavened, their kneading-troughs being bound up in their clothes upon their shoulders. And the children of Israel did according to the word of Moses; and they borrowed of the Egyptians jewels of silver, and jewels of gold, and raiment. And the Lord gave the people favour in the sight of the Egyptians, so that they lent unto them such things as they required. And they spoiled the Egyptians." (Ex. 12:33-36)

Figure 273: Treasures of gold were given to the Hebrews by the Egyptians.

From later events at Mount Sinai we know that this people of slaves had silver, gold cups, finest materials and yarn, precious stones, incense and many other things of great financial value.

24.2. INTERESTING NOTES OF THE IPUWER PAPYRUS

The Ipuwer document consists of a 3.5 m long roll of papyrus, with a lamentation over the situation in Egypt. With the exception of several brief sections which have been damaged, the document is intact and readable. In this long document there are a number of lines which are of particular interest (42).

1. "Let us go plunder", "The mayor of the city goes unescorted".

There is no police force if one can plunder. The military were the police of those days. The Bible describes how the entire army was destroyed.

"There remained not so much as one of them." (Ex. 14:28)

2. "Foreigners have become people everywhere".

The people of Israel, who were foreigners to the Egyptians, increased so greatly that for a time Pharaoh had all newborn boys executed in order to reduce the rate of growth.

"And the people multiplied and waxed very mighty". (Ex. 1:20)

3. "Foreigners are skilled in the works of the Delta".

The people of Israel lived in the delta region, were foreigners and were put to work making bricks, building and in different ways doing work for the Egyptians. (Ex. 5)

4. "What the ancestors foretold has happened".

Joseph, who was second in command in Egypt approximately 260 years earlier, had foreseen that the people of Israel would leave Egypt and this is also mentioned as a promise from the Lord in several biblical texts. According to the Bible, at his death (which must have been an important, well-known occasion in Egypt considering Joseph's position there for about 80 years) Joseph says:

"I die, and God will surely visit you, and bring you out of this land unto the land which he sware to Abraham, to Isaac and to Jacob. And Joseph took an oath of the children of Israel, saying: 'God will surely visit you and ye shall carry up my bones from hence.' So Joseph died, being an hundred and ten years old. And they embalmed him, and he was put in a coffin in Egypt." (Gen. 50:24-26)

So the Exodus was foretold by the minister of state of Egypt.

5. "We don't know what has happened in the land".

When the plagues fall on Egypt, Pharaoh's magicians say to him:

"This is the finger of God" (Ex. 8:19).

By this they probably meant that it was beyond their comprehension and control. Pharaoh and his magicians had good control of all the Egyptian gods otherwise, not least as Pharaoh himself was regarded as an incarnated god (the sun god).

6. "Poor men have become men of wealth", "Gold, lapis lazuli, silver and turquoise, carnelian, amethyst, ibht-stone ... Are strung on the necks of female slaves", "Gold is lacking"

At the Exodus the poor, enslaved people of Israel took with them a large part of the Egyptians' wealth (Figures 273-275).

"And they borrowed of the Egyptians jewels of silver, and jewels of gold, and raiment. And the Lord gave the people favour in the sight of the Egyptians, so that they lent them such things as they required. And they spoiled the Egyptians." (Ex. 12:35-36)

This people of slaves had silver, gold cups, finest material and yarn, precious stones (including the sorts mentioned by Ipuwer), incense and many other things of high, financial value. This is related in the Bible when the people of Israel had arrived at Mount Sinai (Ex. 25:1-9, 11, 17, 24, 29, 31; 26:1, 6, 7, 11, 14, 19, 25; 28: 15-28 etc.)

Figures 274, 275: Treasures were given to the Hebrews. These were made of carnelian and turquoise, as can be seen in these photographs of ancient Egyptian jewellery.

7. "The river is blood"

This is an extraordinary comment. Merely stating that the Nile is full of blood, is a statement that is not found in every text. Furthermore it is exactly what the biblical text mentions as one of the hardships which affects Egypt.

"And Moses and Aaron did as the Lord commanded. He lifted up the rod and smote the waters that were in the river, in the sight of Pharaoh, and in the sight of his servants. And all the waters that were in the river were turned to blood." (Ex. 7:20)

It is also worthy of note that Ipuwer does not say that the river looked like blood, but was blood. This is exactly as the Bible text explain the situation (Ex. 7:20).

8. "There's blood everywhere, no shortage of death".

This comment that there was blood everywhere can have bearing on two things. Firstly, mentioned above, that all the water was turned to blood according to the biblical text. But it can also refer to the extremely fierce hailstorm which kills everything living that is out-of-doors. The latter is perhaps more likely since it also says in the Ipuwer text that there were large numbers of dead. The Bible tells about the hailstorm:

"And Moses stretched forth his rod toward heaven, and the Lord sent thunder and hail, and the fire ran along the ground. And the Lord rained hail upon the land of Egypt. So there was hail, and fire mingled with the hail, very grievous, such as there was none like it in all the land of Egypt since it became a nation. And the hail smote throughout all the land of Egypt all that

was in the field, both man and beast." (Ex. 9:23-25)

9. "Many dead are buried in the river".

The comment that many were buried in the Nile, may imply that so many people died in the plagues that it was impossible to bury them all, so they were thrown into the Nile. If this was the case, it was a marked deviation from the usual way of handling and burying the dead and must indicate that it was an exceptional situation with a large number of dead. The Bible relates that in just one of the plagues at least one in each family dies (every first-born). (Ex. 11:4-10)

10. "Exhausted are materials for every kind of craft", "Lacking are grain, charcoal, irtyw, m3w-wood, nwt-wood, brushwood", "Trees are felled, branches stripped"

After the disaster in Egypt there is a scarcity of almost everything, this section shows that crops were scarce and raw materials for craftsmen, especially wood (the signs quoted show that a translation has not been found for the species that Ipuwer mentions). Trees have fallen down or been knocked down and from the trees that remain standing the branches have been knocked off. The Bible tells of similar consequences to the hailstorm mentioned earlier, which was such as is seldom seen.

"And the hail smote every herb of the field and brake every tree of the field." (Ex. 9:25)

11. "Food is lacking", "Great hunger and suffering", "Ladies say, we want to eat", "Women are barren, none conceive", "Their bodies suffer in rags", "The storehouse is bare".

These quotations from Ipuwer show that there was famine. Food is lacking, people suffer and starve, the stocks are exhausted, so the situation is incredibly difficult. The women may be childless because the children have died, or that starvation has made the women infertile and so unable to have children. This is a probable consequence of the disasters that fall on Egypt, described in the book of Exodus chapters 7 - 12.

12. "See he who slept wifeless found a noblewoman", "See, noblewomen go hungry".

This comment that upper class women are hungry and seek the company of the lower classes indicates two things. That which provided their income is no more, and the upper class men are no more. The upper classes in Egypt mainly consisted of soldiers, officers and high-ranking civil servants seconded to Pharaoh. The Bible reports that the entire Egyptian army perished (Ex. 14:26-29), i.e. a large group, specifically of men, disappears (around 250 000) in addition to what the entire population has suffered.

13. "Scribes are slain, their writings are stolen", "Their books are destroyed".

The chaos which prevails in Egypt also implies a hard blow to the whole of Egyptian culture. Scribes are killed and their work scattered in the wind. This may be a reason why, in spite of everything, there is not very much written about these disasters. The art of writing was a privilege of the few in high positions in Egypt.

14. "One says 'woe' to the place of secrets", "What shall we do about it? All is ruin!" "Gone is what yesterday was seen", "See now, the land is deprived of kingship", "See, all the ranks, they are not in their place, like a herd that roams without a herdsman".

These secret places which were despised refer to the gods worshipped, the wisemen (priesthood) of that time, the secret rituals, the embalming of the dead and the godlike characters that the Pharaohs represented. That which controlled the whole of Egyptian life, now shows itself incapable of standing firm during the crisis which the country is suffering. The population shows contempt which leads to disorder and chaos. It seems as though the entire leadership of the country has disappeared or is not functioning. The whole of the Ipuwer text is about this chaos, which means that in general nothing functions in Egypt. It must have been something very forceful that could crush the super power of that era so completely.

15. "If I knew where god is I would serve him"

This is a strange comment. The Egyptians knew very well where their gods were, in which guise they appeared, which areas of responsibility they had and how one made sacrifices to them. But the Ipuwer text does not ask for these gods. The Egyptians knew that all the people of Israel worshipped the "One God", and they were obviously no longer in doubt concerning whether it was the gods of Egypt who had the power or whether it was the One God.
   The biblical texts tell about all the good that Joseph and the people of Israel did in Egypt. Not least the fact that Joseph saved the whole country of Egypt and gave it great wealth. After a time the Egyptians enslave the people of Israel and later, in spite of being given 10 chances to let the people of Israel leave Egypt, when the biblical texts tell of the anger of the One God expressed in very extraordinary events, they force the people of Israel to stay. They cannot hold them back and soon the Exodus begins, the great migration.
   Finally the entire army of the super power perishes when they try to take back a people of slaves led by a man, Moses, who is only equipped with a shepherd's staff. It is completely understandable that at last the Egyptians realise they have challenged the One God, and their gods were of no help in the struggle. One can really hear the despair in the text. "If I only knew where to find the One God I would serve him."

24.3. DATING OF THE IPUWER PAPYRUS

Ipuwer was a scribe who most probably documented an event that actually occurred. Since Ipuwer is said to have worked during the 19th dynasty (42), this description may well concern events at the end of the 18th dynasty, which also influenced and probably led to the change which is described as a new dynasty, the 19th dynasty. The event, or events were a disaster for Egypt and their consequences tally well with the descriptions in the Bible.

The Exodus, with the events described in that chapter, occurred around 1446 BC according to the biblical texts, which corresponds to the end of the 18th dynasty. The Bible's chronology is described in chapter 44.

25. HOW IS ISRAEL SAVED FROM THE DEATHS OF ALL THE FIRSTBORN?

The Lord speaks to Moses and Moses speaks to Pharaoh:

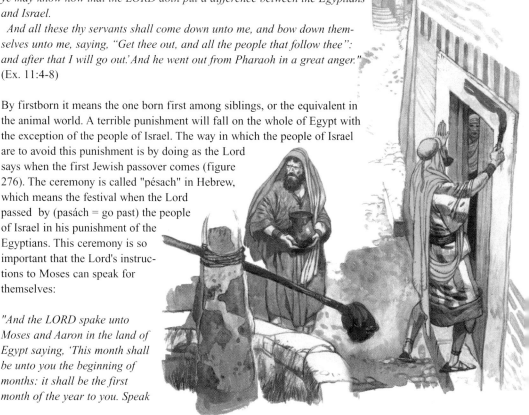

Figure 276: According to the biblical text, the Lord passed over (passover) each house that celebrated passover when he struck the land of Egypt with the death of the first-born.

"And Moses said, 'Thus saith the LORD, "About midnight will I go out into the midst of Egypt: And all the firstborn in the land of Egypt shall die, from the first born of Pharaoh that sitteth upon his throne, even unto the firstborn of the maidservant that is behind the mill; and all the firstborn of beasts."

And there shall be a great cry throughout all the land of Egypt, such as there was none like it, nor shall be like it any more. But against any of the children of Israel shall not a dog move his tongue, against man or beast: that ye may know how that the LORD doth put a difference between the Egyptians and Israel.

And all these thy servants shall come down unto me, and bow down themselves unto me, saying, "Get thee out, and all the people that follow thee": and after that I will go out.' And he went out from Pharaoh in a great anger." (Ex. 11:4-8)

By firstborn it means the one born first among siblings, or the equivalent in the animal world. A terrible punishment will fall on the whole of Egypt with the exception of the people of Israel. The way in which the people of Israel are to avoid this punishment is by doing as the Lord says when the first Jewish passover comes (figure 276). The ceremony is called "pésach" in Hebrew, which means the festival when the Lord passed by (pasách = go past) the people of Israel in his punishment of the Egyptians. This ceremony is so important that the Lord's instructions to Moses can speak for themselves:

"And the LORD spake unto Moses and Aaron in the land of Egypt saying, 'This month shall be unto you the beginning of months: it shall be the first month of the year to you. Speak

ye unto all the congregation of Israel, saying, "In the tenth day of this month they shall take to them every man a lamb, according to the house of their fathers, a lamb for an house: And if the household be too little for the lamb, let him and his neighbor next unto his house take it according to the number of the souls; every man according to his eating shall make your count for the lamb.

Your lamb shall be without blemish, a male of the first year: ye shall take it out from the sheep, or from the goats: And ye shall keep it up until the fourteenth day of the same month: and the whole assembly of the congregation of Israel shall kill it in the evening. And they shall take of the blood, and strike it on the two side posts and on the upper door post of the houses, wherein they shall eat it.

And they shall eat the flesh in that night, roast with fire, and unleavened bread; and with bitter herbs they shall eat it. Eat not of it raw, nor sodden at all with water, but roast with fire; his head with his legs, and with the purtenance thereof."

And ye shall let nothing of it remain until the morning; and that which remaineth of it until the morning ye shall burn with fire. And thus shall ye eat it; with your loins girded, your shoes on your feet, and your staff in your hand; and ye shall eat it in haste: it is the LORD's passover.

For I will pass through the land of Egypt this night, and will smite all the firstborn in the land of Egypt, both man and beast; and against all the gods of Egypt I will execute judgment: I am the LORD. And the blood shall be to you for a token upon the houses where ye are: and when I see the blood, I will pass over you, and the plague shall not be upon you to destroy you, when I smite the land of Egypt.

And this day shall be unto you for a memorial; and ye shall keep it a feast to the LORD throughout your generations; ye shall keep it a feast by an ordinance for ever.'" (Ex. 12:1-14)

Figure 277: The people of Israel are ready to leave Egypt. The powerful Egypt symbolised by the pyramids has severe problems at this time. Northeast of the pyramids in Giza the people of Israel are organized in their families and tribes, and are ready to go into Sinai as soon as orders are given.

"Thus did all the children of Israel; as the LORD commanded Moses and Aaron, so did they. And it came to pass the selfsame day, that the LORD did bring the children of Israel out of the land of Egypt by their armies." (Ex. 12:50-51)

26. How does the Exodus begin?

Egypt is now a country in profound crisis. In addition to all the plagues with poisoned water, invasions of frogs, flies and mosquitoes, the country has been badly damaged by a number of disasters. The plague has killed a large part of the livestock and the whole population has suffered from abscesses and blisters. Hail has broken or killed everything that was out of doors and then there was an invasion of locusts. Three days of darkness came as a sign from the Lord followed by the death of all the firstborn among humans and animals on one and the same night.

26.1. PHAROAH ALLOWS THE HEBREWS TO LEAVE EGYPT

Only then, after ten opportunities to change his mind, does Pharaoh allow the people of Israel to leave Egypt.

"And it came to pass, that at midnight the LORD smote all the firstborn in the land of Egypt, from the firstborn of Pharaoh that sat on his throne unto the firstborn of the captive that was in the dungeon; and all the firstborn of cattle. And Pharaoh rose up in the night, he, and all his servants, and all the Egyptians; and there was a great cry in Egypt; for there was not a house where there was not one dead.

And he called for Moses and Aaron by night, and said, 'Rise up, and get you forth from among my people, both ye and the children of Israel; and go, serve the LORD, as ye have said. Also take your flocks and your herds, as ye have said, and be gone; and bless me also.' And the Egyptians were urgent upon the people, that they might send them out of the land in haste; for they said, 'We be all dead men.'" (Ex. 12:29-33)

It is more than this. They are not only allowed to leave Egypt, the Egyptians do everything they can so that the Israelites will leave Egypt. In addition the people of Israel receive gifts in the form of clothing, silver and gold. The Egyptians give them whatever they ask (Ex. 12:35-36). This can be regarded as payment for all the good that Joseph and Moses have done and payment for all the work that the whole Hebrew nation has had to do as slaves.

26.2. EVERYTHING GOES VERY FAST

Pharaoh must have been close to Goshen (Rameses) since he can call Moses and Aaron to him the same night that this disaster hits Egypt. Pharaoh must at least have been in Memphis, the northern capital of Egypt, but may also have been further north in some other city e.g. Heliopolis, the seat of the high priest in Egypt.

Moses was to see to it that all the people of Israel were ready, that they had prepared the sacrifice (the passover, Ex. 12:1-14, 43-51) and that they would be ready to leave everything in a hurry. The Bible gives the date of this event, the fourteenth day in Nisan (Ex. 12:16), which most certainly was the date since this is still the time of the Jewish passover today, 3450 years later. The month of Nisan is during the period of March-April. Josephus also indicates a few details about how Moses had prepared for the Exodus. Moses divided the people into their twelve tribes, and assembled them within one area (JA 2/14:6).

Figure 278: Pharaoh Thutmosis IV, who according to the hypothesis of this book was the pharaoh at the time of the Exodus. Probably his name was Thutmosis IV as a co-ruler, and Amenhotep III as ruler and pharaoh.

The people of Israel are now completely prepared to begin the Exodus. Moses has used his military experience and organised the people of Israel in a competent way. Each clan leader for Israel's twelve tribes then organises his tribe according to kinship and families. They have also prepared certain equipment such as tents. Most likely the people of Israel were assembled in the eastern part of Goshen close to the Egyptian border, which corresponds to the eastern part of the region of the Nile delta in north-eastern Egypt. The Bible names the place they left "the land of Rameses/-Goshen" (Ex. 12:37), the exact site of which is unknown. The organisation must have been effective because when the marching order comes the whole people of Israel, including all the livestock, are on the other side of the border within a day (Ex. 12:41, 51).

The Exodus, the great migration, has begun.

27. WHO DIED IN EGYPT?

The Bible text is clear regarding those who died in Egypt. That night before the Exodus began, all the firstborn died, i.e. the eldest in each family. The Bible is even more specific when it states:

"And it came to pass, that at midnight the LORD smote all the firstborn in the land of Egypt, from the firstborn of Pharaoh that sat on his throne unto the firstborn of the captive that was in the dungeon; and all the firstborn of cattle." (Ex. 12:29)

The Pharaoh who sat on the throne was not the firstborn as he survived that night (Ex. 12:30-32). According to the hypothesis in chapter 15 this Pharaoh was Amenhotep III. The son, the firstborn son of Amenhotep III was Tutankhamun, which among other things is confirmed by an inscription on the statue of a lion dedicated to the Soleb temple (37).

27.1. THE DEATH OF TUTANKHAMUN

Tutankhamun is remarkable in that one cannot understand how such a young heir to the throne (about 18 years old), who probably had achieved nothing of importance since he had not yet ascended the throne, received such an unprecedented burial. Book after book describes the discovery of the grave in 1922 and all the treasures, often gilded, which were in the grave. The main

Figure 279: All Egyptians, especially the leadership, were affected by the dramatic events at the start of the Exodus. The photograph probably shows the wife of Amenhotep IV from the royal court, with the mission to take over after the collapse of Egypt that followed the Exodus.

reason for all the attention given to Tutankhamun is that his grave was intact and had not been plundered. Nearly every grave has been robbed down through the years just because they contained so many treasures, or alternatively because successors have taken measures to reduce the importance of their predecessors and increase their own importance. (Figure 918)

So the first comment is that Tutankhamun's grave probably does not differ greatly from other graves of members of the reigning family, but it distinguishes itself by not having been robbed. That so much notice is taken of Tutankhamun has nothing to do with political achievement, a long reign, wars of conquest or anything similar but is simply due to the fact that his grave is one of the few that has not been plundered and that it is so lavishly decorated.

According to the hypothesis in this chapter, the scenario which takes place is that Amenhotep III ruled over a great, prosperous and mighty Egypt. As soon as he comes to power, perhaps already when he was still heir to the throne, building is begun on his burial chamber. The Pharaohs' burial chambers with their lavish contents took a long time to finish, and building a burial chamber was one of the important measures a Pharaoh took on coming to power. Amenhotep III, who reigned when things were flourishing, spent a lot on his intended grave and prepared everything well.

Then the events described as the Exodus in this book, the departure of the people of Israel, occur. On the last night all the firstborn die, including Amenhotep's firstborn son Tutankhamun (Ex. 12:29). Pharaoh himself sets off with his entire army to pursue the enslaved people of Israel and bring them back. When the whole of the Egyptian army has almost caught up with the people of Israel, it drowns in the Red Sea and there is not a single survivor, not even Amenhotep III who was leading his army (Ex. 14:26-28).

The Egyptian court then faces a situation where the reigning Pharaoh has drowned and disappeared, so cannot be buried in his lavishly prepared grave. On the other hand, the body of the heir to the throne is there, Tutankhamun for whom probably no grave has been prepared. It would then be easy to decide to let Tutankhamun have his father's grave. All that is personal to Tutankhamun is his own death mask and sarcophagus. This could be a probable explanation of the death of Tutankhamun and why he received such a lavish burial chamber. It is known that Tutankhamon was buried in a tomb that did not belong to him. One reference states the following: "The young king (Tutankhamun, authors comment) was buried in the tomb originally prepared for Ay in the Valley of Kings" (37), although no evidence mentions Ay specifically.

Tutankhamun's own deathmask is impressive, made of pure gold with turquoise insets and weighing about 10.3 kg. This beautiful handicraft is something of a modern symbol for Egypt (figure 280).

It is easy to understand that there was chaos at court. Both Pharaoh Amenhotep III and Tutankhamun, the heir to the throne, died within a couple of weeks.

Figure 280: The death mask of Tutankhamun made of pure gold (10.3 kg) and turquoise. Tutankhamun was buried at the same time of year as the events of the Exodus.

27.2. What happened in Egypt?

Can this scenario be verified in any way? Firstly it can be noted that the successors to the throne deviated from the usual pattern. Instead of members of the reigning family inheriting the throne, it is Ay, an older army officer and counsellor accedes as ruler. After a short time the 18th dynasty comes to an end. This in itself is a sign of the chaos there must have been in Egypt in connection with the Exodus. It is said that Ay hastily married Tutankhamun's wife, Ankhesenamun, so hastily that he is Pharaoh at the burial of Tutankhamun (43).

27.3. When did it all happen?

The biblical text specifies the exact date of the Exodys. It was the 14th day of the month when the people of Israel still celebrate their "pésach". Tutankhamun dies during the night following this day. This date is interesting, since it indicates so precisely a day in spring. Tutankhamun was decorated in many ways, among others with sophisticated and expensive wreathes of flowers. These wreathes were made from fresh plants and flowers as the leaves and parts of the plants have been bent in such a way that only fresh plants can be bent.

Tutankhamun's death was unexpected so it may be surmised that the floral wreathes were made in connection with his death. By determining the species of the flowers and fruits these wreathes were made of, and with information about when these flowers bloomed and bore fruit, it is possible to date the death and/or interment as being between the middle of March and the end of April (44). This strongly supports the hypothesis that Tutankhamun died at a time of year that was exactly, or at least very close to, the time of year of the Exodus.

27.4. A STRANGE LETTER

The person who bore the royal blood, the inheritance, was the royal wife of Amenhotep III, the Pharaoh who was drowned in the Red Sea, and who was the mother of the heir to the throne, Tutankhamun. There is a letter that is preserved in the so-called Tel-Amarna letters (61) sent by this widow of the Pharaoh to the Hittite king Suppiluliumas and preserved by the son of the latter in an inscription:

"...When the people of Misra (Egypt, authors comment) learned the destruction of Amqa, they were afraid, for to make matters worse their master, Bibhuria had just died and the widowed queen of Egypt sent an ambassador to my father and wrote to him these terms:

My husband is dead and I have no son. People say that you have many sons. If you send me one of your sons he will become my husband for it is repugnant to me to take one of my servants to husband. When my father learned this, he called together the council of the great: Since the most ancient times such a thing has never happened before.

He decided to send Hattu-Zittish, the chamberlain, Go, bring me information worthy of belief; While Hattu-Zittish was absent on the soil of Egypt, my father vanquished the city of Karchemish.... The ambassador of Egypt, the lord Hanis, came to him. Because my father had instructed Hattu-Zittish when he went to the country of Egypt as follows: Perhaps they have a prince, they may be trying to deceive me and do not really want one of my sons to reign over them; the Egyptian queen answered my father in a letter in these words;

Why do you say they are trying to deceive me? If I had a son, should I write to a foreign country in a manner humiliating to me and to my country? You do not believe me and you even say so to me! He who was my husband is dead and I have no son. Should I then perhaps take one of my servants and make of him my husband? I have written to no other country, I have written to you..."

Finally Suppiluliumas believes her and sends a son, it is not known what happened to him.

This letter is remarkable because Pharaoh Amenhotep III's widow says that her husband is dead (drowned in the Red Sea), she has no son (Tutankhamun died at the Exodus), and there are only servants left in the country (leaders, ministers, priests, officers drowned in the Red Sea). Bibhuria is probably a linguistic variation among the Hittites for "Neb-maat-Re", one of the names of Amenhotep III. Further, this excludes Tiy as being the widow since she had another son, Akhenaten.

27.5. The threat from the Hittites

At this period in time the Hittites are a potential threat to Egypt. There is every reason in the world for Egypt to hide for as long as possible the fact that the army has been destroyed. The countries existed in relative isolation from each other, it was desert land between them and there were still border posts guarding the borders. After a time, when there is a risk that the truth will leak out that there is no longer a great and mighty army, then this letter can be an invitation to create an alliance (through marriage) with the Hittites before they fully realise what has happened. Obviously the Hittites are surprised ("nothing like this has ever happened before") about the letter and send a messenger to look into the matter.

At the same time this is happening, the cities in Palestine which belong to Egypt are having problems. The Tel-Amarna letters show that among other things these cities were threatened by the Hittites. They begged the Pharaoh in Egypt to send troops, but as it says in one of the letters written during this period, "no help came". The situation was becoming untenable and Egypt was still incapable of sending troops. A strong Egypt with all its mighty army could easily have supported its subject cities in Palestine.

27.6. In summary

Altogether these events show that something dramatic occurred in Egypt at this time. These events were the beginning of the end for the 18th dynasty and include several different incidents which can be connected with each other; letters which state that only servants are left in the country; the time of and reason for Tutankhamun's death; and the absence of help for the cities subject to Egypt.

Similarities to the events described in the Ipuwer document are striking (chapter 24).

28. How numerous were the people of Israel at the time of the Exodus?

At the time of the Exodus the people of Israel were not simply a few families or kinsfolk. They were an entire people, a nation according to the Bible text. Some idea of size is given when the people of Israel leave Egypt:

"And the children of Israel journeyed from Rameses to Succoth, about six hundred thousand on foot that were men, beside children. And a mixed multitude went up also with them; and flocks, and herds, even very much cattle." (Ex. 12:37-38)

"Who formerly could have plundered Tunip without being plundered by Thutmose III? ...and there is no help for us. For 20 years we have been sending to our lord the king, the king of Egypt; but there has not come to us a word – no, not one!" (17) After the powerful Thutmose something happened that destroyed the super power of Egypt and left the colonies without support.

28.1. Different ways to estimate the total number of people

From this information one can estimate the total figure. Firstly about 600 000 men, according to the biblical text above. Equal numbers of both sexes are born, which gives us about 600 000 women. If we assume that there was an even age distribution, that the average length of life was 75 years, and that men were all over 20 years of age, this makes roughly a further 320 000 who are under 20 years. Then the total is just over 1.5 million people. Added to this we have what the Bible calls "a mixed multitude". If we assume that these individuals were one person per Hebrew family and that the 1 520 000 Hebrews consisted of families with an average of 10 people per family, then this multitude was about 150 000 individuals (probably a conservative estimate). Based on these assumptions the total population is about 1.7 million in number.

The estimate could be done in another way as follows: 600 000 men + 600 000 women makes 1.2 million. We also know in connection with Moses' birth that all newborn baby boys were thrown into the river during an unknown length of time. This gives a surplus of women depending on how long the period of time was when newborn boys were killed. If we assume that it lasted for 7-8 years, and that average life expectancy was as above, then there would be a 10% surplus of women or 60 000 individuals. Added to this were children (= did not carry arms), and we use the same number as above for this group, 320 000. If "a mixed multitude" were all sorts of people who just wanted to leave Egypt after all the misery suffered in the country, then it could have been a considerable number of people. If the people of Israel are around 1.6 million (0.6 + 0.6 + 0.06 + 0.32), and to this is added a group said to be large, then this group could be 10-20% of the people of Israel. In this case the total number of people leaving would be about 1.7 - 1.9 million.

The Egyptians were 1.5–5 million people at the time of Exodus (41). The Hebrews were not a part of the Egyptian society, they lived apart from the Egyptians as slaves.

28.2. Are there more references to the number of people?

There is a general reference to the fact that they were numerous when God calls Moses to lead the people of Israel to a "large land" (Ex. 3:7-10). Egypt is a large country and the Nile delta a very large area so if a population group needs more space, it must be a numerous people.

There are a number of biblical texts that suggest - directly or indirectly - that the people of Israel were numerous. Some examples are:

◆ "Surely this great nation..." (Deut. 4:6).

◆ "For what nation is there so great..." (Deut. 4:7).

◆ Calculation of the population down to each family, at least three times (Ex. 38:26, Numb. 1:17-50,3:14-39 and 26:1-65).

◆ "...for every one that went to be numbered from twenty years old and upward, for six hundred thousand and three thousand and five hundred and fifty men." (Ex. 38:26).

◆ "...about six hundred thousand on foot that were men..." (Ex. 12:37).

◆ The whole army of the super power Egypt was needed to bring back the unarmed Hebrews (Ex. 1-15).

◆ The Hebrews had victories over countries, kings and armies. One example is described in Numb. 21:21-35.

◆ Only the elite unit of the most brave Hebrew soldiers was 30 000 men (Josh. 8:3).

◆ Following the Exodus, the Hebrews had victory over 31 kings and their armies under the leadership of Joshua (Josh. 12:7-24).

◆ Huge war trophies were easily absorbed among the Hebrews. In one case this consisted of 675 000 sheep, 72 000 cattle, 61 000 donkeys and 32 000 unmarried females. In addition, there was jewlery and 16 750 shekels of gold, which corresponds to approximately 235 kg of gold (Numb. 31:25-54).

◆ The people of Israel needed a huge area of land for the tribes. The area is described in Numb. 34 and roughly corresponds to todays Israel.

◆ Only one tribe, and one of the smallest, the Levites that served the tabernacle and were not farmers or shepherds, received 48 cities as their share in Canaan. Each city was, with its surroundings outside the wall (for the cattle) approximately 1 x 1 km (Numb. 35:1-8).

These are some examples. When reading the books of Moses after the settlement in Egypt, the end of Genesis, Exodus, Leviticus, Numbers and Deuteronomy, every page is filled with information indicating a great number of people.

28.3. ESTIMATES OF THE NUMBER OF PEOPLE

Estimates can be arrived at in different ways, but the question is whether the number of people can be verified in some way.

Two years after the Exodus a population census was carried out (Numb. 1:17-50). During those two years more children may have been born but on the other hand several things happened which probably reduced the population. This was the actual departure from Egypt, the lack of food and water on a number of occasions and extensive warfare. This means that it is likely that the census two years later showed a lesser population than that at the time of the Exodus.

Added to this was the tribe of Levi, who were not warriors but whose task was to look after the tabernacle. The census of these included all males aged one month or more (Numb. 3:14-39).

We can now make the following assumption regarding the above population figures (Tables 8-10), which were based on a very accurate census of the population:

Table 8. The numbers refer to fighting men over the age of 20 years two years after the crossing of the Red Sea and shown according to the tribe to which they belonged (Numb. 1:17-50).

Tribe	Number
Reuben	46 500
Simeon	59 300
Gad	45 560
Judah	74 600
Issachar	54 400
Zebulun	57 400
Joseph	40 500
Manasseh	32 200
Benjamin	35 400
Dan	62 700
Asher	41 500
Naphtali	53 400
Total	603 550

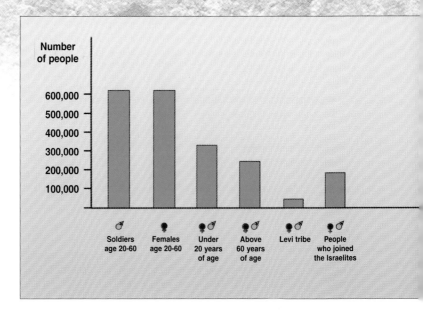

Number of people

600,000 —
500,000 —
400,000 —
300,000 —
200,000 —
100,000 —

| Soldiers age 20-60 | Females age 20-60 | Under 20 years of age | Above 60 years of age | Levi tribe | People who joined the Israelites |

Figure 281: The diagram shows the different sub-groups of people out of the total group that took part in the Exodus. The calculations are based on the biblical texts.

◆ The age for carrying weapons was up to 60 years of age (if this age was lower then it is an under-estimate).
◆ Average life expectancy was 75 years (they became very old, Joseph 110, Moses 120 and Jacob 147 years, to name but a few examples).
◆ An even age distribution.
   ◆ A normal distribution of the sexes (is an under-estimate).
   ◆ "A mixed multitude" corresponding to 10% of the people of Israel (may be much greater, a probable under-estimate).

The total compilation then agrees with Tables 8 to 10. The first estimates came to 1.7 - 1.9 million and the calculation based on the population census came to approximately 2 million. Naturally there are a number of uncertain factors e.g. how large a "mixed multitude" was, if there were other men of the right age who did not carry weapons, if there were more women than men because the Egyptians had killed all newborn boys during an unknown length of time, etc. These factors can give a higher population figure. An approximate figure based on calculations from a very accurate census of part of the population is 2 million.

The basis for these calculations in the biblical texts is very precise, includes many details, is thorough down to the individual family and is made twice during a two-year period. The uncertainty in calculating the total number of people lies in the fact that it is only men of a weapon-bearing age who are counted, and that an unspecified number of people other than the Hebrews ("a mixed multitude") accompanied them (figure 281).

Table 9. The number of men from the tribe of Levi. The census of these included all males older than 1 month (Numb. 3:14-39).

Tribe	Number
Gershon	7 500
Kohath	8 600
Merari	6 200
Total	22 300

The Bible gives further confirmation of the number (Ex. 38:26): it records that there were 603 550 after the Exodus "that went to be numbered, from twenty years old and upward".

The tremendous project to depart with the people of Israel is just as impressive if it were 500 000 or 2 million, but it is worth noting that those who took part in the Exodus were at least about 2 million, and in addition "flocks and herds and many cattle", according to several biblical texts. Just to accomplish this in a desert environment, in a great hurry, and without food for the journey is a miracle in itself. To accomplish this unarmed with the army of a great power on one's heels, must have been considered a completely hopeless enterprise by most people.

Table 10. Calculation of the total number of people based on the population census of fighting men two years after the Exodus (Numb. 1:17-50, 3:14-39).

Fighting men	603 550
Equal number of women	603 550
Under 20 years old	321 900
Over 60 years old	241 400
Levite men	22 300
Equal number of Levite women	22 300
Total number of Hebrews	1 815 000
A "mixed multitude"(assuming that they were 10% of the Hebrew population)	181 000
Total number	1 996 000

28.4. IS THE NUMBER OF PEOPLE REALISTIC IN RELATION TO GROWTH RATE?

The question is whether an estimated population of 2 million is realistic based on possible growth rates. When Jacob's family migrated to Egypt around the year 1706 BC they were 70 individuals (Gen. 46:27, Deut. 10:22) and the question then is whether it is realistic to think that they could have become about 2 million during the 260 years until the Exodus around the year 1446 BC.

The Bible states that they increased greatly and multiplied so that the land was filled with them (Ex. 1:7 and onwards). The more they were oppressed the more they increased (Ex. 1:12), and the people became very numerous (Ex. 1:20). This information, and the fact that the Bible maintains that the Lord granted them prosperity and wealth during the first eighty years (long life when many lived to over 100 years, and large families e.g. Joseph with his 12 siblings) indicate a high growth rate.

Today annual population growth varies from country to country, e.g. USA 1%, Germany 0.6%, Brazil 1.7% and India 1.9%. These figures are based on the yearly mean value during the period 1990-95 (45). In certain countries in South America annual population growth has been up to 3% (figure 282). Around 1990 countries south of the Sahara and in the Arab world had an

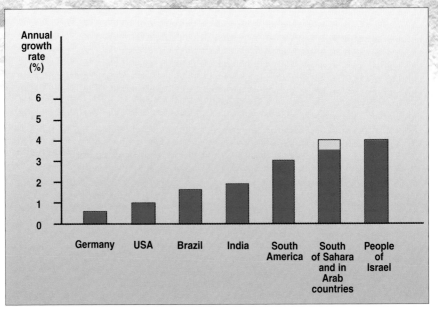

Figure 282: Annual growth rates in different countries, compared to the calculated growth rate of the Israelites at the time before the Exodus. In this calculation the total number at the Exodus was assumed to be 2 million. Since this population also consisted of "a great multitude" of other people the calculated growth rate of the Hebrews is over estimated in this diagram.

annual population growth of 3.5 - 4%. This means that the population doubles every 17 - 20 years. At the end of the 1980s global increase of the world's population was 1.7% annually (46).

The population growth of the people of Israel was very vigorous, since they were very long-lived. They also had the best conditions, at least during the first 80 years while Joseph lived and held his high position in Egypt. We can assume that the growth was over 3%, which South America had during the 1980s when conditions were relatively hard.

Then how numerous were the people of Israel if they were 70 individuals when they arrived in Egypt, and were there for 260 years before the Exodus? A calculation shows that this corresponds to an average annual growth of approximately 4%. This is a vigorous growth rate, which both the biblical texts and Josephus (JA 2/9:1) describe.

The number of people is realistic based on a vigorous annual population growth of approximately 4%, which corresponds to what we have in various parts of the world in modern times. In this figure of 4% is included the group called "a mixed multitude". A group who did not belong to the people of Israel but who accompanied them at the Exodus. This means that the rate of growth given is rather high, and should be reduced depending on how big one assumes this "mixed multitude" was.

28.5. ANOTHER INDICATOR OF THE NUMBER OF PEOPLE

Yet another factor supporting the size of the population is that the super power of that era, Egypt, mobilised its entire super power army of around 250 000 soldiers to bring the people of Israel back to Egypt. This would not have been needed with a little splinter group, but was definitely necessary with a whole people.

Different hypotheses which suggest that the people of Israel were a small group, must disregard a number of biblical texts with direct information about the number of people; a number of biblical texts and historical documents referring to the Hebrews as a great people; and two population censuses, one of which was very comprehensive (covering three chapters in the book of Numbers (Numb. 1-3) with details down to the size of the family) and another census (Ex. 38:26). These hypotheses must also disregard the fact that the super power of that era mobilises its entire army of a quarter of a million experienced, elite soldiers to bring back this unarmed people of exhausted slaves.

28.6. OTHER HYPOTHESES

There is some speculation that the number of individuals in each tribe was a certain number of units of a certain size, instead of the number stated in the text (40). If this were the case, it means the total number of men carrying arms would be around 5500 individuals. This argument falls down because if all these subtotals are added together, a total sum is arrived at which does not tally with the figures given in the Bible text.

The argument that 40500 men (indicating a part of the whole taken as an example from Numb. 2:19-24) could mean 40 units with a total of 500 men falls down because the text states that 40500 + 32200 + 35400 = 108100. With the proposed interpretation of these figures this would be 40 units with a total of 500 men + 32 units with a total of 200 men + 35 units with a total of 400 men, the total sum being 108 units with 1100 men. But this way of calculating does not tally with the total sum in the Bible which is 108100, which in this case would mean 108 units with a total of 100 men. When the biblical texts state the number of individuals (this too a part of the whole, Numb. 3:39) as being 22000, this would then mean that there were 22 units with a total of 0 men bearing weapons (according to this hypothesis).

The continued argumentation that the total sum is an error that was written in much later falls on several points. It suffices to name two of them.

1. Copying of texts was extremely careful, a single mistake and the whole copy was thrown away.
2. One completely disregards later events when first 3000 (Ex. 32:28) and then 14 700 were killed (Numb. 16:49). It is difficult to reconcile this with almost 18 000 killed of the 5500 available, and yet have the entire people more or less intact.

Another hypothesis claims that they could not have been more than perhaps 12 000 because there would not have been room for more than this to encamp at the traditional Mount Sinai. Instead of questioning whether or not one is looking at the right place, one tries to cut up the map and stick it together again in order to make things tally. This argument falls because in all probability one is referring to the wrong place. This will be discussed in detail in Part III of this book.

28.7. IN SUMMARY

To summarise we can say that it was a matter of a very large number, probably around 2 million people. In addition to this, was all the livestock.

29. WHERE ARE THE PEOPLE OF ISRAEL GOING AND IN WHICH DIRECTION?

We know where the people of Israel were going. There are two places. The first place is a mountain. They are to return to the mountain where Moses received his assignment from the Lord to lead the Exodus (Ex. 3:12). The people of Israel are to worship there according to the Lord's command. Mount Horeb, the mountain of God or Mount Sinai, lies in north-western Saudi-Arabia, at that time called the land of Midian. The people of Israel are to walk to this mountain to worship there. The next goal is the land of Canaan (Ex. 6:2-8, 13:11), the land promised by the Lord in his covenant with and promise to Abraham, Isaac, Jacob and Moses.

The question is then which route is the most realistic under the circumstances in which the Lord has placed the people of Israel. The following alternatives are more or less realistic: (figure 188)

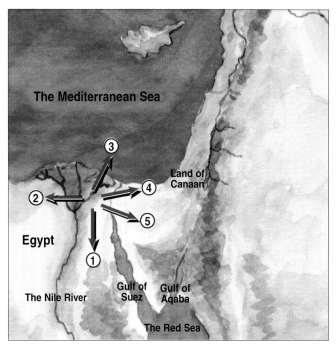

Figure 283: Which direction did the people of Israel take at the Exodus? According to the biblical texts, only alternative 5 is possible.

29.1. Southwards i.e. following the Nile down towards central Africa. Moses knew the area well. Moses had been heir to the throne and, according to Josephus, general at the Egyptian court, and would have had access to maps covering the country and information regarding trade routes etc. Moses had also been general of the Egyptian army in the battles against Ethiopia, and for this reason knew the south of Egypt and Ethiopia very well (JA 2/10:1).

It can only be explained as a huge mistake to embark on a journey towards central Africa with two million people on foot if one is going to Midian and the land of Canaan. Moreover it is stated that the people of Israel crossed the Egyptian border on the first day (Ex. 12:41,51). Had they journeyed southwards they would have gone deeper into Egypt for a long time, and walked towards the most important cities of Egypt.

The only way southwards is through the Nile valley, which means straight through the populated region of Egypt. This route also presupposes that Moses had prepared a crossing over the water further south in the Gulf of Suez. This route would seem to be less likely, or rather most unlikely.

29.2. Westwards, i.e. through north Africa, over Gibraltar, via southern Europe and into Canaan from the north and later down to Midian. This is completely out of the question on practical grounds (an impossible undertaking) and there is nothing in the Bible to support this route historically or in any other way.

29. 3. Northwards to the Mediterranean Sea and then by boat to the land of Canaan. This alternative can be excluded for several reasons. One is that it was completely impossible with this number of people and livestock to find enough boats without prior planning. Moreover they were on the way to Canaan via Mount Sinai (which lay in the opposite direction), and northwards there is only a flat delta landscape as far as the Mediterranean. The people of Israel should go out into the desert. Another reason is that the people of Israel enter the land of Canaan via Jericho (from the east). Further, northwards is not a walking route to the land of Canaan. In addition, they would not cross the border the same day, they would be in Egypt all the time they would be in the delta region.

29. 4. Eastwards would seem to be a logical alternative because it is the nearest route to Canaan. Then they would have followed the Mediterranean coast eastwards and later northwards and entered Canaan through the land of the Philistines. However the Bible states very clearly that they did not take this route:

"And it came to pass, when Pharaoh had let the people go, that God led them not through the way of the land of the Philistines, although that was near; for God said, Lest peradventure the people repent when they see war, and they return to Egypt." (Ex. 13:17)

The people of Israel were unarmed and would not have a chance against an army. Moses also knew that they must go to Midian first to worship at the mountain of God/Mount Sinai/Horeb.

Figure 284: The south east route from Egypt is a very flat land with a hard surface.

29.5. Only one way remains. To make a circular movement by going towards the south-east (and thus to the land of Midian), and later go north at a convenient place to enter into the land of Canaan. This is what the people of Israel did according to the Bible:

"But God led the people about, through the way of the wilderness of the Red sea: and the children of Israel went up harnessed out of the land of Egypt." (Ex. 13:18)

We know that they are on the way to the land of Canaan and that they do not take the nearest route (eastwards) but make a detour via the desert towards the Red Sea. That is to say they go in a south-easterly direction through the area we call the Sinai peninsula today (figures 284-288).

The south-east route would seem to reduce the journey through the Red Sea to a journey through some lake (they were to pass through a sea), which has been suggested as a hypothesis. In the same way the alternative, which entails passing through what we call the Gulf of Suez,

Figure 285: The wilderness of the Sinai desert.

from the west to the east coast, can be eliminated for several reasons. Partly because in this case they would journey towards and not away from the Egyptians (they would have journeyed towards the Egyptian cities and not away from them), and partly because this route would lead to central Africa. Furthermore the people of Israel would not be across the Egyptian border on the same day. Perhaps most importantly, Moses would then have known that he had to go through the sea, which he did not know beforehand.

The most probable conclusion is that the people of Israel, under the Lord's guidance with the pillar of cloud and pillar of fire, went in the

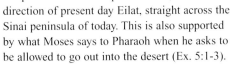

direction of present day Eilat, straight across the Sinai peninsula of today. This is also supported by what Moses says to Pharaoh when he asks to be allowed to go out into the desert (Ex. 5:1-3).

There are many hypotheses which include every possible way out of Egypt. Most of them fall down because of what the biblical texts say and/or, because the route does not lead to the first goal, Mount Horeb (Mount Sinai) in the land of Midian.

30. WERE THE PEOPLE OF ISRAEL ARMED?

The people of Israel are now to the east of Egypt in the region of the Nile delta, and are on the way to the land of Canaan via a detour. In the Swedish Bible, and also in other translations we probably have a wrong interpretation/translation of a word from the original text. In Exodus 13:18 it says that the people of Israel left Egypt armed (or "harnessed" interpreted as being armed). In other translations it says "armed" in this verse. This is not very likely for at least six reasons:

Figures 286-288: The typical landscape of the south east route from Egypt is a very flat land with solid ground. The Sinai peninsula is not a desert in terms of drifting sand, which is the reason it is called a wilderness, but in terms of water the Sinai peninsula is like a desert.

1. The people of Israel were not warriors, they were shepherds, farmers and brick-makers, and they lived as slaves in Egypt. To arm 600 000 men who were of an age to bear weapons in a very short time cannot have been practical, possible in the time, nor politically or financially possible.
2. It is out of the question that the Egyptians would have allowed a large number (a larger number of men able to bear arms than there were in the whole of the great Egyptian army) of oppressed slaves to arm themselves.
3. The people of Israel were to sacrifice and worship in the desert, and for this they did not need weapons. They belonged to Egypt, and Egypt was the military super power of that era. The individuals they might possibly meet in the desert (within the Egyptian sphere of power) would in no way be a threat to some 2 million people.
4. Later on they are armed, which means that they must have been unarmed before.
5. Josephus also mentions that the people of Israel left Egypt unarmed (JA 2/15:3). Again, when the people of Israel and the Egyptian army come closer to each other, the fact that the people of Israel were unarmed is repeated (JA 2/15:4).

6. What then is the meaning of the word in the original text, which is translated "armed" in different editions/translations? The Hebrew word "chamushim" which is found in the original text, only occurs four times in the Old Testament:

◆ Ex. 13:18, the text referred to above, which implies military order or structure. In this context they were grouped according to tribe, kinship and family in a military way.

◆ Joshua 1:14 and 4:12, translated as armed, but these texts concern the time when the people of Israel, with Joshua in the lead, carry out their prayer march round Jericho in military formation. That they had weapons was definitely of secondary importance. However the biblical text is very clear regarding the way in which the week of prayer march was to be carried out. The way they marched was to be in accordance with military order and structure.

◆ Judges 7:11, the same word translated to a military term/strategy.

Here we see an example of the same word being translated as "armed" or "military order/strategy". The correct translation would seem to be "military order", as the two passages in Joshua, where this word occurs, refer to the seven day prayer march round the walls of Jericho. That it was done with the same military order that was decided at Horeb is probable. That they would be armed during the prayer march may be probable, but in this case it would be of secondary importance. The important thing was that in front of and behind the ark of the covenant they should march in strict order, following their tribes and tribal chiefs, and with their trumpeters.

Added to this one can mention that usually in the Pentateuch, and the book of Joshua, the Hebrew word "chalats" is used to indicate armed soldiers. This word is not used in the context describing the departure from Egypt.

The historian Josephus indicates in one clause that the people of Israel were unarmed when they left Egypt. When the Egyptian army started to chase the people of Israel, they believed that it would be relatively easy to succeed in their task, just because the people of Israel were unarmed (JA 2/15:3).

The conclusion would seem to be that they left in military order depending on their tribe and family, and that they were not yet armed. In the new 1999 Swedish translation of the Bible, based on the original text, the word has been changed from "armed" to "marshalled like an army". In the English King James Version the word used is "harnessed".

31. HOW WELL ORGANISED WERE THE PEOPLE OF ISRAEL?

There are many passages in the texts which bear witness to a fixed structure with a sort of order of command during the whole Exodus. It was obviously a very effective order because when Moses called together the elders of the twelve tribes of Israel (Ex. 12:21) to arrange the passover (which was the beginning of the Exodus), and save the people of Israel from the deaths of all the firstborn, word goes out quickly and efficiently to every family in a population of approximately 2 million, even with the communication systems of that epoch. How quickly? The Lord speaks to Moses:

"This month shall be unto you the beginning of months: it shall be the first month of the year to you." (Ex. 12:2)

According to the Bible, the Lord gives instructions to Moses that the first passover is to be celebrated, and he is to tell the people of Israel about it (Ex. 12:3). The Lord says "this month" and then gives instructions about what is to happen that very month, which had just begun.

On the tenth day an unblemished, year-old lamb is to be taken, one for each household. On the fourteenth day it is to be slaughtered and the blood is to be smeared on the doorposts. Afterwards, at night, the roasted lamb is to be eaten with unleavened bread. The people are to be dressed and ready to leave, and eat with great haste. That night all the firstborn in Egypt die but the people of Israel are saved. Within twenty four hours the borders of Egypt have been crossed (Ex. 12:1-42).

Think about it. A new festival is instituted for a whole nation when the Lord speaks to Moses. If the Lord spoke to Moses on the first day of the month (it may have been later i.e. even fewer days in which to inform all the people) then Moses had 10 days at the most to inform all the people of Israel, who were spread out over a wide area, and prepare them to leave.

Figure 289: Where is "Yam suph" (or "Jam suph") or as we call it, the Red Sea, located?

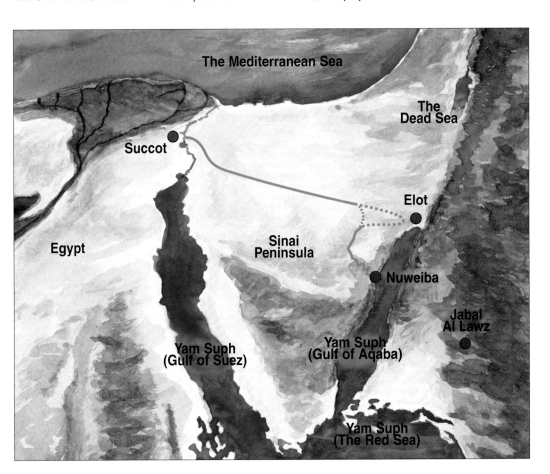

Moses quickly calls together the elders (Ex. 12:21), and within 10 days or less every family among the 2 million individuals has been informed and follows the instructions in detail. This happened 3450 years ago, and affects some 2 million people. There must have been absolutely first-rate military precision in the organisation and lines of communication. Few armies today, with today's communication systems, would be able to improvise and cope with such an assignment under these conditions, and in such a short time.

We can assume that the people of Israel were very well organised.

32. WHERE IS THE RED SEA SITUATED?

The people of Israel are now on the way to the desert. They are on their way to Midian and to Horeb (Mount Sinai, God's mountain). We also know that it is most likely they are going in a south-easterly direction. We do not know exactly which way they choose, but we know that they finally arrive at the Red Sea. Where does the Red Sea lie? This is an important question for the Exodus, and several different hypotheses exist: mainly because not everything has tallied earlier.

The Red Sea is the name of the water separating Africa from the Arabian peninsula. In the northern part the Red Sea has two arms; the Gulf of Suez to the west of the Sinai peninsula, which today divides Egypt into two parts; and the Gulf of Aqaba to the east of the Sinai peninsula, which today separates Egypt from Saudi-Arabia (figure 289).

Earlier we have said that the Gulf of Suez is unlikely as far as the journey through the Red Sea is concerned, for many reasons, amongst others because today it divides Egypt (or Egypt and its sphere of interest), into two parts, as it did 3450 years ago. That here the Bible refers to the part of the Red Sea called the Gulf of Aqaba, which separates the Sinai peninsula from present day Saudi-Arabia, can be considered likely for the following reasons:

32.1. THE TARGET OF THE JOURNEY

The people of Israel are on their way to Mount Horeb/Sinai which lies near the home of the priest Reuel in the land of Midian, where Moses spent his forty years of exile. In all probability these places lie on the eastern side of the Gulf of Aqaba, in northern Saudi-Arabia.

32.2. THE BOOK OF KINGS

In the first Book of Kings it is narrated about King Solomon's fleet:

"And king Solomon made a navy of ships in Eziongeber, which is beside Eloth, on the shore of the Red sea, in the land of Edom." (1 Kings 9:26)

Eloth lay near present day Eilat on the northern point of the Gulf of Aqaba. In the first Book of Kings, in other words, the Gulf of Aqaba is called the Red Sea ("jam suph" in Hebrew). It is also known that the Gulf of Suez was called the Red Sea ("jam suph") (Ex. 10:19). However, what is important to point out is that in the Bible the Gulf of Aqaba is also called the Red Sea.

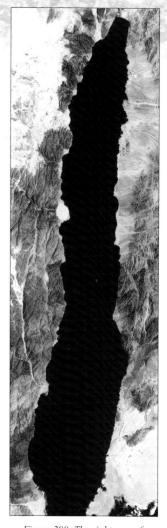

Figure 290: The right arm of the Red Sea, today called the Gulf of Aqaba. The left-hand coast is the Sinai peninsula and the right-hand coast is Saudi-Arabia. At the very northern end two cities are located (seen in red), today's Eilat (left corner) in Israel and Aqaba (right corner) in Jordan. The white Nuweiba peninsula is seen on the Sinai coast in the middle part of the photograph.

32.3. THE BOOK OF EXODUS

In the biblical text it says:

"But God led the people about, through the way of the wilderness of the Red sea: and the children of Israel went up harnessed out of the land of Egypt." (Ex. 13:18)

The people of Israel went through the wilderness and arrived at the Red Sea. Josephus expresses it in the same way, that the people of Israel went through the desert (JA 2/15:3). Through the present day Sinai desert to the present day Gulf of Aqaba (Red Sea). In the English translation it is even more clear where the same text is translated: "through the way of the wilderness of the Red Sea". This wilderness (or desert) surrounded by the Red Sea, "the wilderness of the Red Sea", corresponds most likely to the Sinai peninsula of today.

32.4. THE "JAM SUPH" ISSUE

A number of hypotheses are supported by the thought that the Red Sea is called "jam suph" in Hebrew. This could possibly be translated as the "sea of rushes" (or reeds), and as there are no rushes in the Red Sea but there are some to be found in lakes in northern Egypt, then this translation is put forward.

The important point is that "jam suph" is the name of the sea which we call the Red Sea today, including both the Gulf of Suez and the Gulf of Aqaba. This is what the biblical texts say quite clearly.

The hypotheses which suggest that the people of Israel passed over on some sandbank of a lake at low tide, meet obvious difficulties, not only with a number of passages in the Bible and other documents, but also the fact that the entire Egyptian army of a quarter of a million soldiers and thousands of horses were drowned when the tide turned. The difference in tide levels in that area is about 30 cm, and it applies only to the sea areas. In addition, why should the whole Egyptian army go through the water when they could ride around the lake much faster?

None of these hypotheses are based on archeological discoveries, but are characterised by writing desk theories, where the whole picture does not tally. When the map does not show what one is looking for, it is tempting to change the map, instead of asking if one is looking in the wrong place.

Figure 291: New York city: a Viking settlement or just a Viking name?

32.5. THE MEANING OF A NAME IS OFTEN NOT RELEVANT LATER IN HISTORY

An example which shows the limitations of analysing the name of a place can be illustrated with the following: A Viking from Scandinavia was called Jar. He had a settlement in an occupied area of England by a sea gulf ("vik" in Swedish). The settlement was consequently called Jarvik (the Gulf of Jar). In modern times this name has become York. Later on emigrants took the name with them to America where the name was given to another new settlement, New York. (Figure 937)

The important thing is to know where a place lies, the original meaning of the name may have disappeared or changed during the thousands of years that have passed.

32.6. IN SUMMARY

There is good reason to assume that the part of the Red Sea mentioned in this context, is the part which we call the Gulf of Aqaba today. The question is why this way was chosen. There are three reasons:

◆ The people of Israel, at God's command according to the text, were to journey to Horeb to worship. In order to journey there they had to go through the desert to the northern point of the Red Sea (of the Gulf of Aqaba), where present day Eilat is situated, and then go southwards following the east coast of the Gulf of Aqaba.

◆ This is the most practical (not mountainous), and quickest way to reach the northern point of the Gulf of Aqaba. Moses had taken this route himself on several occasions, and it was a known trade route.

◆ The most important reason, however, is that the Bible claims that the Lord himself guided the people day and night.

33. WHY DID THE PEOPLE OF ISRAEL CHOOSE THE ROUTE THEY TOOK?

It may be easy to forget that both the biblical texts, and the historical writer Josephus, are quite clear that Moses himself did not know which route the people of Israel would follow. Moses knew two things; that first and foremost they would go to Horeb in Midian to pray and worship, and that later

Figures 292-295: The Red Sea is surrounded by mountains that consists of minerals in different red or pink colours. Particulary at sunrise and sunset these mountains can have a deep red colour.

they would go to the promised land, Canaan. But Moses did not know the exact route nor the time schedule. On both these points Moses had a surprise.

The speed of the journey as well as the choice of route were new for Moses. Nor did Moses know anything about the time schedule, that they would be journeying for 40 years before being allowed to enter the land of Canaan.

But the Lord knows what is decided. It is not that Moses sits and chooses the way when they come to valleys, open desert and roadless terrain but, according to the Bible, it is the Lord who leads the people of Israel.

"And the LORD went before them by day in a pillar of a cloud, to lead them the way; and by night in a pillar of fire, to give them light; to go by day and night:" (Ex. 13:21)

The entire people of Israel could follow the pillar of cloud and the pillar of fire. This was what made the choice of route possible, and how Moses would meet the potential difficulties in leading these approximately two million individuals on their journey. It must have been a tremendous feeling for the people of Israel to receive such concrete and clear guidance. It must also have been by divine intervention that they had the strength to journey on during the night and the day. According to the text it was the pillar of cloud and the pillar of fire which determined the speed at which they travelled:

"He took not away the pillar of the cloud by day, nor the pillar of fire by night, from before the people." (Ex. 13:22)

33.1. THEY WALKED DAY AND NIGHT

They could walk both day and night. The Lord must have given the people of Israel the strength to do this, but the Lord had also solved the practical question of how they could journey during the night. The pillar of fire must have been a remarkable sign for them, and it must have been a huge pillar of fire that gave enough light so that two million people could see where to put their feet, which was equally important for the livestock. Night-time in the Sinai area is compact darkness, and there are few places in the world where one feels so enfolded in darkness as in the middle of the Sinai desert. Without light it is useless to move about in the Sinai desert.

According to the biblical texts the pillar of cloud was an angel of God:

"And the angel of God, which went before the camp of Israel, removed and went behind them; and the pillar of the cloud went from before their face, and stood behind them." (Ex. 14:19)

Figures 296-299: Examples of red mountains on the coast of the Gulf of Aqaba.

It may then be logical to assume that the pillar of fire was also an angel since the pillar of fire worked in exactly the same way, except that it worked at night and gave light to the people of Israel. Earlier in the text it says:

"And the LORD went before them by day in a pillar of a cloud, to lead them the way; and by night in a pillar of fire, to give them light; to go by day and night:" (Ex. 13:21)

Here it says that it was the Lord himself who was the pillar of
cloud. Whether it was the Lord himself or an angel messenger
sent by the Lord is of little significance. The important thing is
that the Lord led the people of Israel, himself or with the help of
an angel, in the direction of Mount Horeb, according to the text.

We can note the following: Moses himself did not know the
route to take, which was rather remarkable. The people of Israel
received the strength and ability from the Lord to walk both day
and night, i.e. with double the daily speed of ordinary walkers.
The route chosen was determined by the pillar of cloud/fire and
not by Moses.

34. WHERE WAS ETHAM SITUATED?

Before the people of Israel pitched camp by the Red Sea, they had another
encampment in the area called Etham:

*"And they took their journey from Succoth, and encamped in Etham, in the
edge of the wilderness."* (Ex. 13:20)

Succoth was on the Egyptian border while Etham was much further away.
There is another place in the text which also names Etham:

*"And they departed from Succoth, and pitched in Etham, which is in the edge
of the wilderness. And they removed from Etham, and turned again unto
Pihahiroth, which is before Baalzephon: and they pitched before Migdol. And
they departed from before Pihahiroth, and passed through the midst of the
sea into the wilderness, and went three days' journey in the wilderness of
Etham, and pitched in Marah."* (Numb. 33:6-8)

These passages may seem strange as they pitch camp in Etham, later pass
through the sea at Pi-Hahiroth, and then land in Etham again. If we look at a
map it is easier to understand. Etham was probably an area of land which
consisted of the area north of the Gulf of Aqaba and down along the
coastal areas. Then the Bible passages fit in very well, since the
area of land called Etham probably included both the coastal strips
(figures 292-295).

34.1. ETHAM AND EDOM

Etham may correspond to Edom (current name for part of this area)
which means red. This could then explain the name "Red Sea". The
red colour comes from the red or pink-coloured rock species which
surrounds the Gulf of Aqaba, which in the light of the setting sun
becomes bright red. That the area which became red surrounded
both coasts of the water (Gulf of Aqaba) seems logical.

The people of Israel come via the "southern road", which was a known
route for caravans and troops. In figure 304 this "southern road" can be seen
as it is today. Furthermore, the southern road was south of the dangerous area
which the Philistines controlled. At the same time the route went through the
northern part of what we know today as the Sinai peninsula, which means

*Figures 300-303: The Red Sea
is surrounded by mountains in
different red and pink colours.*

Figure 304: The southern road of today. This road crosses the Sinai peninsula from the northern end of the Gulf of Suez to the northern end of the Gulf of Aqaba. The road of today follows the dotted line in figure 305.

Figure 305: The probable route for the Exodus is shown with the green line.

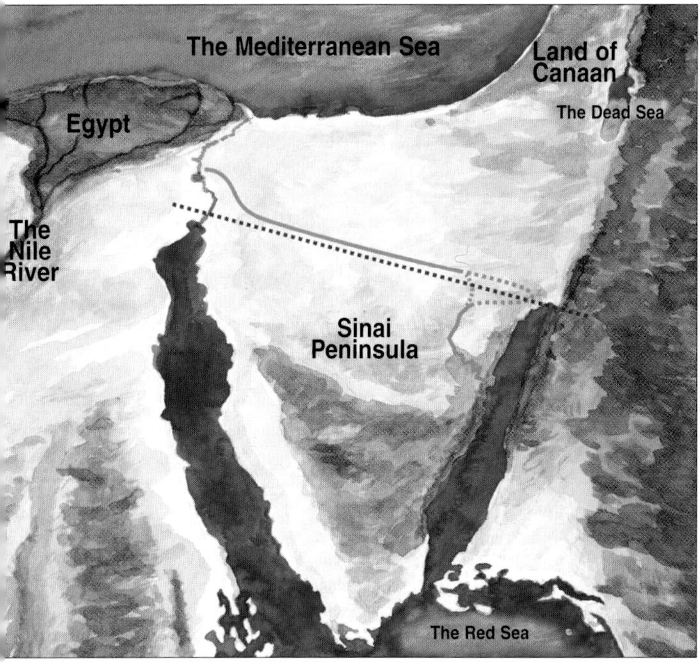

that one avoided the mountains in the centre of the Sinai peninsula. These rocky massifs are very extensive and reach heights of around 2000 m.

34.2. THE SOUTHERN ROAD

When the people of Israel first pitch camp in Etham it is probably on this southern road, west of present day Eilat, which is west of the northern point of the Gulf of Aqaba. Later they turn and go southwards to Pi-Hahiroth. Later, after having passed through the Red Sea they are in the Etham area again, and in the desert of Etham which lay, or began, in the area which corresponds today to the north-western part of Saudi-Arabia.

The Bible says that they encamped in Etham "where the desert began". This can apply to two deserts. They had passed the desert of the Sinai peninsula, or rather travelled through its northern parts. This part of the journey went through a desert (Ex. 13:18). If these words applied to the Sinai desert, the text should have said "where the desert ended". On the other hand, another desert begins at the northern point of the Gulf of Aqaba: the immense desert which includes parts of Jordan and more or less the whole of Saudi-Arabia. It is in the north-western parts that the people of Israel find themselves when they have crossed the sea. If they pitched camp near the northern point of the Gulf of Aqaba, the description fits very well: that they pitched camp "where the desert begins" and then the Bible text means the desert of Etham.

The text can also be interpreted in another way, which is much clearer in the English translation than in the Swedish. There they pitched camp "in the edge of the wilderness" and two verses prior to this the text indicates which wilderness, namely "the wilderness of the Red Sea". The wilderness of the Red Sea was what we call the Sinai peninsula, or the Sinai desert, today. Further support of this interpretation is the fact that Pharaoh exclaimed that "the wilderness hath shut them in". The wilderness to which this refers is what we call the Sinai peninsula.

Whatever the translation and interpretation of the desert referred to, it tallies very well that they pitched camp in the Etham area (which surrounded the inner parts of the Gulf of Aqaba) and that the desert of Etham lay to the east of the Gulf of Aqaba.

The Mediterranean Sea

Land of Canaan

Egypt

The Dead Sea

The Nile River

Sinai Peninsula

The Red Sea

35. Where do the people of Israel encamp?

The people of Israel are most likely journeying right across the Sinai peninsula, from Succoth towards Etham and the northern point of the Gulf of Aqaba. They reach Etham and pitch camp there. They have a comfortable margin between them and the pursuing Egyptian army, something they are not yet aware of, and then the Lord says something to Moses which must have been very odd:

"Speak unto the children of Israel, that they turn and..." (Ex. 14:2)

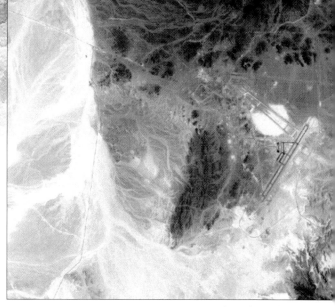

Figure 306: The satellite photograph shows a turning point of the Southern road that still exists today. Across from left to right in the upper part, the Southern road is seen. The turning point is also clearly seen, where the road is directly towards the south. If this road is chosen one comes directly to Nuweiba. The structure in the right part is an air force base.

To turn meant to leave the route. This is odd because the text is very clear on the point that they are to pitch camp by the Red Sea, and now they are to turn and go into the desert again (figure 305). However the pillar of cloud and the pillar of fire guide the people of Israel.

Where did the next encampment lie? We shall consider this question in accordance with what the Bible indicates, based on the geography of the region and what the historian Josephus relates.

1. They are to pitch camp by the Red Sea:

"...and encamp before Pihahiroth, between Migdol and the sea, over against Baalzephon: before it shall ye encamp by the sea." (Ex. 14:2)

2. There are two important factors which are decisive if this is to be possible:

Figure 307: Wadi Watir is the valley between the mountains going from the upper left corner down to the Nuweiba peninsula. This is the way one comes if a turn is made towards the south, as was shown in figure 306. The valley of Wadi Watir is very flat with no obstacles, and is surrounded by high mountain ridges.

    a) It is a matter of finding a place big enough for two million people and all the livestock.
    b) A way of coming to this place must be found.

The coastal area on the western side of the Gulf of Aqaba (Sinai coast), is extremely hilly with mountains of up to 2000 m high, which extend right to the coast. After this coastal stretch of about 200 km, there is only one place which meets the demands, this place can be clearly seen on maps and satellite pictures (figures 307 and 308). It is a very large flat area which today is called Nuweiba. This flat peninsula is about 12 square km in area, it lies right on the coast and could very well provide the space necessary for all the people of Israel and, as we will come to later, the entire Egyptian army. It is also possible to reach this place through the Wadi Watir Valley. In order to enter this system of valleys, which lead to Nuweiba, one must change direction by turning away from the camp in Etham.

Figure 308: This satellite picture illustrates a number of matters. The mountain ridge is the eastern part of the Sinai peninsula with mountains higher than 2000 m. The sea is the Gulf of Aqaba, which is a part of the Red Sea. In the middle, the Nuweiba peninsula is seen with its white surface structure. In the north-south direction the highway is *seen, going from the Israeli border to Sharm El-Sheik. Wadi Watir enters the peninsula from the west. The highway in the Wadi is easy to recognise. On the southern coast of the peninsula, a square shaped object pointing out into the sea can be seen. That is the harbour of Nuweiba where trucks are transported by ferry to Aqaba in Jordan.*

3. The Bible contains an interesting note:

"For Pharaoh will say of the children of Israel, They are entangled in the land, the wilderness hath shut them in." (Ex. 14:3)

From this the following conclusions can be drawn:

a) Pharaoh knows where they are before he has caught up with them, which must mean that he had spies sent out well in advance. Pharaoh may also have had guard posts with signalling systems between the mountain peaks.

b) When they turn and pitch camp, Pharaoh believes that the people of Israel have lost their way. This must mean that Pharaoh feels a degree of certainty that he has the situation under control, he himself has not lost his way. At this stage Pharaoh would be able to take things easy if the people of Israel are lost, while Pharaoh knows where they are.

c) However the most interesting note is that Pharaoh is convinced that the people of Israel have been confined in the desert. They are on the Sinai peninsula. If they are confined there, it means they are south of a line between the northern points of the Gulf of Suez and the Gulf of Aqaba (figure 204). Since the people of Israel were on the way to Midian, were shut in in the desert, and had pitched camp by the sea, then they were on the west bank of the Gulf of Aqaba (figure 305). Or to put it another way, on the east coast of the present day Sinai peninsula.

4. The historian Josephus makes further notes on the place. The encampment was surrounded on two sides by mountains which extended right out to the sea, and could not be passed. The third side was the Red Sea, and the fourth side the valley through which the people of Israel had arrived at the encampment (JA 2/15:3). This description tallies with what Nuweiba looks like. To the north and south the mountains extend to the sea. The only way which existed then was via Wadi Watir, and the Nuweiba peninsula is surrounded by the Red Sea. In figure 307, which is a satellite picture over Nuweiba, it can be clearly seen how the mountain ranges surround the flat Nuweiba peninsula. The Wadi Watir valley is seen as a white line straight through the mountain range.

Figure 309: This is Wadi Watir with a modern highway. As can be seen the valley is very flat and represents in it self a huge highway. The ground is solid and easy to walk on.

Figure 310: This is the end of Wadi Watir. A part of Nuweiba and the Gulf of Aqaba is seen at the end of the Wadi.

Figure 311: Nuweiba seen from the Gulf of Aqaba. The peninsula is very flat and surrounded by high mountain ridges. In the middle of the photograph the end of Wadi Watir can be seen.

Figure 312: The Nuweiba peninsula seen from the north. To the left is the Gulf of Aqaba and to the right the mountain ridges are seen. The Nuweiba peninsula represents a huge plain.

It is not strange that the people of Israel become furious and despondent that they have been led into a dead end. For without a doubt, this is a dead end (figures 307-311). The sea in front of them, high mountains on either side and Wadi Watir behind them, the valley through which they have just passed. How could they find such a bad place to pitch camp? And how could they go on?

36. WHY DO THE PEOPLE OF ISRAEL TURN ?

The Bible relates that the people of Israel follow the pillar of cloud by day and the pillar of fire by night. In this way the Lord leads them by day and by night. Moses and the people are completely convinced that they are under the Lord's guidance. Moses knows this because the Lord has spoken directly to him, and the people of Israel have both a pillar of cloud and a pillar of fire to follow. In particular the pillar of fire at night must have been something altogether extraordinary.

Figure 313: Close to the entrance of Wadi Watir the land is broad and flat.

The simple answer to the question as to why they turned, (Ex. 14:2) is that they just followed the pillars of cloud and fire, or in other words they were guided by the Lord. However Pharaoh is confused and believes that they are lost (Ex. 14:3). It must have been an extraordinary decision to turn and go southwards.

Why does the Lord lead the people of Israel in this way so that they turn? The answer is probably found in the text, i.e. that the Lord wants to punish the army which is out to capture the people of Israel who, after a long time in captivity as slaves, have finally become free. The Egyptian army without doubt had plans, under Pharaoh's leadership, to kill a large number of the people and take the rest back as slaves. Already at an earlier date, we know that for a period of time, all newborn Hebrew males were killed by the Egyptians, so that the people would not increase in number. But the text says that the people of Israel were under the Lord's protection, and if the Egyptian army tries to carry out its plans, the Lord will stop them:

Figure 314: There are some minor oases in Wadi Watir, which is the reason some palm trees can be found.

"... and I will be honored upon Pharaoh, and upon all his host; that the Egyptians may know that I am the LORD ..." (Ex. 14:4)

There are at least three reasons why God leads the people of Israel so that they turn southwards:

◆ To confuse Pharaoh and his army.
◆ To allow the Egyptian army to catch up with the people of Israel.
◆ To lead the Egyptian army to a place where they can be punished if they continue their pursuit.

37. DOES THE ENCAMPMENT HAVE A NAME?

Modern Nuweiba had no name at that time that we know of, but there are three points of reference in the Bible and we shall look at these more closely.

In the Bible several places are mentioned as indications of how the people

of Israel pitched camp just before crossing through the Red Sea. The Lord speaks to Moses regarding the encampment:

"Speak unto the children of Israel, that they turn and encamp before Pihahiroth, between Migdol and the sea, over against Baalzephon: before it shall ye encamp by the sea." (Ex. 14:2)

It is not known where these places were, but let us look more closely at the names:

37.1. Migdol

To begin with, Migdol must lie some distance from the coastal/shore area as the people of Israel were to pitch camp between Migdol and the sea. Migdol is Hebrew and means tower. It could have been a watch tower up on one of the mountains, or some sort of watch tower at the mouth of the valley near the encampment on the coast. Migdol is referred to as a fortress on Egypt's north-eastern border (47). If Sinai is included in Egypt's sphere of interest, which Sinai was (not least due to the copper mines and quarries of semi-precious stones such as turquoise), then the place assumed to be that of the crossing (Nuweiba) can be described as being situated at the north-eastern border of Egypt.

Figure 315: The mouth of Wadi Watir seen from the Nuweiba peninsula.

37.2. Pi-Hahiroth

The meaning of this name could either be of Hebrew origin, and signify "the caves' mouth", or of Egyptian origin and signify "a grassy place" (47). The caves' mouth could mean the way out of the Wadi Watir valley, surrounded by high mountains, to the flat area which is Nuweiba.

It is a very dry area but if grass is to be found anywhere it is in the valleys and the way out of the valleys, where water can be found at certain times of the year, visible or under the surface. Although it is uncertain both these descriptions could fit the place of encampment.

Hahiroth is indicated as a place on the west coast of the western arm of the Red Sea, the Gulf of Suez (47), but this is an assumption based on the biblical text and in that case assumes that the part of the Red Sea that the people of Israel crossed was the Gulf of Suez. There is no evidence that the place lay there, but it is known that the place was by the crossing. It then depends on where one believes that the crossing through the Red Sea lay, when one indicates the locality.

Figure 316: Camels are the only large animals found in Wadi Watir.

37.3. Baalzephon

Baalzephon would lie opposite the place of encampment, which can be assumed to mean on the other side of the Red Sea, about 14 km away, on the eastern shore of the Gulf of Aqaba. Baalzephon is Hebrew and means "lord of the north" (47), it is pointed out as a cult site where an idol was worshipped and human sacrifice was practised. The locality of the site is not known.

Perhaps the name of the place can be traced in another way. Zephon was one of the sons of Esau's son Eliphaz, who was a tribal prince in Edom (47). Edom is an area described as lying between the Dead Sea and the Gulf of

Aqaba, and also further down along the coastal area of the Gulf of Aqaba. Edom, which means red, may comprise the same area as Etham, i.e. the coastal area of the Gulf of Aqaba. Baal-Zephon would then indicate a cult site for the god Baal in the area of Zephon (Baalzephon). If this is the case then this place could have been on the north-east coast of the Gulf of Aqaba, opposite the suggested place of encampment of the people of Israel.

37.4. ARCHEOLOGICAL DISCOVERIES

The interpretation of where these three places were situated is uncertain, but it is worth noting that all three could very well have defined the suggested place of encampment, Nuweiba. Added to this, Moses knew where these places were, since he was in Midian during his forty years of flight. According to the hypothesis presented here, these places were in Midian (Baalzephon), or in sight (14 km across the sea) of Midian (Migdol and Pi-Hahiroth).

Are there more factors which support the theory that Nuweiba was the place of encampment? Let us look at archeological remains.

1. In the northern part of Nuweiba there are the ruins of a Turkish fort, which probably stands on the foundations of an Egyptian fort. This fort must have blocked possible attempts to pass over the mountain ridge to the north. Moreover the fort must have had some form of communication with Egypt. Perhaps it was horsemen (or fire signals between the mountain peaks) from this fort, which informed the pursuing Egyptian army that the people of Israel had pitched camp in Nuweiba?

It is likely that this is the Egyptian fort which may have been Pi-Hahiroth. This name may have significance with both Hebrew and Egyptian origins, while the other names are Hebrew. This too points to the probability that Pi-Hahiroth was of Egyptian origin. For this reason it is probable that the people of Israel pitched camp in the southern part of Nuweiba, as far as possible from the enemy. A factor that suggests that this fort has been of impor-

Figures 317-320: The ruins of a fort which probably stands on the foundations of an old Egyptian fort. There is an ancient well within the fort that is still used by the bedouins. This well was vital, to enable a settlement in ancient times. Otherwise there have only been small groups of beduoins living in the area. This ruin might be the biblical Pi-Hahiroth.

tance for a long time is that there is an old well in the courtyard. Wells were of the highest importance for building, or for establishing any form of settlement in this area. Although the fort is in ruins, this well is still used today by the local bedouins (figures 317-320).

2. Migdol was probably a watch tower on one of the mountain tops. It is not known if there are any ruins on these peaks, but it is known that the Egyptians had watch towers on the mountain peaks in Sinai which could communicate with each other with light signals (reflections of the sun) in the daytime and fire signals at night.

3. Opposite Nuweiba on the east coast of the Gulf of Aqaba, in present day

Saudi-Arabia, there is a possible ruin on the shore. This may have been a cult site of the Midianites dedicated to Baal within the area of Zephon (Baalzephon). The expression "over against" probably means opposite, which implies straight across the Gulf of Aqaba.

Interestingly, there is a place in Saudi-Arabia just opposite Nuweiba a few km inland that today - in Arabic - is called "Saraf al-Bal". In this name we have the Bal/Baal connection. "Zephon" in English, is written "Sefon" in other languages. It is not unlikely that this could be spelled/pronounced "Saraf" in Arabic some 3500 years later.

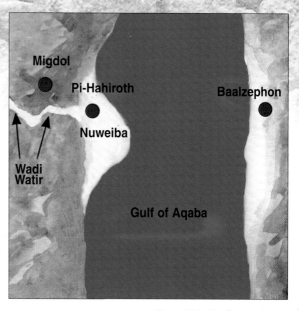

If these places are Pi-Hahiroth and Baalzephon respectively, and it is assumed that Migdol was a watch tower, then the Lord's command to Moses would have been (figure 321): "Tell the

Figure 321: On the map the possible locations of the biblical reference points are shown.

people of Israel to turn and pitch camp in front of the Egyptian fort Pi-Hahiroth, between the watch tower Migdol and the Red Sea (Gulf of Aqaba). Opposite Baalzephon in northern Saudi-Arabia, just by the sea". Today the command in this case would have been "pitch camp in Nuweiba".

These names, their origins, the place called Nuweiba, the valley leading to it, the description with mountains, sea and ruins are indices. Are there more? Yes, there are more. But before we deal with that, we shall look more closely at what happened in Egypt.

38. What happens in Egypt?

At this point in time Egypt is a ravaged country. In addition to the diseases from which the Egyptians suffer; most of the livestock is dead; the trees are beaten down as well as the crops; locusts have eaten up almost everything; plus the firstborn of both people and animals have died. This means that every family was in mourning, and busy with funeral arrangements.

38.1. The death of the firstborn

The eldest son often earned a living as an officer. Another occupation for the eldest son was to take over a farmholding. That night the eldest child in every family had died. Many of the country's leaders had also died the night when the Jewish passover was instituted. It is highly likely that the leadership and the administration of the country were facing a crisis.

When all the firstborn died in Egypt, this applied to Pharaoh and his family too. Pharaoh himself, most likely Amenhotep III, was not firstborn since, according to the Bible, he survived that night. That Pharaoh was not firstborn is clear from the brief statement:

"And it came to pass, when Pharaoh had let the people go, that God led them not through the way of the land of the Philistines," (Ex. 13:17)

This is said after the night when all the firstborn died, and it was Pharaoh who finally allowed the people of Israel to leave Egypt. In other words, Pharaoh Amenhotep III was not himself the eldest in the family in which he grew up, but on the other hand Pharaoh's eldest son, Tutankhamun, was a firstborn child.

38.2. MOBILISATION

Pharaoh learns that the people of Israel have fled and this ignites the fury and lust for revenge of Pharaoh and his counsellors. The Bible relates:

"And it was told the king of Egypt that the people fled: and the heart of Pharaoh and of his servants was turned against the people, and they said, Why have we done this, that we have let Israel go from serving us? And he made ready his chariot, and took his people with him." (Ex. 14:5-6)

Pharaoh mobilises his entire army to pursue the people of Israel and to force them back to Egypt. Egypt, even if ravaged, was the super power of that time and Pharaoh takes with him all his army, the world's greatest military force at that time. The army was great:

"And he took six hundred chosen chariots, and all the chariots of Egypt, and captains over every one of them." (Ex. 14:7)

"But the Egyptians pursued after them, all the horses and chariots of Pharaoh, and his horsemen, and his army,.." (Ex. 14:9)

The historian Josephus gives further information regarding the military power of Egypt at that time. The army consisted of 600 chariots with their 50 000 soldiers and 200 000 infantry troops. All of them were armed (JA 2/15:3). In modern military terms Pharaoh had a fighting force of about 50 brigades. The 600 chariots mentioned were not horse and wagon as we perhaps imagine them, but were the "tanks" of those times. They were warhorses with a little chariot, with one or more heavily armed soldiers in heavy armour. To confirm their strength psychologically the chariots and horses were often decorated in various ways, and some of the chariots were gilded (figure 322).

To give further light on the balance of power, the people of Israel were unarmed, had no military training, were without war chariots, and were now pursued by a well-trained, élite army, driven on by a great fury and lust for revenge that had grown from all they had suffered. Not least was the fact that every Egyptian family had lost its firstborn on that fateful night before Pharaoh finally allowed the people of Israel to leave the country. Thus, every Egyptian soldier had very strong personal reasons for avenging what each and everyone had suffered.

Figure 322: The elite army of Egypt was impressive in terms of number of horses, chariots, and soldiers, but also in terms of how advanced the equipment was.

In addition there were very strong political motives and reasons of prestige: that large numbers of unarmed slaves just walk away from a super power, and that a large part of the manpower which built up the country is lost. All the prestige of Egypt and its role as a super power was at stake. At this point the people of Israel turn in their desert journey, and Pharaoh receives the message that the people of Israel have lost their way and are enclosed in the wilderness.

It is presented to them on a plate. Never has a mighty army had such an easy target. Unarmed, enclosed with absolutely no vegetation in which to hide, tired after a long journey with very little to eat and drink, the people of Israel await their destruction.

39. How long does it take the Egyptians to catch up with the Israelites?

The people of Israel had permission to go three days journey into the desert to sacrifice and worship (Ex. 8:27). It is not indicated if Pharaoh knew where they were going, except that they were going into the desert to sacrifice and worship. We can therefore assume that there was no particular reaction during the first three days. Moreover the Egyptians were fully occupied with all the disasters which had hit them. Not least, every family, including Pharaoh, had a funeral to arrange.

39.1. To report to Pharaoh

But Pharaoh was the leader of a super power and he was without doubt both energetic and surrounded by a well-trained army. It is likely that he sent out spies to travel with the people of Israel, or to follow them at a distance. When the third day draws to a close and the people just continue their journey, these spies must have reacted. If some of them immediately ride back to report to Pharaoh we can assume that they rode as quickly as possible in that terrain. The spies could also have sent signals between the possible watch towers along this route.

"And the LORD went before them by day in a pillar of a cloud, to lead them the way; and by night in a pillar of fire, to give them light; to go by day and night." (Ex. 13:21)

39.2. How fast did the people of Israel travel?

If the people of Israel journeyed day and night for three days, this corresponds to six days of travel on foot. We must not forget that they had the pillar of fire by night, and continued to walk both day and night, according to the text. The horsemen who ride back cannot ride by night since they only have the daylight on which to depend. In the thick darkness which prevails in the area, no transport can be carried out at night. Nor can they urge their horses on too much in the heat, which prevails during the day in this desert area. But of course the horsemen can travel much more quickly than the people on foot. We can assume that these six days of travel on foot could be

Figures 323, 324: High mountains enable rapid communication between the mountain peaks: in the daytime with mirrors or smoke signaling and at night by signaling with fires.

done in two days on horseback.

Thus when these horsemen return to Pharaoh, a further forty-eight hours has passed, and the people of Israel have put behind them the equivalent of four days more travel. By the time the horsemen reach Pharaoh, the people of Israel are 4-5 days journey (on foot) into the desert, corresponding to 8-10 "day distances".

39.3. THE REACTION AT THE COURT OF PHARAOH

How does Pharaoh react to the news that the people of Israel are not going to return? Pharaoh mobilises the whole of his army. As has been mentioned earlier, according to Josephus, this was an army of a great power, even by today's standards.

◆ 600 selected war chariots and all the chariots in Egypt, plus the 50 000 soldiers belonging to them.
◆ 200 000 infantry soldiers.
◆ All the troops were armed.

A week is a very short time to mobilise such an army. In addition to putting in order all the fighting equipment, there were two things that determined how long the mobilisation of the army would take:

◆ The aftermath of all that had happened in Egypt regarding the plagues, including the death of many officers and administrators.
◆ The likelihood of speedily assembling necessary stores, including water for both horses and men, in view of the amount needed and also of the fact that the resources of the entire country had been laid waste.

This must have been a very difficult and complicated enterprise. But if we assume that:

◆ The majority of the army was stationed in the eastern border area
◆ All the equipment was in place and could be put in order quickly
◆ They had stored supplies for a big military operation
◆ The deaths among all the officers, soldiers and administrators did not affect the mobilisation to any great extent. If we add to this a great anger and lust for revenge, then perhaps the mobilisation of a powerful army could be managed in a few days. This is a very short time since they were not prepared for it, and it was a military operation entailing a quarter of a million soldiers who needed to have everything with them for transport, maintenance and battle in the desert area.

39.4. HOW FAST DID THE ARMY OF EGYPT MARCH?

During these days of mobilisation the people of Israel managed to journey further away. With the days travel they had already managed to accomplish, the people of Israel were now far out in the desert. The speed of the Egyptian army's march was not determined by the horsemen, but by how quickly the stores could be transported. Presumably this was done by oxen and wagons, and in the desert climate this type of transport is not much quicker than

Figure 325: Many armies have been interested in the Gulf of Aqaba. One example is the crusaders, their fortified island can still be seen.

going by foot.

But let us suppose that the army could travel, at any rate, twice as quickly as the people of Israel. Then they covered two days journey on foot in one day. The people of Israel went at half that speed, but on the other hand they travelled both day and night, i.e. two days journey on foot in twenty-four hours. It would take a very long time to catch up with the people of Israel, and the decisive factor is if and when the people of Israel pitched camp.

We can calculate with various figures but all is guesswork. The simple conclusion is that the pursuing army had great difficulty in catching up with the people of Israel, unless the people of Israel stopped and pitched camp. If we assume that the people of Israel travelled at a speed of two km an hour, and journeyed five hours each day and five hours each night, they had 14 hours to rest every twenty-four hours. Thus they could move themselves about 20 km every twenty-four hours. In this case, by the time the Egyptian army began its march, the people of Israel would have been able to reach any place in the wilderness of the Red Sea (today's Sinai peninsula). Roughly speaking, from then on both the Egyptian army and people of Israel covered the same distance each day.

The conclusion is that the people of Israel could have reached anywhere they chose within the area we call the Sinai peninsula today, since at its widest it is 230 km (if one draws a straight line between present day Suez and Eilat). The critical stage arises at the point when the people of Israel pitch camp, while the Egyptian army continues its march (figure 305).

Figures 326, 327: Egyptian war chariots at the Karnak temple in Luxor.

39.5. IN SUMMARY

How far do the people of Israel manage to move before they are overtaken? Calculated from the area where it is considered that Succoth was situated (close to today's Suez canal), which was the starting point of the Exodus, the people of Israel could have crossed the Sinai peninsula with a good margin and reached Nuweiba without the Egyptian army having much chance of catching up with them.

40. HOW DO THE EGYPTIAN ARMY AND THE PEOPLE OF ISRAEL MEET?

According to the biblical text, the Egyptian army catches up with the people of Israel at the encampment on the coast of the Red Sea:

"But the Egyptians pursued after them, all the horses and chariots of Pharaoh, and his horsemen, and his army, and overtook them encamping by the sea, beside Pihahiroth, before Baalzephon." (Ex. 14:9)

Figure 328: Wadi Watir just before Nuweiba. The Red Sea is seen in the background (Gulf of Aqaba).

The people of Israel discover the Egyptian army when it is very close, which may imply that the Egyptians were hidden until they were almost on them:

"And when Pharaoh drew nigh, the children of Israel lifted up their eyes, and, behold, the Egyptians marched after them..." (Ex. 14:10)

This agrees with the assertion that the Egyptians emerged from a valley surrounded by mountains, which also fits the suggested locality, Nuweiba. The

speed is implied when the Bible says that the Egyptian army "marched". It was not a question of horsemen galloping, which supports the hypothesis regarding the length of time the Egyptian army needed. Also, the fact that they did not catch up before the people of Israel pitched camp at the Red Sea, shows that the Egyptian army could not keep up a fast pace.

Figure 329: The mouth of Wadi Watir seen from the Red Sea.

40.1. THE PEOPLE OF ISRAEL WERE DESPERATE

The people of Israel are terribly afraid, and turn to Moses in anger and desperation. They are convinced that the Egyptian army will kill a large number of the people and take the rest back as slaves:

"... and they were sore afraid: and the children of Israel cried out unto the LORD. And they said unto Moses, Because there were no graves in Egypt, hast thou taken us away to die in the wilderness? wherefore hast thou dealt thus with us, to carry us forth out of Egypt?" (Ex. 14:10-11)

According to the Bible however, Moses remains confident of the Lord's guidance and tells the people of Israel to stand fast.

"The LORD shall fight for you, and ye shall hold your peace." (Ex. 14:14)

Figure 330: At Nuweiba the Egyptian army caught up with the people of Israel, but they never came in contact with one another.

The simple answer to the question regarding how the Egyptian army and the people of Israel meet, is that they do not meet at all. When the Egyptian army has caught up with the people of Israel, and has emerged on to the great plain of Nuweiba on the Red Sea (figure 330), they only look at each other from a distance.

Pharaoh, who led the army, must have been completely sure of victory. The entire people of Israel were shut in. Mountains on two sides, the sea on another, and all the Egyptian army on the fourth side (according to Josephus (JA 2/15:4)). So when the Egyptian army comes out on the Nuweiba peninsula they think they have everything under control and pitch camp, meaning to do battle the following day (JA 2/16:1).

40.2. READY FOR BATTLE

We have now followed the people of Israel from Rameses to Succoth. From there to Etham where, after having pitched camp, they turned and went southwards to Nuweiba where they pitched camp by the sea. The Egyptian army finally caught up with the people of Israel at Nuweiba.

A battle on a gigantic scale now takes place, but not the slaughter and capture the Egyptian army had planned for these approximately two million, unarmed Israelites, who now stand completely enclosed in front of them.

The battle which takes place (according to the Bible text) begins when the Egyptian army attacks that which the Lord has chosen to protect, and in such

a battle there is only one victor. According to the Bible, the Egyptians place themselves in a situation which they had had every opportunity to avoid. But the lust for power, prestige and vengeance is their guiding star, and finally becomes their destruction.

41. WHAT HAPPENED AT THE CROSSING SITE?

The Egyptian army seems to have been completely certain of victory. They pitched camp so they could deploy themselves in peace and quiet, rest, eat, and gather their strength for the great battle that was expected. But there was something else that happened.

41.1. ENCLOSED IN DARKNESS

The pillar of cloud, which had gone in front of the people of Israel moved, and it is said to have brought darkness over the Egyptian army, while the people of Israel had light:

"And the angel of God, which went before the camp of Israel, removed and went behind them; and the pillar of the cloud went from before their face, and stood behind them: And it came between the camp of the Egyptians and the camp of Israel; and it was a cloud and darkness to them, but it gave light by night to these: so that the one came not near the other all the night." (Ex. 14:19-20)

As a result, the Egyptian army must not have been able to do much more than pitch camp in the darkness. However, the people of Israel could move about freely, in the light of the pillar of fire. What it all looked like is difficult to imagine, but the result is clearly pointed out in the following text:

"...so that the one came not near the other all the night." (Ex. 14:20)

41.2. MOSES STRETCHES HIS HAND OVER THE SEA

In what is a completely hopeless situation when something begins to happen. Firstly, the Egyptians are wrapped in total darkness, and the people of Israel receive maximum light from the pillar of fire. Moses turns to the Lord and the Lord replies:

Figure 331: Moses was most likely standing on the shore of Nuweiba, looking at the coast of Saudi-Arabia. Initially he had no idea what to do in this situation.

"And the LORD said unto Moses, 'Wherefore criest thou unto me? speak unto the children of Israel, that they go forward: But lift thou up thy rod, and stretch out thine hand over the sea, and divide it: and the children of Israel shall go on dry ground through the midst of the sea.'" (Ex. 14:15-16)

Moses does as the Lord says, he stretches out his staff and his hand, and the sea divides itself. The Lord has spoken his Word, and so nothing else remains but to act as Moses does, according to the text. In addition to the fact that it is highly improbable the Red Sea divides itself, we may note two things: According to the text, the sea is cloven in two, not pushed to one side. Nor does the bottom rise up, but it is the sea which divides itself. Moreover, it is noted that the people of Israel were able to go through the Red Sea on dry land. Which sea-bed becomes dry solely because the water is removed? Most often there are several metres of sediment and mud on the sea-bed.

This means that it is not a question of tidal water. Typically, the turning of the tide causes large quantities of water to be displaced. It is easy to establish that there is no natural phenomenon where large quantities of water are cleft. Furthermore, it is a question of a special type of sea-bed with firm ground and no sediment.

Figure 332: Nuweiba and the suggested crossing site seen from the Nuweiba peninsula. The sun is rising above the mountains of Saudi-Arabia.

41.3. How long did the people of Israel have to cross the sea?

When reading the text, it seems as if one night was the time available for the crossing. But there might also have been a more stretched out scenario in terms of time.

If the biblical text is analysed in more detail the text opens up a time scale that actually could have taken three days from the start of events until it is all over. This data is summarised in figure 333.

When the Egyptian army arrives at the campsite it is clear that the army and the people of Israel do see one another. This is day one. The people of Israel are terrified while the Egyptian army slowly march into the area and decide to camp. The army is tired and needs rest before the huge battle that will take place, with the purpose to take control of the slaves that have escaped and bring them back to Egypt.

The people of Israel are terrified (Ex. 14:10-12). But Moses receives instructions from the Lord according to the text. First the pillar of cloud separates the two camps. The Egyptians are covered in darkness and consequently cannot do anything but wait. Moses then stretches out his hand and the waters are divided. The whole night a strong wind is blowing towards the west. Most likely the purpose with the wind was to make the sea-bed dry. It is out of the question that there would be an unbelievably strong wind that would blow a ditch in the sea and that people still could camp in the direction of the wind. If we assume that there was such a strong wind that could separate the deep waters, it is out of the question that people would survive being in the blown "ditch" in such a wind. It is more likely that the purpose of the wind was to make the sea bed dry, since it is stated several times that they crossed on dry ground.

"And the children of Israel shall go on dry ground through the midst of the sea." (Ex. 14:16)

This strong wind did blow the whole first night and the two camps were separated the whole night.

"...and the pillar of cloud went from before them and stood behind them. So it came between the camp of the Egyptians and the camp of Israel." (Ex. 14:19-20)

"...so that the one did not come near the other all that night." (Ex. 14:20)

This is the first day and night.

Day two the people of Israel starts the crossing, probably very early in the morning since it is said that the wind only blew during the night. Still the camps are separated by the pillar of cloud, and the people of Israel can go undisturbed across the sea with their leader Moses in the front. It is said that it was "a great way", "dry land" and that there were "no obstacles" on the sea-bed. They are surrounded by "walls" of water to the right and to the left. It is interesting to note that there were walls (Ex. 14:22, 29) of water. That means that the water was cut apart as if with a knife. Since the pillar of smoke separated the camps, the pillar of smoke must have been on land until the last Hebrew went out into the dried sea-bed. The people of Israel were guided by the pillar of fire during the night, so they could have been crossing the sea from the morning of the second day including the following night, night two.

In the morning (of the third day according to this hypothesis), at the morning watch, the Lord sends confusion to the Egyptian army according to the biblical text. Wheels fall off and the army is grabbed by panic. They are now in the middle of the sea with the whole army and decide to retire back to the land from where they came. Moses stretches out his hand again on the Lords command, according to the text, and the water returns. Not from the sides, but as a huge wave from the west that refills the whole sea road ditch with water. All the Egyptians die and are washed by the stream and winds towards the east coast of the Gulf of Aqaba, where the people of Israel have camped. This is indicated by two factors, first the wave that flows from the west towards the east and secondly, that the people of Israel can see all the soldiers on the beach. They cannot see bodies on a shore 14 km away, on the opposite side. These are the events of the third day.

If this hypothesis is correct the people of Israel had approximately 24 hours available for the crossing. From the morning of day two until the morning watch of day three. This is a summary of the biblical text (Ex 14: 1-30) with some comments from the historian Josephus (JA 15-16) as shown in a graphic manner in figure 333.

To summarise: The shortest time for the crossing was one night, but the text also opens up an alternative scenario which would have given them approximately 24 hours (one day and one night).

Figure 333: With the scenario shown in the figure, the time for crossing was approximately 24 hours. Numbers in parenthesis relate to the verses in Exodus, chapter 14. Red: The people of Israel. Blue: Egyptian army.

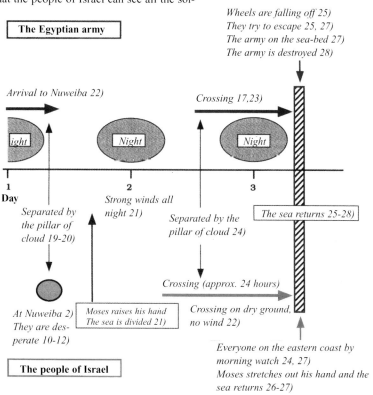

The Egyptian army

Wheels are falling off 25)
They try to escape 25, 27)
The army on the sea-bed 27)
The army is destroyed 28)

Arrival to Nuweiba 22)

Crossing 17,23)

light *Night* *Night*

1 **Day**   2   3

Separated by the pillar of cloud 19-20)

Strong winds all night 21)

Separated by the pillar of cloud 24)

The sea returns 25-28)

At Nuweiba 2) They are desperate 10-12)

Moses raises his hand The sea is divided 21)

Crossing (approx. 24 hours)

Crossing on dry ground, no wind 22)

The people of Israel

Everyone on the eastern coast by morning watch 24, 27)
Moses stretches out his hand and the sea returns 26-27)

42. How did the people of Israel cross the Red Sea?

The Gulf of Aqaba is part of a long rocky cleft, the Rift Valley, which stretches from present day Israel way down to Africa. The cleft is due to the fact that there are two continental plates here, which each move in their own direction. The Gulf of Aqaba is therefore deep, with a maximum depth of 1900 metres surrounded by high mountains of up to 2500 metres in height. Now if the water divided itself, it would not be the solution to the Israelites' problem. With a depth of water of about 1900 metres even with all the water gone, an enormous cleft faces the people of Israel.

42.1. An underwater bridge

It so happens that at Nuweiba there is a flat underwater bridge across the Red Sea. Typical of the Gulf of Aqaba are high mountain ranges up to 2500 metres in height which enclose the gulf. These mountains mostly go straight down into the sea. The Gulf of Aqaba has two deep basins: the northern is approximately 900 metres deep, and the southern approximately 1900 metres deep. The usual maritime maps of the area are of limited value. The reason is that it is so deep and with no islands (except for a few close to the coast), so there have not been any detailed surveys. Therefore, it is not unusual that relatively large vessels have no sonars or maritime maps when trafficking the Gulf of Aqaba.

At Nuweiba the coast is totally different. The Nuweiba peninsula is very flat and goes 3.5 km straight out into the gulf. This peninsula is so big that it is easily recogniseable on all maps and from satellites. From the Saudi-Arabian side it is a similar, although not so pronounced, situation. The Saudi-Arabian coast opposite Nuweiba is very flat and also similar to the Nuweiba character. Massive erosion has over the ages washed out huge amounts of sand and gravel from the surrounding mountains via the wadis. This has generated the flat areas on both sides. Consequently one can expect these flat areas to continue under water.

Is this the case at Nuweiba? Official data from the US National Geophysical Data Center suggest that there is a distinct underwater bridge from coast to coast with a maximum depth of approximately 100 metres. However, this data is not reliable since there is some 9 km between each point of measurement, and the computerised extrapolation of data based on such great distances between points of measurements is statistically weak.

Maps of unknown identity actually show an underwater bridge character at Nuweiba. In figure 334 an example of such a map is shown. In figure 335 a Russian map suggest an underwater shallow area between Nuweiba and the Saudi-Arabian coast. At Nuweiba, the distance from coast to coast is approximately 14 km. From the Saudi-Arabian coast it is as shallow as 87 m 4 km out from the coast line. If this is correct and transferable to both sides, it corresponds to a gradient of 2.2%.

After studying the underwater bridge from the Nuweiba side by a remote controlled underwater camera, the following data was acquired.

The bottom was followed every meter at 0.458 nautic mile (848 metres) with the camera. The starting point was approximately 1200 metres from the coast line. The depth at that point was 28 metres. From this point the bottom

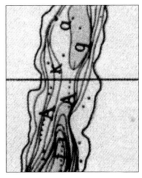

Figure 334: A map of unknown identity showing an underwater bridge at Nuweiba. Nuweiba is the peninsula seen along the left coastline.

was extraordinary flat to the end of the measurement where it was 82 metres deep. The depth was confirmed by the depth from the camera transferred to the surface and the length of the cable to the camera. The sea-bed was similar to the peninsula (see the cover of this book) in terms of the character of the ground, as well as in width and the very pronounced flatness with no obstacles. In figures 336 and 337 the character of the sea bed can be seen. Figures 336 and 337 represent overviews of the sea-bed down to 82 metres. The very flat

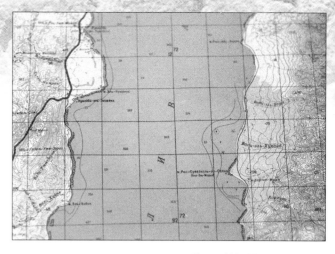

Figure 335: A Russian map shows a shallow region on the Saudi-Arabian side of the Gulf of Aqaba, opposite Nuweiba.

Figures 336, 337: The common characteristic of the sea-bed of the Gulf of Aqaba is very steep gradients. It is like the mountain ridges go straight down into the gulf and continue as steep under water canyons. Figures 336 and 337 show the general sea-bed east of Nuweiba down to 82 metres. These are representative photographs of the investigated area. There are no corals or vegetation in deeper waters due to the limited amount of light. Down to 82 metres there was very limited vegetation (small grass-like plants in some areas) and no corals, except very close to the shore. Since erosion has created this very flat sand and gravel character of the sea-bed and gravity together with currents move material towards the bottom, there are good reasons to assume that this sea-bed character continues into deeper waters. The sea-bed is made up by sand.

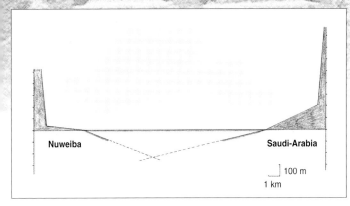

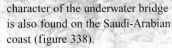

character of the underwater bridge is also found on the Saudi-Arabian coast (figure 338).

The change in depth from 28 to 82 metres (54 metres) at a distance of 848 metres (determined by satellite navigation) indicates a gradient of 6.4%. Or from the shore to the end of measurement it corresponds to 4.0%.

In figure 339 a graphic presentation is shown of this data. The solid curve in the left part (the Sinai coast) is from measurements by the underwater camera, and the similar curve from the east coast (Saudi-Arabia) is from the Russian map of figure 334. The dotted line is an extrapolation of the curves assuming that they continue with the same grade. If this is the case, the maximum depth is approximately 240 metres.

Figure 339: Measured gradients (solid lines) across the Gulf of Aqaba at Nuweiba. Note that the gradient is graphically over expressed in the figure. The realistic gradients are shown in figure 340. If the gradients would go across the gulf the maximum depth would be approximately 240 metres (dotted lines).

A map produced by J.K. Hall and Z. Ben-Avraham at The Israel Geological Survey exists. This map, which is based on the best available data and the survey, can confirm two matters: a broad underwater bridge at Nuweiba between the Nuweiba peninsula and the Saudi-Arabian coast; and a flat gradient. This data is in accordance with the underwater camera measurements and the Russian data although the Israeli measurements were done more extensively and in deeper waters. The Israeli data suggest a maximum depth at approximately 800 metres. It should be noted that the actual curves from the Israel Geological Survey have been extrapolated from a number of measurements, and that there might be more shallow areas at the suggested crossing site. A calculation of the crossing, based on the Israeli data, indicate a mean downhill gradient of 12% (west coast) and an uphill (east coast) gradient of 15% (70). The American "Disability Act" accepts a gradient range of 8.3-12.5% (new and old buildings, respectively) for disabled people (38). These gradients or slopes are graphically shown in figure 340, showing that even when the suggested deepest scenario have been used, the limits are very close to the American gradients accepted for disabled people.

The underwater land bridge of the investigated area has the following characteristics:
◆ Very limited vegetation (some grass-like plants in limited areas)
◆ No corals (except at the coast line)
◆ No pieces of rock
◆ No mountainous formations
◆ No steep slopes
◆ No organic sediments (like mud)
◆ Extremely flat
◆ Very broad (at least 2 km)
◆ The sea-bed is covered by sand and gravel

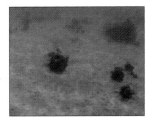

Figure 338: The sea-bed is similar on the Saudi-Arabian side as can be seen on this underwater photograph.

This means that if the water is removed and the sand is dried, there is solid ground to walk on. Further, the calculated gradient (based on the deepest depth scenario) is close to what is accepted for disabled people. The gradient corresponds to a change of 22-150 metres per km (or 2-15 cm/linear meter) with the deepest depth scenario. With a very flat area and no obstacles this gradient is possible to walk across. From the texts (Exodus and Josephus) it is clear that there were no obstacles on the sea-bed suggesting a flat sea-bed.

The total distance with the different calculations of gradients is in the range of 14.5-22 km if the Israelites walked straight across.

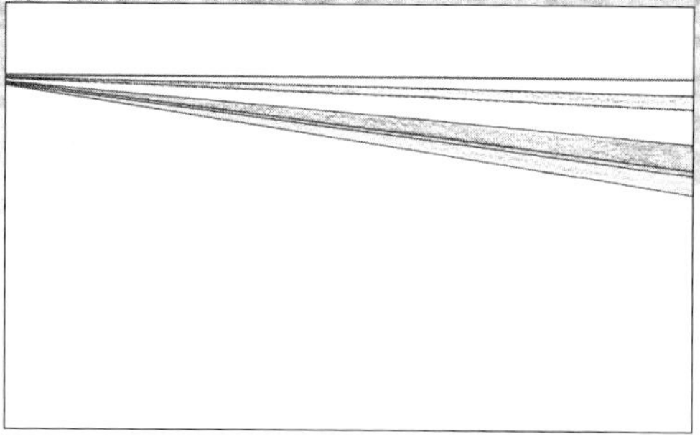

One can make different calculations but there are three important issues concerning this matter.

◆ The unusual character of the sea-bed making it look like a highway or a very wide (at least 2 km wide) underwater bridge.
◆ There is no natural explanation to how the water (according to the text) was cut apart.
◆ If the water was cut apart there would be a dry solid ground and the gradient would be possible to walk or ride across.

Figure 340: The gradients of the sea-bed discussed in the text. The blue line on top represent the water surface while the other lines represent the gradient of the sea-bed across the Gulf of Aqaba at Nuweiba. The black lines represents the gradients of the scenario of figure 339 extrapolated across the gulf, while the blue lines represent the gradients of the deepest scenario based on data from the Israeli Geological Survey. The red lines represent the range of gradients accepted for disabled people in the US. In this figure the gradients are realistic while they are over expressed in figure 339.

42.2. HOW WAS THE WATER CLEAVED?

So what did the Lord do to cleave the water? The text describes how a strong east wind blew the whole night and made the sea dry land:

"And Moses stretched out his hand over the sea; and the LORD caused the sea to go back by a strong east wind all that night, and made the sea dry land, and the waters were divided." (Ex. 14:21)

This event can be interpreted, and commented on with the following:

a) There is no wind that can blow a 14 km long, and several hundred metres deep, ditch through a sea, where people can walk at the same time. This is out of the question. Such a strong wind would wipe out every living thing. Most probably, the purpose of the wind was to dry the sea-bed.

b) A tide water phenomenon can be eliminated. If one plays with the thought that it was a tide after all, with a difference in height of several hundred metres, it is very difficult to picture this, as it is the moon's force of gravity which directs the tidal currents. The moon's force of gravity has a constant cycle at respective places on earth/water surfaces.

If one supposes that the bridge of land at that time was only a metre deep, and that an unusually strong tide (the normal tide water variation in the region is about 0.3 metres) opened up a way, this might possibly explain how the people of Israel could pass. However, it is completely impossible to explain how the entire Egyptian army could be wiped out by such a small difference in the tide waters.

Nor is it so simple to explain that this possible shallow passage was unknown. Had it been known the people of Israel would have had no problem of being shut in, and Pharaoh would never have believed that they were shut in. Pharaoh would surely have known about it with all the troops

Figure 341: Going through the Red Sea. This is what it could have looked like, although the walls of water were probably higher and the "sea road" much wider, probably at least one km.

that were usually found in the area, and moreover, probably a fort at the place. Had there been a superficial land bridge with such shallow water, neither would king Solomon have placed his port and large fleet in Elot, inside this land bridge.

c) The explanation nearest to hand for this phenomenon, must be that the Lord had taken the people of Israel to Nuweiba because they were to cross the Gulf of Aqaba precisely there. Moses was not prepared for this, which is shown both in the biblical texts and by the historical writer Josephus. If they were pursued by the Egyptians, then the Lord would punish the latter.

If the Lord is the Lord and creator of all, which the bible text claims, then it cannot be a big problem to keep two masses of water separate. We do not need to understand how the Lord did it, just as we do not understand how all the plagues the Egyptians suffered came to be. Either all this is a falsification or else it is a matter of God being God, and acting according to his own judgment to suspend the laws of nature He himself created.

Further on in the Bible there is a more poetic description of the parting of the water, when Moses and the people of Israel sing praises to the Lord:

"And with the blast of thy nostrils the waters were gathered together, the floods stood upright as an heap, and the depths were congealed in the heart of the sea." (Ex. 15:8)

Figure 342: The water came back early in the morning when the Egyptian army was in the middle of the Red Sea, according to the biblical text. The photograph shows the Nuweiba beach and the sunrise over the Saudi-Arabian mountain ridges on the opposite side of the Gulf of Aqaba.

This text implies that the waters were held apart in an extraordinary way, as if the water congealed, or perhaps it was angels who held the waters apart? At the Lord's command Moses has cleft the Red Sea. The people of Israel then march quickly behind Moses, who goes first, through the Red Sea on what Josephus calls "a divine path" (JA 2/16:2-3). And so the people of Israel enter Etham and the land of Midian, on the way to Mount Horeb, God's mountain, to worship the Lord.

43. WHAT HAPPENS TO THE EGYPTIAN ARMY?

When the darkness of the pillar of the cloud and the night are at an end for the Egyptians and the people of Israel pitch camp on the other side of the Red Sea, the Egyptian army resumes the pursuit. Not even then, when the entire Red Sea has been cleft in two and saved the people of Israel, do Pharaoh, the priesthood, the counsellors and all the officers understand that they are struggling against the Lord himself.

43.1. AN ATTACK ON A WIDE FRONT

According to Josephus, the Egyptians rush forward with the war chariots in
the lead (JA 2/16:3). Soon the entire Egyptian army is gathered on the path,
on the bed of the Red Sea: at least 600 war chariots, besides all the chariots
of Egypt with 50 000 soldiers belonging to them, and 200 000 infantry
troops. All of them armed and under the command of the priesthood and
Pharaoh Amenhotep III himself. Since the sea is still cleft in a way that made
it possible for roughly 2 million Israelites to cross, the Egyptian army can
also attack in formation and on a wide front.

Josephus expresses this in a way the Egyptians ought to have seen: "...but
the Egyptians were not aware that they chose a way that had been made for
the Hebrews and not for others, that this way was made for the liberation of
those in danger and not for those who wanted to use it to kill others." (JA
2/16:3).

According to the Bible, the entire Egyptian army was out in the middle of
the dried-out Red Sea bed, while Moses stood on the other shore. Then the
Lord sent confusion amongst the Egyptian army:

*"And it came to pass, that in the morning watch the LORD looked unto the
host of the Egyptians through the pillar of fire and of the cloud, and troubled
the host of the Egyptians, And took off their chariot wheels, that they drave
them heavily: so that the Egyptians said, Let us flee from the face of Israel;
for the LORD fighteth for them against the Egyptians."* (Ex. 14:24-25)

At this point the Egyptians understand that they have fought against the Lord,
and not against mere humans:

*"And took off their chariot wheels, that they drave them heavily: so that the
Egyptians said, Let us flee from the face of Israel; for the LORD fighteth for
them against the Egyptians."* (Ex. 14:25)

But it is too late for the Egyptians. They have passed the limit set by the
Lord according to the text. They have made themselves gods, and they now
see that they are nearing their destruction. The Lord says to Moses:

*"And the LORD said unto Moses, Stretch out thine hand over the sea, that
the waters may come again upon the Egyptians, upon their chariots, and
upon their horsemen. And Moses stretched forth his hand over the sea, and
the sea returned to his strength when the morning appeared; and the
Egyptians fled against it; and the LORD overthrew the Egyptians in the
midst of the sea. And the waters returned, and covered the chariots, and the
horsemen, and all the host of Pharaoh that came into the sea after them;
there remained not so much as one of them."* (Ex. 14:26-28)

Thus the Red Sea swallows up the entire Egyptian army including Pharaoh
and the priesthood.

Figure 343: "...thunder was in the heaven, the lightnings lightened the world..."

43.2. How did they die?

The question is, did the Egyptians drown? Most likely we can assume that they could not swim, they were trained to fight in desert environments. Moreover, they were weighted down with weapons bound to their bodies, and had shields and many other heavy objects. But it is not certain that they drowned. They were enclosed by the Red Sea at a depth of up to several hundred metres. Because of the changes in pressure, ascent from such a depth causes serious injuries followed by unconsciousness and death. A direct ascent of the type to which the soldiers were exposed, would cause their lungs to burst. This is a risk at only 10 meters depth. The way in which the Egyptians died is not crucial, but the text tells us that there was not a sole survivor (Ex. 14:28).

43.3. Stormy waters

The Bible relates that simultaneously, as the waters of the Red Sea flowed back, there was a storm, rain, thunder and lightning as a sign from the Lord.

"The clouds poured out water: the skies sent out a sound: thine arrows also went abroad. The voice of thy thunder was in the heaven: the lightnings lightened the world: the earth trembled and shook. Thy way is in the sea, and thy path in the great waters, and thy footsteps are not known. Thou leddest thy people like a flock by the hand of Moses and Aaron." (Ps. 77:17-20)

It can be speculated that it was an earth quake at this moment. Vulcanic activity faded out a long, geological time ago in this region, but an earth quake induced by a movement of the earth's crust is possible.

43.4. The people of Israel become armed

The Egyptians floated up and were washed up onto the shore, where the people of Israel had pitched camp:

Figure 344: Strong winds blew the Egyptian bodies to the eastern shore, where the Israelites collected the weapons.

"Thus the LORD saved Israel that day out of the hand of the Egyptians; and Israel saw the Egyptians dead upon the sea shore." (Ex. 14:30)

The historian Josephus has an interesting note, which is linked to chapter 30 in this book, where the hypothesis is put forward that the people of Israel were unarmed at the Exodus. Josephus says: "The next day Moses had all the Egyptians' weapons collected up and taken to the Hebrew encampment with the help of sea currents and strong winds, and he declared that this too happened through divine intervention so that they would not be without arms. So when he had ordered the Hebrews to arm themselves with these he led them to Mount Sinai..." (JA 2/16:6).

Here we have the explanation of how the people of Israel could depart unarmed, but nonetheless be armed when they fought the Amalechites (chapter 62); soon after reaching Midian having passed through the Red Sea. This is the only note with bearing on how all the people of Israel were able to arm themselves in this desert region to which they had come unarmed.

The weapons the Egyptians had were in the main attached to their bodies. This applied particularly to the soldiers in the war chariots, who needed free hands. But without a doubt, even the infantry soldiers would have had their weapons attached or in some way fastened to the body, just as the soldiers of today carry their arms. When the bodies floated up, very little wind was needed to drive them into the shore. The Bible relates that there was a mighty storm when the waters closed, and so there were strong winds which drove floating objects onto the shore in this narrow strait. Presumably the people of Israel had large heaps of soldiers from whom to pick weapons. These weapons were mainly swords, daggers, spears, bows and arrows.

44. What do the people of Israel do?

When the people of Israel see how God has saved them from the Egyptian army in this extraordinary and mighty way, they sing praises to God. This song of praise is cited in the book of Exodus:

44.1. A song of praise

"Then sang Moses and the children of Israel this song unto the LORD, and spake, saying, 'I will sing unto the LORD, for he hath triumphed gloriously: the horse and his rider hath he thrown into the sea. The LORD is my strength and song, and he is become my salvation: he is my God, and I will prepare him an habitation; my father's God, and I will exalt him. The LORD is a man of war: the LORD is his name.

Figure 345: The wind blew towards the east, and caused the remains of the Egyptian army to be blown towards the coast of today's Saudi-Arabia.

Pharaoh's chariots and his host hath he cast into the sea: his chosen captains also are drowned in the Red sea. The depths have covered them: they sank into the bottom as a stone. Thy right hand, O LORD, is become glorious in power: thy right hand, O LORD, hath dashed in pieces the enemy.

And in the greatness of thine excellency thou hast overthrown them that rose up against thee: thou sentest forth thy wrath, which consumed them as stubble. And with the blast of thy nostrils the waters were gathered together, the floods stood upright as an heap, and the depths were congealed in the heart of the sea.

The enemy said, "I will pursue, I will overtake, I will divide the spoil; my lust shall be satisfied upon them; I will draw my sword, my hand shall destroy them." Thou didst blow with thy wind, the sea covered them: they sank as lead in the mighty waters.

Who is like unto thee, O LORD, among the gods? who is like thee, glorious in holiness, fearful in praises, doing wonders? Thou stretchedst out thy right hand, the earth swallowed them. Thou in thy mercy hast led forth the people which thou hast redeemed: thou hast guided them in thy strength unto thy holy habitation. The people shall hear, and be afraid: sorrow shall take hold on the inhabitants of Palestina.

Then the dukes of Edom shall be amazed; the mighty men of Moab, trembling shall take hold upon them; all the inhabitants of Canaan shall melt

Figure 346: The waters of the Red Sea calmed, and the people of Israel were protected by the water barrier. This photograph was taken from the Saudi-Arabian side, facing Nuweiba.

away. Fear and dread shall fall upon them; by the greatness of thine arm they shall be as still as a stone; till thy people pass over, O LORD, till the people pass over, which thou hast purchased.

Thou shalt bring them in, and plant them in the mountain of thine inheritance, in the place, O LORD, which thou hast made for thee to dwell in, in the Sanctuary, O LORD, which thy hands have established. The LORD shall reign for ever and ever. For the horse of Pharaoh went in with his chariots and with his horsemen into the sea, and the LORD brought again the waters of the sea upon them; but the children of Israel went on dry land in the midst of the sea.'" (Ex. 15:1-19)

44.2. ON THE WAY TO THE MOUNTAIN

There is reason to note several points in this song of praise. It is implied here that the Egyptians were heavily armed, they "sank to the bottom as a stone", "they sank as lead in the mighty waters".

It was not a matter of the waters being driven aside, but "the depths were congealed in the heart of the sea". With a depth of up to several hundred metres, and earlier texts stating that the sea was a wall to the right and to the left of them, the picture described is clear, "the waters congealed".

The song of praise goes on:

"Thou shalt bring them in, and plant them in the mountain of thine inheritance, in the place, O LORD, which thou hast made for thee to dwell in, in the Sanctuary, O LORD, which thy hands have established." (Ex. 15:17)

It is clear in the biblical text that they are on the way to Mount Sinai/Horeb after going through the Red Sea. The mountain to which Moses went earlier, and the mountain which the Lord made his own, Mount Horeb or Mount Sinai. The mountain which Moses had been given the task of leading the Israelites to, in order to worship there.

In Christian tradition the rescue through the Red Sea depicts baptism, through water to salvation. In Jewish tradition this becomes the birth of the Israelite nation. They enter the sea-bed as persecuted slaves and stand on the further shore as a liberated nation, which is shortly to receive its fundamental law.

45. WHEN DOES THE EXODUS TAKE PLACE?

In the biblical texts there is a basis on which to draw up a chronology for the periods of time with which this book deals. Important key events can also be verified with other historical sources.

45.1. THE DESTRUCTION OF JERUSALEM

The destruction of Jerusalem by Nebuchadnezzar in 586 BC (48), is the starting point of this chronology. This event is referred to in the Bible and is named in a definite way in historical sources. These sources originate from Babylonian documents, with astronomic references to points in time.

Ordinary encyclopedias also give this date for the destruction of Jerusalem. This date is discussed thoroughly in literature. The destruction of Jerusalem occurs, and the captivity in Babylon begins, in the 19th year of the reign of Nebuchadnezzar, and the 11th year of Zedekiah's reign (II Kings 25:2).

45.2. THE BOOKS OF KINGS

King Zedekiah was reigning in Jerusalem when Nebuchadnezzar invaded the city, and the incidents occured which led to the destruction of Jerusalem (II Kings 25:1-17). This is the last event mentioned in chapter 25 of the second book of Kings. Every preceding king is mentioned in the two books of Kings: 47 chapters in all. If one counts back from king Zedekiah through the books of Kings, one comes to the beginning of the first book of Kings, which refers in detail to king Solomon.

Every king in between is specified, especially with regard to the length of his reign. Furthermore, during many years the country was divided into two kingdoms, Israel and Judah respectively. This means that there are two parallel royal lines, which make a number of cross references possible since at regular intervals they refer to each other or to other events. Some things remain uncertain, but these lie within relatively narrow margins (when one refers to the thorough, parallel royal lines), in spite of the length of the period and the fact that the events occured several thousand years ago.

45.3. KING SOLOMON

To the year 586 BC (the destruction of Jerusalem), can be added approximately 384 years (from the royal lines), which gives us approximately 970 BC as the first year of the reign of Solomon. King Solomon reigned for 40 years.

Later, in the first book of Kings a precise comment is made, which relates the reign of king Solomon to the date of the Exodus:

"And it came to pass in the four hundred and eightieth year after the children of Israel were come out of the land of Egypt, in the fourth year of Solomon's reign over Israel, in the month Zif, which is the second month, that he began to build the house of the LORD." (I Kings 6:1)

"The house of the Lord" is the temple in Jerusalem. To arrive at the fourth year of king Solomon's reign, four years are subtracted from approximately 970 BC, giving us approximately 966 BC. That year, states the biblical text (I Kings 6:1), it was exactly 480 years since the Exodus took place. Then approximately 966 can be added to 480, giving approximately 1446 BC. According to this chronological calculation, the Exodus occurred in approximately 1446 BC.

According to the calculation in figure 347, in this book the Exodus is said to have occurred in approximately 1446 BC. There is some uncertainty about this date. Firstly there are four uncertain years (miscount) during the last 2000 years, connected with the birth of Jesus and the founding of Rome respectively. This uncertainty is generally known. With regard to other years given in figure 347, 480 years and 36 years are individual indications (not calculated/worked out). In the presentation of the royal lines, there may be a

There is a growing support of an approximate year of 1446 BC for the Exodus compared to other suggestions (25). Furthermore, 14C-dating of remains of Jericho suggests the destruction to have happened around 1400 BC (27). The destruction of Jericho would, according to the hypothesis of this book, have occurred approximately 1406 BC.

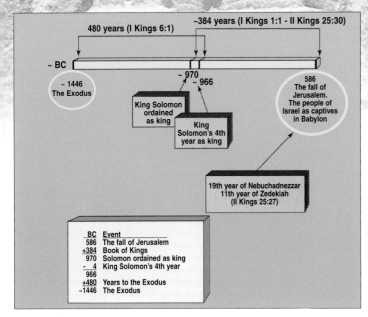

480 years (I Kings 6:1)

~384 years (I Kings 1:1 - II Kings 25:30)

~ BC

~ 1446
The Exodus

~ 970
~ 966

King Solomon
ordained
as king

King
Solomon's 4th
year as king

586
The fall of
Jerusalem.
The people of
Israel as captives
in Babylon

19th year of Nebuchadnezzar
11th year of Zedekiah
(II Kings 25:27)

BC	Event
586	The fall of Jerusalem
+384	Book of Kings
970	Solomon ordained as king
- 4	King Solomon's 4th year
966	
+480	Years to the Exodus
~1446	The Exodus

Figure 347: A summary of how to calculate the approximate year of the Exodus, according to the biblical texts.

margin of error of about a decade. This figure is an estimate. With 4 + 10 years presumed uncertainty, there may be a total of around 15 years uncertainty in the years given in figure 347.

45.4. ESTIMATION OF THE PERIOD IN CAPTIVITY

When we now know the probable point in time of the Exodus (approx. 1446 BC), the next step is to begin to count from the birth of Abraham. We put Abraham's birth at the year 0, and count forwards according to the biblical texts. Isaac is born when Abraham is 100 years old (Gen. 21:5), Jacob is born when Isaac is 60 (Gen. 25:26) and Joseph is born when Jacob is 91 years old (Gen. 41:46-47; 45:6, 9-10; 47:9). Furthermore, Joseph attains his high position in Egypt when he is 30 years old (Gen. 41:41), and Jacob and his family move to Egypt when Joseph is 39 years old (Gen. 47:9). As is shown in figure 348, this gives a total period of 290 years.

There are now two time axes which must be linked together. The biblical texts give three different passages which directly indicate a time span from an event with Isaac to the year of the Exodus. The first of these passages is:

"And he said unto Abram, 'Know of a surety that thy seed shall be a stranger in a land that is not their's, and shall serve them; and they shall afflict them four hundred years; And also that nation, whom they shall serve, will I judge: and afterward shall they come out with great substance.'"
(Gen. 15:13-14)

Here Abraham receives a prophecy from the Lord which contains a great deal of information, but the prophecy is couched in general terms. Abraham learns the following:

1. Abraham's offspring (Isaac and onwards) will live in a foreign country, but it is not said in which foreign country/countries.
2. They will be subject to the laws of that country.
3. They will be slaves, but it is not indicated in which country nor for how long.
4. Later they will leave this country with great possessions.
5. This will, taken all together, happen during a period of about 400 years.

They would not be slaves all the time nor would they be in Egypt all the time and a rounded figure of the length of time is given. They learn of this in general terms and this prophecy lives on among the people of Israel. When

Event	Number of years	Sum of years	Comments
Birth of Abraham	0 =	0	
Birth of Isaac, Abraham 100 yrs. (Gen. 21:5)	+100 =	100	
"Sacrifice" of Isaac (Gen. 22:1-19)		120 ←	The "sacrifice" of Isaac: If Isaac was 20 yrs., Abraham was 120, 290 - 120 = 170 yrs. before Jacob and his family moved to Egypt (430 years before the Exodus (Ex. 12:41)
Birth of Jacob, Isaac 60 yrs. (Gen. 25:26)	+60 =	160	
Birth of Joseph, Jacob 91 yrs. (Gen. 41:46-47, 45:6, 9-10, 47:9)	+91 =	251	
Joseph appointed to his position in Egypt at age 30 (Gen. 41:41)	+30 =	281	
Jacob and his family move to Egypt when Jacob is 130 and Joseph is 39 (Gen. 47:9)	+9 =	290	

Figure 348: A summary of the chronology from Abraham to Joseph, according to the biblical texts.

Joseph dies in Egypt the people of Israel have to promise on oath to take Joseph's bones with them when they leave the country later on, although this date is some 190 years in the future.

One can understand the suffering of the people of Israel as slaves in Egypt, and that this became particularly hard when 400 years had passed and still nothing happened. But something was happening. Moses had been in the land of Midian for about 10 years, having fled from the Egyptian army.

At the Exodus reference is made to this prophecy:

"Now the sojourning of the children of Israel, who dwelt in Egypt, was four hundred and thirty years. And it came to pass at the end of the four hundred and thirty years, even the selfsame day it came to pass, that all the hosts of the LORD went out from the land of Egypt." (Ex. 12:40-41)

It should be noted that they kept a careful check on the prophecy. It was exactly on the day, 430 years later, that everything was fulfilled. A foreign country implies that one lives in someone else's country, i.e. one does not have a country of one's own. They became slaves and they also received many possessions as gifts from the Egyptians.

The question is to which event the prophecy refers. The event would have happened 430 years before the Exodus, which gives us about the year 1876 BC. In the epistle to the Galatians Paul gives the following interpretation:

"Brethren, I speak after the manner of men; Though it be but a man's covenant, yet if it be confirmed, no man disannulleth, or addeth thereto. Now to Abraham and his seed were the promises made. He saith not, And to seeds, as of many; but as of one, And to thy seed, which is Christ. And this I say, that the covenant, that was confirmed before of God in Christ, the law, which was four hundred and thirty years after, cannot disannul, that it should make the promise of none effect." (Gal. 3:15-17)

To summarise, these passages tell us the following:

1. There were 430 years between when the law was given, and the prophecy to Abraham concerning his offspring (Isaac). Here Paul refers to the passage discussed above (Ex. 12:40-41).

2. So what happened with Isaac that these passages refer to? That which happened about 1876 BC?

3. In the biblical text Gen. 22:1-19 this event is dealt with under the heading: "Abraham commanded to offer Isaac". We have touched on this event in chapter 4.

45.5. THE "SACRIFICE" OF ISAAC

The Bible text tells us the following:

"And it came to pass after these things, that God did tempt Abraham, and said unto him, 'Abraham': and he said, 'Behold, here I am.' And he said, 'Take now thy son, thine only son Isaac, whom thou lovest, and get thee into the land of Moriah; and offer him there for a burnt offering upon one of the mountains which I will tell thee of.'

And Abraham rose up early in the morning, and saddled his ass, and took two of his young men with him, and Isaac his son, and clave the wood for the burnt offering, and rose up, and went unto the place of which God had told him. Then on the third day Abraham lifted up his eyes, and saw the place afar off.

And Abraham said unto his young men, 'Abide ye here with the ass; and I and the lad will go yonder and worship, and come again to you.' And

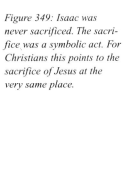

Figure 349: Isaac was never sacrificed. The sacrifice was a symbolic act. For Christians this points to the sacrifice of Jesus at the very same place.

Abraham took the wood of the burnt offering, and laid it upon Isaac his son; and he took the fire in his hand, and a knife; and they went both of them together.

And Isaac spake unto Abraham his father, and said, 'My father': and he said, 'Here am I, my son.' And he said, 'Behold the fire and the wood: but where is the lamb for a burnt offering?' And Abraham said, 'My son, God will provide himself a lamb for a burnt offering': so they went both of them together. And they came to the place which God had told him of; and Abraham built an altar there, and laid the wood in order, and bound Isaac his son, and laid him on the altar upon the wood.

And Abraham stretched forth his hand, and took the knife to slay his son. And the angel of the LORD called unto him out of heaven, and said, 'Abraham, Abraham': and he said, 'Here am I.' And he said, 'Lay not thine hand upon the lad, neither do thou any thing unto him: for now I know that thou fearest God, seeing thou hast not withheld thy son, thine only son from me.'

And Abraham lifted up his eyes, and looked, and behold behind him a ram caught in a thicket by his horns: and Abraham went and took the ram, and offered him up for a burnt offering in the stead of his son. And Abraham called the name of that place Jehovahjireh: as it is said to this day, In the mount of the LORD it shall be seen.

And the angel of the LORD called unto Abraham out of heaven the second time, and said, 'By myself have I sworn, saith the LORD, for because thou hast done this thing, and hast not withheld thy son, thine only son:

That in blessing I will bless thee, and in multiplying I will multiply thy seed as the stars of the heaven, and as the sand which is upon the sea shore; and thy seed shall possess the gate of his enemies; And in thy seed shall all the nations of the earth be blessed; because thou hast obeyed my voice.'

So Abraham returned unto his young men, and they rose up and went together to Beersheba; and Abraham dwelt at Beersheba." (Gen. 22:1-19)

To summarise, these events concern the following:

1. Abraham shows his readiness to sacrifice his son Isaac in a blood sacrifice on Mount Moriah. Human sacrifices were common in the area, but this was only a test for Abraham.
2. On that day 430 years later, a lamb without blemish was to be sacrificed (blood sacrifice) in every family of the people of Israel, to avoid the death of every firstborn. It is the institution of the Jewish passover, and the beginning of the Exodus. The promise given to Abraham is fulfilled that year, with liberation from slavery, and the covenant given with the stone tablets on Mount Sinai.
3. As Paul explains (Gal. 3:15-17), on precisely the same day and the same mountain, slightly more than 1900 years later, Jesus Christ is sacrificed on the summit of Mount Moriah in a blood sacrifice with the promise of liberation, and the institution of the new covenant. It is the institution of the Christian Easter.
4. It is on Mount Moriah that old Jerusalem is built. The site of the temple was up on Mount Moriah. Here the Jews have the western wall as a sacred

place, the part of the temple which is still standing today. Here the Muslims have two mosques on the site where the temple stood. Close by, also on Mount Moriah, the Christians have Golgotha (the place of sacrifice) and the empty grave.

It is this event, the "offering" of Isaac, which permeates the whole Bible, and is indicated as the point of reference for these 430 years. We can then, with relative precision, put together these two time axes (figures 347, 348).

45.6. How old was Isaac?

The question then remaining is what age Isaac was when he was to be "sacrificed".

The following four alternatives spring to mind:

1. Isaac argued logically with his father Abraham. Isaac should then have been at least 10 years old. However there is no specific reference to age.
2. One might speculate that Isaac was as old as Jesus Christ when he was sacrificed at the same place. In that case Isaac was 33 years old, but there is no reference to this age either.
3. Isaac has to carry all the firewood the last part of the way to the place of sacrifice. A relatively large amount of firewood was needed for the sacrifice, so it must have been heavy to carry. This implies that Isaac was physically stronger than Abraham, who carried only the fire and the knife. According to this comment Isaac would have been in his late teens.
4. But there is a reference to another age. In order for the sacrifice of Isaac (which did not need to be carried out) to be righteous, then Isaac should have been adult and responsible for his actions. The Bible gives us several references as to when a man was considered adult and independent.
a) To enlist as a soldier a man had to be 20 years old (Ex. 3:11-15).
b) In a census men old enough to bear arms were counted (Ex. 38:26).
c) The age at which the people could be penalised was 20 (Numb. 14:29, 32:11).

Based on this argument Isaac should have been between 10 and 33 years old. Most probably Isaac was 20 years old, since he would have been responsible for his actions, adult enough to take the consequences of his decisions, and of the age to be penalised when it was a matter of a vicarious sacrifice (punishment for the sins committed by the people).

45.7. Combining the time axes

In the link between the two time axes in figures 347 and 348, the age of 20 has therefore been used for the point in time (the "sacrifice" of Isaac) to which the Bible refers. The total time axis can be seen in figure 350. Approximately 10 years of uncertainty should be added to the time axis in figure 350, because of the uncertainty about Isaac's age at the "sacrifice" on Mount Moriah.

Therefore, the total time axis in figure 350 has an estimated uncertainty of about 25 years altogether. In Table 11, details of the calculation of the royal lines of Judah and Israel are shown.

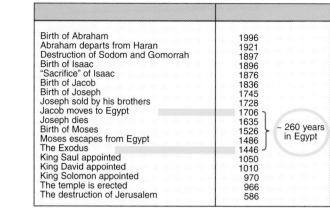

Birth of Abraham	1996
Abraham departs from Haran	1921
Destruction of Sodom and Gomorrah	1897
Birth of Isaac	1896
"Sacrifice" of Isaac	1876
Birth of Jacob	1836
Birth of Joseph	1745
Joseph sold by his brothers	1728
Jacob moves to Egypt	1706
Joseph dies	1635
Birth of Moses	1526
Moses escapes from Egypt	1486
The Exodus	1446
King Saul appointed	1050
King David appointed	1010
King Solomon appointed	970
The temple is erected	966
The destruction of Jerusalem	586

~ 260 years in Egypt

Figure 350: A combination of the time axis in figures 224 and 225.

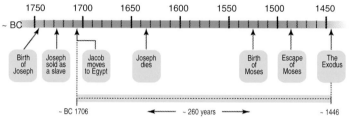

Table 11. A summary of the cronology according to the hypothesis in this book. All years are approximate, for comments on this matter, see the text in chapter 45.

Person/Event	Approx. Year BC
Birth of Terah	2126
Birth of Abraham	1996
Abraham leaves Haran (Gen. 12:4)	1921
Birth of Ishmael (Gen. 16:16)	1910
Destruction of Sodom and Gomorrah (Gen. 17:21-25)	1897
Birth of Isaac (Gen. 21:5)	1896
"Sacrifice" of Isaac (Gen. 22:1-19)	1876
Isaac marries Rebecca (Gen. 25:20)	1856
Birth of Jacob and Esau (Gen. 25:26)	1836
Abraham dies	1821
Birth of Joseph (Gen. 41:46-47, 45:6-10, 47:9)	1745
Joseph sold by his brothers (Gen. 37:2)	1728
Isaac dies	1716
Joseph promoted in Egypt (Gen. 41:46)	1715
Jacob arrives to Egypt (Gen. 47:9)	1706
Joseph dies	1635
Birth of Moses	1526
Moses escape from Egypt	1486
EXODUS	1446
Moses dies (Deu. 34:7), Entry into Canaan	1406
Joshua dies (Josh. 14:10)	1377

cont.

continued Table 11

- Period of Judges -

King Saul	1050
King David	1010
King Solomon	970
Construction on the temple starts	966
Israel divided into Israel and Judah	931

- Kings of Israel -	BC	- Kings of Judah -	BC
Jeroboam	930-909	Rehoboam	930-913
		Abijah	913-910
		Asa	910-869
Nadab	909-908		
Baasha	908-885		
Elah	885-884		
Zimri	884		
Omri	884-873		
Ahab	873-852	Jehoshaphat(1)	873-848
Ahaziah	852-851		
Joram(2)	857-845	Jehoram(3)	853-846
		Ahaziah	845
Jehu	844-818	Athalia	844-838
Jehoahaz	818-802	Joash	838-799
Jehoash	802-786	Amaziah(4)	800-772
Jeroboam(5)	798-758	Uzziah(6)	796-745
Zechariah	758		
Menahem	758-748		
Pekahiah	747-746		
Peka(7)	747-728	Jotham(8)	747-731
		Ahaz(9)	739-723
Hosea	727-719	Hezekiah(10)	725-697
Conquered, ceases to exist			
		Mannaseh	696-642
		Amon	641-640
		Josiah	639-609
		Jehoahaz	608
		Jehoiakim	608-598
		Daniel to Babylon	605
		Jehoiachin	597
		Zedekiah	597-586

Israel into Babylonian captivity	586
Nebudchadnezzar destroys the temple	586

(1) co-rules 4 y with Asa. (2) co-rules with Ahab and Ahaziah. 3) co-rules 5 y with Jehoshaphat. (4) co-rules 2 y with Joash. (5) co-rules 13 y with Jehoash. (6) co-rules 25 y with Amaziah. (7) co-rules 2 y with Pekahiah. (8) co-rules 2 y with Uzziah. (9) co-rules 8 y with Jotham. (10) co-rules 3 y with Ahaz.

(see also (49)

46. ARE THERE ANY ARCHEOLOGICAL FINDS TO CONFIRM THE CROSSING THROUGH THE RED SEA?

There are a number of archeological finds and contexts, which support the hypothesis that the Red Sea was crossed at Nuweiba. Earlier, the encampment site was discussed with the connected archeological finds and the origin of names. In chapter 42 the underwater bridge which stretches across the Red Sea at Nuweiba was discussed.

The actual encampment site; the way there; the origin of the names which define the encampment; the ruins of a fort and a probable location for the worship of Baal; the fact that there was room for both the people of Israel and the Egyptian army at the site; Wadi Watir as the only way to reach the site, which meant that the people of Israel had to turn back; the underwater bridge through the Gulf of Aqaba; and that all this leads to Mount Horeb in the land of Midian have been dealt with so far. All of these events tally with what is decribed in the biblical texts, and by the historical writer Josephus. The question that arises is whether this dramatic event left any traces at Nuweiba, in the Red Sea or on the other side in Saudi-Arabia.

The answer is that there are a number of different traces and archeological finds, besides those mentioned earlier, which we shall now look at more closely.

Figure 351: A column was raised on the shore of Nuweiba.

47. COLUMNS RAISED AT THE PLACE OF THE CROSSING THROUGH THE RED SEA

On the shore at Nuweiba there is an approximately 4.7 metre high column, with a diameter of roughly 90 cm (figure 351). The column is cylindrical in shape and made of red granite. The style of the column resembles more what is to be found in Israel, and does not look Egyptian. During the time that the Sinai peninsula was occupied by Israel, the column was discovered lying at the edge of the water. It was raised up again near the place where it had fallen over.

The column is large, with an estimated weight of 11.5 tons, and must have meant a great deal to the person who made it and set it up. The material, red granite (figures 352-354), is not found in the area and must come from somewhere else. The column has no inscriptions, or the movement of the sea has rubbed them away during the course of time, since one side of the column is badly eroded (figures 359, 360).

Another alternative is that possible inscriptions have been chiselled away, and the column knocked over purposely. From the shape of the column it seems that one side has been eroded, since it has an uneven surface and the round shape in that part of the column is more oval. It may also be that the column fell over into the water on the edge of the shore as the result of an earthquake.

This column is interesting in itself, but the question is why it has been erected on this spot. To procure good quality red granite from far away, perhaps from southern Egypt, to fashion a column weighing roughly 11.5 tons and then transport it to this place, must mean that whoever did this felt the place was worthy of marking in a way that cost a great deal of money. This place has not been inhabited, but has only had temporary bedouin visits and

Figures 352-354: The column was made out of red granite, a material not found in this area. The red granite most likely has its origin in Egypt. The left figure shows the red granite from the Nuweiba column. The right side shows red granite from the Karnak temple in Southern Egypt.

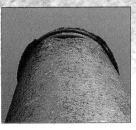

Figures 355-358: In Ashkelon, on the Mediterranean coast of today's Israel, there are a large number of columns that are made of granite and look very similar to the column at Nuweiba.

Figures 359-361: The column at Nuweiba showing the limited decorations.

possibly a military unit in the fort, at the other end of the Nuweiba peninsula.

In Ashkelon, on the Mediterranean coast of present day Israel, there are a number of columns closely resembling the column in Nuweiba (figures 355-358).

The similarities include:

- Shape
- Height and diameter
- Material (granite)
- Lack of decorations
- A simple border high up on the pillar

The only type of decoration is the border ornamenting the upper part of the column. Similar decorations can be seen on the columns in Ashkelon (figures 357, 358). It may be assumed that it was the same cultural sphere which created the column in Nuweiba, this would mean within the area corresponding to present day Israel.

47.1. TWO COLUMNS

What the column in Nuweiba really means has not been known. However, the situation changed completely when an identical column was found on the other side of the Red Sea, exactly where the people of Israel were expected to have come ashore and pitched camp after crossing the Red Sea, in north-western Saudi-Arabia. Two identical columns, made of the same material and the same size, erected on either side of the Red Sea exactly where the people of Israel are assumed to have crossed. Is this a memorial? If so, erected by whom?

The place where they passed through the Red Sea was known by all the Hebrew people, and it is very probable that they retained this knowledge through the ages. The event was absolutely decisive for the continued existence of the people of Israel, and the place of the event was easy to identify and remember.

The column discovered on the eastern shore was in a better state, since it was still standing and had not lain in sea-water and eroded. The column on the Saudi-Arabian side was taken down as soon as it was identified by the Saudi-Arabian authorities, and is now only marked by a metal flag and plate at the place where the column was erected (figures 364, 365).

47.2. Who erected these columnns?

Saul was the first king of Israel, followed by David and then Solomon. King Solomon became the king of Israel in about 970 BC, and he reigned for 40 years. The building of the temple in Jerusalem began in the fourth year of King Solomon's reign, with the aim of housing the Ark of the covenant, which the people of Israel made at Mount Horeb. Solomon became king of Israel 476 years after the Exodus.

Figure 362: A typical column in Ashkelon, with similar decorations as the column in Nuweiba.

The suggested explanation of these columns, is that King Solomon erected them in memory of the deliverance of the people of Israel by going through the Red Sea. The columns were raised on either side of the crossing through the Red Sea. The erection of these columns probably took place about 3000 years ago, during the reign of King Solomon, perhaps simultaneously with the beginning of construction of the temple under King Solomon's direction. King Solomon was also familiar with the waters of the Gulf of Aqaba, and had the equipment to transport these columns:

"And King Solomon made a navy of ships in Eziongeber, which is beside Eloth, on the shore of the Red sea, in the land of Edom. And Hiram sent in the navy his servants, shipmen that had knowledge of the sea, with the servants of Solomon." (I Kings 9:26-27)

Elot was situated in the vicinity of today's Eilat on the northern point of the Gulf of Aqaba, in present day Israel. Since King Solomon had his own fleet in the Gulf of Aqaba, and moreover was very rich and influential, it could not have been any great problem to manufacture these columns, and transport them to the respective places by sea. The site of the crossing through the Red Sea (Nuweiba) is only roughly 70 km south of the northern point of the Gulf of Aqaba, Eilat of today.

Figure 363: The columns in Ashkelon are numerous, and found at many places, even on the beach.

These columns suggest that this place, on either side of the Gulf of Aqaba, has been marked by a rich and influential person with access to shipping vessels. In this region it is almost impossible to take these columns by land, as the mountain ridges reach right down to the edge of the sea (figure 366).

The red granite may have come from southern Egypt. This is not unlikely since King Solomon was rich, had his own fleet and built the temple in Jerusalem to house the Ark of the covenant, and to honour the Lord. In addition, it can be mentioned that Solomon was married to the daughter of the Pharaoh then reigning in Egypt, and thus had excellent contacts with the Egyptians through his father-in-law:

"And Solomon made affinity with Pharaoh king of Egypt, and took Pharaoh's daughter, and brought her into the city of David, until he had made an end of building his own house, and the house of the LORD, and the wall of Jerusalem round about." (I Kings 3:1)

In the first book of Kings one can read about King Solomon's tremendous wealth, wisdom and desire to glorify the Lord. It might very well have been King Solomon, who had these columns erected. In any case he had the

Figures 364, 365: The identical column found on the Saudi-Arabian beach, was taken down as soon as it was discovered. The location is marked by a metal flag and a metal plate.

Figure 366: It is almost impossible to transport heavy material such as a column by land, since the mountains go directly down into the sea in most places. It is most likely that the columns were transported to their positions by a sea vessel.

Figures 367-370: The Egyptian war chariots are found everywhere in ancient Egyptian inscriptions, and in a few examples from royal tombs.

resources, the practical requirements, and was deeply involved in drawing attention to the work of the Lord through building, according to the biblical texts.

48. The causeway on the Red Sea bed

The sea-bed has been examined at the site of the crossing. There one can observe an interesting sea-bed formation. Stones and blocks have been "ploughed" aside like snow drifts, to form a path on the bed of the Red Sea. Since the people of Israel were in a hurry, it is not very likely that they had time to remove various blocks of stone.

One possibility is that the Egyptian army had advance troops, who cleared the passage of stone blocks so that war chariots, and the ordinary chariots drawn by horses, could move along it more easily and more quickly. However, this is not very likely as the people of Israel also had wagons, and they were first to cross over on the sea-bed. Nevertheless, Josephus relates that the Egyptian army pursued the people of Israel in great haste, and that they had horses in front (JA 2/16:3). This implies that the way was already cleared to allow the chariots to pass.

Then it may be that when the Lord shaped this passage through the water (according to the text), stone blocks and other things were cleared away at the same time. Perhaps it is this to which the Bible refers when it says there was a strong wind which formed the passage.

Precisely how this happened is hidden from us, but it is worth noting that there is a sort of cleared way on that part of the sea-bed, which has been examined.

49. Finds from the Red Sea bed - chariot wheels

49.1. War chariots in the Egyptian army

The Egyptians had war chariots in their army and these, together with all the Egyptian chariots, were used by the Egyptian army when they pursued the people of Israel.

"And he made ready his chariot, and took his people with him: And he took six hundred chosen chariots, and all the chariots of Egypt, and captains over every one of them." (Ex. 14:6-7)

The historian Josephus mentions the same number of chariots, and also that there were 50 000 horsemen and 200 000 infantry soldiers (JA 2/15:3).

These war chariots were intended for quick battles and often had two soldiers; one who drove the chariot, and one who fought from the chariot with sword, bow and arrow. These chariots were relatively light, the "body work" or the chariot basket was made of wood and leather. The flooring was of wood, and the wheel axle was fastened to the underside of the floor. The wooden shaft leading to the horses, of which there were two,

Figure 371: An example of a chariot that was found in one of the pharaonic tombs.

Figure 372: The chariot wheels had different designs. This is an example of a wheel from a light weight chariot, probably used for ceremonial purposes.

was also attached under the floor. The soldiers were so much the heavier with different sorts of armour, shields, swords and other weapons. These war chariots are depicted in many contexts in various types of inscriptions. In figures 367-370 there are several examples.

In figure 371 there is a sketch of Tutankhamun's ceremonial chariot, which was found in his burial chamber. A close-up of the wheel construction is shown in figure 372. This chariot can be taken as a general picture of chariot construction, however it is small in comparison with the actual war chariots. It is important to realize that all the chariots that are found in tombs belonged to Pharaohs, and were ceremonial to their character. A similar comparison could be made with the horse-driven wagon queen Elisabeth uses in different ceremonies and parades in London, and corresponding horse-driven wagons used during the first world war. Basically it is the same, but the equipment used for soldiers is more solid in construction.

The different parts of the chariot can be clearly distinguished. In all probability the war chariots were stronger and simpler, with metal pieces e.g of bronze. Figure 373 shows a side of the chariot which belonged to Thutmosis IV, here eight and four-spoke wheels are depicted. In the centre of the wheel there were hub-caps, which have been preserved until modern times (figure 374). Egyptian reliefs show examples of the production of chariots and chariot wheels with four spokes (figure 379).

Figure 373: Eight- and four-spoked chariot wheels from the time of Thutmosis IV.

In addition, the Egyptian army must have had a large number of chariots as supply vans, i.e. maintenance for the whole of this army. These chariots were intended for the transport of food, water, and equipment like tents, and without doubt were solid in construction. Very probably the wheels of these chariots were, at least partly, cast in bronze in order to carry the weight.

The priesthood also took part in fighting campaigns, but kept to the back. Their task was not to fight, but to inspire courage in the soldiers and to see that the gods were on their side. There is good reason to suppose that their chariots had a more symbolic function, which would reflect power and the support of the gods.

The biblical texts relate that the sea closed, and the entire Egyptian army was destroyed. The question which then arises, is whether remains of these chariots can be found on the Red Sea bed at the site of the crossing at Nuweiba, which is the working hypothesis of this book.

Figure 374: Hub caps from Egyptian wheels of a more solid character, compared to the wheel shown in figure 372.

49.2. Chariot wheels on the sea-bed

It is important to note that the sea-bed was "scraped clean". Corals are found everywhere in the Red Sea, but in order to grow they must have something on which to fasten. Corals do not begin to grow on sand, or anything of that kind. It might thus be generally assumed that since the sea-bed was scraped clean at the crossing, and there are now a great deal of corals in the area, these corals have fastened to objects which ended up on the sea-bed, when the Egyptian army perished there.

The problem is that it becomes difficult to identify different objects, since the corals have grown over them, besides this they have often grown into other corals. If corals start to grow on organic material like wood, the wood will be consumed by coral growth, and after a certain amount of time only the shape remains. It must also be noted that there are strong currents in the area, and the water is deep. Altogether this makes it difficult to identify structures.

There is good reason to suppose that many of the lighter objects have been taken down into the deep trenches, alongside the underwater bridge, by the strong tidal currents. These deep trenches are up to 1900 metres in depth, and it is completely impossible to investigate these depths without very special equipment e.g. such as was used to find the "Titanic".

The most simple structures to recognise are the wheels, and there are a number of wheels on the underwater bridge. Coral does not grow on structures in the silt, which means that the gilded wheel in figures 380 and 382 can be clearly seen. The wheel is roughly a metre in diameter and has four spokes. The frame is of wood and the entire wheel is gilded. The wheel is of a strong construction, and is probably more representative of wheels used in warfare and long distance transport, than the ceremonial wheels found in the graves of several pharaohs (figures 371, 372). It should be noted that so far, no wheels have been found anywhere other than in a few pharaonic burial chambers.

The gilt wheel was attached to a chariot towards the rear of the troops, and probably belonged to the priesthood. The higher officers and Pharaoh himself, who possibly had gilt wheels, were probably much further forward in the troop formation.

The gilt wheel is unique in many ways:

Figures 375-378: Different examples of Egyptian war chariots. The lower figure illustrates a war chariot on an Egyptian bank note.

1. It is the first wheel discovered anywhere other than in a burial chamber.

2. It is the first gilt wheel that has been found.

3. The construction differs from the wheels found in burial chambers, with regard to the actual wheel ring (stronger), the spokes (more robust) and the hub, which has a different technical construction to the ceremonial chariots. On the other hand, it is very similar to what is found in Egyptian inscriptions.

4. There is no reason for it to lie on the Red Sea bed, other than as a result of an accident/disaster. It is not easy to find a natural explanation for the fact that a chariot has been way out to sea, and then sunk to the bottom, particularly a gilt chariot which was of great symbolic value as well as material worth.

5. This wheel can be clearly identified, since it has been in the silt, and therefore has no coral growing on it.

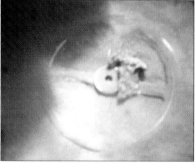

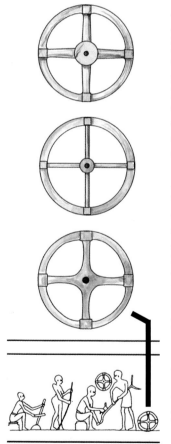

The wheel is very fragile, since the wooden remains have decomposed to a great extent. It is known from inscriptions that gilded chariots existed. There is an inscription concerning Thutmosis III (18th dynasty), which speaks of golden chariots in many different situations. This is repeated several times in the document (50).

In figure 379 a comparison is seen between the goldplated wheel (figures 380-382), and a drawing made from a modern military illustration of an Egypt war chariot from approximately 1430 BC (51). These wheels look very similar. In the same figure there is a drawing from an Egyptian inscription (52) from the 18th dynasty. The inscription illustrates Egyptians producing four-spoked wheels of a similar character as the wheel found on the sea-bed.

During the 18th dynasty, Egypt was a powerful nation with a strong army. They had a lot of chariots, either produced in Egypt or as war trophies. In one battle, to take an example, the war trophy was 2041 horses (51), suggesting that it also included a number of chariots as well.

The biblical text (Ex. 14:6-7) says that "600 chosen chariots" (probably the best chariots with their elite soldiers) were used in the

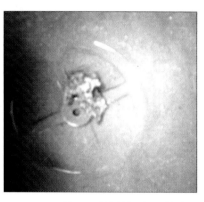

Figures 380-382: This gilded chariot wheel was found on the sea-bed. The wheel has been in the silt, and has only one coral growing on it. There is no doubt that it is a four-spoked wheel. All the different parts of the wheel are recognisable, and the diameter is approximately one meter.

Figure 379: The upper wheel is the gilded wheel front on the sea-bed; the middle is from an illustration of wheels from around 1430 BC; and the lower is from the inscription shown (18th dynasty).

Exodus campain in addition to "all the chariots" of Egypt. "All the chariots" must have included all the chariots taken as war trophies during the campains, suggesting a great variety in design.

In figure 387 there is another wheel. This is a wooden wheel covered with coral growth. The round, symmetrical shape of the wheel can be distinguished, as well as the raised hub and the spokes. Part of the wheel is missing at the lower edge. The next figure (figure 388) is a drawing of the wheel, and from the position of the spokes it can be seen that there would have been eight to this wheel.

Figure 383 shows an unusual coral formation, which is probably a pair of wheels, with the axle intact, standing and resting on one wheel. The round wheels as well as the axle can be seen. The rightangle between wheel and axle is important. In figure 384 a sketch has been made to show what it could have looked like when this pair of wheels landed on the sea-bed.

In figure 385 two wheels can be seen. These two wheels are a part of a pile of objects that will be discussed in the coming chapters. The wheels are seen from a distance, and are standing up or leaning towards the pile of other objects. The wheels have been coloured to make it easier to distuingish them from all the other objects. The right wheel has six spokes. Note the similarity between the right wheel and the wheel in the illustration (figure 386) that was done based on general knowledge of wheel construction. The illustration was made before the wheels in figure 385 were discovered.

In figure 393 it seems as though a whole chariot is lying on its side. It might be a war chariot but it could also be a transport chariot. Towards the back a circular shape can be seen, which might very well be a wheel. In the front part, a probable axle can be seen standing straight up with

Figures 383, 384: This is probably two wheels that stand up, resting on one of the wheels with an intact axle at a 90 degree angle, which connect the two wheels.

Figures 385, 386: Two wheels (coloured pink) in a pile of objects that will be discussed later. These are six-spoked wheels. Note the similarity of the right wheel and the illustration made before the discovery of these wheels, and based on a general understanding of Egyptian wheel construction.

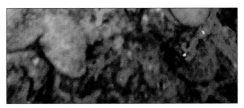

Figures 387, 388: The wheel is covered with coral. The raised hub can be seen as well as spokes in different directions. The circular shape of the wheel is also apparent. At the lower edge a part of the wheel is missing. This is an eight-spoked wheel.

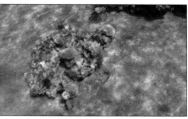
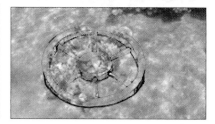

Figures 389, 390: This wheel is lying flat on the sea-bed and is less intact as in figure 387. The circular shape and the hub can be seen. In addition there are other objects on top of the wheel. This is a six-spoked wheel.

Figures 391. 392: The axle between the two wheels is broken with one wheel lying flat with the axle sticking straight up. The outer part of the wheel is clearly seen while the spokes are over grown with coral.

the possible remains of a spoke and part of the hub. Between them there is what could be the remains of the body of a chariot.

The wheel is a characteristic shape to look for, and is an important part of the war chariot. The Bible too refers to the wheel, in particular with the comment that the Lord let the wheels fall off to create confusion in the army (Ex. 14:24-25). There are many separate, loose wheels on the bed of the underwater bridge.

The wheels in figures 380-388 and 393 are found on the west side of the underwater bridge, in other words from chariots at the rear of the troops. The finds in figures 389-392 and 394-404 are from the east part of the landbridge, which means the front of the troops.

In figure 389 a wheel lying on the sea-bed is shown. The round, symmetrical shape of the wheel is seen as well as the spokes. The wheel has six spokes. The position of the hub is also seen in the raised part in the centre of the circle of the wheel. In figure 390 an explanatory sketch is shown.

Figure 391, with the sketch pertaining to it (figure 392), shows another pair of wheels. The axle is broken and one wheel is lying down on the sea-bed, while the remains of the axle stick straight up. The shape of the wheel can be

Figure 393: An object completely overgrown with coral. There are strange shapes of the object like a possible body of a chariot, a round wheel-like structure and a probable axle standing straight up with the possible remains of a spoke and parts of the hub.

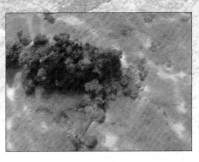

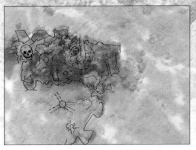

Figures 394, 395: This is an example where the flat sea-bed has no corals. This object is not typical for corals and a lot of strange patterns are seen like right angles, wheel-like structures etc. It is most likely that there are a number of objects on top of one another.

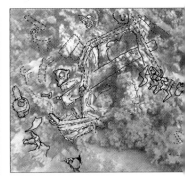

Figures 397, 398: This might be the frame of a transport wagon. The right angles and structures of possible planks can be seen. Across the structure is a possible wheel axle. The object is over grown with coral. Note the object in the sand in the lower left part, which is magnified in figure 396.

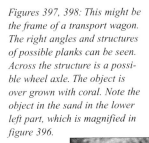

Figure 396: This is most likely a human skull underneath the larger object of figure 397. The skull is seen from above and if there were a skeleton it would be under the major object of figure 397.

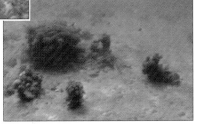

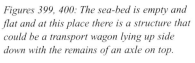

Figures 399, 400: The sea-bed is empty and flat and at this place there is a structure that could be a transport wagon lying up side down with the remains of an axle on top.

Parts of wheels are spread around. The wheel structure to the right has been standing up and still one spoke can be seen.

clearly seen with both the outer and the inner sides of the wheel visible. The second wheel is still standing upright with the other part of the axle at a right angle to the wheel.

The object in figures 399 and 400 is lying isolated on an otherwise empty, flat bottom (as many other objects). Close to what could be a transport chariot, four possible wheels are lying. Everything is covered in coral, but the shapes of broken wheel rings are clear.

In figures 397 and 398, also from the east side of the landbridge, a strange object can be seen in the middle of the picture. It may have been the frame of a transport chariot with a possible axle underneath, in the middle of the chariot. Once again the right angles should be noted between the parts, which probably consist of coral-covered wood. It looks as though parts of the chariot, probably the sides of the chariot body, were built of planks. At the bottom of the picture (separate small picture) what is probably a human skull can be discerned. It is partly hidden by sediment from the sea-bed at the corner of the chariot, and is seen diagonally from above, from the position of the photographer. The rest of the body is trapped under the remains of the chariot.

In figures 394 and 395 there is a formation that is also difficult to describe, but it differs from the ordinary sea-bed structures. Perhaps it is the under-part of a war chariot? It could be the remains of an axle with its attachment. In front of the part which is possibly a chariot, there are several finds in the layer of sediment. Here one can see right angles, which are not usually found among corals. Possibly these are remains of four-spoke wheels.

Figures 401 and 402 show a typical find from the sea-bed at the place of the crossing. On an otherwise empty and smooth sea-bed there is a curiously shaped object. Although covered in coral, several of the shapes can be dis-

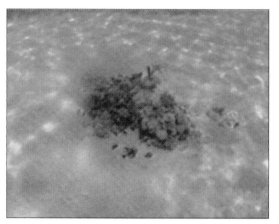

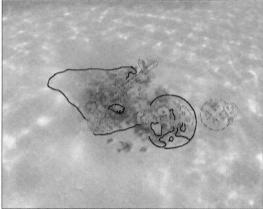

Figures 401, 402: As in many other cases the sea-bed is clear except for a strange object. This object resembles a chariot lying upside down. An axle with a wheel can be seen. The body of the chariot can be seen as a structure under the axle. Interestingly, on the side of the chariot a structure very simi-

lar to a quiver (for a bow and arrows) is visible. This seems to be a light-weight war chariot with four-spoked wheels. Wheels and other structures tend to be thicker due to over growth of coral.

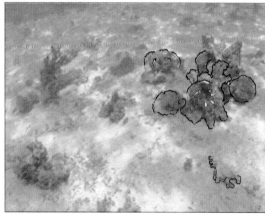

Figures 403, 404: Also in this case the sea-bed is empty except for the objects close together. It seems like a chariot with wheels. Note the right angle of the chariot floor. The possible shaft leading to the horses (on top) is twisted a bit.

The circular tube-like object is a typical connection between the body of the chariot and the shaft to the horses. The position of this connector could suggest that the chariot is standing up side down with the floor collapsed.

cerned. Possibly it is an overturned war chariot with remains of the chariot body, and a quiver of arrows at the side. Under the chariot a possible axle can be seen with the remains of a wheel. In this case it is a four-spoke wheel. In front of the chariot the remains of two other possible wheels can be seen, one of them is lying on the sea-bed covered in coral, but the typical wheel shape can be clearly seen. The other wheel is covered in sediment, but the spokes can be clearly seen with angles of 90 degrees between them, i.e. a four-spoke wheel.

Another find, which resembles figure 401, can be seen in figures 403 and 404. Here again the sea-bed is empty except for the objects which lie collected close together. It looks like an almost intact war chariot, which is standing on its wheels. On top of the chariot there is a possible axle from another chariot, or something else which is hard to identify. Around the chariot there are possible remains of several wheels, which are either standing straight up or lying on the sea-bed.

Altogether, there are many different types of finds on the sea-bed. Sometimes these finds are very difficult to identify. However, several finds differ so markedly from the surroundings that it is evident the coral growth has taken the shape of some foreign object e.g something completely round, square, which had right angles, or which showed traits of chariots, wheels, harnesses and so on. In odd cases the finds are so clear that one can say with complete certainty that "this is a wheel", for example. Such a clear and obvious example can be seen in figures 380-382 discussed earlier.

50. DATING THE WHEELS ON THE SEA BED

Can these wheels tell us anything about the date of the event which caused them to end up at the bottom of the Red Sea?

The number of spokes is of great importance in determining the date. It is believed that these war chariots came to Egypt via the Hyksos people, and were probably of Syrian origin. They were introduced into Egypt towards the end of the 17th dynasty (Pharaoh Kamosis, the last ruler of the 17th dynasty), and the beginning of the 18th dynasty (Pharaoh Amosis, the first ruler of the 18th dynasty). The four-spoke wheels were used in the beginning, and are regarded as an indication of the date of the early period of the 18th dynasty. They were used until the time of Thutmosis IV (53). The eight-spoke wheels can be seen on the chariot bodies of Thutmosis IV's war chariots (figure 373), and are considered to be a short-lived experiment during a brief spell of his reign. After Thutmosis IV only six-spoke wheels were used. However, these were already sometimes used at an earlier date during the reign of Thutmosis IV (53, 54).

Altogether, this establishes the date of the wheels discovered as within a limited period, which is summarised in figure 405. The four-spoke wheels were used until the time of Thutmosis IV. The eight-spoke wheels were used during a short period of time, probably only during the reign of Thutmosis IV. The six-spoke wheels began to be used during the 18th dynasty, particularly after Thutmosis IV, but they also existed to a limited extent before Thutmosis IV. Hoffmeier (53) expresses his conclusions as follows: "Another picture source from the reign of Thutmosis IV is the workshop scene from Hepus' grave. Here the wheel constructors are working with four-spoke

wheels. This signifies that four-spoke wheels
were in use during a limited period after
1400 BC. From then onwards, for the
remainder of the 18th dynasty, chariot wheels
are normally depicted with six spokes."

Wheel type	Number of spokes	Thutmosis IV
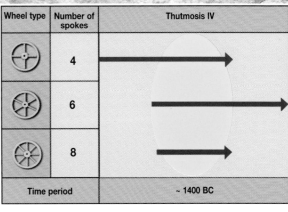	4	
	6	
	8	
Time period		~ 1400 BC

Figure 405: The number of spokes enable dating of the chariot wheels.

During the succeeding dynasties the six-
spoke wheel dominated. This means that
there was a change in the number of spokes
during a short period. There was a gradual
transition from four-spoke to six-spoke
wheels at the beginning of the 18th dynasty,
and during a brief period (Thutmosis IV)
there was also an eight-spoke wheel.

The reign of Thutmosis IV is said to have been from 1419 to 1386 BC (43).
However, it is probable that this reign was at a somewhat different time,
depending on how one interprets reigns and names, which are discussed in
chapter 12.

The wheels found on the bed of the Red Sea represent wheels with four, six
and eight spokes. This gives a date during part of the 18th dynasty, most likely during the reign of Thutmosis IV or shortly before it. Several different
varieties of chariots and wheels were to be expected at the Exodus since all
the chariots in Egypt were mobilised (Ex. 14:7).

Dating the events in the Red Sea, which resulted in the defeat of the
Egyptian army, can then be summarised as follows (Table 12):

Table 12. Three datings of the wheels on the sea-bed (53, 54, 71).

	Year BC
Wheel spokes:	18th Dynasty
During the reign of Thutmosis IV	1419-1386 BC (*)
Chronology which dates Exodus according to the books of the Bible (chapter 44 in this book):	Approx. 1446 BC

(*) This dating is probably not as exact as shown, see discussion chapter 12 concerning
Thutmosis IV, but as a rough estimate it is most likely correct.

It can be assumed with good reason that the Exodus took place some 1450
years BC, and that the chronology calculated with the help of biblical texts
agrees well with the wheel dating.

It should be noted that only eleven war chariots have been preserved until
modern times. All of these are from graves, and four of these eleven are from
Tutankhamun's burial chamber. No war chariots or wheels have been discovered from anywhere else except these graves. The chariots found in the

graves were for the pharaohs, and had a ceremonial purpose and/or were intended for the pharaohs' death journey. Inscriptions show other wheel types as well.

51. Parts of human skeletons from the Red Sea bed

The next question which arises, regarding finds one can expect, concerns the remains of humans, oxen and horses. Are there any remains of humans, oxen or horses on the bed of the Red Sea, at the place of the crossing?

Figures 406, 407: A human femur bone, several hundred years old (brown), from a Swedish tomb compared with what is an almost certainly human femur (white) from the sea-bed of the underwater landbridge, of the Gulf of Aqaba. The skeletal parts are discussed in the text.

51.1. Petrification and coral growth

Firstly, most skeletal parts that have ended up in the Red Sea have become petrified if embedded in oxygen free sediments. This entails a form of fossilisation. The Red Sea has a high salt content, and contains a great deal of calcium carbonate ($CaCO_3$). The Red Sea is a tropical sea with a high degree of biological activity, and it has an abundance of microscopic organisms which bore into objects. This means that sea water can quickly force its way in, and have an effect on substances that find themselves in the water. This leads to a relatively quick process of petrification; from a geological point of view.

If skeletal parts lie open and accessible, and are not buried in sediment, then corals settle and begin to grow. This can make it very difficult to find identifiable skeletal parts. There is a large quantity of skeletal parts on the sea-bed at the place of the crossing, but they are often piled up together in large heaps and covered in corals, which makes the precise identification of individual skeletal parts well nigh impossible. But there are also several examples of skeletal parts which can be identified.

51.2. A human femur bone

In figures 406 and 407 there is a thigh-bone (femur), which is almost certainly human. Next to the coral-covered thigh-bone from the Red Sea bed (the lighter one), there is a human thigh-bone (the darker one). These bones show identical characteristics on several points:

1. The general impression, when the complete bone is shown, is that it closely resembles a human thigh-bone.
2. The ball and socket joint is still there (figure 406).
3. The outgrowth to the left of the ball and socket joint is there (figure 406).
4. The turn of the bone, and the proportions directly under the ball and socket joint are, in the main, identical to the reference bone (figure 406).
5. The length and proportions of the bone tally (figure 407).
6. The inside of the knee-joint (indistinct part in figure 407) consists of two

larger parts with a depression between. The depression and the (in the picture) right raised part are intact. The left raised part is missing however.

7. The proportions of the bone in the narrower and wider parts tally.

8. Both bones show the typically, human arching of the thigh-bone when seen laterally (chimpanzees and gorillas have straight thigh-bones in this respect).

9. The length of the femur bone tallies with a human being, which can be seen from the figures and the measurements. The length of the thigh-bone corresponds with that of a person with a height of 166-173 cm. The span takes into account the margin of doubt in the tables, and which tables of reference that are relevant (the tables are based on Caucasian- and Afro-Americans, and males and females, respectively). The estimated length tallies with what might be expected regarding Egyptian soldiers. Egyptian mummies represent wealthy individuals, who have had no difficulty in obtaining food. There is good reason to suppose that soldiers were well-trained and had sufficient food, and thus are exemplified by the mummies discovered as far as height is concerned. Dunand and

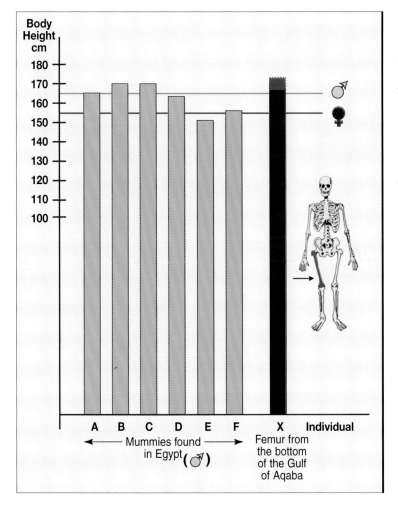

Figure 408: A-F represent the body height of male mummies (representing the suspected genotype and individuals well-nourished, as the soldiers were) from Egypt. X represents the calculated body height based on the found femur, which should be a male if it represents an ancient Egyptian soldier. The two lines indicate mean body height of male and female mummies, respectively.

Lichtenberg (55), in their survey of mummies, indicate how tall these were. Individual heights are given for six men, while the average height is said to be 1.65 m for men. For women the average height is 1.55 m. This information is shown graphically in figure 408. As can be seen in the figure the calculated body height corresponds to a male.

Regarding the age of the thigh-bone one can only say that it is very old, which should mean several thousand years.

51.3. HUMAN SKELETON AND SKELETAL PARTS

Normally, if anything is normal in this place, large quantities of skeletons lie in piles, which have "grown together" by becoming covered in corals.

Nonetheless, in figure 409 there is an exception to this, where individual skeletal parts can be identified in a large heap of skeletons found on the west side of the sea-bed. When studying figure 409, one should take into consideration that it is difficult to judge distances under water. The photograph covers a large heap of skeletons photographed from above. The light parts are closest to the camera, while the dark parts are both further away and also sloping downwards, illustrated in Figure 410. The fish (Pterois volitans) in the picture is very poisonous with poison in the tip of each individual part of the fin. The fish is nearest the camera and is about 30-40 cm long.

When the skeletons are covered in corals they lie still as though moulded together, but before this happens there are several factors which determine how parts can be moved around. Without a doubt the chaos and panic (Ex. 14:24-28) with horses, chariots and human beings, caused injuries in various ways. In addition, are the forces that came into play when the waters closed together again. When the acute situation has passed, there are the processes of decay, the attacks of animals and the water currents, which can all affect the way in which skeletal parts are scattered and broken up.

On top of the pile of skeletons there is one skeleton (A-E coloured yellow in figure 409) which has a skull, where the eye-holes, nasal opening, mouth and jaw can be seen. Just below the skull the remains of the spinal column (backbone) can be seen, and even individual vertebrae. It seems as though the skull has been pulled away from the rest of the body: when one considers the distance between the vertebrae and the distance between the skull and the thorax. The thorax (rib-cage) is very clear, and one can distinguish individual ribs on both sides of the breastbone. The shape is very like the thorax of a human being, as is the v-shaped opening in the thorax below the breastbone. The parts near the cervical column, which stand up more, are probably the collarbones. Behind/under the thorax one can discern the backbone, which goes down to the triangular-shaped rump bone (sacrum). The pelvis has partly disappeared, but near the rump bone parts can be seen that are probably from the pelvis.

With detailed observation one soon discovers further skeletal parts from other individuals. A possible skull (F, coloured orange) is lying upside down with the upper jaw visible; in the darker part of the lower side of the picture.

Immediately above the fish there is a possible piece of backbone with a skull; seen diagonally from behind and beneath (G, yellow). To the right of this find there are yet more remains of a backbone (H, pink) with formations

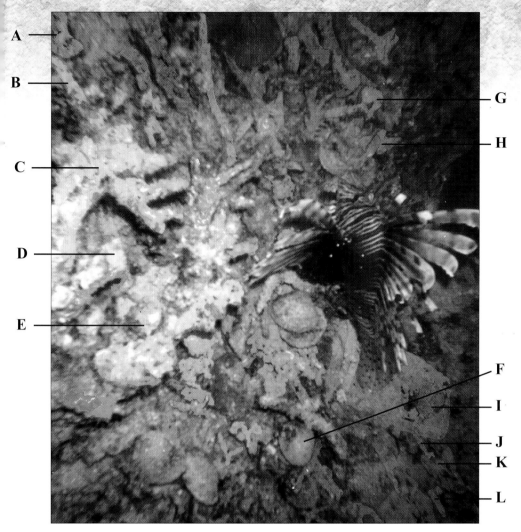

Figure 409: A-E represent a human skeleton, see text for comments. A possible skull (F, coloured orange) is lying upside down with the upper jaw visible; in the darker part of the lower side of the picture.

Immediately above the fish there is a possible piece of backbone with a skull; seen diagonally from behind and beneath (G, yellow). To the right of this find there are yet more remains of a backbone (H, pink) with formations on top, which may very well be shoulderblades. Below the shoulderblades the skull can be seen. Both the skeletal remains are lying flat.

Under the fish, to the left the triangular shape, could be a rump bone or a spearhead (blue). The shape on the lower, left side of the picture (blue) could be another rump bone (or spearhead).

In the right of the picture is what may be a skull with the remains of the backbone and hipbone (I-L, orange). It looks as if these skeletal parts are lying over the edge of another strange object (to be commented on later).

on top, which may very well be shoulderblades. Below (in the photograph) the shoulderblades the skull can be seen. Both the skeletal remains are lying flat.

Under the fish, to the left the triangular shape, could be a rump bone or a spearhead (blue). The shape on the lower, left side of the picture (blue) could be another rump bone (or spearhead).

Figure 410: The diver's position in figures 409, 418 and 428.

In the right of the picture is what may be a skull with the remains of the backbone and pelvis bone (I-L, orange). It looks as if these skeletal parts are lying over the edge of another strange object (to be commented on later).

This pile of skeletons probably represents several different individuals, and if the whole heap consists of human remains then it is a very large number of individuals. These bones are covered in coral. This formation probably represents a number of individuals, at least three and possibly many more, who have met their death under special circumstances, and ended in a large heap. This event must have taken place several thousand years ago. Further comments on this picture are found in the following chapters.

52. PARTS OF CATTLE SKELETONS FROM THE RED SEA BED

In figures 411-413 another interesting find is shown. This piece of a skeleton is petrified, but has lain protected by sediment and thereby been shielded from coral growth. The skeleton piece is in very good condition since each individual bone cell has filled with calcium carbonate during the process of petrification. Thus the original appearance and shape of the bone are preserved in such a way, that on superficial observation, the skeleton piece looks exactly as if it is composed of bone. One part of the bone is completely intact with the surface of the joint (figure 412), while the other end is broken. This fracture probably occurred before petrification since petrified bone is very resistant, hard and stable. According to the hypothesis discussed in this book, fractures of skeletal parts are to be expected considering the chaos and panic which preceded the disaster.

From which type of animal does this bone come? The bone is typical of cattle, and it is part of a right leg. In figures 414-416 the petrified bone is seen photographed alongside a corresponding bone from a Swedish cow. From comparisons of dimensions, joint surfaces, bone

Figures 411-413: A petrified radius and elbow bone from a bull/cow/ox, most likely several thousand years old and found on the sea bed.

ridges and many other details it is very probable that this is a radius and elbow bone from a bull/cow/ox.

The petrified bone (white) is from an adult animal but smaller in size than the reference bone (brown), which exemplifies a modern Swedish cow produced through intensive breeding. The size of the bone is closer to that of a

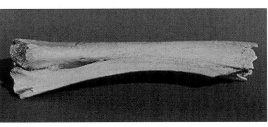

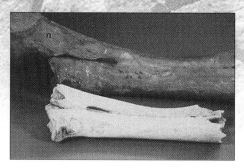

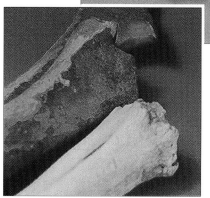

mediaeval Swedish cow. The sex is not apparent from an elbow and radius bone, one can only speculate. If the animal was there as a draught animal, it is likely that it was a bull or an ox. However, it could also have been a cow for milk production, and a mobile larder for the soldiers. It could have been a great advantage to have part of the provisions in a form which could transport itself, keep fresh and be slaughtered should the need arise.

Figures 414-416: The petrified bone (white) compared to a similar bone (brown) from a modern Swedish cow. The size of the adult bone from the Red Sea corresponds in size to a Swedish mediaeval cow.

In great probability, this bone represents a petrified radius and elbow bone from a cow/bull/ox, which most likely is several thousand years old.

53. Parts of horse skeletons from the Red Sea bed

We now return to the pile of skeletons which are depicted earlier in figure 409. Those which are probably human remains are discussed in section 51.3., but there is reason to speculate about other pieces of skeleton in that pile.

The remains which are coloured yellow, directly below the fish (figure 418), could very well be the thorax (A, rib cage, yellow) of a horse in cross-section. The size and shape tally with the thorax of a horse. Below on the left there probably is a broken rib (B, yellow), while the thorax, as such, shows three visible rib bones (to the right and to the left of the picture). In figure 424 a rib cage from a horse can be seen.

Halfway up the pile (C-D, pink) there is a pair of what are probably skeletal parts, which might also be the upper parts of a thorax with vertebrae (which have upward-pointing outgrowths), and parts of the ribs. Just above this pair is a possbile third (E) structure of similar shape. Two identical sets lying on each other, and a third just beside, further support the theory that they are parts of a backbone/thorax. The thin rib bones seem to have broken apart. In figure 420 an example is shown from a horse vertebrae with ribs, and the skeletal part that points upwards. The more solid skeletal part seen in figure 420, is magnified in figure 419. In figure 417 the upper part of a horse rib cage can be seen. Note

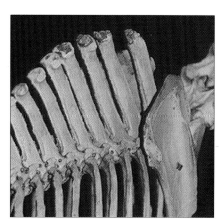

Figure 417: The upper part of a rib cage from a horse.

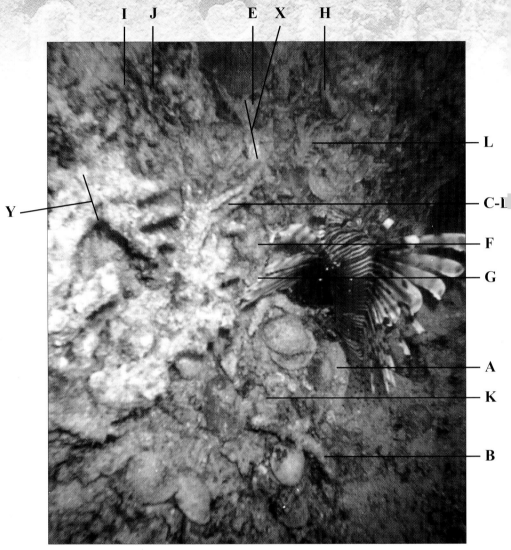

Figure 418: The remains which are coloured yellow, directly below the fish, could very well be the thorax (A, rib cage, yellow) of a horse in cross-section. The size and shape tally with the thorax of a horse. Below on the left there probably is a broken rib (B, yellow), while the thorax, as such, shows three visible rib bones (to the right and to the left of the picture).

Halfway up the pile (C-D, pink) there is a pair of what are probably skeletal parts, which might also be the upper parts of a thorax with vertebrae (which have upward-pointing outgrowths), and parts of the ribs. Just above this pair is a possbile third (E) structure of similar shape. Two identical sets lying on each other, and a third just beside, further support the theory that they are parts of a backbone-/thorax. The thin rib bones seem to have broken apart.

Further details are found in the text.

Figure 419: The more solid skeletal part of the rib cage magnified from figure 420.

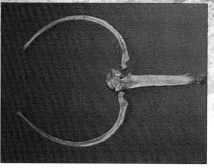

Figure 420: A horse vertebrae with a pair of ribs and the more solid skeletal part that points upwards (compare to figures 417 and 419).

the skeletal structure in the shoulder region, pointing upwards.

When vertebrae C-D is compared to the human rib cage, directly to the left (yellow), a size comparison could be made. The upward pointing outgrowth of the horse vertebrae (X) should be approximately the same length as the distance between the V-shaped part of the human rib cage, and the upper part of the rib cage (Y). The lenghts X and Y are very similar, which is a further indication that these skeletal remains fit the expected size and origin.

Next to these possible vertebrae remains, a little to the right of these parts, one can see what is probably the skull of a horse (F, pink) seen from above. It is not the eye-holes that can be seen. It is more likely the openings on the side of the skull where the jaw bone is connected. The nose of the skull is

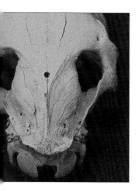

Figures 421, 422: A horse skull photographed from a similar angle as seen in figure 418.

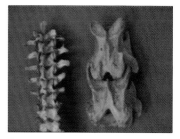

Figure 423: A comparison between a horse (right) and a human vertebrae (left).

Figure 424: A shoulder blade and part of the rib cage of a horse.

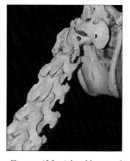

Figure 425: A backbone of a horse.

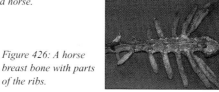

Figure 426: A horse breast bone with parts of the ribs.

Figure 427: A pelvis bone from a horse.

covered by possible ribs (C-D). Figures 421 and 422 show a horse skull, photographed from a similar angle.

In the neck area of the possible Red Sea horse skull there is something
which might very well be the backbone (G, pink), which on the picture is
bent to the left. The size and proportions of the possible vertebrae, and how
they are connected to the skull is similar to a horse. In Figure 423 a comparison of human and horse vertebrae can be seen.

Straight above the fish, in the upper edge of the picture, a possible shoul-
der-blade and the remains of a possible horse's bow-shaped cervical column
can be seen (H, green). A comparison with a horse shoulder blade can be
seen in figure 424. Two possible backbones of horses can be seen in the
upper left corner of the figure (I-J, green), which can be compared to the
back bone of a horse in figure 425. A possible horse pelvis bone can be seen
close to the rib cage (K, yellow). Although not distinct, it is symmetric, has
the right size and proportions, and has the characteristic V-shaped part in the
more narrow section of the bone. Figure 427 shows a pelvis bone from a
horse as a comparison.

To the right of the possible vertebrae (E), there is a structure very similar to
the breastbone of a horse (L, pink). It fits the size of a horse brestbone in
comparison with the possible human backbone and skull (yellow) directly to
the right, and looks very similar to the horse breastbone in figure 426.

In this pile of skeletons there are very probably bones from a number of
horses, which most likely are several thousand years old.

54. OTHER FINDS IN THE PILE OF SKELETONS

Scattered about in this great heap of remains a number of objects can be
seen, which may represent various types of relics as seen in figure 428.

At the bottom of the picture, a relatively long way from the photographer,
two wheels (A-B, pink) can be clearly seen. These wheels have six spokes.

Below the fish there is a larger flat part which is coloured green. It begins
in the far right (C), then goes below the big yellow ribs, and is seen again
just to the left as separate planks (D). This may very well be the flooring of a
war chariot. Just underneath, above one of the wheels (B) that is located far
deeper, there is a construction that is a possible part of a chariot (E). This
object has a T-shape with right angles, and could be a part of the axle and/or
the construction of the under part of a chariot.

Just below the thorax of what is the remains of a human being, there is an
object which is coloured pink (F). This might be the remains of a dagger,
which has been attached to a waist belt. Size, shape, and localisation on the
body all fit a typical dagger for an Egyptian soldier.

Possible spearheads (G-H) have been coloured blue.

In addition, there are a number of different formations, which may be skeletal parts and/or the remains of various types of equipment, scattered about in
this pile. Some of these objects have been coloured.

Altogether, this pile of skeletons shows the remains of a number of human
beings, possible horses and equipment that have collected in a large heap,
following some sort of disaster several thousand years ago.

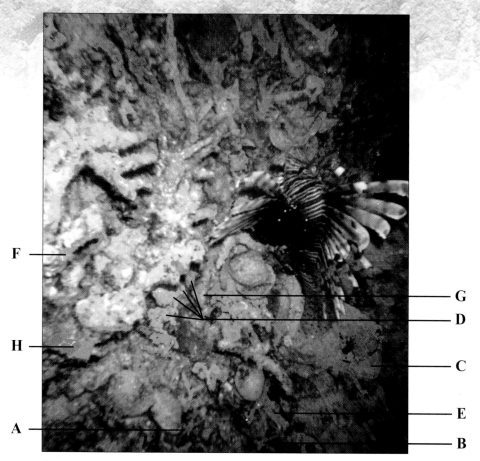

F

H

A

G

D

C

E

B

Figure 428: Scattered about in this great heap of remains a number of objects can be seen, which may represent various types of relics.

At the bottom of the picture, a relatively long way from the photographer, two wheels (A-B, pink) can be clearly seen. These wheels have six spokes.

Below the fish there is a larger flat part which is coloured green. It begins in the far right (C), then goes below the big yellow ribs, and is seen again just to the left as separate planks (D). This may very well be the flooring of a war chariot. Just underneath, above one of the wheels (B) that is located far deeper, there is a construction that is a possible part of a chariot (E). This object has a T-shape with right angles, and could be a part of the axle and/or the construction of the under part of a chariot.

Just below the thorax of what is the remains of a human being, there is an object which is coloured pink (F). This might be the remains of a dagger, which has been attached to a waist belt. Size, shape, and localisation on the body all fit a typical dagger for an Egyptian soldier.

Possible spearheads (G-H) have been coloured blue.

In addition, there are a number of different formations, which may be skeletal parts and/or the remains of various types of equipment, scattered about in this pile. Some of these objects have been coloured.

55. How long does the process of petrification take?

When part of a skeleton or other organic material (e.g. wood) becomes petrified, it means that the structure of the organic material is replaced by minerals, with calcium carbonate ($CaCO_3$ = limestone) or silicon dioxide (SiO_2 = quartz) being the most abundant. These may contain a number of different metals, which can give different colours. Processes of petrification are assumed to be processes that take a very long time. However, this is unlikely.

If the conditions for petrification (no oxygen) are there then it probably happens relatively quickly (from a geological point of view). This can be shown by a simple fact, which can be seen in figure 429. The figure shows petrified wood, something which can also be called wood turned to stone. In this case, there is a piece of wood from the USA that has been exposed to wind and water (which has given it its rounded shape), and a piece of wood from Denmark (figure 430). The example from Denmark shows something that looks like a flat piece of wood, chopped from a block of firewood or something similar.

What the figures show is obvious. The process of petrification must have been quicker than the process of decomposition of the organic material, otherwise they would never appear as they do. In this case, the silicon dioxide has transformed the wooden material so that it has become an exact copy made of stone. The petrified piece of wood from the USA resembles wood so closely that one has to hold it in order to realise that it is a stone.

Since the process of petrification results in an exact copy of the organic material (bone in figures 411-413 and wood in figures 429, 430), by definition the process of petrification must be quicker than the process of decomposition of the organic material. If the conditions for preserving the organic material are optimal, then it may be a matter of a few thousand years.

Figure 429: Petrified wood from the US.

Figure 430: Petrified wood from Denmark.

56. Skeletons in a sea environment

The question as to whether a skeleton can be preserved for a long time in the sea is justified. Let us look at the sea environment in the vicinity of the Red Sea.

Off the Mediterranean coast of Israel, there is an historical place called the "Maritime Atlit site", which is about 10 km south of present day Haifa. It is the largest and best preserved prehistoric settlement that has been found on the sea-bed, and the only one that has graves (56). The reason why the settlement is found on the sea-bed (8-10 m depth) is that it was established before all the ice from the latest ice age had melted. Many thousands of years ago, the Mediterranean Sea was roughly 30 m shallower for this reason, and the settlements which were on the coast at that time are now on the sea-bed.

At this place 15 skeletons have been found in graves, which represent an era before the level of the Mediterranean Sea rose to the present day sea-level, and turned the area into sea-bed. The age of these skeletons (based on C14 dating of carbon remains around the skeletons and other organic material) indicates a period of several thousand years. Complementary dating has been done via other discoveries of ceramics etc. (56).

In a sea environment, similar in salt content and temperature to the Red Sea, skeletons are preserved for several thousand years. If corals grow there later on, it is because the skeletal parts are exposed. If they are lying under sediment they will not become covered in corals.

Althogether, it can be said that there is a large quantity of skeletons and skeletal parts on the underwater bridge in the Gulf of Aqaba. It is highly probable that these skeletal parts represent human beings, horses and cattle. Some skeletal parts are petrified and thus probably several thousand years old. Most of the skeletal parts are thickly covered in corals. The strange thing is that the skeletons and skeletal parts are collected in heaps, and in mixtures of skeletons from humans, horses and draught animals. Obviously, a number of humans, horses and draught animals lost their lives on the same occasion, and landed in large heaps. This event lies several thousand years back in time.

THE EXODUS
A SUMMARY

Part II consists of a long series of events linked to various archeological finds. We have followed Moses and his career at the Egyptian court. The hypothesis about Moses in Egyptian history has been presented with examples from chronology, names, history, kinship, graves etc.

The land of Midian, to which Moses fled, has been discussed in detail regarding its whereabouts. We have also followed the extraordinary events in Egypt prior to the beginning of the Exodus - the great march of the people of Israel. A number of important aspects such as the number of people, the route of the migration, what influenced the choice of route, encampments and aspects of time have also been discussed.

The site of the crossing through the Red Sea has been described from both geographic, and technically possible aspects. Geographical names, pillars, and the point in time of the Exodus have been discussed in detail.

Finally, the actual site of the Red Sea crossing has been shown to have a number of marine archeological remains, from some sort of disaster. This disaster included a large number of animals, horses, human beings, chariots and wheels, which are lying on the sea-bed of the underwater bridge. Some skeletal parts are petrified which implies that the event took place several thousand years ago. Possibilities of identifying finds vary (because of the coral covering them), from being absolutely certain that it is a gilt wheel, for example, to having great difficulty in giving an opinion other than: these formations are different and curious. The finds are scattered over a wide area, from the west side (the coast of the Sinai peninsula) to the east side (the coast of north west Saudi-Arabia) and imply a very extensive disaster. With a length of approximately 14 km and a width of approximately 5 km, the total area covers some 70 km^2.

Figure 431: A hidden disaster under the surface of the Gulf of Aqaba?

Altogether, these finds give a picture of a disaster that probably occurred at the time of what the Bible calls the Exodus: the departure of the people of Israel followed by the destruction of the Egyptian army in the Red Sea.

The people of Israel are now on the other side of the Red Sea and on the way to their first goal, Mount Horeb. Here await special events, to say the least.

The Exodus now enters its second dramatic phase.

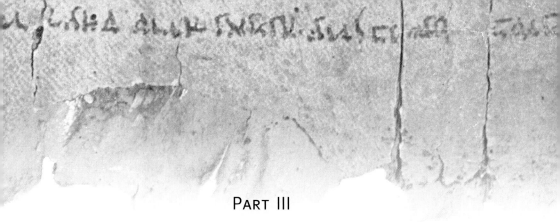

PART III

AT THE MOUNT
OF GOD

Figure 432

FROM THE RED SEA
TO MOUNT SINAI

AT THE MOUNT OF GOD

The people of Israel are now encamped on the east coast of the Gulf of Aqaba, facing Nuweiba. They have experienced a period of upheaval with strong manifestations of the Lord's guidance and protection, according to the biblical text. The people of Israel are now a nation, armed, well-organised and of good courage.

They know where they are going, at least Moses and Aaron know; firstly to worship at Horeb and then to the land of Canaan, the land that will flow with milk and honey, which the Lord promised in his covenant with the fathers of Israel, Abraham, Isaac and Jacob.

But the people of Israel are unaware of what awaits them, regarding both difficulties, suffering and the dramatic intervention of the Lord, according to the biblical text.

The people of Israel now break camp to go on to a very special mountain. But once again Moses is not allowed to choose the shortest and quickest way. According to the Bible, the Lord also holds this part of the journey completely in his hands.

Figure 433

57. Where do the people of Israel go after crossing the Red Sea?

From the biblical texts we know the places to which the people of Israel went. However, it is difficult to say exactly where they were situated. The people of Israel left the Red Sea and entered the wilderness of Shur:

"So Moses brought Israel from the Red sea, and they went out into the wilderness of Shur; and they went three days in the wilderness, and found no water." (Ex. 15:22)

This means that very close to the place where they came ashore, on the east coast of the Gulf of Aqaba, there was a wilderness. This wilderness is facing Nuweiba (figures 434-435), in the north western part of present day Saudi-Arabia. This wilderness is also called the wilderness of Etham (Numb. 33:8). This may sound confusing since the people of Israel pitched camp in Etham (Ex. 13:20) just before they turned and went southwards on the Sinai peninsula to Nuweiba, where they crossed through the Red Sea. How could the people of Israel be in "Etham" before the crossing of the Red Sea, and be in the "wilderness of Etham" after the crossing? The answer is that Etham was probably not a town, but an area that surrounded the northern part of the Gulf of Aqaba.

With this localisation of Etham there is no problem with the narration that they left Etham and then, after having crossed the Red Sea, were still in Etham.

To the east of the Gulf of Aqaba there is a very extensive desert and wilderness area, which more or less covers the whole of present day Saudi-Arabia and parts of Jordan. One major part of this wilderness is called (in Arabic) "Sirhan" today. It is possible that this name could

Figures 434, 435: On the opposite side of Nuweiba there is a similar plain. This huge plain area is about the same size as Nuweiba, but stretches out along the shore. Otherwise, high mountains are found along the coastlines. In the lower photograph the Nuweiba peninsula can be seen on the opposite coastline.

Figure 436: A large cargo vessel shown on its way north to Aqaba, in front of the Saudi Arabian mountains.

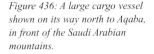

234

Figure 437: This satellite photo shows the northern part of the Gulf of Aqaba. The colours illuminate vegetation. Everything that is red is vegetation. It is easy to see that the only vegetation is at the northern tip of the Gulf of Aqaba. Two cities are located at the northern tip. To the west is Eilat (Israel) and to the right is Aqaba (Jordan).

In the left part of the photograph is the wilderness of the Sinai peninsula (Egypt). The regular shaped object is an airport. The white dots on the sea are vessels, and even the waves generated by the vessels can be seen as long tails. Interestingly this part, especially the north-eastern part of the photograph, was named on the map of R.F. Burton (from 1878) as Etham (both a mountain peak and a wadi). This connects to the hypothesis that Etham was an area that surrounded the upper part of the Gulf of Aqaba.

be related to the 3500 year old name "Shur".

The journey through the wildernesss of the Red Sea (the Sinai peninsula of today) went relatively quickly. Now, after the Red Sea crossing, a laborious period begins which was very demanding for the people of Israel. The first place we know about is called Marah.

58. WHAT HAPPENS IN MARAH?

After passing through the Red Sea the people of Israel journey three days in the desert of Etham or the desert of Shur. It is worth noting that the biblical text gives both these names for this desert (Ex. 15:22, Numb. 33:8). It cannot have been easy to journey with an entire nation and their livestock in a large desert/wilderness region. The first limitation would have been the water supply.

Figure 438: This is probably the eastern beach of Etham with the mountain ridges of Saudi-Arabia further east.

58.1. BITTER WATER

Josephus relates that the people of Israel had water with them for the journey in Sinai (JA 3/1:1). It is probable that they had waterbags made of sheepskin with them, but this water is now finished. After three days without water the situation is critical. Scouts are sent on ahead but they do not find any good water, so the people are obliged to stay in a place where there is only bad water.

The people are dejected, angry and exhausted. One can imagine the despair which spread amongst them when they could only find bitter water and two million people and all the livestock are dying of thirst.

The Bible text explains that the Lord is testing his people, and Moses turns to the Lord in prayer:

"And he cried unto the LORD; and the LORD shewed him a tree, which when he had cast into the waters, the waters were made sweet: there he made for them a statute and an ordinance, and there he proved them" (Ex. 15:25)

The Bible states that the water was bitter and therefore the place was called Marah. "Mar" is Hebrew and means bitter. Mar, and different variants of the word, is the name used in various languages for the sea (mare, meer etc.). The water in Marah was probably salty and tasted bitter like seawater. Saltwater has the characteristic of not being able to quench the thirst of either humans or cattle, which Josephus also notes regarding the water in Marah (JA 3/1:1).

It is difficult to speculate about what the piece of wood represented, which was thrown into the water and made it sweet. The most simple explanation is that it was a sign of the Lord's intervention following the prayer of Moses.

58.2. THE WATER CONSUMPTION

A rough estimate of the daily consumption of drinking water (excluding all other uses of water) is three litres per person a day, for two million people. If we assume that there were 200 000 cattle, with a daily consumption of about

10 litres of water per animal, this gives a total for both human beings and animals of approximately eight million litres per day, or 8000 cubic metres. This is a very conservative estimate. By way of comparison, in Sweden about 100 times more water is consumed every day for personal use, but then shower/bath, usage of dish-washers, etc. are included.

If we then assume that they also needed to store water for the continuation of the journey, and this supply was intended to be five days' rations, then 40 000 cubic metres were necessary.

We know of no species of tree of which a small specimen can purify such huge amounts of water by simply being thrown in the water. It was Moses who threw the tree in the water, which suggests a small piece of wood. The water immediately became sweet. The function of the piece of wood as water purifier must have been negligible with the given conditions, and was if anything a symbol or a sign of the Lord's intervention as it is described in the Bible.

On local maps there is a place near Jabal Al Lawz called "Ain Marra". It is not known if this is the Marah of the Bible, but it is worth noting that the name is almost identical. "Ain" is Arabic and means a spring. In other words "Ain Marra" means "the bitter spring".

59. THE WELLS AT ELIM

After journeying further, the people of Israel come to Elim. Elim was a place with 70 palm trees and 12 springs of water (Ex. 15:27). Today there are several hundred palm trees and 12 wells at an oasis in the area where the people of Israel were travelling. In figure 439 the possible location of Elim can be seen. In this oasis the 12 wells are still in use. The palm trees found in this oasis are rare for the region.

When they depart from Elim they have travelled for 30 days, since they departed the 15th day of the first month, and depart from Elim on the 15th day of the second month.

Figure 439: This is an oasis in the area with several hundred palm trees and 12 springs of water. The biblical text mentions a place with 70 palm trees and 12 springs (Ex. 15:27).

"...on the fifteenth day of the second month after their departing out of the land of Egypt." (Ex. 16:1)

60. WHERE DOES THE FOOD COME FROM?

After staying a short time in Elim, the people of Israel leave and journey on to the desert of Sin, situated between Elim and Mount Sinai (Horeb). According to Numb. 33:8-14, the people of Israel encamp at the Red Sea, the desert of Sin, Dophkah and Alush. In Ex. 16 and 17 it is described in more general terms, they journeyed from "encampment to encampment".

60.1. THE PEOPLE OF ISRAEL ARE DESPERATE FOR FOOD

It may appear a little strange that the people of Israel journey around in a seemingly muddled way. They are not particularly far from Mount Horeb (Mount Sinai), and Moses knows these parts well. But it is the Lord who leads the people of Israel, with the pillar of cloud and the pillar of fire, and it seems as though the Lord wants to test his people (according to the biblical text). It is still the pillar of cloud and pillar of fire that lead the people of Israel on their journey, according to the biblical text. They continue until patience wears thin and thirst burns their throats, then Moses prays to the Lord for a solution and the Lord meets their needs in various ways. When the people of Israel are in the desert of Sin, it seems as though their strength is at an end. Their feelings are revealed in the biblical text:

"And the children of Israel said unto them, Would to God we had died by the hand of the LORD in the land of Egypt, when we sat by the flesh pots, and when we did eat bread to the full; for ye have brought us forth into this wilderness, to kill this whole assembly with hunger." (Ex. 16:3)

When the people of Israel say "ye" they mean Moses and Aaron. The people of Israel protest, are doubtful of what they are really doing and would rather just die. It is natural that the leaders, and Moses in particular, would be the scapegoats for all these hardships. Then the Lord speaks to Moses:

"Then said the LORD unto Moses, Behold, I will rain bread from heaven for you; and the people shall go out and gather a certain rate every day, that I may prove them, whether they will walk in my law, or no. And it shall come to pass, that on the sixth day they shall prepare that which they bring in; and it shall be twice as much as they gather daily. And Moses and Aaron said unto all the children of Israel, At even then ye shall know that the LORD hath brought you out from the land of Egypt: And in the morning, then ye shall see the glory of the LORD; for that he heareth your murmurings against the LORD: and what arewe, that ye murmur against us?

And Moses said, This shall be, when the LORD shall give you in the evening flesh to eat, and in the morning bread to the full; for that the LORD heareth your murmurings which ye murmur against him: and what are we? your murmurings are not against us, but against the LORD.

And Moses spake unto Aaron, Say unto all the congregation of the children of Israel, Come near before the LORD: for he hath heard your murmurings. And it came to pass, as Aaron spake unto the whole congregation of the children of Israel, that they looked toward the wilderness, and, behold, the glory of the LORD appeared in the cloud.

And the LORD spake unto Moses, saying, I have heard the murmurings of the children of Israel: speak unto them, saying, At even ye shall eat flesh, and in the morning ye shall be filled with bread; and ye shall know that I am the LORD your God." (Ex. 16:4-12)

60.2. MEAT TO EAT

The Bible relates that the Lord sees what the people of Israel need. The Lord says firstly that he will put them to the test and try their faith, and then that he will meet their needs. The Lord promises that they will receive meat to eat that very evening, and they will receive bread the following day. According to the Bible, it happens just as the Lord has said. In the evening a cloud of quail (figure 440) covers the encampment.

The quail is a small bird. If we assume that the people of Israel received a quail each, at least about two million quail fell down on the encampment. Since they were starving, and would normally have eaten two quails each, there may have been up to four million quail. Whatever the precise number it was not a matter of a few birds, but a gigantic flock of several million quail, which dropped down from the sky on to the encampment of the people of Israel. The biblical text indicates that the quail covered the encampment.

Josephus implies that the quail flew in from the Arabian gulf (JA 3/1:5). This indication further points out that the people of Israel were on Arab territory, on the Arabian peninsula.

60.3. BREAD TO EAT

The following morning the dew falls. The dew disappears leaving something which is described as scales or hoar-frost. The people of Israel wonder what it is, which under-lines that it was something they had not seen previously. Moses explains that it is the bread that the Lord has sent:

Figure 440: Millions of quails cover the encampment and provide the people of Israel with meat.

"And it came to pass, that at even the quails came up, and covered the camp: and in the morning the dew lay round about the host. And when the dew that lay was gone up, behold, upon the face of the wilderness there lay a small round thing, as small as the hoar frost on the ground. And when the children of Israel saw it, they said one to another, It is manna: for they wist not what it was.

And Moses said unto them, This is the bread which the LORD hath given you to eat. This is the thing which the LORD hath commanded, Gather of it every man according to his eating, an omer for every man, according to the number of your persons; take ye every man for them which are in his tents.

And the children of Israel did so, and gathered, some more, some less. And when they did mete it with an omer, he that gathered much had nothing over, and he that gathered little had no lack; they gathered every man according to his eating.

And Moses said, Let no man leave of it till the morning. Notwithstanding they hearkened not unto Moses; but some of them left of it until the morning, and it bred worms, and stank: and Moses was wroth with them.

And they gathered it every morning, every man according to his eating: and when the sun waxed hot, it melted. And it came to pass, that on the sixth day they gathered twice as much bread, two omers for one man: and all the rulers of the congregation came and told Moses.

And he said unto them, This is that which the LORD hath said, Tomorrow is the rest of the holy sabbath unto the LORD: bake that which ye will bake to day, and seethe that ye will seethe; and that which remaineth over lay up for you to be kept until the morning. And they laid it up till the morning, as Moses bade: and it did not stink, neither was there any worm therein. And Moses said, Eat that to day; for to day is a sabbath unto the to day ye shall not find it in the field. Six days ye shall gather it; but on the seventh day, which is the sabbath, in it there shall be none.

And it came to pass, that there went out some of the people on the seventh day for to gather, and they found none. And the LORD said unto Moses, How long refuse ye to keep my commandments and my laws? See, for that the LORD hath given you the sabbath, therefore he giveth you on the sixth day the bread of two days; abide ye every man in his place, let no man go out of his place on the seventh day. So the people rested on the seventh day.

And the house of Israel called the name thereof Manna: and it was like coriander seed, white; and the taste of it was like wafers made with honey. And Moses said, This is the thing which the LORD commandeth, Fill an omer of it to be kept for your generations; that they may see the bread wherewith I have fed you in the wilderness, when I brought you forth from the land of Egypt.

And Moses said unto Aaron, Take a pot, and put an omer full of manna therein, and lay it up before the LORD, to be kept for your generations. As the LORD commanded Moses, so Aaron laid it up before the Testimony, to be kept. And the children of Israel did eat manna forty years, until they came to a land inhabited; they did eat manna, until they came unto the borders of the land of Canaan." (Ex. 16:13-35)

This passage describes what the people of Israel came to call manna. Manna is described in several places in the Bible. The 78th psalm concerns the whole Exodus and manna is described as:

"Though he had commanded the clouds from above, and opened the doors of heaven, And had rained down manna upon them to eat, and had given them of the corn of heaven. Man did eat angels' food: he sent them meat to the full." (Ps. 78:23-25)

60.4. THE MANNA WAS UNKNOWN

The manna is described as something which came from the Lord in a way unknown to human beings. Furthermore, a certain quantity of manna came for five days, double the quantity on the sixth day and nothing on the seventh day. It is difficult to find a natural phenomenon which manifests itself in this way and with this rythm. In addition, the manna follows the people of Israel on their journey to different places, and continues to do so for forty years until the people of Israel enter the land of Canaan. Then, in a day, the manna disappears.

"And the manna ceased on the morrow after they had eaten of the old corn of the land; neither had the children of Israel manna any more; but they did eat of the fruit of the land of Canaan that year." (Josh. 5:12)

The word "manna "is Hebrew and can be traced to the word "man", which means "what". There was reason to ask "what is this?" when they saw the manna fall as hoar-frost the first time.

60.5. SIMILAR TO FROST AND CORIANDER SEED

The appearance of manna is compared to hoar-frost and coriander seed. The picture of hoar-frost probably has something to do with the fact that the manna could only be collected in the morning, because when the heat of the sun came what was left melted away. Coriander seed is probably a measure of size. The Bible text describes the manna as;

"...it was like coriander seed..." (Ex. 16:31)

Josephus refers to it in this way: "as big as coriander seed" (JA 3/1:6)

It was sweet tasting like honey, and it appears they could either eat the manna as it was or bake bread with it. It would seem to be a rather limited diet, but it probably was not for two reasons. A diet which did not provide the nutrition the Israelites needed would have destroyed the people. Manna was their basic diet for forty years. Moreover, Josephus makes a comment that the manna stayed the hunger for other foods (JA 3/1:6), which must have been a work of the Lord. No dish, however good, is enjoyable several times a day, but this was not just for several days or weeks, but for forty years.

What were the dietary recommendations? Here too, there were direct instructions from the Lord. One omer per person, per day. An omer was a measure of volume, and corresponded to about 2.2 litres. If the people of Israel were roughly two million, and they needed an omer per person every day, then this meant 4.4 million litres, or 4400 cubic metres, were needed. Every day, except the sixth day when double the amount was needed and then nothing on the seventh day, the day of rest. Besides this was all that was not gathered, which disappeared in the heat of the sun.

Figure 441: Coriander seeds are from 3-6 mm in diameter. Coriander seed was given as a size marker for manna (Ex. 16:31, JA 3/1:6).

60.6. FOOD FOR THE CATTLE?

Something which is not mentioned in the text, is what the animals ate. There was a little grass in the area but was it sufficient for the Israelites' herds of cattle? Could it be possible that the animals were also able to eat manna? Manna was an adequate diet for humans and stayed their hunger for all other foodstuffs, so manna could have served in the same way for animals. The cattle could eat the manna straight from the ground in the morning when it fell like dew. We can only speculate about this question since the Bible does not give any indication of how this problem was solved in the desert.

If the animals also ate the manna, then much more was needed than the amount given above for the people of Israel. If we assume that there were fewer animals than people, but that they ate much more, then they may have needed the same amount per day as the people. There was also a surplus of manna, which fell like dew and disappeared later in the day. This means (using the example calculated and on the basis of the biblical text) that at least 10 000 cubic metres of manna fell each weekday, with the exception of the day before the sabbath when twice as much manna fell.

60.7. MANNA, A SECRETION FROM A PLANT?

Certain hypotheses claim that the manna was some kind of secretion from a plant which grew there naturally. This however causes a number of difficulties. One difficulty is that twice as much manna fell on the day before the sabbath. A further problem is the enormous amount of manna that fell each day. If a lorry can hold 10 cubic metres, then the volume of manna that fell each day corresponds to the loading capacity of 1000 lorries. In addition, this manna fell within a limited area, which meant that no removal was required as the manna could be gathered within walking distance. It is very difficult to imagine a natural ecological process behind this course of events: manna that fell every day, in a specific way, and in such enormous quantities.

An important point is the emphasis on the day of rest. Every day they received what they needed but they could not save any. All that was saved was destroyed by maggots and began to stink. It was only on the sixth day, the day before the day of rest when they received a double ration, that it could be saved for the next day. The reason for this was that they were not to work on the day of rest, the seventh day. This was a clear decree from the Lord, which we shall see in the Commandments from God in chapter 70.

60.8. SHOW BREAD

In modern everyday language there is an expression "just for show". In Swedish it is translated "show bread", meaning only on display, not to eat. This is something one can only look at, not eat or use in another way. This expression originates from the command that one omer of manna was to be set aside, so that the Israelites could look at this bread (manna) as a reminder of what the Lord had given them to eat during their travels in the desert (Ex. 16:32-34).

What happens concerning the manna must also be the work of the Lord. The manna comes suddenly one day, gives a perfectly satisfactory diet, follows the people of Israel on their journey for forty years, and then disappears in a day. Furthermore, the manna comes for five days, twice the amount on the sixth day and nothing the seventh day. The quantity of manna is enormous to feed the entire people. The manna described in the Bible is completely different from the vegetation in the Mediterranean region, which later came to be called manna or some similar name. If the manna had been a natural phenomenon, the whole of northern Saudi-Arabia might have been densely populated on account of the rich supply of food. However, all this part of Saudi-Arabia is exceptionally sparsely populated, no-one lives on any manna found in the desert.

Once again we face a situation where either the biblical texts must be correct or they must be false. Nonetheless, the fact remains that in some way roughly 2 million people were fed in the desert.

61. WHAT HAPPENS IN REPHIDIM?

After the people of Israel had journeyed from encampment to encampment, according to the Lord's command, they pitched camp in a place which came to be called Rephidim (Ex. 17:1-2). Rephidim is Hebrew and means encampment (57).

What came to denote this place, was that once again the people of Israel were without water. They had their daily food from the manna that fell on the ground every morning, but water was still a problem. As has been mentioned earlier, the question of water was a big problem and the Israelites directed their anger against Moses once again. The people of Israel seem to have already forgotten that so far the Lord has provided them with everything they need, and so they complain to Moses:

"And the people thirsted there for water; and the people murmured against Moses, and said, Wherefore is this that thou hast brought us up out of Egypt, to kill us and our children and our cattle with thirst?" (Ex. 17:3)

With hindsight it may be easy for us to think that the people of Israel often whined about things. But to travel in the desert and almost die of thirst, can make anyone desperate. Once again, according to the biblical text, it becomes clear that the Lord is testing his people. Moses turns to the Lord in prayer and the Lord replies to Moses:

"And the LORD said unto Moses, Go on before the people, and take with thee of the elders of Israel; and thy rod, wherewith thou smotest the river, take in thine hand, and go. Behold, I will stand before thee there upon the rock in Horeb; and thou shalt smite the rock, and there shall come water out of it, that the people may drink. And Moses did so in the sight of the elders of Israel." (Ex. 17:5-6)

The Lord calls the rock "the rock of Horeb". This rock is not to be confused with Mount Horeb. Horeb is the same mountain as Mount Sinai. The name "the rock of Horeb" indicates two things: firstly that it was a rock (and not a mountain), and secondly that it is the rock of "Horeb". Therefore this rock should lie quite close to Mount Horeb.

  The Bible relates that Moses does as the Lord has told him. Moses gathers the elders together and strikes the rock with his staff, and water pours out from it. The quantity of water is enough to quench the thirst of all the Israelites and all the cattle they have with them.

  Josephus mentions that the people of Israel were to receive water from a place where they least expected it (JA 3/1:7). Water that pours out of a rock would certainly not be expected, as it was usual to dig for water. This time the water is clear, of good quality and runs abundantly. Josephus uses the term "river" when he describes the flow of water (JA 3/1:7).

  The translator of Josephus' historical scripts, William Whiston (who lived 1667-1752) makes a comment (58) that this rock could still be seen by travellers visiting the area. He describes the rock as being too big to be moved by horse and cart. However, it is not known if this was really the right rock, what was believed to be "Horeb's rock", since Whiston does not give any further details regarding where the rock could be seen.

62. IS IT POSSIBLE TO VERIFY THE ROCK OF HOREB ARCHEOLOGICALLY?

Can Rephidim and the rock of Horeb be found today? Let us see what defines this place and the rock of Horeb.

62.1. WHAT IS SAID ABOUT THE ROCK OF HOREB?

1. The rock must lie near Mount Horeb (because of the name "Horeb's rock"

Ex. 17:6).

2. It must be a rock. A rock is either part of a mountain, or a separate block of stone which is distinguishable from the surroundings (Horeb's rock).

3. In the same section as the narration about the rock of Horeb, the battle against the Amalekites is described. At this battle Moses climbed to the hilltop in Rephidim (Ex. 17:9-10). In other words there must be a hilltop in Rephidim. Possibly it is the same hill on which Horeb's rock is found.

4. Within sight of this hilltop there must be a plain where the battle between the Amalekites and the people of Israel took place. We do no know how many Amalekites there were, but we know that they were a warrior people, and the warriors more or less equalled the warriors of Israel since the fighting took a whole day. Moses stood on the hilltop, and from there could follow the entire battle (Ex. 17:10-13).

5. Moses built an altar to give thanks to the Lord for victory over the Amalekites. It is very likely that Moses erected this altar close to the hilltop where he lifted his hands in prayer during the fighting (Ex. 17:8-16).

6. If Whiston's comment is correct, that travellers could see the rock of Horeb, then we can note that:
   a) It must have been an obvious rock and one possible to recognise.
   b) The rock was too big to be "moved away by horse and cart".

7. If a large quantity of water was able to flow from the rock (Jospehus uses the term "river"), to provide water for all the Israelites and their cattle, then it should be possible to see signs of this on the rock. It was not a case of a small crack with a trickle of water, but something much bigger.

8. Josephus indicates that water was to pour out from a place where the people of Israel least expected it. From this we can draw the conclusion that it was to be a remarkable or odd place to find water.

Figure 442: The probable rock of Horeb is the hill in the middle part of the photograph with a huge rock (1-2 mm in size, seen from a large distance) on the left side. The photograph is taken from the ridge of Jabal Al Lawz towards the west.

62.2. On the west side of Mount Horeb

On the western side of Mount Horeb there is a place that was probably Rephidim. The area is characterised by a plain with several hills that are off-shoots from Mount Horeb. On one of these hills there is a rock which can be seen from a distance, and which is remarkable in several ways. In figure 442 this hill can be seen in the distance, photographed from Mount Horeb. When one gets nearer to this hill, the rock pointing straight up from the hill can be seen (figures 443-445).

In various parts of the world lava paths can be seen. The surrounding mineral is weathered away, and hills or peak formations remain. In other places one can see that certain minerals have become crystallised as great pillars with a later weathering of softer surrounding minerals so that formations like pillars are formed.

The rock in Rephidim does not resemble any of these natural formations. It looks more like a gigantic block which has been erected on this hill. The rock species is the same as that of the hill itself. The rock is as high as a six-storey building i.e.18-20 metres.

This is a large rock formation on a hill, situated on a plain, on the western side of Mount Horeb. The rock can be clearly seen by anyone passing, and it is certainly too large to be carried away by horse and cart. Thus several of the points listed above tally with this rock formation.

But the rock must have other factors defining it as the rock of Horeb. The Bible says that Moses struck the rock with his staff, and the split rock poured out large quantities of water. In figure 446 it can be clearly seen that the whole rock is split from top to bottom. It is no ordinary little crack but rather the rock is cleft as if by the stroke of an axe, vertically from its top to its foot. It is understandable that, according to Josephus, the people of Israel were amazed. If a six-storey high, split-rock, standing on a hill in a desert area, suddenly has large quantities of water pouring out of it, it must appear very strange indeed. The rock is very high,

Figures 443-445: The same hill as shown in figure 442, but now seen from the surrounding plain. The rock is more obvious the closer one gets to the hill. The Jabal Al Lawz mountain ridge is seen in the background.

which can be seen in figure 447, where the size of a human is shown.

Figure 447 illustrates how it might have looked for the Israelites when they saw a river of water emerging from the split rock. Figure 448 shows how the rock at the foot of the crack has eroded. It resembles rock formations on dried-out riverbeds, with smoothed and hollowed out blocks of rock. Below the rock, it looks as if water poured out in such large quantities that even now, 3500 years later, it still resembles the source of a river. The Bible recounts how, after finding no water, the people of Israel were ready to stone Moses in desperation:

Figures 446-448: The upper photograph shows the split rock. The lower photograph shows the erosion seen at the base of the crack. The middle illustration show a size comparison with a human (encircled), and how it could have looked with a river coming out of the rock (according to the biblical text). It is an unlikely place for a spring: from a split rock, on top of a hill in a desert.

"And Moses cried unto the LORD, saying, What shall I do unto this people? they be almost ready to stone me. And the LORD said unto Moses, Go on before the people, and take with thee of the elders of Israel; and thy rod, wherewith thou smotest the river, take in thine hand, and go. Behold, I will stand before thee there upon the rock in Horeb; and thou shalt smite the rock, and there shall come water out of it, that the people may drink. And Moses did so in the sight of the elders of Israel." (Ex. 17:4-6)

It is very probable that large quantities of water have poured out from this extraordinary rock, which several of the points listed above indicate.

62.3. THE WAR WITH THE AMALEKITES

The Bible records that fighting broke out with the Amalekites, exactly at the place which was called Rephidim. Amalek was a distant relation of the people of Israel. Amalek was of Esau's line (figure 449). Esau was the brother of Jacob. It was the concubine of Esau's son who gave birth to the tribal prince Amalek, who settled in the vicinity of the Gulf of Aqaba (Gen. 36:1-8).

The Amalekites, named after their forefather Amalek, lived in Arabia. They raised camels and lived from assault and robbery. In Arab tradition the Amalekites are referred to as the oldest tribe in Arabia, and founders of Medina (57). The enmity of the Amalekites against the people of Israel led to many wars over a long period of time, Israel's king Saul was later killed by an Amalekite (1 Sam. 30:1-20, 2 Sam. 1:1-16, 8:11-12, 1 Chron. 4:42-43).

The battle against the Amalekites in Rephidim, underlines yet again, that the people of Israel were in Arabia (the land of Midian) after the crossing of the Red Sea. The Amalekites would never have been able to carry out such a concentrated attack on the Sinai peninsula, close to the Egyptian copper mines which were under the military guard of Egypt, the super power of the day.

When the people of Israel were attacked by the Amalekites in Rephidim, two things should be noted. Firstly, the people of Israel were armed, which they were not when they left Egypt. The weapons came from the dead Egyptians who floated ashore after they had perished in the Red Sea. Secondly, it was a curious battle in which the Lord protected the Israelites from the attack in a particular way (Ex. 17:8-16. JA 3/2:1-5).

62.4. MOSES ON THE HILLTOP IN REPHIDIM

Moses appoints Joshua as commander of Israel's army, and then climbs to the hilltop in Rephidim. He lifts up his hands in prayer for the people of Israel, a people of slaves who are now to go into battle without any military training or experience of weapons. The battle is to be against a warrior people accustomed to fighting, who support themselves by conquering and plundering. This warrior people, the Amalekites, have attacked the people of Israel. As long as Moses holds up his hands in prayer, the people of Israel have the advantage. The battle continues all day, and Moses holds up his hands with the help of his brother Aaron and his brother-in-law Hur. They have to keep his hands raised in prayer throughout the entire battle.

Figure 449: Amalek was of the same family origin as Moses, which can be traced back to Abraham.

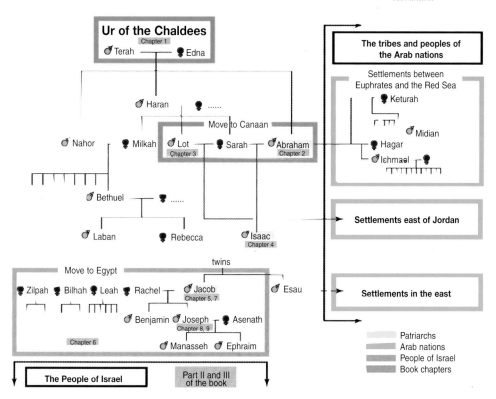

62.5. An altar

According to Josephus, the people of Israel are victorious, and obtain a great deal of equipment and valuables in the plunder they take from the Amalekites (JA3/5:4). The Bible tells that Moses erects an altar in the Lord's honour. An altar to which Moses gives the name "The Lord my banner" (Ex. 17:15).

Close to the rock of Horeb, a few hundred metres away on the plain, stands a stone altar which can be seen in figure 450. It is well-known that the people of Israel erected altars in the Lord's honour on special occasions, and the victory over the Amalekites was very special. It is very probable that Moses stood on this hill near the rock during the battle. Josephus states that women and children were assembled round the Rephidim rock during the fighting.

Figure 450: According to the biblical text, Moses erected an altar on the hill in Rephidim, where he watched over the battle. A few hundred meters away from the split rock in figures 307-312, this ancient altar has been erected.

Part of Israel's armed troops were set aside to protect them from attack during the battle (JA 3/2:3). If Moses was to erect an altar in this place, it can be assumed on good grounds that it would have been very close to Horeb's rock. The stone altar found close to this hill is about one metre high.

Several of the points above indicate that Rephidim would be characterised by a hill, from which Moses could direct the battle (near the rock of Horeb, according to Josephus). The hill must be surrounded by a flat area, which can be seen in figures 443-445. The area is a flat, sandy/gravel area with a hill in Rephidim that sticks up. The area is easily reached via valleys which go in different directions. Later, close to the rock of Horeb, Moses was to have erected an altar of thanksgiving in honour of the Lord. There is a stone altar standing very close to the rock of Horeb.

Altogether there are a number of factors and archeological discoveries which support the hypothesis that the place described is Rephidim. All the specifications named in the biblical text and by the historian Josephus regarding the place tally in detail. In addition, Rephidim was the last encampment before Mount Sinai (Mount Horeb). The encampment at Horeb was on the other side of Mount Horeb, to the east, while Rephidim lay to the west of Mount Horeb.

63. Who visits Moses and the people of Israel in the desert?

Moses was in the land of Midian during his 40 years of exile. It was in the land of Midian, on Mount Horeb (Mount Sinai) that the Lord appeared in the burning bush, and Moses received his assignment to lead the people of Israel out of Egypt, according to the text.

63.1. Moses family sent ahead to Midian

The people of Israel were to journey to the promised land of Canaan, but first they were to go to Mount Horeb to worship. Moses was aware of this all the time. We see this in the biblical text where the Lord commissions Moses

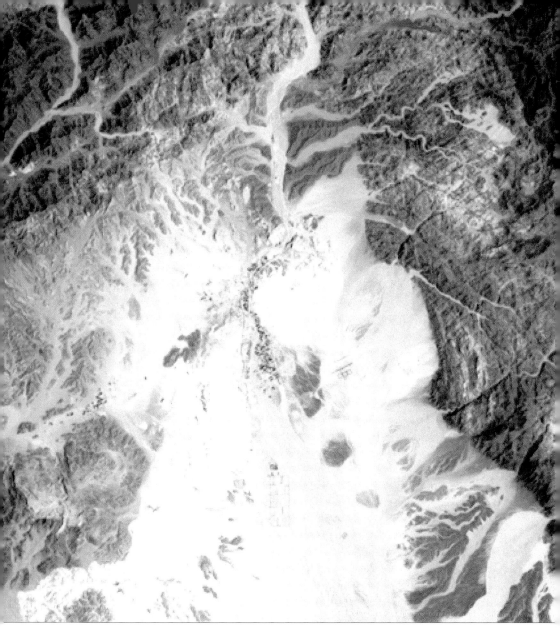

Figure 451: The location of the land of Midian has been discussed earlier, and it is obvious from maps printed in the last 450 years that it was on the east side of the Gulf of Aqaba. The area shown above is the only place for a permanent settlement in the region. This is for one reason: access to drinking water. No permanent settlement was possible without wells for drinking water since there were no lakes, rivers or other open sources of water. Moses' father in law (Jethro) was the high priest of Midian. The high priest probably lived in the "capital" or permanent settlement of the region. The only place this could be is what is called Al Bad today, which is the area in red. Red marks vegetation on this map. Interestingly, the investigation of the land of Midian by R.F. Burton in 1878, revealed the position of what was called "Moses' Well". This well was located in the middle, red coloured region of this satellite photograph, i.e. in Al Bad. Right beside "Moses' Well", on the map from Burton's investigation, is a wadi named "Wadi El Bada".

to return to the mount of God with the people of Israel. However, we can also see it in a side-note in the text, when the people of Israel are in the desert near Mount Sinai.

"Then Jethro, Moses' father in law, took Zipporah, Moses' wife, after he had sent her back, And her two sons; of which the name of the one was Gershom; for he said, I have been an alien in a strange land: And the name of the other was Eliezer; for the God of my father, said he, was mine help, and delivered me from the sword of Pharaoh:

And Jethro, Moses' father in law, came with his sons and his wife unto Moses into the wilderness, where he encamped at the mount of God: And he said unto Moses, I thy father in law Jethro am come unto thee, and thy wife, and her two sons with her.

And Moses went out to meet his father in law, and did obeisance, and kissed him; and they asked each other of their welfare; and they came into the tent. And Moses told his father in law all that the LORD had done unto Pharaoh and to the Egyptians for Israel's sake, and all the travail that had come upon them by the way, and how the LORD delivered them.

And Jethro rejoiced for all the goodness which the LORD had done to Israel, whom he had delivered out of the hand of the Egyptians."
(Ex. 18:2-9).

In other words, Moses had sent his wife Zipporah and his two sons ahead to their home, the home in Midian. This underlines once more that Moses knew where the people of Israel were going (however Moses did not know the route in advance). It was to Mount Horeb in Midian. Moses understood that it was to be a difficult journey, he not only sent his family on in advance, but he sent them to the place where they had grown up. Moses' wife and two sons were then under the protection of the high priest Reuel (also called Jethro), Moses' father-in-law.

In this passage the names of the sons are given, Gershom and Eliezer. From earlier passages in the Bible it is clear that Moses took his family with him from Midian to Egypt (Ex. 4:20), but there is no mention of Moses having sent the family on ahead to Midian, until it recounts how they saw each other again (Ex. 18:2). The only way of travelling from Egypt to Midian via the Red Sea, would have been by crossing what is today called the Gulf of Aqaba. When Moses sent his family on in advance, they naturally travelled the ordinary way by land via present day Eilat; the route Moses followed until the Lord led them to turn, and thus become shut in at Nuweiba.

63.2. Moses meets Jethro

When Jethro meets Moses he comes to the encampment at the mountain of God, which must have been Rephidim since they have not yet moved to the place in front of the mountain of God, Horeb. The rock of Horeb was in Rephidim, and Rephidim was to the west of Horeb. However, the people of Israel have not reached the eastern side of Mount Sinai, where great miracles and signs await the people.

The meeting between Jethro and Moses is a joyful occasion. They greet each other with respect, Jethro follows Moses into his tent and Moses relates all that has happened. Jethro already knows this in general as the Lord had called Moses during his time in Midian, and so Moses had already told Jethro of his assignment. Moses' narration greatly impresses Jethro:

"And Moses told his father in law all that the LORD had done unto Pharaoh and to the Egyptians for Israel's sake, and all the travail that had come upon them by the way, and how the LORD delivered them. And Jethro rejoiced for all the goodness which the LORD had done to Israel, whom he had delivered out of the hand of the Egyptians.

And Jethro said, Blessed be the LORD, who hath delivered you out of the hand of the Egyptians, and out of the hand of Pharaoh, who hath delivered the people from under the hand of the Egyptians. Now I know that the LORD is greater than all gods: for in the thing wherein they dealt proudly he was above them. And Jethro, Moses' father in law, took a burnt offering and sacrifices for God: and Aaron came, and all the elders of Israel, to eat bread with Moses' father in law before God." (Ex. 18:8-12)

Jethro is the one who suggests that Moses should institute a system with judges and leaders. These can then deal with minor problems and conflicts, so that only the important questions, or those that are difficult and unsolved, are taken to Moses (Ex. 18:13-27).

64. Do the people of Israel reach Mount Sinai?

The short and simple answer to the question as to whether the people of Israel reached Mount Sinai is: yes, they reached it. According to the biblical texts, eight weeks to the day after leaving Egypt the people of Israel arrive at the first goal of their journey - Mount Sinai - to hold a service of worship. They departed the 15th of the first month, and arrived on the 15th of the third month.

"In the third month, when the children of Israel were gone forth out of the land of Egypt, the same day came they into the wilderness of Sinai. For they were departed from Rephidim, and were come to the desert of Sinai, and had pitched in the wilderness; and there Israel camped before the mount. And Moses went up unto God, and the LORD called unto him out of the mountain, saying, Thus shalt thou say to the house of Jacob, and tell the children of Israel;" (Ex. 19:1-3)

Figures 452, 453: The black upper part of the Jabal Al Lawz mountain ridge, seen from the camp area in front (east) of the mountain.

"And they departed from Rameses in the first month, on the fifteenth day of the first month; on the morrow after the passover the children of Israel went out with an high hand in the sight of all the Egyptians." (Numb. 33:3)

Concerning the time of the journey, we can note that it probably took only

about a week from the land of Rameses to the site of the crossing at Nuweiba. The remainder of the time, about seven weeks, was spent in various places in north-western Saudi-Arabia, or journeying between these places. During this time, after crossing the Red Sea, the people of Israel were tested by the Lord in different ways. Their trust in the Lord was really put to the test through hunger, thirst and a great battle when, unprepared, they were attacked by a great warrior people. Exactly eight weeks after leaving, they arrive at Horeb.

In Egypt Moses asked for permission from Pharaoh to go out into the desert to worship the Lord. Pharaoh refused to allow the people of Israel to do this, which was the reason for all the plagues Egypt suffered. Now the people of Israel have reached Mount Sinai, and it is time to worship. However, this worship will be very different from what the people of Israel expect. Nevertheless, before we go into this we must look more closely to see if this Mount Sinai in northern Saudi-Arabia (figures 454-456) tallies with the descriptions given in the Bible, and by Josephus as well as what archeological discoveries and popular tradition say.

The mountain has three names in the Bible: "God's mountain", "Mount Horeb" and "Mount Sinai". Besides this is the modern name of the mountain "Jabal Al Ławz". From now on this mountain will be called "Horeb" because it is short, simple, and is not confused with the traditional Mount Sinai on the Sinai peninsula. Horeb is Hebrew and means "dry" or "desolate". Both these descriptions fit the site of Mount Horeb very well.

Figures 454-456: The mountain peak of Jabal Al Lawz (lower), the plateau on the way to the peak with the campsite in the background (middle), and the holy area close to the mountain base with the campsite seen behind (upper). The upper photograph was taken from a position close to the plateau (middle photograph).

65. WHAT DID HOREB (MOUNT SINAI) LOOK LIKE?

The biblical texts give a number of descriptions of Mount Horeb. Some of these are direct descriptions, in other cases it is a matter of the conditions

Figures 457-458: The satellite photograph in the lower left corner gives an overview of the Gulf of Aqaba. At the very northern tip the cities Eilat (Israel) and Aqaba (Jordan) are located (shown in red). The Nuweiba peninsula (Egypt) is easily seen as the white peninsula on the west coast. From west to east at Nuweiba, is the under water bridge ending on the plain of the east coast (Saudi-Arabia). Al Bad is seen as the white area with a red area in the middle, in the lowest part of the photograph. The Jabal Al Lawz mountain ridge is seen as the black section in the lower right corner. The campsite is seen as the white area east of the black mountain ridge.

The big satellite photograph is a magnification of the Jabal Al Lawz mountain ridge, seen as the black area in the lower left part of the photograph. The white area east of the black mountain ridge is the suggested campsite.

that must exist. In addition to the biblical texts, are the comments of Josephus, popular tradition, and a reference to the Koran. There are more descriptions of Horeb, and its immediate surroundings, than one would imagine. This makes it even more incredible that the traditional site on the Sinai peninsula has been accepted, since in the main none of the criteria below have been satisfied by this location.

65.1. AN ENCAMPMENT

The entire people of Israel were to pitch camp in front of Mount Horeb (Ex. 19:2, JA 3/5:1). The entire people of Israel, roughly two million people, and all the livestock were to find space in front of the mountain. A large area was needed for this.

In figure 456, the picture over the area is taken from the plateau on Horeb, and faces directly eastwards. In the valleys to the right, left and straight on, is a very large area on which to put up tents and keep cattle. The satellite pictures (figures 457, 458) show this clearly as a white area. The encampment area is at least 40 square kilometres, and even larger if the valleys in all directions are included.

In the encampment area, part (roughly a quarter) of a millstone was found, a stone that together with a piece of log (mortel and pestle) or a stone, was used for grinding flour (figures 459, 460). In this case it was probably used for preparing the manna to make bread. In figures 461 and 462 a corresponding millstone from ancient Egypt is shown. As can be seen these two millstones were made in the same way suggesting an Egyptian origin.

Along the route of the Israelites stone-circles have been found. For example in the Negev desert, and other places in todays Israel. At Mount Horeb there is a huge number of stone circles, but they are located on the west side of the mountain, the "back" side or around the place that most likely was Rephidim (figures 463-467).

There is speculation as to whether these stone circles could have encircled tents. In figure 463 a large stone can be seen erected in the middle of a circle. Perhaps this was to hold up the cloth of the tent, which was then stretched over the stones and afterwards kept taut and held down by stones laid on it (figure 468). The stone circles may also have been there to support the tent pole holding up the roof of the tent.

The biblical texts and Josephus indicate that the people lived in tents. The function of the stone circles may have been to keep the cattle out of the tents, which did not always have closed sides all round. But since it is stated in the biblical text that the people of Israel encamped in front of the mountain;

"...Israel camped before the mount..." (Ex. 19:2)

(to the east of the moun-

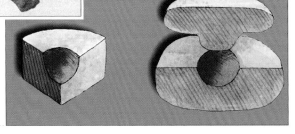

Figures 459, 460: A part of a millstone found at the campsite. The sketch shows how the millstone once looked.

Figures 461, 462: An ancient Egyptian millstone, with its two parts. The right part was placed on top of the left, and was moved in circles to grind the seeds.

tain), and no stone circles are found there it could have been a totally different situation. The stone circles could have been made to keep the animals in place, which could have been kept at the west side of the mountain, while the people had their campsite on the other side, the east side, in front of the mountain.

We can only speculate on the exact function, but it is obvious that around Mount Horeb a great number of people thought it was important to erect a huge number of these stone circles. Otherwise, this is an uninhabited wilder-

Figures 463-467: A large number of stone circles are found on the west side of the mountain.

ness.

In addition, there is no doubt that space for an encampment was unlimited at this location.

Another theory could be that the stone circles were the home of the highpriest in Midian, Moses' father-in-law, Jethro.

65.2. A BOUNDARY AROUND THE MOUNTAIN

Moses was to mark out a boundary so that people would not come into contact with the foot of the mountain. The mountain was so holy that if any unauthorised person were to come into contact with Mount Horeb they would die, according to the biblical text. Therefore it was important to have a marked boundary, a fence or something similar, so that no-one came too close.

Figure 468: The sketch shows a possible function of the stone circles.

"And thou shalt set bounds unto the people round about, saying, Take heed to yourselves, that ye go not up into the mount, or touch the border of it: whosoever toucheth the mount shall be surely put to death:" (Ex. 19:12)

"And Moses said unto the LORD, The people cannot come up to mount Sinai: for thou chargedst us, saying, Set bounds about the mount, and sanctify it." (Ex. 19:23)

The Bible does not state what type of fence or demarcation Moses had put up. However, several conclusions can be drawn. The people of Israel had no fencing material with them from Egypt, so the raw material would have to be found locally in the vicinity of Mount Horeb. There are a few trees but their number is very limited. On the other hand, there was an unlimited supply of stones of all sizes. In the pictures in figures 456 and 469 black bands of stone can be seen along the side of the mountain in the middle of the lighter, brownish stones. This could be the remains of some sort of stone wall built of untreated natural stone. But the more interesting find is the block of stone with a special type of inscription (figure 470).

The inscription is a mark of a foot or a shoe. This mark is interesting because it existed in Egypt, and there it was used to mark a holy place. The origin may be that in a holy place one took off one's shoes, of which the Bible gives an example when Moses receives his calling at Mount Horeb (Ex. 3:5).

Thus the inscription might represent an untied shoe. In figure 470 one can partly see the strap for the big toe, the leather sole and two shoe-straps. As the inscription signified holy ground in Egypt (59), and the Bible indicates that shoes should be removed at sacred places, it is highly likely that the inscription marked the boundary of something holy. There is a large number of stone blocks below Horeb with this inscription. These blocks of stone alone may have been the boundary mark, or they may have been part of a stone wall built there.

Figure 469: There are rows of darker stones at the base of Mount Horeb that could have been walls in ancient times.

65.3. THE HEIGHT OF THE MOUNTAIN

Josephus states (JA 3/5:1) that Horeb was the highest in the area. This tallies with the Jabal Al Lawz mountain ridge which, with its height of 2580 metres, raises itself above all the other mountain ridges in the area. The traditional Mount Sinai is not the highest in the area.

65.4. THE APPEARANCE OF THE MOUNTAIN

The mountain is said to have been difficult to climb because of its height, and the problem of climbing all the vertical rocks (JA 3/5:1). In figure 471 it can be seen that a large part of the mountain is composed of huge steep rocks with vertical sides. This applies particularly to that part of the moun-tain which more people than Moses climbed (the 70 elders, Ex. 24:9). The actual area at the top, at a higher level, consists of fewer stones and is more flat in character.

65.5. AN ALTAR

There must be an altar below Mount Horeb and that altar must satisfy certain requirements according to the Bible.

"And Moses wrote all the words of the LORD, and rose up early in the morn-ing, and builded an altar under the hill, and twelve pillars, according to the

Figure 470: There are several stones at the base of Mount Horeb with a shoe inscription. This was used in ancient Egypt as a sign for a holy place (shoes should be taken off).

Figure 471: The mountain had vertical rocks that made it hard to climb, which is seen at Jabal Al Lawz mountain ridge.

twelve tribes of Israel." (Ex. 24:4)

The Bible tells us that Moses built an altar below Horeb, and at the foot of this mountain there is an altar. In figures 472 and 473 this can be seen photographed from the mountain. From that distance and seen from above, the altar is formed in an angle like the letter L upside down. The Lord is very detailed when he gives Moses the instructions of how this altar is to look:

"An altar of earth thou shalt make unto me, and shalt sacrifice thereon thy burnt offerings, and thy peace offerings, thy sheep, and thine oxen: in all places where I record my name I will come unto thee, and I will bless thee. And if thou wilt make me an altar of stone, thou shalt not build it of hewn stone: for if thou lift up thy tool upon it, thou hast polluted it. Neither shalt thou go up by steps unto mine altar, that thy nakedness be not discovered thereon." (Ex. 20:24-26)

The altar is to be of earth, if stones are used they are to be uncut stones (stones found in nature), and the altar is to be low.

Below the mountain, just where the side of the mountain comes down to the more level ground inside the holy

Figures 472, 473: The upper photograph is taken from the mountain towards the mountain base. The altar is seen at the tip of the arrow. The lower picture is a magnification of the same photograph.

Figure 474: The structure of the altar seen from the east (from the camp). The length of one side is approximately 18 m. The altar section is the right part.

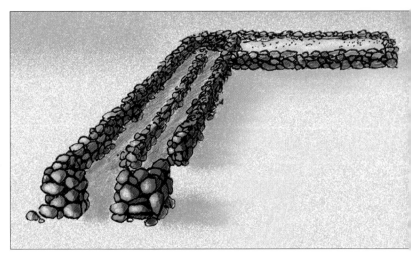

Figure 475: A photograph taken from the side of the "corridor" section of the altar (see figure 474).

(demarcated) area, stands the altar. The altar is low. It is difficult to determine its exact height, but the altar may have been roughly one metre high: if one bases it on the outer stone wall. There are no stones scattered about to imply that it has collapsed and was much higher when it was in use, so the altar there now satisfies the condition of being low.

The wall is built of natural stone (uncut stone), which is erected both as a wall and as a border. From this aspect too the existing altar satisfies the conditions.

The altar is in two parts, which can be seen in the simplified sketch in figure 474. The lefthand part consist of some form of pathway. It may be that animals were led in along two separate paths. Bulls along one path and sheep/lambs along the other. It may have been practical at the time to separate these animals. Another possibility is that animals were led in along one path, and those who held the animals went back along the other path. With this solution too this represents a practical solution for handling the large number of animals sacrificed at this place.

The altar itself is the higher part (right part) seen in figure 474. This part is enclosed by a stone wall and is filled up with earth, or rather gravel and sand. From this aspect also, the altar at the mountain satisfies the requirements of the biblical text.

Figure 475 shows a close-up picture of the altar. This picture was taken after a certain amount of excavation had been done by Saudi Arabian archaeologist's. The actual altar part has been completely dug out, and the earth is lying in a pile outside the altar.

Scattered about below the altar, are broken columns of marble. Comments on these will be made in section 65.12.

65.6. TWELVE STONE PILLARS
According to the biblical texts there should be 12 stone pillars below Mount Horeb.

"And Moses wrote all the words of the LORD, and rose up early in the morning, and builded an altar under the hill, and twelve pillars, according to the twelve tribes of Israel." (Ex. 24:4)

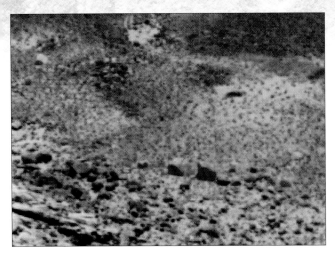

Figure 476: A semi-circle of stone pillars at the base of the mountain. Moses raised 12 stone pillars according to the biblical text (Ex. 24:4).

Within the sacred area just below the rock face there are the remains of stone pillars. The stones are standing in a semi-circle. Some of the stones have fallen over, and are more or less hidden by sand and gravel. The row of stone pillars is coloured yellow in figure 476. This picture taken in an eastward direction from the plateau on Horeb, shows that the stone pillars are along the same rock face as the altar.

Several of the stone pillars are standing upright and some have fallen over. Sand and gravel in varying degrees have covered parts of the stone pillars. Ten stone pillars are standing in marked semi-circles, and there are two empty places as though two stone pillars are missing.

Twelve stone pillars were to be erected at the foot of Horeb. It is probable that these are the stone pillars mentioned in the Bible.

65.7. A PLATEAU ON THE MOUNTAIN

There should be a plateau on the mountain, large enough for Moses, Aaron, Nadab and Abihu, as well as the seventy elders (Ex. 24:1-18). Assuming that this total of 74 people each needed 5 square metres (they must have been able to fall to the ground in prayer without knocking one another off the mountain), then this plateau needed to be at least approximately 400 square metres large.

In figure 477 there is a picture taken towards the encampment area from the top of the ridge of Jabal Al Lawz. There is a large plateau on the side of the mountain marked with an arrow. This plateau covers an area of several thousand

Figure 477: Mount Horeb should have a plateau that could accomodate at least 74 people.

square metres, which means that there was plenty of space for the 74 individuals who were allowed on the mountain. The photograph shown in figure 472, looking down towards the sacred area, is taken from the mountain plateau.

Horeb should have a relatively large plateau a little way up the mountain, but clearly separate from the mountain peak. The mountain range Jabal Al Lawz has such a plateau.

65.8. THE CAVE

There should be a cave on Mount Horeb, where the prophet Elijah lived for a while when many years later he met the Lord on that mountain:

"And he arose, and did eat and drink, and went in the strength of that meat forty days and forty nights unto Horeb the mount of God. And he came thither unto a cave, and lodged there; and, behold, the word of the LORD came to him, and he said unto him, What doest thou here, Elijah?"
(1 Kings 19:8-9)

In figure 478 there is a picture taken looking towards the sacred area. The black top of Horeb can be seen in the background, and the double peaks with the cleft can be seen to the right. The higher of the two peaks has a cave straight down from the top. In figures 479 and 480 there is a detailed picture

Figure 478: The sacred area at the base of the mountain, seen from the campsite. In the upper left area the plateau can be seen.

of this peak. The opening to the cave is marked with an arrow. The cave is larger than one realises. The best idea of size is obtained by comparing the mouth of the cave with the tree growing between the gigantic rocks at the top.

The Jabal Al Lawz mountain ridge, which the hypothesis of this book claims is Horeb, also has a cave as Horeb should have, according to the Bible.

65.9. THE WATER SUPPLY

A stream of water poured down from Mount Horeb to give water to the people of Israel and their livestock (Deut. 9:21). It must have been an enormous amount of water since this source was to satisfy all the needs of two million people as well as a large number of cattle.

There are obvious traces of the stream of water and of the pond (lake), where the water collected below Horeb. In figure 456 there is a picture taken from the plateau on Horeb, look-

Figures 479, 480: Mount Horeb should have a cave on the side, where the prophet Elijah stayed long after the events discussed in this book. The arrow indicates the opening of the cave. The lower photograph is a magnification of the entrance to the cave.

Figure 481: The riverbed at the base of the mountain has been "filled with water" in this illustration. The dots are wells discussed later in this section.

Figure 482: Wells were located along the shoreline of the water. These wells had two walls with a sand filter between. The illustration shows the design. The diameter was approximately 6 m.

ing directly eastwards. At the foot of the mountain the stream of water can be seen as a dried up river-bed winding through the sacred area below the mountain. Note that the small green pieces of fluff in the river-bed are tall trees and bushes several metres high. The best idea of size is obtained by comparison with the car tracks in the lefthand part of the sacred area. In figure 481 the stream and the pond have been marked.

The water did not flow away but was dammed up in a lake, which made it easier both to fetch water for all the people, and to give the herds of cattle water. The depth of the pond can only be roughly estimated. The difference in level between the "banks" and the "bed" of the pond is about 7 metres, which meant a considerable amount of water.

The water sprang from the middle of the rock face on Horeb, an equally remarkable situation as in Rephidim with the rock that split and became a source of fresh water for the entire people of Israel. In figure 481 the water is marked along the highest waterline. The water flowed across to the left of the picture.

To ensure good quality drinking water, double-walled wells were dug along the banks. Outline sketches for these wells can be seen in figure 482. The wells had an outer wall of stone, an interspace filled with gravel and sand and an inner wall of stone. To reach the wells the water had to pass through ground consisting of sand and gravel. This filter system can resemble what we have in modern times for the purification of drinking water (sand filters).

In figures 483 and 484 enlargements (indistinct, circular tops of wells) of pictures taken from Mount Horeb can show some of these wells. The wells had a large capacity,

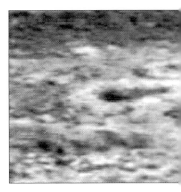

Figures 483-485: The upper two photographs are magnifications of pictures taken far away from the wells. The circular shapes are the upper parts of the wells. The third (lowest) shows a section of a well wall, seen as a half circle in the right part of the photograph.

with a diameter of approximately 6 metres. A partly collapsed well can be seen in figure 485. In figure 481 the positions of the wells are shown as dots along the banks of the dammed lake below Mount Horeb.

The capacity of the water supply and the advanced technological design imply that the people of Israel represented a large number of individuals.

Figure 486: This is the view that Moses would have had if this is Mount Horeb. Moses was on his way down, and saw that something was going on in the camp. The worship of the golden calf (encircled).

65.10. THE ALTAR TO THE GOLDEN CALF

The people of Israel made themselves an idol of gold, a golden calf (Ex. 32:1-35, Deut. 9:6-29) when they thought that Moses had disappeared during his 40 days on Horeb. They wanted an image of the God who had brought them out of Egypt. The calf that was made of gold was according to the Egyptian cult of Apis (bull cult). They sacrificed burnt offerings to this golden calf on an altar which Aaron built after great pressure from the people (Ex. 32:5). The position of the golden calf and its altar was such that Moses saw it when he went down Mount Horeb (Ex. 32:17-29, Deut. 9:15-16), this means east of the mountain peak.

In figure 486 the photograph shows an overview of the sacred area, and the encampment spreading out into the valleys

around Horeb. This was the view Moses had as he went down from Mount Horeb. Moses sees that there is a feast underway in the camp. Joshua who is accompanying Moses believes that it is a war cry that they hear in the camp. As Moses gets nearer, he sees dancing and feasting around the golden calf.

The people of Israel did not believe that Moses would return from the mountain, and so they made themselves this bull-calf. This was a custom they knew from Egypt, where the bull cult permeated the whole of Egyptian society. It may have been Hebrews who took the initiative in making this

Figure 487: This is most likely the altar of the golden calf fenced by the Saudi-Arabian authorities. The altar in itself is not critical, it is the typical Egyptian bull inscriptions (the Apis cult) that are extraordinary, since they are not found on Arabian territory except at this location.

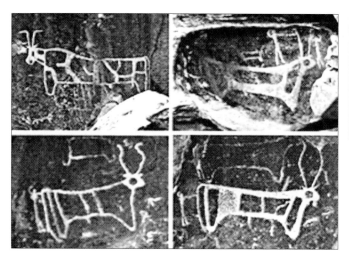

Figures 488, 489: Bull inscriptions at the altar. These are typical Egyptian Apis bull inscriptions.

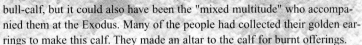

bull-calf, but it could also have been the "mixed multitude" who accompanied them at the Exodus. Many of the people had collected their golden earrings to make this calf. They made an altar to the calf for burnt offerings.

The circle in figure 486 indicates the altar to the golden calf, exactly where the Bible relates Moses would have seen it as he went down the mountain. Of course the golden calf is not left since Moses according to the text crushed it and ground it to powder. But the altar remains. In figure 487 is the altar itself with inscriptions of bulls. In the detailed pictures in figures 488 and 489, some of the inscriptions can be seen on the stone blocks connected with this altar.

This is the only known place in Saudi-Arabia where inscriptions of this type have been found, according to Saudi Arabian archaeologists. Apis bulls are extremely common in Egyptian culture, which can be seen in figures 490-499. It should be particularly noted that it was usual to depict these bulls with a sort of squared pattern (or other patterns), both in the making of statues and on inscriptions and other images (figures 500-502).

The altar as such consists of a number of very large natural blocks of stone, which were suitable to use as an altar. On the sides of the large blocks of stone inscriptions of bulls were made in various configurations. On one stone close to the altar is the inscription shown in figure 503. One of these inscrip-

tions is especially interesting (figure 504) where a person is "lifting" a bull in worship. This type of inscription can be found in Egypt, an example is shown in figure 505.

One block of stone at the altar had a slight depression and after a brief shower something glistened at the bottom, which turned out to be small flakes of gold. This rock could well have been the place where Moses ground the golden calf to powder (Ex. 32:20).

It should be noted that this Egyptian bull cult was not

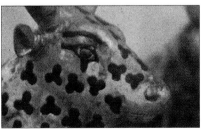

Figures 490-499: Examples of the Egyptian Apis cult (worship of bulls).
Note the typical, strange patterns of the bulls as also is seen in the inscriptions.

found in this area or anywhere else in Arabia, while it completely dominated religious life in Egypt.

The presence of this altar with all its inscriptions and its position, which completely tallies with the biblical description of its position when Moses went down from Horeb, means that this find very strongly supports the hypothesis that this mountain is the mountain called God's mountain, Mount Sinai or Horeb in the Bible.

65.11. The cleft in the mountain

There should be a cleft in the side of the mountain, where Moses stood when he spoke with the Lord on one occasion:

"And the LORD said, Behold, there is a place by me, and thou shalt stand upon a rock: And it shall come to pass, while my glory passeth by, that I will put thee in a clift of the rock, and will cover thee with my hand while I pass by: And I will take away mine hand, and thou shalt see my back parts: but my face shall not be seen." (Ex. 33:21-23)

Horeb has a cleft on the mountainside just by the plateau (section 65.7.). The cleft in the mountain can be seen in figures 477 and 478. This cleft is seen from the plateau in figure 504. This seemingly irrelevant note in the biblical text also tallies with what Jabal Al Lawz, or Horeb, looks like today.

65.12. A further archaeological discovery

In close-up pictures of the altar (figures 507, 508) there are a number of objects which do not belong to the place (the altar is seen in the background). They are pieces of white marble and parts of marble columns. In the figures it can be seen that these broken pieces are scattered below the altar. Firstly, it can be stated that marble is not found in the area. Marble was something which came from

Figures 500-502: Typical patterns depicted on Egyptian bulls.

Figure 503-505: Another inscription at the location shows a number of bulls. Note the one that is magnified in the upper right photograph. This illustrates typical worship of bulls in Egypt. The lower right illustration shows an inscription from Egypt illustrating the very same situation ("lifting" a bull in worship).

Figure 506: Jabal Al Lawz has a cleft just by the plateau.

a long distance and was expensive. The find at this place shows that there were probably six double columns in a circle with a domed marble roof, erected near the altar (figure 509).

The person who erected this must have considered this desolate place as holy, must have known what place it was, must have had large resources to procure marble, transport it to the place and build this monument there. The person who organised this must have believed in the Lord because only a person with faith in the Lord regards this place as holy. On certain marble finds there are ancient Hebrew letters.

The assumption could be made that this was a memorial place that king Solomon wanted to mark out. The mighty and rich king Solomon had his fleet in the Gulf of Aqaba, and built the temple in Jerusalem to the glory of the Lord. According to the hypothesis in chapter 47, king Solomon also erected the columns which have been identified on either side (Egyptian and Saudi-Arabian) of the crossing of the Red Sea at Nuweiba.

The reason why the monument is broken, according to local Bedouins, is that the marble was used when a mosque was built in Al Haql not too far from Horeb. As has been said, marble is not natural to the area and it is expensive to produce. In figure 509 there is a sketch of what this memorial probably looked like.

Altogether the mountain ridge of Jabal Al Lawz has all the characteristics, descriptions etc. that Horeb, Mount Sinai or God's mountain have in the biblical texts. Moreover there are further archeological finds which support the hypothesis that this mountain is the Horeb or Mount Sinai of the Bible. There is a total of at least 12 characteristics of Horeb. Jabal Al Lawz has all 12 characteristics. The traditional Sinai only complies with the odd one of these characteristics.

Figures 507, 508: White marble pieces are spread around the altar at the base of the mountain.

Figure 509: A suggested reconstruction of what the marble memorial looked like before it was all crushed into pieces.

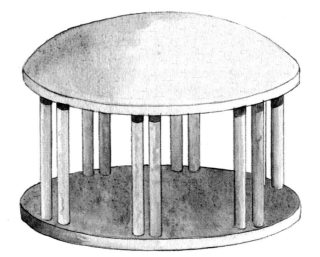

Figure 510: The traditional Mount Sinai on the Sinai peninsula.

66. WHAT IS MOUNT SINAI ON THE SINAI PENINSULA?

The traditional location of Mount Sinai (figure 510) is in the middle of the southern part of the Sinai peninsula, which is marked in figure 511. Traditionally this mountain has been considered to be Horeb, Mount Sinai or the mountain of God described in the Bible. This book discusses other hypotheses only to a limited extent, but it can be valuable to look at the background of the traditional Mount Sinai on the Sinai peninsula.

This mountain is a popular place to visit, and has been so for a long time. It should be noted that in general this mountain is always called the "traditional" Mount Sinai, i.e. the one decreed by tradition. One never refers to archeological discoveries. On the contrary, there is a great deal of literature which questions this localisation. A few examples of this uncertainty are the following:

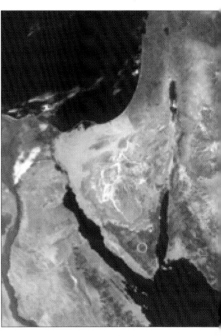

Figure 511: The satellite photograph shows the traditional location of Mount Sinai on the Sinai peninsula. The upper left photograph shows the traditional Mount Sinai.

◆ In the report of a Danish expedition (which took place between 1761 and 1767 and was reported in "Arabia Felix" (60), this comment is made about the traditional Mount Sinai close to the monastery of St. Catherine: "I have observed earlier that we could not possibly be at Mount Sinai. The monastery was situated in a narrow valley, which was not even large enough for a medium-sized army to be able to camp in, let alone the 600,000 men that Moses had with him, who, together with their wives and children, must have come to over 3,000,000."

◆ There is no Jewish tradition regarding the geographic position of Mount Sinai, according to The Jewish Encyclopedia (61).

◆ G.Larsson, a Swedish theologian who has been the principal of the Swedish Theological Institute in Jerusalem for many years and who is very familiar with Christian and Jewish tradition, notes in his 340-page commentary on the book of Exodus (62) that at least nine different suggestions for the location of the Red Sea have been put forward, and thirteen theories about the position of Mount Sinai.

So how was the traditional Mount Sinai arrived at as the mountain described in the book of Exodus?

In the fourth century AD, Helena the mother of Constantine the Great, built a chapel on the north-west slope of the mountain on the Sinai peninsula. The monastery of St.Catherine (figure 512) which is still there, can be dated to about 527 AD, and was founded by the Emperor Justinius. In the monastery of St.Catherine there are a number of very old manuscripts, amongst others the famous "Codex Sinaiticus" was found here.

Figure 512: The St. Catherine Monastery located at the base of the traditional Mount Sinai at the Sinai peninsula.

In other words, the monastery was founded just over 2000 years after the events at Mount Sinai occurred. The chapel was built roughly 1750 years after the events in the book of Exodus. The position of the chapel and monastery is not based on archeological finds, but on a vision Emperor Constantine had in the fourth century.

Altogether it may be noted that the localisation cannot be traced further back than to about 1750 years after the events in the book of Exodus, and that there has always been a great deal of doubt as to the actual position of the mountain. Figure 513 shows the position of Horeb (Mount Sinai) which is the working hypothesis of this book, the mountain range Jabal Al Lawz.

67. ARE THERE REFERENCES TO HOREB IN ANCIENT LITERATURE AND POPULAR TRADITION?

"Horeb" denotes the place put forward by the hypothesis presented in this book, which means that Horeb, Mount Sinai or the mountain of God is the mountain in north-western Saudi-Arabia known today as Jabal Al Lawz. The following comments and notes are examples of popular tradition and ancient literature, which link the location of Horeb to Saudi-Arabia and Jabal Al Lawz.

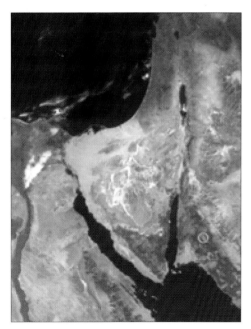

Figure 513: The location of Mount Sinai according to the hypothesis discussed in this book. This location is in today's Saudi-Arabia.

◆ Charles Doughtery travelled in the Arab regions including Saudi Arabia. In his book from 1888, "Travels in Arabia Deserta", he states that the local tradition in north-western Saudi Arabia was "... a tradition amongst their ancestors that very anciently they occupied all that country about Maan, where also Moses fed the flocks of Jethro the Prophet" (63).

◆ H. St. John Philby has carried out extensive investigations of the land of Midian in north-western Saudi-Arabia, which have been published under the name "The Land of Midian". Philby states that Jethro (Moses' father-in-law who lived in the land of Midian) lived and worked in north-western Arabia: "From here my guide and I climbed up the cliff to visit the circles of Jethro on the summit of Musalla ridge, from which we climbed down quite easily to our camp on the far side... A cairn marked the spot where Jethro is supposed to have prayed, and all round it are numerous circles..." (64).

◆ In the same work as above, while Philby is at the ridge with the circles of Jethro, he says with regard to Jabal Al Lawz (Horeb): "...I had a magnificent view of the whole of the Midian mountain range, with Lauz [Lawz] and its sister peaks in the northeast and Maqla a very little north of east, with the valley of al-Numair separating the latter from the low ridge of All Marra, extending from east to south-east, where the two peaks of Hurab stood out in front of the great range of Zuhd, which runs down to a point not far from the sea to our southward... the spot that held my imagination was the smooth, double-headed, granite boss of Hurab, an obvious candidate for identification with the Mount Horeb of the Exodus... the only candidate for the honour which can claim to have preserved the name... According to Hasballah the name of Hurab applies primarily to the wadi, while he called the mountain itself Al Manifa." (64). This comment is interesting since according to Philby the name Hurab was still used in modern times.

R. F. Burton, who made the first scientific investigation of Midian, was convinced that this was the home of Moses.

The "circles of Jethro" mentioned by Philby (64) could be the same circles as shown in figures 463-467.

◆ In his book "On the Track of the Exodus" (65), C.C. Robertson states: "The Biblical references connecting Sinai with Mount Seir, Edom and the land of Midian seem clearly to indicate this region east of the Aelanitic Gulf [Gulf of Aqaba] as pointed out by Beke (1834), Walhausen (1886), Sayce (1894), Moore (1895), Shede (1897), Gall (1898), Gunkel (1903), Edward Meyer (1906), Schmidt (1908), Gressman (1913), Haupt (1914) and by Alois Musil in The Northern Hegaz (1911).

Figure 514: A tree grows between the huge pieces of rock on top of the peak just beside the plateau of the Jabal Al Lawz mountain ridge.

◆ On Horeb there is a small peak on the plateau. At the top of this peak there are two very large rocks, and the remarkable thing is that a tree is growing here (figure 514). If there is anywhere where water cannot be found, it is on a rock on a mountain peak in a desert environment. Nevertheless a tree is growing here.

The tree on the peak is how it is identified locally, since there is no other mountain in the area with a tree on the top. Certain trees can grow to be very old, e.g. an olive tree can be a couple of thousand years old. But has this tree been there for a long time?

The Koran, written between 610 and 632 AD, has an interesting clause in a section about Mount Sinai: "...and a tree issuing from the Mount of Sinai that bears oil and seasoning for all to eat." (66). This comment may be symbolic and refer to the life which springs forth from Mount Sinai. But it may also be that Mohammed, who moved about in this area, had been to the site of Mount Sinai. The local inhabitants had probably already noticed that that mountain had a tree on its peak.

One can only speculate about this connection but the tree is there, olive trees found in this area can be older than the Koran, and the Koran mentions a tree on Mount Sinai. That Mohammed was in this area at least once is supported by the fact that he participated in a peace treaty with Christians in Aqaba, and Jews in the Maqna oasis. Mount Sinai lies between these two places.

◆ During a visit to the area in 1985 the local population (bedouins) related that even today Jabal Al Lawz (Mount Horeb) is known by the inhabitants as "Jebel Musa", which means "Moses' mount". There are also caves in a south-west direction, which are considered to be Moses' caves. According to the Bible, Moses lived in this area for forty years.

◆ The historical writer Josephus recorded over 1900 years ago that people in the area were afraid of Mount Sinai because of the rumour that circulated that God lived on the mountain (JA 3/5:1).

In figure 515 a number of the finds at Horeb are summarised.

68. WHAT HAPPENS AT GOD'S MOUNT HOREB?

The Bible gives a vivid description of what happened at Mount Horeb. The people of Israel arrive at the mountain exactly eight weeks after they left Egypt. In many ways the journey has been extraordinary, hardly a moment has been normal. Eight weeks of severe testing, and now the people of Israel have arrive the first important goal of their journey.

They arrived at the mountain where Moses saw "the burning bush", or rather where the Lord manifested himself and gave Moses the assignment of liberating the people of Israel. Even Moses must have been amazed many times during that journey.

Moses now finds himself in his home district, where he had lived for forty years. The mountain to which they have come has many names. In the biblical texts it is called Horeb, Mount Sinai or God's mountain. In modern times the mountain has been given the name Jabal Al Lawz and is called Jebel Musa (Moses' mount) by the bedouins. In addition, the wadi to the north was called Hurab as late as the last century.

Figure 515: A summary of some of the finds at Mount Sinai. The altar at the base (red), the marble (three black dots), the river bed (blue), the wells (violet), the campsite (yellow), the pillars (green), and the altar of the golden calf (violet circle).

Moses was doubtful when the Lord called him and would much rather have avoided the call. He had long discussions with the Lord. Now it is different, Moses is the leader of the nation and has been sorely tested under very special circumstances. When they arrive at Horeb it records very bluntly:

"And Moses went up unto God, and the LORD called unto him out of the mountain, saying, Thus shalt thou say to the house of Jacob, and tell the children of Israel;" (Ex. 19:3)

According to the Bible the Lord speaks directly to Moses, and gives him instructions about what he is to say to the people of Israel. The Lord says that he has carried the people of Israel on the wings of eagles, an expression signifying speed, protection and with prophetic clarity. The Lord tells Moses that he wants to establish a covenant with the people.

"And ye shall be unto me a kingdom of priests, and an holy nation. These are the words which thou shalt speak unto the children of Israel." (Ex. 19:6)

"Holy" means set apart for the Lord. Moses climbs down the mountain and calls together the elders. The people respond, saying they want to do whatever the Lord wills, and Moses goes back up the mountain with this reply.

The Lord says that he will come before the whole people in a cloud and speak, so that not only Moses but all the people hear his voice. Moses is given the task of sanctifying the people because the Lord will appear on the third day. Sanctification entailed a form of fasting and preparation. They also received strict orders not to come near the mountain itself. It is then that Moses demarcates a boundary for the holy (set apart) area (section 65.2).

On the third day the Lord appears:

"And it came to pass on the third day in the morning, that there were thunders and lightnings, and a thick cloud upon the mount, and the voice of the trumpet exceeding loud; so that all the people that was in the camp trembled." (Ex. 19:16)

The people went to the foot of Horeb led by Moses:

"And mount Sinai was altogether on a smoke, because the LORD descended upon it in fire: and the smoke thereof ascended as the smoke of a furnace, and the whole mount quaked greatly. And when the voice of the trumpet sounded long, and waxed louder and louder, Moses spake, and God

Figure 516: The peak of the Jabal Al Lawz mountain ridge, which is the highest in the area. In the upper left corner the plateau can be seen, and behind the plateau the campsite.

answered him by a voice. And the LORD came down upon mount Sinai, on the top of the mount: and the LORD called Moses up to the top of the mount; and Moses went up." (Ex. 19:18-20)

In figure 516 the top of Horeb is shown. The upper part of the mountain ridge is black while the rest of the mountain is golden brown in colour. There is a clear line between the different colours on the mountain, so that it almost looks as though a huge projected shadow is resting over the top. In figure 517 there is a photograph of a stone from the top. It is speculation as to how the upper part has been transformed by heat, but the Bible uses a "furnace" as a picture of the heat, and the top is quite different from the rest of the mountain. The black stone is obsidian or volcanic glass, a mineral formed at high temperatures.

Figure 517: A specimen of the black mineral of the upper part of the Jabal Al Lawz mountain ridge. It is a mineral (obsidian) formed at high temperatures.

The Lord tells Moses that no-one, not even the priests may come near the mountain. Moses may only take Aaron with him. Then the Lord speaks.

Moses must be in a place where he can speak to the people so that what he says can be heard. Josephus writes that "they were assembled and he stood raised up so that all could hear him" (JA 3/5:3). In figures 478 and 506 the cleft can be seen, which lies above the encampment and the holy area. The cleft is just by the plateau where the 70 elders probably stayed when they were on their way up Horeb (figure 477).

It has not been tested at exactly this place but similar places in this area have very good acoustics. A person can make himself heard in an inexplicable way since the sound rebounds along bare mountainsides. An ordinary voice with raised pitch can be heard several kilometres away. If Moses stood in this mountain cleft, which seems like a natural rostrum raised above the whole camp, then it is probable that he could reach the entire people with the natural acoustics provided by this place.

69. Satellite information from Jabal Al Lawz

There are several finds around Jabal Al Lawz, which according to the hypothesis of this book is Mount Sinai referred to in the biblical texts. Could these finds be confirmed by additional methods? This chapter presents data from a new satellite that can give high resolution four-colour pictures. High resolution in this respect means one meter.

69.1. The general area

Figure 518 is a Landsat-satellite photograph of the area of the Jabal Al Lawz mountain ridge and surroundings. The mountain ridge is pitch black on its upper part. The two arms of the black ridge, which stick out into the white area in a V-shaped pattern (in the middle part of the photograph), are magnified in the large photograph taken by the Ikonos satellite.

When studying the two arms one can easily see that the black arms are not the mountain ridge itself, but the upper part of the ridge. The sharp border between the black and gray-brown area of the mountain can be seen. In the previously discussed figure 453 the same area can be seen from below show-

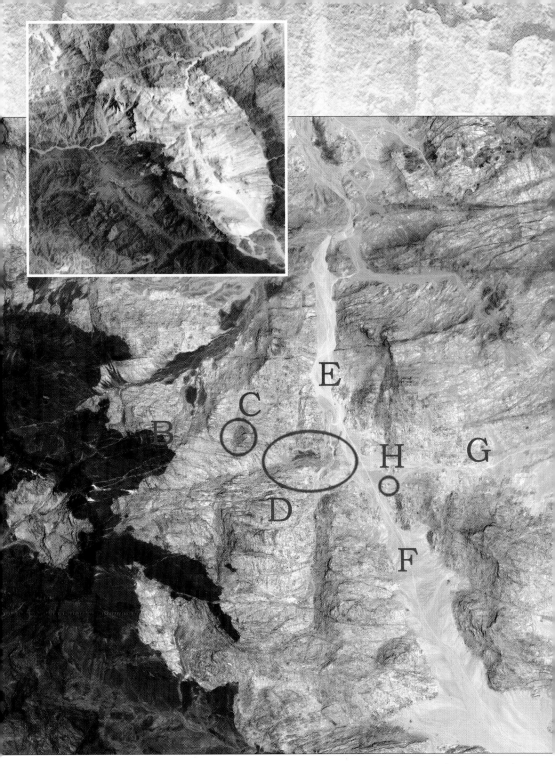

Figures 518, 519: The previously shown satellite photograph is shown in the upper left corner. The natural colours show three different areas. The black mountain ridge in the lower left part, the white round area east of the ridge, and the remaining areas in brown. In the right part of the black mountain ridge there are two arms sticking out in a V-shaped pattern, in the middle part of the photograph. This V-shaped area is shown in the other satellite photograph. For explanations and discussions see the text.

ing the outer part of the upper outstretched arm. The peak shown in figure 453 is not Jabal Al Lawz. The peak marked "A" is Jabal Al Lawz and the peak marked "B" is the peak seen in figure 453.

The plateau is marked "C". The encircled area is the flat part (D) below the mountain where the altar, marble pieces etc. were found. The differences in altitude are great. The difference in altitude between the Jabal Al Lawz peak (A), and the encircled area (D) below the mountain is more than 2000 m. If this is Mount Sinai, the encampment area was to the north (E), east (G) and south (F) of the encircled area. This is supported by the location of the probable golden calf altar, marked "H", which according to the biblical text was in the camp opposite the place where Moses descended from the mountain.

69.2. THE AREA IN FRONT OF THE MOUNTAIN

Figure 524 is a further magnification of the Ikonos satellite photograph from figure 519. The following finds can be seen from the satellite;

The square shaped area represents the flat area at the base of the mountain, where several finds have been found. The curve shaped line (M) represents the base of the mountain, or expressed in another way, the borderline between the flat area and the mountain. The mountain peaks "A" and "B" and the plateau (C) shown in figure 519 is out of the figure 524, but the golden calf altar can be seen (H). Around the golden calf altar Saudi-Arabian authorities have raised a fence to protect archeological finds. The fence (I) is seen as the thin line surrounding the altar.

The possible campsite was surrounding the golden calf altar according to the biblical text. At this location it would be represented by the wide wadis to the north (E), the south (F) and to the east (G). These flat areas widen into huge areas as can be seen in figure 519.

Within the square shaped area the altar at the base of the mountain is located at "J". At "K" the marble remains are spread out. The wells can be seen from the satellite in the area "L".

When the Saudi-Arabian authorities were informed about the finds at this mountain they fenced the area. To protect the area, guards with machine guns are constantly stationed at this location. The position of the fence is marked "N", and the guardhouse is marked "M". The object marked "P" will be discussed below.

69.3. FURTHER MAGNIFIED SATELLITE PHOTOGRAPHS

The finds discussed in the figures above were magnified further, and the detailed photographs verify and add new information.

The altar (J) at the base of the mountain is clearly seen in figure 522. In the satellite photograph the altar is seen from a different angle than in figure 473, when it was photographed from the mountain ridge west of the altar. The shape and structure fits well into the drawing of figure 474. Beside the altar are remains of marble, as shown earlier in figures 507 and 508. The marble pieces are too small to be seen from the satellite, but there is a whitish area close to the altar (figure 522).

The upper part of the wells are in the area marked "L". In figure 523 it is possible to see these round structures located in line. The guard house (M) is seen at the northern part of the fenced (N) area (figure 524). The fence stretches across the whole opening of the wadi, which is the flat area at the base of the mountain. The fence reaches the mountain side north of the guard house, and south of the flat area. The river bed is shown in detail in figure 525.

In figure 527 the suggested altar of the golden calf is seen. First the huge blocks of rock are easily recognised, as discussed earlier in figure 487. On these rocks the bulls of figures 488 and 489 are inscribed. In figure 487 the fence surrounding the golden calf altar is clearly seen. In figure 527 this fence can be seen as the dark line around the pieces of rock.

69.4. ADDITIONAL FINDS
In figure 520 a find was marked "P". In figure 526 a magnification can be seen. The photo shows a man-made object, in a square shape with 90 degree angles. This is most likely a wall made of pieces of rock. Interestingly, at this

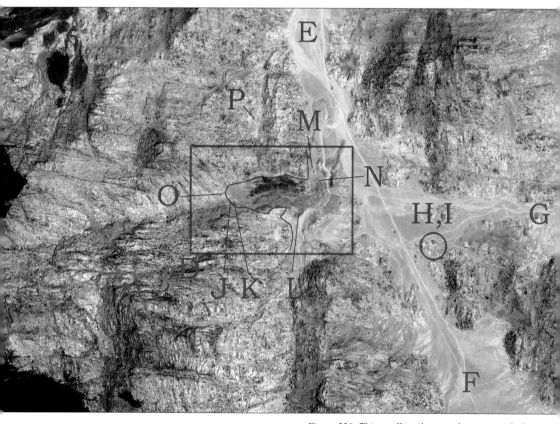

Figure 520: This satellite photograph is a magnified section of the flat area at the base of the mountain ridge. The area is marked "D" in figure 519. The different letters represent finds that are discussed in the text.

Figure 522: Satellite photograph of the altar at the base of the mountain ridge.

Figure 524a: The guardhouse with fence.

Figure 524b: Satellite photograph of the guardhouse and fence. The fence is seen as a thin line going from the upper part to the lower.

Figure 523: Satellite photograph of the upper part of the wells.

Figure 525: Satellite photograph of the riverbed at the base of the mountain ridge.

Figure 521

Figure 526: Satellite photograph of a walled area. The thin wall is seen as a square area.

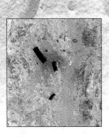

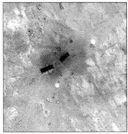

Figures 528, 529: Are these structures small mines or excavations? They are approx. 15-20 meters long and found at several places in the area.

Figure 527b: The golden calf altar and fence.

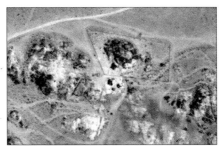

Figure 527a: Satellite photograph of the golden calf altar and fence. The dark blocks are seen in the middle of the photograph. The thin line around these blocks is the fence.

part of the mountain a wall was observed, which was built around something that probably was once in the middle of the walled area. This side of the mountain is not steep and can be reached by the wadis from the north. It is speculation, but if this represents another place of memorial it could be the place of the burning bush. It is clear from the biblical text that the burning bush was close to the home of Jethro, in a desert area and that it was at the mountain of God/Horeb (Ex. 3:1-2). It is common in the Middle East to see flocks of sheep walking up and down in wadis, and even far up on the mountain sides to look for the tiniest area of grass or dry bush. This location represents a relatively flat area that can be reached by a nearby wadi without climbing. In addition, there are some strange structures in the area that look like small mines or excavations (15-20 metres), as shown in figures 528 and 529. The areas look like shafts where some dark material is brought up and then spread around the shaft. It is uncertain what these structures represent.

70. WHAT WERE THE COMMANDMENTS FROM GOD?

According to the Bible, these are the Commandments given by God before the entire nation assembled together. Note that there are edited/rewritten versions in different traditions, but this is what the Bible relates:
"And God spake all these words, saying,

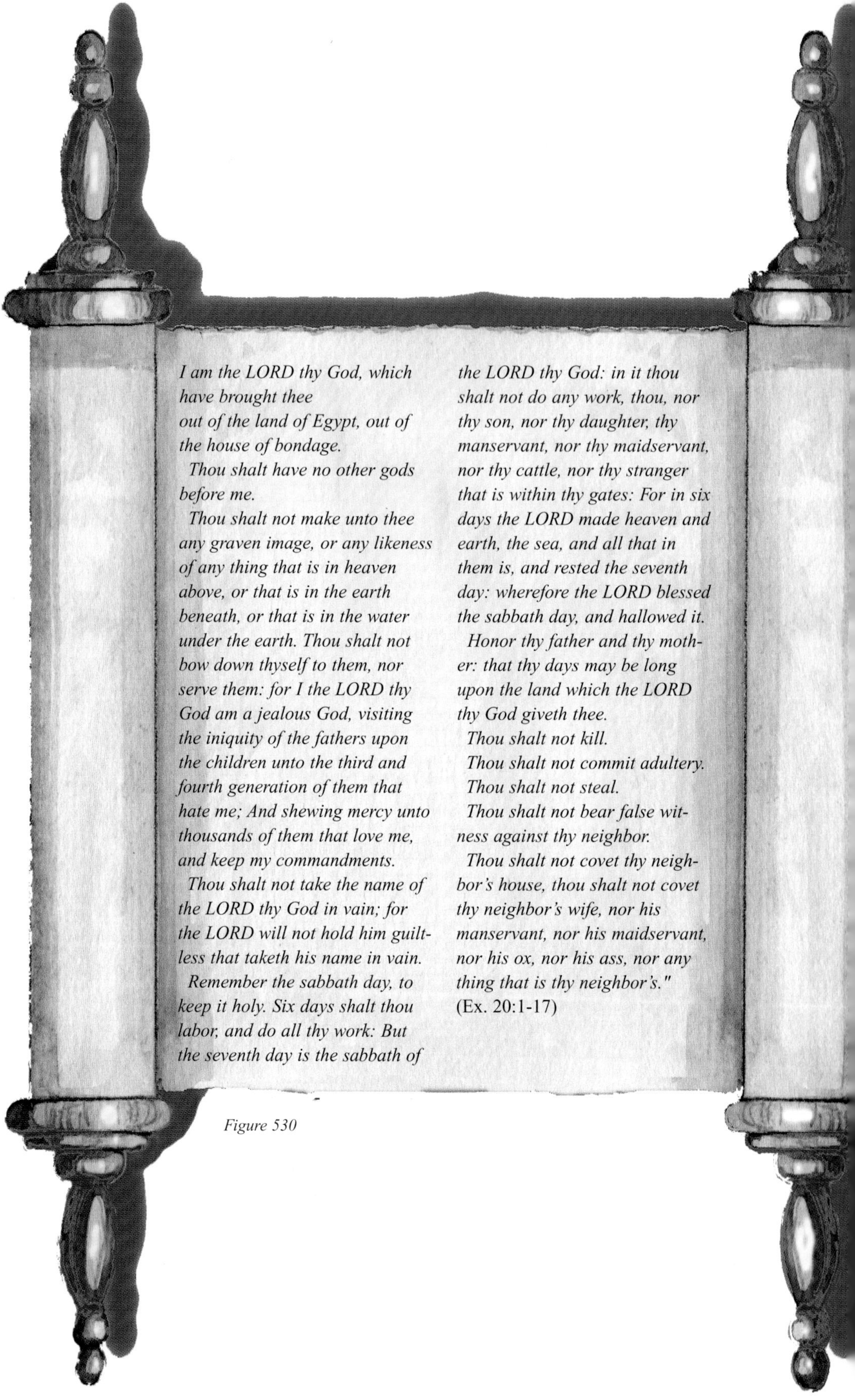

I am the LORD thy God, which have brought thee out of the land of Egypt, out of the house of bondage.

Thou shalt have no other gods before me.

Thou shalt not make unto thee any graven image, or any likeness of any thing that is in heaven above, or that is in the earth beneath, or that is in the water under the earth. Thou shalt not bow down thyself to them, nor serve them: for I the LORD thy God am a jealous God, visiting the iniquity of the fathers upon the children unto the third and fourth generation of them that hate me; And shewing mercy unto thousands of them that love me, and keep my commandments.

Thou shalt not take the name of the LORD thy God in vain; for the LORD will not hold him guiltless that taketh his name in vain.

Remember the sabbath day, to keep it holy. Six days shalt thou labor, and do all thy work: But the seventh day is the sabbath of the LORD thy God: in it thou shalt not do any work, thou, nor thy son, nor thy daughter, thy manservant, nor thy maidservant, nor thy cattle, nor thy stranger that is within thy gates: For in six days the LORD made heaven and earth, the sea, and all that in them is, and rested the seventh day: wherefore the LORD blessed the sabbath day, and hallowed it.

Honor thy father and thy mother: that thy days may be long upon the land which the LORD thy God giveth thee.

Thou shalt not kill.

Thou shalt not commit adultery.

Thou shalt not steal.

Thou shalt not bear false witness against thy neighbor.

Thou shalt not covet thy neighbor's house, thou shalt not covet thy neighbor's wife, nor his manservant, nor his maidservant, nor his ox, nor his ass, nor any thing that is thy neighbor's."
(Ex. 20:1-17)

Figure 530

71. Did the people of Israel receive further instructions?

The Commandments were the basis of the covenant between the Lord and mankind, according to the biblical texts, and the Lord speaks these commandments directly to the nation. The first four commandments regulate the relationship between God and mankind, the other six commandments regulate relations between people.

In addition, the previously enslaved people of Israel received instructions to follow in order to become a nation. The Lord speaks to Moses, who then takes this to the people.

"Now these are the judgments which thou shalt set before them." (Ex. 21:1)

Then two and a half chapters follow with instructions regulating possession, economy, scales of punishment, justice and instructions on cultivating the ground (Ex. 21:1-23:13). These regulations are followed by the institution of commemorative times, and the promise of assistance from the Lord.

Later, Moses comes before the people and presents what the Lord has said to them. The people of Israel reply:

"And Moses came and told the people all the words of the LORD, and all the judgments: and all the people answered with one voice, and said, All the words which the LORD hath said will we do." (Ex. 24:3)

The following morning Moses has an altar built, and has the twelve stone pillars erected (Ex. 24:4), one for each tribe. Both the altar and the stone pillars are erected at the foot of Mount Horeb. The covenant between the Lord and the people of Israel is later confirmed by a great sacrifice of bulls.

"And Moses took the blood, and sprinkled it on the people, and said, Behold the blood of the covenant, which the LORD hath made with you concerning all these words." (Ex. 24:8)

The Bible then relates how the Lord speaks to Moses about the tablets of stone:

"And the LORD said unto Moses, Come up to me into the mount, and be there: and I will give thee tables of stone, and a law, and commandments which I have written; that thou mayest teach them." (Ex. 24:12)

"And Moses went up into the mount, and a cloud covered the mount. And the glory of the LORD abode upon mount Sinai, and the cloud covered it six days: and the seventh day he called unto Moses out of the midst of the cloud. And the sight of the glory of the LORD was like devouring fire on the top of the mount in the eyes of the children of Israel. And Moses went into the midst of the cloud, and gat him up into the mount: and Moses was in the mount forty days and forty nights." (Ex. 24:15-18)

It is during this period of forty days that the people of Israel believe that

Moses has disappeared, and so they make the golden calf dealt with in section 65.10.

Moses receives many instructions from the Lord during his 40 days on the top of Horeb, which are included in the biblical texts Ex. 25:1-31:18.

Moses is very clear concerning the fact that it was not him but the Lord who wrote on the tablets of stone with his finger.

"And he gave unto Moses, when he had made an end of communing with him upon mount Sinai, two tables of testimony, tables of stone, written with the finger of God." (Ex. 31:18)

Table 13. A comparison between the Commandments ("fundamental law"), and the judgements and statutes for the people of Israel. The purpose of the judgements and statutes was to transform this people of slaves into a nation.

The Words from God	Judgements and Statutes
1. God speaks directly to the people.	1. God speaks to Moses who then speaks to the people.
2. Written on the tablets of stone.	2. Written on scrolls.
3. Written by God, "God's finger".	3. Written by Moses.
4. Purpose universally applicable and timeless.	4. Law/order/hygiene for slaves to become a nation.
5. Demanded sanctification of the people before the Words were given.	5. Given by Moses in the presence of the people.
6. Written in stone.	6. Written in ordinary script.
7. The tablets of stone were broken once.	7. Nothing mentioned about the regulations with regard to this.
8. The tablets of stone were in the Ark of the covenant.	8. The scripts were kept close to the Ark of the covenant (in a box on the side of the ark).

This means that the Commandments are universally applicable and timeless, and can be regarded as a contract or agreement.

The temporary nature of the judgement and statutes was to bring about structure and order amongst the people in the situation which prevailed. This does not mean that the regulations are unimportant, but they must be regarded from the point of view of the situation at the time.

The Commandments can be likened to a country's constitution, while the judgement and statutes are to be likened to regulations of the authorities. A constitution cannot be changed, but regulations are issued according to the local circumstances and problems which exist. A regulation can also be compared to a speed limit. On a bad road the speed limit is lower, while on a motorway very high speeds are permitted. Therefore, no speed limit is absolute. On the other hand, everyone is responsible for adjusting the speed according to the conditions prevailing on a certain stretch of road.

72. THE BUILDING OF THE TABERNACLE

The Tabernacle was a sanctuary for the Lord, according to the biblical text, and a type of portable temple. The Lord shows Moses models, so that the Tabernacle and everything that is to be within the Tabernacle area will be exactly as the Lord directed (Ex. 25:1-8). Moses receives a comprehensive description of how all these parts of the Tabernacle are to be formed. In chapters 25 - 31 of the book of Exodus this is described in detail. The parts to be made were the following:

72.1. THE ARK OF THE COVENANT

The Ark of the covenant was the most important part of the Tabernacle. "Ark" means a chest or box in which the tablets of the law were to be kept. The other texts were kept in a recepticle on the side of the ark.

"And it came to pass, when Moses had made an end of writing the words of this law in a book, until they were finished, That Moses commanded the Levites, which bare the ark of the covenant of the LORD, saying, Take this book of the law, and put it in the side of the ark of the covenant of the LORD your God, that it may be there for witness against thee." (Deut. 31:24-26)

But according to the biblical texts, this was not just any chest. The Lord himself was to have this ark as a throne, and there manifest his presence. Since the Lord was holy, only certain individuals were allowed to come near. One of the functions of the Tabernacle was to avoid unnecessary deaths because people came close to the Lord without being specially sanctified. In order for this to work, the entire tribe of Levi was given the task of taking care of the Tabernacle and its function. However, it was only a very few of the Levites who were allowed to come near the ark of the covenant.

Figure 531: Acacia, the only source for wood in the wilderness around the Red Sea.

The ark was made of acacia wood, the only tree commonly found in this desert environment (figure 531). It cannot have been easy to make all the parts of the Tabernacle described by the Bible from pieces of the acacia tree, since it is difficult to find straight pieces of the tree. The tree is relatively low and often bent in various ways. The raw materials for the entire Tabernacle were collected as an offering from the people of Israel, and include gold, silver, copper, different coloured linen, goat hair, ram skins, tahas skins, acacia wood, oils, spices and precious stones (Ex. 25:1-8).

The construction of the Ark of the covenant is descibed in detail in Ex.

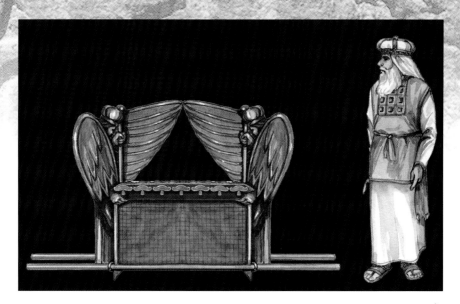

Figure 532: The Ark of the Covenant made out of acacia wood and covered with gold. Inside the box was the place for the stone tablets. The person is shown as a comparison concerning the size, but this is probably how the high priest looked.

25:10-22. The measurement which indicates the scale on which the ark is to be built is given as the cubit, which is approximately 52 cm. The ark was made of acacia wood overlaid with gold. Two poles were to be used to carry the ark. The ark itself was a chest that was to contain the evidence from the Lord, amongst other things the tablets of stone.

On top of the chest was the mercy seat. The mercy seat was both a lid for the chest and a throne for the Lord. On each side stood an angel made of gold, which spread one wing over the ark of the covenant. The Lord would appear between the angels and talk to Moses, and later the high priest. Figure 532 is a representation of the Ark of the covenant.

72.2. THE SHOW TABLE

A table was also to be made of acacia wood overlaid with gold, where the showbread could be placed (Ex. 25:23-30). The "showbread" was bread baked from manna, which was placed on this table. The bread was only to be looked at and not eaten, but lay there before the face of the Lord to remind the people of Israel that the Lord had provided them with bread during the time in the desert, and to indicate their total dependence upon the Lord.

The table was roughly 105 x 52 cm and about 78 cm high. In each corner there was to be a gold ring into which the gilded poles were threaded in order to carry the table. According to the biblical texts (Levit. 24:5-9), 12 loaves of bread, one for each tribe, were laid on the show table every sabbath day. The bread that had lain there previously was to be eaten by Aaron and his sons, the Levites, whose task it was to take care of the Tabernacle.

72.3. THE CANDLESTICK

A seven-armed candlestick was to be made in pure gold (Ex. 25:31-40). This candlestick has become a symbol for Israel and is called Menorah. Menorah is the Hebrew word for this candle holder or candlestick. The shape of the candlestick is described in detail in the Bible. The seven-armed candlestick was large, heavy, hollow and weighed 30-60 kg, which corresponds to the weight measure "a talent" in the Bible. The candlestick was not like a candlestick of today, but was a holder for oil lamps which burned olive oil.

This candlestick was to be kept burning every day with olive oil given by the people of Israel to the Levites (Ex. 27:20-21). The seven-armed candlestick can be seen in figure 534. In figure 533 a modern picture of the seven-armed candlestick can be seen on an Israeli postage stamp. In front of the Knesset, the Israeli parliament in Jerusalem, a Menorah several metres high stands today.

72.4. The Tabernacle

The Tabernacle was what we could describe as a mobile unit, which about 3450 years ago meant a tent construction combined with wooden walls to be assembled, and legs of gold, silver and copper. Even the construction of the Tabernacle is described in detail.

Figure 533: The Menorah is still an official symbol of Israel, as seen on this stamp.

"Moreover thou shalt make the tabernacle with ten curtains of fine twined linen, and blue, and purple, and scarlet: with cherubims of cunning work shalt thou make them. The length of one curtain shall be eight and twenty cubits, and the breadth of one curtain four cubits: and every one of the curtains shall have one measure. The five curtains shall be coupled together one to another; and other five curtains shall be coupled one to another.

And thou shalt make loops of blue upon the edge of the one curtain from the selvedge in the coupling; and likewise shalt thou make in the uttermost edge of another curtain, in the coupling of the second. Fifty loops shalt thou make in the one curtain, and fifty loops shalt thou make in the edge of the curtain that is in the coupling of the second; that the loops may take hold one of another.

And thou shalt make fifty taches of gold, and couple the curtains together with the taches: and it shall be one tabernacle. And thou shalt make curtains of goats' hair to be a covering upon the tabernacle: eleven curtains shalt thou make. The length of one curtain shall be thirty cubits, and the breadth of one curtain four cubits: and the eleven curtains shall be all of one measure.

And thou shalt couple five curtains by themselves, and six curtains by themselves, and shalt double the sixth curtain in the forefront of the tabernacle. And thou shalt make fifty loops on the edge of the one curtain that is outmost in the coupling, and fifty loops in the edge of the curtain which coupleth the second.

And thou shalt make fifty taches of brass, and put the taches into the loops, and couple the tent together, that it may be one. And the remnant that remaineth of the curtains of the tent, the half curtain that remaineth, shall hang over the backside of the tabernacle.

And a cubit on the one side, and a cubit on the other side of that which remaineth in the length of the curtains of the tent, it shall hang over the sides of the tabernacle on this side and on that side, to cover it.

And thou shalt make a covering for the tent of rams' skins dyed red, and a covering above of badgers' skins.

And thou shalt make boards for the tabernacle of shittim wood standing up. Ten cubits shall be the length of a board, and a cubit and a half shall be the breadth of one board. Two tenons shall there be in one board, set in order one against another: thus shalt thou make for all the boards of the taberna-

cle.

And thou shalt make the boards for the tabernacle, twenty boards on the south side southward. And thou shalt make forty sockets of silver under the twenty boards; two sockets under one board for his two tenons, and two sockets under another board for his two tenons.

And for the second side of the tabernacle on the north side there shall be twenty boards: And their forty sockets of silver; two sockets under one board, and two sockets under another board. And for the sides of the tabernacle westward thou shalt make six boards. And two boards shalt thou make for the corners of the tabernacle in the two sides. And they shall be coupled together beneath, and they shall be coupled together above the head of it unto one ring: thus shall it be for them both; they shall be for the two corners.

And they shall be eight boards, and their sockets of silver, sixteen sockets; two sockets under one board, and two sockets under another board. And thou shalt make bars of shittim wood; five for the boards of the one side of the tabernacle, And five bars for the boards of the other side of the tabernacle, and five bars for the boards of the side of the tabernacle, for the two sides westward. And the middle bar in the midst of the boards shall reach from end to end.

And thou shalt overlay the boards with gold, and make their rings of gold for places for the bars: and thou shalt overlay the bars with gold. And thou shalt rear up the tabernacle according to the fashion thereof which was shewed thee in the mount. And thou shalt make a vail of blue, and purple, and scarlet, and fine twined linen of cunning work: with cherubims shall it be made:And thou shalt hang it upon four pillars of shittim wood overlaid with gold: their hooks shall be of gold, upon the four sockets of silver.

Figure 534: The Menorah, a huge oil lamp made out of pure gold.

And thou shalt hang up the vail under the taches, that thou mayest bring in thither within the vail the ark of the testimony: and the vail shall divide unto you between the holy place and the most holy. And thou shalt put the mercy seat upon the ark of the testimony in the most holy place.

And thou shalt set the table without the vail, and the candlestick over against the table on the side of the tabernacle toward the south: and thou shalt put the table on the north side. And thou shalt make an hanging for the door of the tent, of blue, and purple, and scarlet, and fine twined linen, wrought with needlework.

And thou shalt make for the hanging five pillars of shittim wood, and overlay them with gold, and their hooks shall be of gold: and thou shalt cast five sockets of brass for them." (Ex. 26:1-37)

The Tabernacle was the site of the Ark of the covenant. Where the Ark of the covenant stood was the most holy place, which was set apart by a curtain (the veil). On the other side of the veil was the holy place where the show table and the seven-armed candlestick stood. The textile hangings measured roughly 14 x 2 metres, and were made of twined linen yarn that was dark blue, purple and scarlet. The roof was made of goat hair covered with ram skins dyed red and another layer of tahas skin. The meaning of "tahas" is not absolutely clear but it was probably a type of sea cow found in the Red Sea. The skins were considered valuable, which is also evident in the book of Ezekiel (Ez. 16:10).

72.5. THE SACRIFICIAL ALTAR
An altar was also to be made for the Tabernacle (Ex. 27:1-8). The altar was to be made of acacia wood, overlaid with copper and was to have four horns. The altar was to measure approximately 2.5 x 2.5 metres, with a height of about 1.5 metres. The altar was to be carried in the same way as the Ark of the covenant, but with acacia poles overlaid with copper. These poles were to be threaded into rings, and the altar accessories were also to be made of copper. The altar was to be used for burnt offerings of animals.

72.6. THE INCENSE ALTAR
The incense altar (Ex. 30:1-10) was also to be made of acacia wood, and was to measure 0.5 x 0.5 metres with a height of 1 metre. This altar was also to have four horns, and the entire incense altar was to be overlaid with gold. Gold rings at the sides made it possible to carry the altar with gilded poles of acacia wood. The incense altar was to be placed in front of the veil, the hanging in front of the entrance to the holy of holies. Every day the high priest was to burn incense, both morning and evening.

72.7. THE COPPER BASIN
The priests had strict orders to wash their hands and feet each time they entered the tent of revelation (Ex. 30:17-21). For this purpose a copper basin was made with a copper foot, and was placed between the tent of revelation and the altar. There is no description of what this looked like, but it could have resembled a round washbasin made of copper.

72.8. THE COURT OF THE TABERNACLE
Around the Tabernacle itself a courtyard was to be built (Ex. 27:9-19). The courtyard was a large area of roughly 1370 square metres surrounded by pillars with sockets of copper. Between the pillars there were textile hangings made of white twined linen yarn. The height of the enclosure was approximately 2.6 metres. The gate of the court was covered in a hanging of twined yarn in dark blue, purple, scarlet and white linen yarn. The sockets were made of copper as were all the other accessories in the court of the Tabernacle. It is interesting to note how the Tabernacle is situated in relation to the points of the compass. The Bible describes in detail how the Tabernacle was placed with the entrance to the east (Ex. 26:1-37). The historian Josephus also mentions the position of the Tabernacle, with the front side to the east (JA 3/6:3).

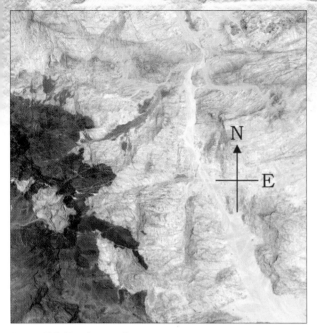

Figure 535: The photograph with the compass shows that the flat area at the base of the mountain ridge was due east.

From these texts we can see that the sacred area below Horeb must have satisfied the requirements in that it was to be facing east. In that way the people were turning their backs towards the rising sun, which represents their turning away from worshipping the sun, which was very important in Egypt.

In figure 535 it can be established that the sacred area's opening from Horeb is due east. Furthermore, the photograph taken from Horeb directly above the place where the Tabernacle stood (if the hypothesis is right that this mountain is Horeb) shows in figures 536 and 537 that there is an opening between two mountain ridges right in front of the sacred area. In between there is a large flat area which was the encampment, and due east there is a mountain ridge.

This is another factor that supports the hypothesis that Jabal Al Lawz is Mount Horeb.

72.9. THE PRIESTS' VESTMENTS

The Levites (Hebrews of the tribe of Levi) were to carry out the priestly service in the Tabernacle, and they had detailed instructions for this service (Ex. chapters 28-30). The vestments of the high priest were specified in detail. The garments consisted of five parts, breast-plate, ephod, cowl, bodice, mitre and girdle. In addition, there were breeches made of linen. Dark blue, purple, scarlet and white linen yarn were to be used for the garments as well as gold.

The bodice was the garment worn next to the skin, and was made of white yarn. The mitre was also to be of white linen yarn. A gold plate was to be attached to the mitre with a blue band. On the plate was to be engraved "Holy to the Lord".

Figure 536: A photograph taken in an eastern direction (towards the campsite) from the Jabal Al Lawz mountain ridge.

Figure 537: Sunrise seen from the flat area at the base of the mountain ridge.

The ephod robe was worn over the bodice, and was made entirely of dark blue material. In the centre of the robe there was an opening for the head edged with a woven border. To the lower hem pomegranates and small golden bells were attached. The sound of the bells would save the high priest's life when he entered the holy of holies.

Over the bodice and the ephod robe, the ephod was worn. The ephod was a sort of coat for the high priest, which hung over the shoulders and covered the chest and back. The ephod was made of gold and white, dark blue, purple and scarlet twined linen yarn. The belt fastened round the waist to hold the ephod in place was of the same material. Two onyx stones were fastened to the shoulders with entwined gold. On each stone were engraved the names of six of the tribes of Israel. There was also a more simple type of ephod worn by the priests, and this was made of white linen yarn.

The breastplate was an important part of the vestments. It was not made of metal but was of the same material and colours as the ephod. The breastplate was square-shaped, the sides measuring about 25 cm. Precious stones were sewn into the breastplate in four rows with three stones in each row, and in the upper corners of the breastplate there were two gold rings which were tied to the shoulders of the ephod with woven bands of gold.

These precious stones represented the twelve tribes of Israel. It is difficult to determine what exactly these stones were. In different languages, cultures and in different eras precious stones have had different names, and so it is today. One example is the sapphire, which is generally associated with a blue colour. But sapphire includes all the varieties of colour of aluminium oxide crystals except red, which is called ruby. If a ruby is pale red, then this colour too is called sapphire. Sapphires can be anything from black to blue, green, yellow, pink, to completely colourless.

When the biblical texts mention different stones sometimes it can be difficult to translate the names correctly and even if the name is correct, it can be difficult to know which colour or variety of stone is concerned. This is to explain why it is impossible to say exactly which stones were found in the breastplate.

The stones of the breastplate consisted of a wide spectrum of colour, and each of the stones was the symbol of one of the tribes of Israel.

"And the curious girdle of the ephod, which is upon it, shall be of the same, according to the work thereof; even of gold, of blue, and purple, and scarlet, and fine twined linen. And thou shalt take two onyx stones, and grave on them the names of the children of Israel: Six of their names on one stone, and the other six names of the rest on the other stone, according to their birth. With the work of an engraver in stone, like the engravings of a signet, shalt thou engrave the two stones with the names of the children of Israel: thou shalt make them to be set in ouches of gold.

And thou shalt put the two stones upon the shoulders of the ephod for stones of memorial unto the children of Israel: and Aaron shall bear their names before the LORD upon his two shoulders for a memorial."
(Ex. 28:8-12)

"And they wrought onyx stones inclosed in ouches of gold, graven, as signets are graven, with the names of the children of Israel. And he put them on the shoulders of the ephod, that they should be stones for a memorial to the children of Israel; as the LORD commanded Moses." (Ex. 39:6-7)

73. WHICH STONES WERE INCLUDED IN THE BREASTPLATE?

In Table 14 the stones named in the Swedish translation of the Bible are listed. The same stones are named in the latest Swedish translation of the Bible, which is based on the original text and was completed at the end of 1999. If we look at translations of the Bible in other languages, there are several different variations in the list of stones that were used.

Table 14. Breastplate stones according to the latest official Swedish translation, from 1999, based on the original text.

Row 1.

Cornelian
Is a reddish-orange variety of quartz (rock crystal), which is semi-transparent. Cornelian is always this colour, but otherwise is the same type of stone as agate and chalcedony.

Topaz
The colour spectrum of topaz is wide and includes yellow, pink, blue and green. Topaz is a precious stone.

Emerald
This stone is always as green as grass, and a stone of great worth. Its green colour has given rise to the expression "emerald green". In ancient times emerald may have meant any green stone.

Row 2.

Ruby
Is a specified name which applies to the red stone ruby, a name used also in modern times. It is possible that in ancient times ruby related to red stones e.g. garnet, ruby or red spinel.

Sapphire
Is the crystal of aluminium oxide and can be of any colour except red. Today in general, the blue variety is meant, but during antiquity sapphire could mean lapis lazuli, which is an opaque sea-blue semi-precious stone. Next to the diamond, sapphire is the hardest (precious) stone.

Chalcedony
A stone that is hard to define. Chalcedony is the same thing as agate, onyx, cornelian and jasper, and with this collective name it is difficult to determine the colour and appearance. Chalcedony is a variety of quartz and may indicate a light blue stone.

Row 3.

Hyacinth
Today this is the name of a reddish-brown variety of zircon. It is difficult to conclude what this name meant historically.

Agate
Like chalcedony this stone is difficult to specify with such an indefinite name. Agate is an opaque variety of quartz, which can have any colour.
Amethyst
This is a violet form of rock crystal, which is a semi-precious stone.

Row 4.

Chrysolite
This stone is olive to grass green in colour and is a variety of quartz with magnesium and iron, which is used as an ornament. It is also called peridot and olivine.
Onyx
Opaque quartz which can differ in colour, but which is striped. Stripes are usually black/white or brownish-red/white. In ancient times this mostly related to the clear variety of quartz, rock crystal.
Jasper
Jasper is a type of chalcedony, which today is used to designate a brick-coloured stone. However, during antiquity it was the name given to transparent green stones.

73.1. CONFUSION CONCERNING THE STONES

In Table 15 the list of stones is shown from seven translations of the Bible. The names of the stones are written in the original language of the respective translations. The stones are partly listed in different order, but it is obvious that it is difficult to translate the names of the stones into their current analogues. The following nine stones are found in most translations: (I) cornelian/sard, (II) topaz, (III/IV) carbuncle/ruby, (III/IV) emerald, (V) sapphire, (VIII) agate, (IX) amethyst, (XI) onyx and (XII) jasper.

Most stones belong to the same quartz family. The quartz mineral is composed of silicon dioxide (SiO_2), and is classed as a semi-precious stone. Cornelian is a red-brown variety of quartz defined by its colour. The colour scale can range from orange-brown to red-brown (figure 538).

Agate is the general designation of a group of quartz minerals. Colours and patterns can be infinitely varied depending on where they were found, and which metals are present as "pollution". Therefore, agate does not designate either pattern or colour. Several examples can be seen on next page.

Figure 538: Cornelian

Onyx (XI) is a specific variety of quartz which is currently defined as having a pattern of parallel bands, most often black and white (figure 543). But in ancient times onyx was a more general term for quartz (figure 549). It is worth noting that the two stones on the shoulders of the ephod were also onyx/quartz. Quartz in its pure form is what we know today as rock crystal.

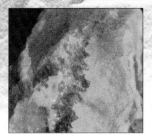

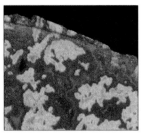

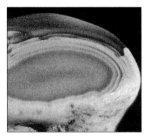

Figures 539-542: Different types of agate.

Figure 543: Onyx, a striped agate most often in black and white.

Rock crystal looks like ice and has no colour. There are at least four reasons that suggest that this stone was rock crystal.

1. When the Lord looked upon the people via the priest that made offerings for their sins, the people were considered clean, pure and free of their sins according to the biblical text. It is logical to assume that a crystal clear stone would symbolise this.

2. Stone number XI, which was the stone for the tribe of Joseph, was of the same kind as the shoulder stones. This suggests that the representative of that tribe had a special role, symbolised by the purity of that stone. Joseph fulfilled the Lord's purpose in a very special way (as discussed in the first part of this book). The stone representing Joseph is different from the other stones in that it is crystal clear, and without colour.

3. The stones on the shoulders of the priest's ephod were the same, and of this onyx/quartz type. When the Lord looked upon the crystals on the ephods shoulder pieces, which were clear, all the inscribed names of the tribes would be seen. In other words, there was no front or back to the stones.

4. It is clearly described in the biblical text that six tribe names were written on each of the two stones, in total 12 names, one for each tribe. Interestingly the crystal formation of a rock crystal is six-sided (figure 549) . The structure of rock crystal forms six flat surfaces, where an inscription easily could be made.

Taken all together, it was probably the case that this stone was what we call rock crystal today.

Jasper (XII) is also a quartz mineral which has rather dark, dull colours. It can be dark green, brick-red or golden-brown. Sometimes these colours are found blended together (figure 544). Jasper was found in ancient Egypt, most often as the brick-red variet. Jasper mines were located in the south of Egypt.

Amethyst (IX) is easier to define. It is a rock crystal "polluted" by manganese, which gives the stone a very beautiful violet colour (figure 545). The amethyst has been a popular jewel for a long time, and was found in ancient Egypt; where the people of Israel obtained their precious stones as gifts at the beginning of the Exodus.

Aluminium oxide (Al_2O_3) in crystal form is a precious stone (figure 546). It is the group of precious stones next to the diamond in hardness. There is a large variety of colours, but the red ("polluted" by iron) is known as ruby. All the other colours are called sapphires, which can range from clear as glass to greenish black. However where jewelry is concerned, one generally means the clear blue or sea-blue coloured stone, when talking about sapphires (V) today (figure 550).

Topaz (II) is a precious stone that is more difficult to define as a historical name. Today it is defined by its chemical formula $Al_2[SiO_4](F,OH)_2$. The colour can be almost anything. However light brown, yellow and blue are the most common varieties (figure 547). It is difficult to trace the name topaz to any specific colour.

Emerald (III/IV) is somewhat simpler to define. The emerald is a beryl, and the chemical composition is $Al_2Be_3[Si_6O_{18}]$. The emerald is a precious stone that is always as green as grass (figure 548). The colour comes from the chrome "pollution". Nonetheless, in ancient times,

Table 15. The stones of the breastplate according to seven different translations. The names are given in each language, respectively.

Row 1.

(I) Reuben	(II) Simeon	(III) Levi
Sardius*	Topaz*	Emerald*
Karneol*	Topas*	Smaragd*
Sardius*	Topaz*	Carbuncle**
Sardius*	Topaz*	Carbuncle**
Sardica*	Topacio*	Carbunclo**
Sardoin*	Topaz*	Emerald*
Sardius*	Topaz*	Carbuncle**

Row 2.

(IV) Judah	(V) Dan	(VI) Naphtali
Turquoise	Sapphire*	Diamond*
Rubin (karbunkel**)	Safir*	Kalcedon
Emerald*	Sapphire*	Diamond*
Emerald*	Sapphire*	Diamond*
Esmeralda*	Zafiro*	Diamante*
Carbuncle**	Sapphire*	Diamond*
Emerald*	Sapphire*	Diamond*

Row 3.

(VII) Gad	(VIII) Asher	(IX) Issachar
Jacinth*	Agate*	Amethyst*
Hyacint*	Agat*	Ametist*
Ligure	Agate*	Amethyst*
Jacinth*	Agate*	Amethyst*
Rubi	Agata*	Amatista*
Opal**	Agate*	Amethyst*
Opal**	Agate*	Amethyst*

Row 4.

(X) Zebulon	(XI) Joseph	(XII) Benjamin
Beryl*	Onyx*	Jasper*
Krysolit**	Onyx*	Jaspis*
Beryl*	Onyx*	Jasper*
Beryl*	Onyx*	Jasper*
Berilo*	Onix*	Jasper*
Chrysolite**	Onyx*	Jasper*
Beryl*	Onyx*	Jasper*

The translations are the following (in descending order of each list of stones); Hebrew/English Bible (New King James 1982), New Swedish official translation from the original language (1999), with translation from the 19th century in parenthesis, King James, revised (1962) version from 1611, The American Standard Bible, La Santa Biblia, Spanish translation (1909), Darby Translation Of The Old Testament and Youngs Bible translation (1863).

For each stone, * and ** indicate the same stone in different languages/spellings.

Figure 544: Jasper.

Figure 545: Amethyst.

Figure 546: A ruby crystal.

Figure 547: An example of topaz crystals.

it is probable that a number of green stones were called emeralds.

The remaining three stones are very unclear in translation. These three are those corresponding to stones VI, VII and X in most translations. From now on these stones will be designated by their numbers.

73.2. STONE NO. VI

This stone is alternately referred to as a type of agate (chalcedony), or a diamond (figure 551). The only statement one can make is that it is most unlikely this was a diamond (crystallised carbon). The stones were approximately 2-3 cm long, a diamond of that size would mean it was in the same class as the very large diamonds known today, which are of enormous financial worth. At that time diamonds were hardly in circulation as precious stones, and the only known source of diamonds until the eighteenth century AD was India. Precisely what stone no. VI was is difficult to say. However, many of the other stones belonged to the quartz family, so the translation which gives the name chalcedony - a form of quartz - may be considered more likely.

73.3. STONE NO. VII

This stone is difficult to comment upon regarding which stone is concerned since translations range over a variety of stones. Today hyacinth is a reddish-brown variety of zircon (zircon silicate), while the opal is a shimmering red/blue/green quartz with so-called crystal water (figure 552). The Spanish translation calls this stone a ruby, which is a red aluminium oxide crystal. "Ligure", which is the name used in two translations, is an old name no longer used to designate precious stones. In the main, it is impossible to deduce which stone is meant.

73.4. STONE NO. X

This stone is said to be beryl or chrysolite. Today we usually refer to beryl as a precious stone that is light blue and called aquamarine. The most common forms of this precious stone are light blue, but there are also green, yellow, pink and transparent varieties. Chrysolite is easier to define as far as colour is concerned since it is olive green. Chrysolite is also called olivine and peridot (figure 553). In ancient times the name chrysolite was used for a number of green stones. An interesting note about chrysolite is that it is found in abundant quantities in a 3500 year old location: a volcano in the Red Sea. The fact that chrysolite was quarried in Egypt during the time the biblical texts

Figure 549: Rock crystal, a six-sided, ice-clear stone.

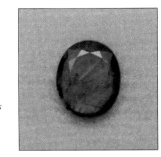

Figure 548: Emerald, always grass-green.

were written, is good reason to assume that stone no. X was chrysolite rather than beryl.

73.5. IN SUMMARY

Altogether these twelve stones can be said to include the ornamental stones, semi-precious stones and precious stones known in the region at that time. Most probably the Hebrews received these stones as part of the gifts the Egyptians gave them when they left Egypt. To summarise, one cannot deduce with any certainty exactly which stones, in modern terminology, correspond to those in the breastplate. In modern times we have scientific definitions such as chemical composition, hardness and wavelength spectrum concerning colour, to name but a few. Historically one used colours as the main definition. This makes it difficult to specify the exact stones used. On the other hand, what we can say is that the stones represented the precious stones of those days, which then, as now, represented some of the main groups of precious stones. For example the quartz group which completely dominates, and the aluminium oxide group.

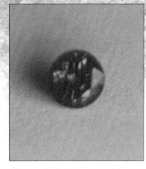

Figure 550: A blue sapphire.

The stones that can be identified with some certainty are amethyst, cornelian and chrysolite since these stones definitely existed in Egypt during the period of time with which this book deals. Sapphire may have been a name for lapis (blue) or turquoise (blue-green) since these stones were common in Egypt, and found within the surrounding region.

Figure 551: Diamond crystals (octahedron crystals).

It may be noted that in the last book of the Bible, Revelation, John meets some angels in a vision and sees the new Jerusalem. This is a long section of 22 chapters. In chapter 21 the new Jerusalem is described in the following way:

"And the foundations of the wall of the city were garnished with all manner of precious stones. The first foundation was jasper (XII); the second, sapphire (V); the third, a chalcedony (VI or VIII); the fourth, an emerald (IV); The fifth, sardonyx (I); the sixth, sardius (I); the seventh, chrysolyte (X); the eighth, beryl (X); the ninth, a topaz (II); the tenth, a chrysoprasus (III?); the eleventh, a jacinth (VII); the twelfth, an amethyst (IX). And the twelve gates were twelve pearls: every several gate was of one pearl: and the street of the city was pure gold, as it were transparent glass." (Rev. 21:19-21) (Roman numbers refer to Table 15)

Figure 552: A "black" (left) and a white (right) opal.

In the biblical text, there is a great resemblance between the new Jerusalem's foundation stones, and the precious stones of the breastplate. It is worthy of note that diamond is not mentioned here (see 73.2 for discussion). "Chrysoprasus" is a green stone looking similar to the green emerald (III), which could explain the use of another word for the same stone.

Figure 553: Peridot (also called olivine or chrysolite).

74. The stone tablets

When Moses, according to the biblical text, has received instructions about how everything is to be made and the procedures to sanctify these objects, the Lord tells him of the importance of keeping the sabbath day (Ex. 31:12-17). Keeping the sabbath day holy (distinct from other days) is to be a sign.

  Later on, Moses receives that which the Lord puts tremendous value on: the Commandments. They were written by the finger of God, on what we have come to call the stone tablets:

"And he gave unto Moses, when he had made an end of communing with him upon mount Sinai, two tables of testimony, tables of stone, written with the finger of God." (Ex. 31:18)

The Bible says here that there were two stone tablets. The tablets were made of stone, and God himself had written the text. A little further on in the Bible we read the following:

"And Moses turned, and went down from the mount, and the two tables of the testimony were in his hand: the tables were written on both their sides; on the one side and on the other were they written. And the tables were the work of God, and the writing was the writing of God, graven upon the tables." (Ex. 32:15-16)

Figure 554: The stone tablets were approximately 60 x 70 cm and the text was written on both sides.

  The tablets had writing on both sides, according to biblical texts, and it was not Moses who had made the inscriptions on the tablets. The Bible is clear regarding who had made the inscriptions on the tablets, it was the Lord himself who had written them.

  When Moses comes down from Mount Horeb he sees that the people have made a golden calf as their idol. Moses throws the law tablets down and breaks them in his anger. Then he smashes the golden calf, grinds it to powder and sprinkles it on the water the people of Israel then have to drink.

  Moses begs the Lord to forgive the people of Israel for what they have done.

Then the Lord renews his covenant with the people (Ex. 34:10-27), and Moses is given the task of making two new stone tablets:

"And the LORD said unto Moses, Hew thee two tables of stone like unto the first: and I will write upon these tables the words that were in the first tables, which thou brakest." (Ex. 34:1)

Moses places the stone tablets in the Ark of the covenant (Deut. 10:5). Moses was 80 years old when he made these stone tablets. Then he had to carry them up the mountain, where the Lord inscribed the text. The tablets cannot have been particularly big and heavy. Furthermore, there had to be enough space for them in the Ark of the covenant, which also limited their size. The outer measurements of the ark of the covenant were 131 cm in length and 78 cm in height and width.

From these measurements the thickness of the sides of the Ark of the covenant must be subtracted, and there must be enough space for the fingers between the stone tablets and the inside walls if the tablets were to be lifted out. This limits the stone tablets to measure roughly 60 x 70 cm at the most if they were to be laid down in the ark of the covenant. Figure 554 shows what the stone tablets may have looked like.

75. The Tabernacle erected and sanctified

It took time to make everything that was to be in the Tabernacle, as well as the Tabernacle itself. The entire people of Israel had to contribute with everything from olive oil, skins, acacia wood and copper to gold and precious stones. A whole chapter lists all the articles that were to be in the Tabernacle (Ex. 40).

When all was ready it was to be sanctified. To sanctify, make holy, means to set apart. The Tabernacle with all its different parts was to be sanctified by anointing with oil. Those who were to officiate were to be chosen, and were to be of the tribe of Levi. They were to be dressed in holy (set apart) vestments, and to be anointed with oil and washed in water.

"Then a cloud covered the tent of the congregation, and the glory of the LORD filled the tabernacle. And Moses was not able to enter into the tent of the congregation, because the cloud abode thereon, and the glory of the LORD filled the tabernacle.

And when the cloud was taken up from over the tabernacle, the children of Israel went onward in all their journeys: But if the cloud were not taken up, then they journeyed not till the day that it was taken up.

For the cloud of the LORD was upon the tabernacle by day, and fire was on it by night, in the sight of all the house of Israel, throughout all their journeys." (Ex 40:34-38)

"And it came to pass on the twentieth day of the second month, in the second year, that the cloud was taken up from off the tabernacle of the testimony. And the children of Israel took their journeys out of the wilderness of Sinai..." (Ex 10:11-12)

76. WHO WAS THE AUTHOR?

There are basically three different alternatives in terms of authorship of the first five books of the Bible.

1. These books represent a mixture of different texts that at some point in history were put together. This is one possibility.

2. Moses had a scribe, a kind of secretary, who wrote down what Moses dictated. This is possible since it was common in ancient Egypt for important people to have scribes. Common people could not write at all, it was an exclusive right that belonged to the very upper segment of society. Moses had learned the wisdom of Egypt from the very best teachers in the land, and with this background he was almost certainly an experienced reader and writer. Although, after an additional 40 years in the wilderness as a shepherd, he definitely did not have a scribe. According to the text, Moses' brother Aaron frequently communicated whatever needed to be said, but no scribe is mentioned.

3. Moses was the author. This is a possiblity.

The question of whether Moses had a scribe to help him or not, is impossible to answer. This is not important in terms of understanding the text. However, it is probable that Moses did not have a scribe, as will be discussed later in this chapter.

76.1. A MIXTURE OF DIFFERENT TEXTS ?

There are different hypotheses that claim that the Pentateuch (the first five books of the Bible) have a great variety of authors. It is claimed that the Pentateuch was compiled some 1,000 years after Moses death, by editing processes organised by priests.

The basis for hypotheses like this is that when analysing the text, different varieties of words or expressions are found. These sections are then subtracted from the text to form a new text. In this way, it can be claimed that there were different authors that wrote different parts, and at a certain point these

Figure 555: Each chapter of Exodus 1-10 coloured according to the following; Matters known to people of that time (yellow), only known to a limited number of people (orange), or only known to Moses (red).

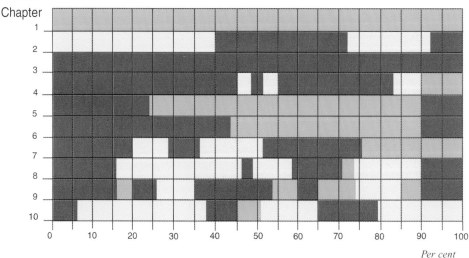

Exodus

Chapter

Per cent

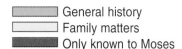

General history
Family matters
Only known to Moses

parts were edited into one document.

The problem is that it is a subjective selection of these different uses of words, and therefore the creation of new documents is subjective by definition. In addition, there are no such ancient documents found. They are created in very recent history, i.e. the last 100 years. To create such documents and then claim it must have been an editing process, because the created documents must fit the original in some way is, to say the least, speculative.

W.F. Albright, former professor of Semitic Languages at John Hopkins University, was considered to be one of the foremost biblical archeologists during a long period of time in the 20th century. He has commented upon this way of dealing with a text, and his opinion can be summarized in one sentence; "Unfortunately all of this was developed in the infancy of archaeology and was of very little value in interpreting history" (67).

Another way of dealing with biblical texts is to consider the text to be invalid as a historical document until another texts can support the content. This is a very non-scientific approach. To transfer the issue to the practice of law, everyone should be considered guilty until proven innocent. In addition, this approach os illogical since other texts are considered valid, until the opposite is proven.

Other types of criticism suggest that the high level of law, order and structure could not relate to the time of Moses. At the same time, other documents present a similar level of social order at that time. Examples are the Code of Hammurabi (2,000-1,700 BC) from Mesopotamia, and the Ras Shamra Tablets (approx. 1,400 BC) (68). So this type of criticism is less relevant.

76.2. WHO WAS THE AUTHOR?

There are different approaches to deal with this issue.

1. Who had knowledge of these events?
To write down a series of events, one must have information on how it all took place. In figure 555 a relative comparison has been made concerning the first 10 chapters of Exodus. Each chapter is calculated in terms of each verse that contains "General information" (known to people living at the time), "Family matters" (known only to Moses and Aaron, or similar limited groups like meetings between Moses and Pharaoh), and "Moses matters" (only known to Moses).

As seen in the figure, a substantial part of information could only have been known to Moses. In figure 556 this is summarized. Approximately 1/4 of all the information in Exodus chapters 1-10 was generally known by the people at the time, and consequently could have been written by anyone able to write. Another 1/4 could only have been written by Moses or his very close family, like Aaron. About half of all this information was only known to Moses.

Based on this information there are three conclusions to be drawn;

a) The text is fiction, written by someone who wanted to create an interesting story for the Hebrews.

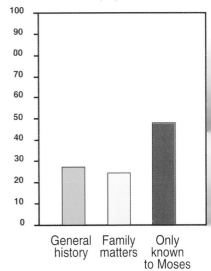

Figure 556: A summary of figure 555. Exodus 1-10 coloured according to the following; Matters known to people of that time ("General history", yellow), only known to a limited number of people ("Family matters", orange) or only known to Moses (red).

Per cent

General history   Family matters   Only known to Moses

b) Moses shared all the information he had access to with a person who wrote it down.

c) Moses recorded the events himself.

2. What is written in the biblical text in terms of authorship?

Moses is ordered to write down all the events by the Lord;

"And the LORD said unto Moses, Write this for a memorial in a book..." (Ex. 17:14)

The law is another name of the Pentateuch, the five books of Moses;

"And Moses wrote this law, and delivered it unto the priests the sons of Levi, which bare the ark of the covenant of the LORD, and unto all the elders of Israel." (Deut. 31:9)

This book should be kept in a box on the side of the ark of the covenant;

"And it came to pass, when Moses had made an end of writing the words of this law in a book, until they were finished, That Moses commanded the Levites, which bare the ark of the covenant of the LORD, saying, Take this book of the law, and put it in the side of the ark of the covenant of the LORD your God, that it may be there for a witness against thee." (Deut. 31:24-26)

According to the biblical text, Moses was writing until his 120th year and he was clear in mind until his death.

"And Moses was an hundred and twenty years old when he died: his eye was not dim, nor his natural force abated." (Deut. 34:7)

Moses wrote all the words of the Lord;

"And Moses wrote all the words of the LORD, and rose up early in the morning, and builded an altar under the hill, and twelve pillars, according to the twelve tribes of Israel. And he sent young men of the children of Israel, which offered burnt offerings, and sacrificed peace offerings of oxen unto the LORD. And Moses took half of the blood, and put it in basons; and half of the blood he sprinkled on the altar. And he took the book of the covenant, and read in the audience of the people: and they said, All that the LORD hath said will we do, and be obedient." (Ex. 24:4-7)

Again, the commission to write...

"And the LORD said unto Moses, Write thou these words: for after the tenor of these words I have made a covenant with thee and with Israel." (Ex. 34:27)

A number of subjects were to be written by Moses, here it is a song;

"Now therefore write ye this song for you, and teach it the children of Israel: put it in their mouths, that this song may be a witness for me against the children of Israel." (Deut. 31:19)

Moses is supposed to write down a report of their journeys. It is this report which the book of Exodus is based on;

"And Moses wrote their goings out according to their journeys by the commandment of the LORD: and these are their journeys according to their goings out." (Numb. 33:2)

In addition to these biblical texts, there are at least 60 other references in the Old and New testament of the Bible that refer to Moses as the author of the first five books of the Bible.

One biblical reference is from the gospel of John, quoting Jesus;

"Do not think that I will accuse you to the Father: there is one that accuseth you, even Moses, in whom ye trust. For had ye believed Moses, ye would have believed me; for he wrote of me. But if ye believe not his writings, how shall ye believe my words?" (Joh. 5:45-47)

So, who was the author of the Pentateuch? There is no doubt what the biblical texts are stating: the author was Moses. It is not until the very end of the fifth book (Deuteronomy), that Moses' second in command, Joshua, adds the details of Moses death (Deut. 34:5-12) as a bridge over to the next book; the book of Joshua.

AT THE MOUNT OF GOD
A SUMMARY

We have now followed the Hebrews from the crossing site to the Mount of God, also called Horeb and according to the hypothesis of this book Jabal Al Lawz.

There are a number of matters which support the hypothesis that today's Jabal Al Lawz is the biblical Mount Sinai. The oasis with palm tree's and 12 wells that corresponds to Elim. The split rock with water erosion at the back side of Horeb (The rock of Horeb), together with an ancient altar. The highest mountain in the area with a number of finds.

These finds represent a campsite (where a mill stone was found) in front of a mountain that is considered a holy mountain by locals. After the discovery, the area was fenced and protected by Saudi-Arabian guards with machine guns, since this is considered to be an archeological site, according to signs on the fence.

The site fits very well with the biblical description of the mountain, the following are examples of the characteristics;

◆ The highest mountain in the area.
◆ Huge blocks on the side of the mountain.
◆ A cave.
◆ A cleft.
◆ A plateau.
◆ An altar at the base.
◆ An altar for worship of the Egyptian Apis (bull) cult.
◆ A river bed.
◆ Remains of wells.
◆ Stone circles.
◆ Raised pillars.
◆ A large area for a campsite.
◆ The flat area faces east.
◆ The split rock with an altar.
◆ In the Land of Midian.
◆ Very close to the place where Jethro is most likely to have lived.

Photographs document the finds, as well as satellite photographs where applicable.

CONCLUSIONS

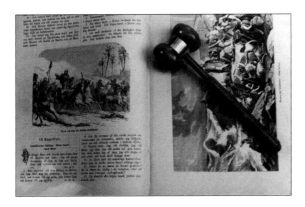

The title of this book is "The Exodus Case". You could look upon the book as a court case. The court trial deals with whether the text of Genesis 11:27 to Exodus 40:38 is a true historical document. That was the hypothesis. That was the case presented.

There is one factor which makes it hard to prove beyond all doubts that the hypothesis is correct. The events the trial deals with took place some 4000 years ago. Therefore there is not a single object, a single event or a single text to show as THE proof.

Instead a chain of events, circumstances, chemical analyses, names, maps, photographs, satellite photographs and finds have been presented. One, or a few of them could be invalid: mistakes, overinterpretation or falsifications. But this book presents the following, among many other things, and each point can be divided into a number of sub parts;

◆ Ur of the Chaldees.

◆ Rain of burning sulphur.

◆ Joseph in Egypt.

◆ Moses in Egypt.

◆ The route of the Exodus.

◆ The crossing site of the Red Sea.

◆ Horeb or Mount Sinai in Saudi-Arabia.

To explain the finds, the biblical text has been shown together with presentation and discussion. In addition **572** illustrations, photographs, tables and graphic illustrations have been presented.

You are the jury. You have to come to a conclusion. You must understand that you actually have three possibilities to confront:

1. The first possibility deals with the statement that the biblical texts referred to are not correct. A statement that could identify this possibility are; The "Red Sea" means a lake with reeds, in the northern part of Egypt. In general this approach, when faced with a suggested theory that does not fit into the biblical text, changes, modifies or neglects the biblical text. This is often given the stamp of science. This kind of statement could be applied to all the issues brought up in this book. That is possibility number one.

2. The second possibility is that the whole biblical text referred to is a falsification, which was presented by a small tribe in the Middle East that needed an impressive history. This possibility faces an increasing number of problems. To name but one, the British Museum (London) has published a book (69) in which 60 finds from the museum give support, to different extents, to the historical events described in the biblical texts. This is possibility number two.

3. The third possibility is what is presented in this book. This possibility is defined by the hypothesis that the biblical text referred to represents true historical events. In some cases information is given from different sources that can confirm an event, connect a place or a name to the biblical text, or document finds that fit into the biblical text. In other cases there are no possibilities to verify an event either because by its nature it is impossible to verify, or because the time span of up to 4000 years has made it impossible. The data that has been found is presented in this book. This is possibility number three.

You are the jury.

You have to decide if the biblical text referred to is a historical document. Use the same criteria as you would use for similar events that took place some 3500-4000 years ago. The level of proof should be the same for all possibilities in this trial.

If there is one situation presented, in which the biblical text seems to be historically correct, then you cannot say beyond all doubt that the biblical text is a falsification. So what is your verdict?

Take your time. Take all the time you need. But do not leave this room without a verdict.

You are the jury in the Exodus Case.

REFERENCES

THE BIBLE

The Bible is referred to at many places in the book. In the beginning of a Bible all biblical books are listed. The five books of Moses are the first books of a Bible. These books are named Genesis (Gen.), Exodus (Ex.), Leviticus (Lev.), Numbers (Numb.) and Deuteronomy (Deut.). These books are referred to many times, especially Genesis and Exodus. Biblical books are referred to with the abbreviation of the book, normally the first 3-4 letters, followed by chapter and verse. An example is "Gen. 32:1." (Genesis, chapter 32, verse 1)

JOSEPHUS

Flavius Josephus (AD 37-100) is the author of the most significant extra-biblical writings of the first century. He was a Jew and son of a priest. His writings were based on several historical documents that existed some 1900 years ago in addition to the general historical knowledge of that time. Most of the writings were done in Rome. One book is named "The Antiquities of the Jews", abbreviated "JA" in this book. References are given as "JA1/15", meaning "The Antiquities of the Jews, book 1, chapter 15". The references are from the English translation made by William Whiston that first appeared 1736. The updated edition used is from 1987 and published by Hendrickson Publishers Inc., USA. This translation covers 525 pages, divided into 20 books and further divided into chapters. This edition also includes other texts from Josephus like "The War of the Jews". In total the book covers 927 pages. ISBN 1-56563-167-6.

MAPS

Historical maps are referred to with the name of the person who made the map and the year. An example is "Antonio Zatta, 1784". These maps from the last 500 years are not easy to find and are mostly part of different collections. All map data are from the original maps.

REFERENCES SHOWN AS NUMBERS IN THE TEXT

1. J. McDowell (1993), A Ready Defense, Thomas Nelson Publishers, Nashville, USA.

2. The New Encyclopedia Britannica, 15th edition (1985), London, England.

3. R. deVaux (1978) The early history of Israel, Darton, Longman and Todd, London, England.

4. J.N. Postgate (1992) Early Mesopotamia, Routledge, London, England.

5. Biblical Archaeology Review, June 1977.

6. Book of Jubilees (second century BC), (1985) The Old Testament Pseudoepigrapha, vol. 2, p 52-, editor J.H. Charlesworth, Doubleday, New York, USA.

7. D. Collon (1995) Ancient Near Eastern Art, British Museum Press, London,

England.

8. M. Caygill (1999) A-Z Companion, British Museum Press, London, England.

9. C.B.F. Walker (1998) Reading the Past Cuneiform, British Museum Press, London, England

10. Book of Jubilees (second century BC), (1985) The Old Testament Pseudoepigrapha, vol. 2, p 43-, editor J.H. Charlesworth, Doubleday, New York, USA.

11. Flavius Josephus (AD 37 - circa 100), The Wars of the Jews, book 4, chapter 8, translation by William Whiston (1667-1752), 1995 printing, Hendrickson Publishers, USA.

12. A.H. Sayce (1972) Records of the Past, Benjamin Blom Inc., New York, USA.

13. E. During (1999) Cremated Skeleton Material (in Swedish), Archaeo Osteological Reserach Laboratory, University of Stockholm.

14. L. Casson (1969) The Search for Imhotep, Horizon, vol XI, No.3.

15. The Ancient Near East (1958) vol 1., p 24-, Editor J.B. Pritchard, Princeton University Press, Princeton, USA.

16. M. Lichtheim (1980) Ancient Egyptian Literature, vol III, University of California Press, Berkeley, USA.

17. B. Mertz (1996) Temples, Tombs and Hieroglyphs, Michael O'Mara Books Ltd, London, England.

18. J.F. Nunn (1996) Ancient Egyptian Medicine, British Museum Press, London, England.

19. J.W. Estes (1993) The Medical Skills of Ancient Egypt, Science History Publications, Canton, USA.

20. The Ancient Near East (1958) vol 1., p 234- , Editor J.B. Pritchard, Princeton University Press, Princeton, USA.

21. A. Silotti (1997) Pyramids of Egypt, The American University in Cairo Press, Cairo, Egypt.

22 W.C. Hayes (1990) The Scepter of Egypt, vol. II, The Metropolitan Museum of Art, New York, USA.

23. Hatshepsut's Temple Inscription at Speos Artemidos, translated by Goedicke.

24. E. Anati (1986) The Mountain of God, International Publications Inc. Rizzoli, New York, USA.

25. A.J. Hoerth (1998) Archaeology and The Old Testament, Baker Books, Grand Rapids, USA.

26. R. Parkinson (1999) Cracking Codes, British Museum Press, London, England.

27. B.G. Wood (1990) Dating Jericho's destruction, Biblical Archaeology Review, 5.

28. E.A. Wallis (1989) The Mummy. The original published 1925 by Cambridge University Press, Dover Publications, Mineola, New York, USA.

29. G. Hart (1991) Pharaohs and Pyramids, The Herbert Press, London, England.

30. Seattle Art Museum, USA, Tablet, Purification for a Priest, Catalog #95.

31. A. de Selincourt (1979) Herodotus - The Histories, Penguin Books, Harmondsworth, England.

32. M. Collier and B. Manley (1998) How to Read Egyptian Hieroglyphs, British Museum Press, London, England.

33. E.A. Wallis (1978) An Egyptian Hieroglyphic Dictionary, vol. 1, section XVI, (originally published 1920), Don Mills, Toronto, Canada.

34. J.H. Breasted (1921) A History of Egypt, Hodder and Stoughton, London, England.

35. J. Tyldesley (1998) Hatchepsut, the Female Pharaoh, Penguin Books, Harmondsworth, England.

36. F.F. Bruce (1963) Israel and the Nations, The Paternoster Press Ltd., Exeter, England.

37. F. Tiradritti (1999) The Cairo Museum Master Pieces of Egyptian Art, Thames and Hudson, London, England.

38. Accessibility Guidelines for Buildings and Facilities (ADAAG) (1988), USA.

39. J.E. Harris (1973) X-Raying the Pharaohs, Scribner, New York, USA.

40. G.E. Mendenhall (1958) The Census Lists of Numbers 1 and 26, J. of Biblical Literature, 77, 52-66.

41. B. Manley (1996) The Penguin Historical Atlas of Ancient Egypt, Penguin Books, London, England.

42. M. Lichtheim (1973) Ancient Egyptian Literature, vol. 1, University of California Press, Berkeley, USA.

43. P.A. Clayton (1994) Chronicle of the Pharaohs, Thames and Hudson Ltd., London, England.

44. F.N. Hepper (1990) Pharaoh's Flowers, Royal Botanic Gardens, Kew, London, England.

45. The Swedish Bureu of Statistics (1999), Stockholm, Sweden, personal communication.

46. The Swedish National Encyclopedia (1990) In Swedish, Bra Böcker, Höganäs, Sweden.

47. The Complete Biblical Library, the Swedish edition (1988), Illustrert Bibelleksikon AS, Ski, Norway.

48. J.R. Bartlett (1997) Archaeology and Biblical Interpretation, Routledge, London, England.

49. E.R. Thiele (1951) The Mysterious Numbers of Hebrew Kings, University of Chicago Press, Chicago, USA.

50. The Ancient Near East (1958) vol 1., p 175-183, Editor J.B. Pritchard, Princeton University Press, Princeton, USA.

51. M. Healy and A. McBride (1992) New Kingdom Egypt, Osprey Publishing Ltd, London, England.

52. J. G. Wilkinson (1837) Manners and Customs of Ancient Egyptians, London, England.

53. J.K. Hoffmeier (1976) Observations on the Evolving Chariot Wheel in the 18th Dynasty, JARCE, 13.

54. Y.Yadin (1963) The Art of Warfare in Biblical Lands, Weydenfeld and Nicholson, London. England.

55. F. Dunand and R. Lichtenberg (1993) Les momies, un voyage dans l'éternité, The Swedish translation by P. Nyquist, Berghs Förlag, Stockholm, Sweden.

56. The New Encyclopedia of Archaeological Excavations in the Holy Land (1993) E. Stern (ed), The Israeli Exploration Society and Carta, Israel.

57. N. Reeves and R.H. Wilkinson (1996) The Complete Valley of the Kings, p 91, Thames and Hudson Ltd, London, England.

58. Flavius Josephus (AD 37 - circa 100), The Antiquities of the Jews, translation by William Whiston (1667-1752), notes by Whiston, 1995 edition, Hendrickson Publishers, USA.

59. R. Keating (1963) Nubian Twilight, Harcourt, Brace and World Inc., New York, USA.

60. Arabia Felix (1964) The Danish Expedition of 1761-1767, translated by J. and C. McFarlane, Collins, England.

61. J.B. Pritchard (1969) Ancient Near Eastern Texts, Princeton University Press, Princeton, USA.
62. G. Larsson (1993) Uppbrottet (In Swedish), Verbum Förlag, Stockholm, Sweden.

63. C. M. Doughty (1979) Travels in Arabia Deserta (originally published 1888), Dover Publishing Inc., New York, USA.

64. H.J. Philby (1957) The Land of Midian, E. Benn Ltd., England.

65. C.C. Robertson (1990) On the Track of the Exodus, Artisan Sales, Thousand Oakes, California, USA.

66. The Koran, section XXIII, translation by A.J. Arberry, 1983, Oxford University Press, Oxford, England.

67. W.F. Albright (1966) Historical Analogy and Early Biblical Tradition, Louisiana State University Press, Baton Rouge, USA.

68. J.P. Free (1969) Archaeology and Bible History, Scripture Press, Wheaton, USA.

69. T.C. Mitchell (1988) The Bible in the British Museum, British Museum Press, London, England.

70. J. Harned (2000), Discovery Media Productions, Los Angeles, USA, personal communication.

71. R. Partridge (1996) Transport in Ancient Egypt, The Rubicon Press, London, England.

INDEX
Numbers refer to pages or chapters (chp.)

PHOTO CREDITS

ILLUSTRATION CREDITS

Anni Mikkelsen
12, 15, 33, 40, 47, 69, 70, 93, 109, 110, 111, 119, 120, 124, 125, 128, 132, 136, 138, 152, 154, 155, 156, 181, 191, 192, 193, 195, 196, 197, 198, 207, 208, 211, 213, 219, 227, 245, 257, 266, 281, 282, 283, 289, 292, 295, 305, 321, 330, 344, 347, 348, 350, 371, 379, 405, 408, 410, 447, 449, 460, 468, 474, 482, 500, 501, 502, 505, 509, 530, 532, 534, 537, 555, 556.

Lennart Möller
199, 333, 339, 338, 340.

Cecilie Olesen
384, 388, 390, 392, 395, 398, 400, 402, 404.

José Pérez Montero
10, 113, 130, (part of 136, 138 = small illustrations), 147, 222, 276, 322, 341, 349, 386, 440, 554.